THE CLEAN BODY

A MODERN HISTORY

PETER WARD

McGill-Queen's University Press
Montreal & Kingston • London • Chicago

© McGill-Queen's University Press 2019

ISBN 978-0-7735-5938-7 (cloth)
ISBN 978-0-2280-0062-4 (ePDF)
ISBN 978-0-2280-0063-1 (ePUB)

Legal deposit third quarter 2019
Bibliothèque nationale du Québec

Printed in Canada on acid-free paper that is 100% ancient forest free
(100% post-consumer recycled), processed chlorine free

This book has been published with the help of a grant from the Canadian
Federation for the Humanities and Social Sciences, through the Awards to
Scholarly Publications Program, using funds provided by the Social Sciences
and Humanities Research Council of Canada.

Funded by the   Financé par le
Government   gouvernement   Canada Council   Conseil des arts
of Canada   du Canada   for the Arts   du Canada

We acknowledge the support of the Canada Council for the Arts.
Nous remercions le Conseil des arts du Canada de son soutien.

Library and Archives Canada Cataloguing in Publication

Title: The clean body : a modern history / Peter Ward.
Names: Ward, W. Peter, author.
Description: Includes bibliographical references and index.
Identifiers: Canadiana (print) 20190132876 | Canadiana (ebook) 20190132884
  | ISBN 9780773559387 (cloth) | ISBN 9780228000624 (ePDF) | ISBN
  9780228000631 (ePUB)
Subjects: LCSH: Hygiene—Western countries—History. | LCSH: Laundry—Western
  countries—History. | LCSH: Bathing customs—Western countries—History.
Classification: LCC RA780 .W37 2019 | DDC 613/.4—dc23

This book was typeset in 10.5/13 Sabon.

A M'ARCORD

Al so, al so, al so,
Che un om a zinquent'ann
L'ha sempra al mèni puloidi
E me a li lèv do, tre volti e dè,

Ma l'è sultènt s'a m vaid al mèni sporchi
Che me a m'arcord
Ad quand ch'a s'era burdèll.

Federico Fellini

CONTENTS

Preface: Beginnings   ix

Introduction: Contexts   3

PART ONE | CLEANLINESS AS TRADITION

1 Before the Deluge   11

PART TWO | CLEANLINESS AS HABIT

2 Public Places, Private Spaces   49
3 Clothes and Their Cleaning   84
4 The Soap Trade and the New Hygiene   107
5 The Educators   131

PART THREE | CLEANLINESS AS COMMODITY

6 Bathrooms and Bathing   158
7 The Laundry Revolution   174
8 Cleanliness and the Beauty Business   202
Conclusion: Making the Modern Clean Body   231

Acknowledgments   237
Appendix   239
Notes   243
Index   309

PREFACE

BEGINNINGS

This book takes its origins from two small incidents in my own life, one at either end of my professional career. The first was a casual remark by my grandfather. When a student in the early 1970s, I taped an interview with him for an oral history project run by an archive in the western Canadian province where he lived. They were documenting the community's past through interviews with older residents and, having lived there for most of his adult life, he certainly qualified. A successful small businessman and community leader, he was typical of many who came west from central Canada during the early years of the century. The interview must have been an important occasion for him because he dressed for it in his Sunday best, even though we were meeting at home. The conversation itself was a pleasure as he journeyed back and forth across the broad plains of his memory, from his childhood in Montreal's Griffintown through his farmboy adolescence on a back concession in eastern Ontario and his early years as a mine worker in the Rockies to his long odyssey as a hardware merchant and local notable in small-town Alberta. No expert interviewer, I simply let him tell me his story, and he did.[1] Today I remember little of what he said apart from an offhand remark about his youthful bathing habits. "Facilities such as we know them today," he told me, "were unknown at that time. You had a bath maybe once in six months. We must have smelled to high heaven although I never noticed it." Since then I've often wished I'd had the wit to pursue the subject with him but, still learning my craft and a neophyte with a tape recorder and microphone, I let the opportunity slip. Yet the comment itself lingered in the back of my mind, teasingly, for decades.

Some forty years later the tease had become a curiosity and I'd begun to explore the long history of personal cleanliness. My wife Patricia and I had rented a quirky flat just a few steps from London's verdant Hampstead Heath while I trolled through the British Library. The daily commute to Euston Road was relatively short and I had the choice between the bus and the Underground to vary the routine. While the tube station was a bit farther from our apartment and the journey just a rattling rush through a long dark tunnel, usually it was the better choice during the heavy morning traffic, though you never really could be sure. Large creaking elevators connected the Hampstead station with the platforms below, and at peak hours, commuters crammed themselves in, sharing a closeness with strangers they'd never accept otherwise. One morning I missed my timing and arrived at the station just at the height of the rush. I wedged myself into the next elevator, heard the door slam shut, and felt the usual lurch as it began its descent. Pressed tightly against my nearest neighbours, I caught a whiff of the English middle class setting off for a day at the office. I sniffed gently, then breathed deeply, and what did I smell? Coffee. Someone with a more tutored nose than mine might have parsed the bouquet de Hampstead Village more subtly, sensing perfumes and soaps, lotions and hair preparations of delicacy and refinement. But for me the overwhelming aroma of the moment was coffee, certainly not any of the body's natural odours. On that short journey from Hampstead station down to the platform below I learned a lesson that only experience could have taught: the modern Western body has lost its own aromas and is now overwhelmed by the scents offered by the age of mass consumption.

For me these two short encounters raise the main question of this book: how have we come to be so clean? My grandfather must have had a pong as a boy, but by the time I knew him his personal habits were well above reproach. He bathed often and changed his clothes regularly just like everyone else I knew. At some point in his young life he must have learned new habits. Presumably the change was part of growing up: like Fellini, he adopted adult ways of being. No doubt he shared the common experience of children and youths in his own time, learning the lessons of cleanliness current in late Victorian Canada. But his personal growth merely begs larger questions. After all, standards of personal hygiene were in flux across the Western world in his time. By then they'd been in evolution for generations, as they'd remain for most of the next century. How was the body cared for before the great hygienic transformation? What broader influences underlay the changes that then occurred? When and where and how and why did traditional notions of bodily care become today's grooming practices? What material conditions underlay these processes? What ideas shaped beliefs about the clean body, who circulated them, and why did they do so? How was the cleanliness revolution connected to the coming of the modern age? In short, what was the larger historical meaning of my brief elevator ride at the Hampstead tube station on that sunny October morning in the early twenty-first century?

Plate 1 | Bartolomeo Pinelli, *La famiglia dei pedochiosi* [The family with lice], late eighteenth/early nineteenth century. Wellcome Collection, CC BY.

Plate 2 | Guercino (Giovanni Francesco Barbieri), *Landscape with Bathing Women*, c. 1621. Museum Boijmans Van Beuningen, Rotterdam, the Netherlands.

Plate 3 | Théodule-Augustin Ribot, *The Morning Wash* (*The Children's Home*), c. 1863). Montreal Museum of Fine Arts, gift of Lord Strathcona and Family. Photo MMFA.

Plate 4 | Kitchen in a cellar apartment at Pücklerstraße 14, Berlin, 1905.
Photo: akg-images.

Plate 5 | The *lavoir* at Roscoff, Brittany, at the turn of the twentieth century.
Author's collection.

C. A. Pini - Bologna. BOLOGNA - Lavatoio della Grada.

Plate 6 | The *lavatoio* della Grada, Bologna, at the turn of the twentieth century. Collezione Brasa, Bologna, Italy.

Plate 7 | *Boy Blowing Bubbles*. After J. E. Millais. Pears Soap advertisement, c. 1888. Photo: akg-images, Fototeca Gilardi.

Plate 8 | Sun Court Cleansing Station, London: children are washed in a bathroom, 1914. London Metropolitan Archives (City of London).

Plate 9 | Cristiano Focarile, *Igiene innanzi tutto* [Hygiene first of all], daily washing routines in an Italian *colonia estiva*, 1920s. Cristiano Focarile, *La funzione sociale della cooperazione fascista per il potenziamento della stirpe* (Roma: Esperienza cooperative, 1930), 25.

PACENTRO - *Lavatoio pubblico i Canaj in Contrada della Porta del Castello*

Plate 10 | The *lavatoio* at Pacentro, Abruzzo, in the early twentieth century. Courtesy of L'Associazione Culturale Pacentrana, Pacentro (AQ), Italy.

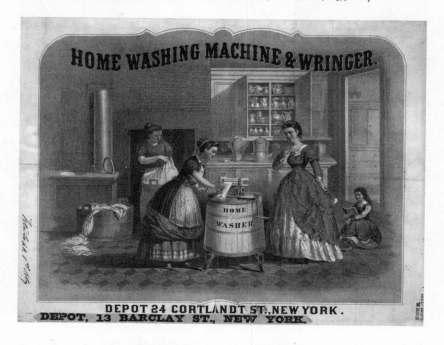

HOME WASHING MACHINE & WRINGER.

HOME WASHER

DEPOT 24 CORTLANDT ST., NEW YORK.
DEPOT, 13 BARCLAY ST., NEW YORK.

Plate 11 | American home washing machine and wringer, 1869. Library of Congress, Prints and Photographs Division, LC-DIG-pga-03845.

Plate 12 | Persil, *Die Weiße Dame* [The white lady], detergent advertisement, 1920s. Copyright Henkel AG & Co., KGAA, Düsseldorf, Germany.

THE CLEAN BODY

CONTEXTS

The development of modern personal hygiene has been one of the great cultural transformations in the Western world over the past two centuries. With passing time older habits of body care have gradually given way to new ones and in turn these have yielded to still newer ones. Each generation of customs has been more scrupulous than the one it replaced, each has expressed a new engagement with the self and its social relations. Compared with some of modernization's revolutions this has largely been a personal matter, for the most part unfolding in the domestic sphere and in the life of the individual. The habits it fashioned and refashioned were private, often intimate. Fundamentally they expressed the regard individuals had for their own bodies and how they presented themselves in the public realm. But private though these customs were, they were pervasive as well, touching the lives of all. By the late twentieth century regular handwashing, frequent bathing, and wearing freshly laundered clothes had become routine for virtually everyone in Europe and North America, standards of comportment that framed the ordinary actions of everyday modern life.

Grooming is an activity we share with many animal species, and though it seems to be innate, its forms vary widely. Among humans it is a set of cultural practices influenced by needs, beliefs, understandings, and traditions, as well as environmental settings. Its basic activities are habitual, most often learned in childhood, and passed informally from parents to children during the early course of life. They form part of a cluster of seldom-articulated customs that we gradually absorb as we grow up. At the same time our grooming behaviours are shaped by broader factors encountered more often in adolescence and adulthood, and these amplify the lessons we learn in early life. As a result, however private our hygienic practices may be, they also have a public character that opens them to social influences. The interplay between these elements, public and private, has been the driving force behind the cleaning of the body for centuries, though their relative weights have shifted over time.

The discussion here centres on two broad themes: clean bodies and clean clothes – the skin and its envelope. Personal cleanliness has always involved them both, though the balance between them has varied across the centuries. The two have separate yet braided pasts, and over time the social meanings of being clean have assumed various forms. Traditional concepts of cleanliness – ideas about the meaning of "clean" – form our point of departure. Past beliefs about cleanliness were embedded in understandings about the body and its care widely held in their times. Then, as now, popular notions were based on contrasts between clean and unclean, though the specific meanings of the two terms differed greatly from those we now accept. The concept of the clean body is a construct, one that has evolved slowly over time. It has found its clearest expression at the level of practice, for hygienic customs inevitably reflect the sensibilities of their era.

From the seventeenth century onward new beliefs about care of the body came to shape the progress of personal hygiene everywhere in the Western world. The sites and symbols of clean and unclean oscillated between the body and its covering. Before the modern age the state of the visible underclothes expressed the body's hygiene most clearly, at least among those wealthy enough to afford such luxuries, while that of the skin was of little concern. Clean clothes spoke to the body's condition. But by the close of the eighteenth century the virtues of a cleansing bath were beginning to gain acceptance within these same social circles, and during the coming century, they won an ever wider following. The new upper-class views about bathing's benefits were embedded in broader class identities; they were elements of display that distinguished the clean bourgeois self from the unclean lower-class other. Over the nineteenth century they gradually descended the social hierarchy, winning slow, sometimes grudging, acceptance from those who usually faced great practical challenges in washing themselves. During the second half of the century these beliefs gained new support from an emerging medical science of hygiene – the germ theory in particular – which enlisted scientific understanding in aid of personal cleanliness. They gained further allies from the ranks of authorities, both public and private, who directed institutions to further the cause, most often through schools and other organizations for the young. By the later decades of the century another powerful group of promoters had also joined the movement: the makers of soaps – voluble advocates of cleanliness with commercial gain in mind. And their influence came to dominate over the decades to come, as the soap trades became the loudest voice in the cleanliness crusade.

At the same time, the evolving material conditions of daily life gradually widened the opportunities that entire populations enjoyed to bathe conveniently. The slow but steady spread of civic water and sewer systems was a primary building block of modern urban life, one that had touched the lives of every city, town and village dweller by the time the process reached its conclusion. By degrees the new utilities introduced fresh water into the dwelling and removed the foul water it produced. A condition that was a rare privilege during the early nineteenth century had become an entitlement by the late twentieth. Meanwhile, what the city as a whole experienced on a grand scale, the individual dwelling knew in microcosm. Once connected to the urban network, the house channelled water in and out of its interior, supplying with ease what formerly had cost great effort – and considerable sums as well. In important respects the Western home itself had to be reconceived in order to reap the fruits of the hydraulic miracle. The diffusion of household plumbing, both the hidden networks of pipes and tubes and the visible ones of porcelain fixtures, required major renovations to existing housing stocks as well as substantial change to new building designs and construction techniques. The provision of hot water at the turn of a tap, needed for convenient bathing, added a further challenge. Most important of all, the home now had to offer the privacy of a bathroom, a separate space for the intimacies of the bath.

Change on this scale involved millions of buildings across Western Europe and North America, an immensely costly enterprise that took decades to achieve. In some places the process trailed well behind the new culture of cleanliness that took form during the nineteenth and early twentieth centuries, and many families lagged the aspirations they no doubt had formed, though their numbers dwindled with passing time. For those who lacked a fully serviced bathroom of their own, one alternative was an improvised arrangement of tubs and curtains in the family kitchen. Another, for urban dwellers at least, was the public bath or community swimming pool, available in growing numbers from the late nineteenth century on. Yet another was a quick rinse in a basin or sink. In the early 1970s I met an Italian American in Florence who had just visited his family there after many years' absence and he told me about the process he'd observed: "First you wash up as far as possible and then down as far as possible, and then you wash the possibles." But the universal wish remained the private use of a bathroom.

As well, change on this scale was gradual, incremental more often than rapid, evolutionary much more than revolutionary. While a broad gulf divided the end points of the process, the transformation of personal cleanliness was much more a matter of small steps than of giant strides. Before the coming of the modern age, body care was governed by traditions whose obscure origins lay in the deep past. Bathing was highly exceptional, washing irregular, and cleanliness mostly a matter of appearances. Though far from universal, these were the commonplace practices of the pre-industrial Western world. By the late-eighteenth-century political revolutions, however, understandings of personal hygiene had started to change. Growing numbers of the middle classes in all Western nations began to see a virtue in full-body bathing that lay beyond older assumptions about the benefits of a medicinal bath. Throughout the nineteenth century more and more Westerners came to accept the intrinsic value of the clean body and to recognize the need for routine habits to maintain it. Those that bathed regularly began to encourage others to do so too. They preached, taught, coerced, enticed, and ultimately convinced the unwashed. By the early twentieth century the majority had come to accept the truth of the new hygiene, and those who had not soon would. By this time, too, cleanliness had become a commercial product, widely advertised and sold in the flourishing consumer markets of the Western world. As it remains today.

Writing about the history of personal hygiene has a history of its own. This isn't the first book on the subject and I expect it won't be the last. A glance at the notes will reveal my dependence on those who have gone before me. What follows differs from their work in two main respects. While most of what has been written till now examines the story as it unfolded in a single country, I've taken the Western world as my canvas, or at least as much of it as I could explore. In particular I've chosen the larger nations – France, Germany, Great Britain, and Italy in Europe, the United States in North America – as my primary concern. Western Europe, in particular, provides a range of cultural differences, political and economic histories, institutional frameworks, and living standards that offer instructive contrasts. Inevitably, modern historians tend to know more about lives lived in great cities than in small ones, in towns than in countrysides, and that fact has shaped my inquiry too. Given my reliance on the work of so many others, I have more to say about the history of big city cleanliness than about the subject in other settings. But whatever the limitations imposed by this imbalance, it also offers an advantage because cities were the primary sites of innovation in the hygiene revolution.

The other major difference is the time frame I've chosen: from the mid-seventeenth century to the recent past. It would have been possible – and an attractive possibility at that – to begin with the Roman bath, one of the great institutions of antique Western civilization. But I wanted to avoid a broad survey in favour of a more focused study on the modern age, when the habits and understandings of cleanliness we now know gradually took their present form. I also intended to make good an omission in much of what others have written on the subject. Most seem to have abandoned their efforts at the end of the nineteenth century or the early years of the twentieth, as if the modern clean body were in place by then. But the transformation of personal hygiene in thinking and practice has continued until our own time, not simply as an epilogue to earlier change but as a growing expression of our own individuality.

PART ONE

Cleanliness as Tradition

Before the dawn of the modern age, long-standing traditions framed Western habits of body care and the ideas on which they rested. Popular beliefs about health kept company with those of medical science, and both informed common understandings of personal cleanliness. Across the Western world everyday wisdom about the body suffused rural lifeworlds while scientific knowledge remained the domain of urban intellectuals. The popular mind held ambivalent notions about dirt and filth, some even stressing their positive value for health. It commonly held water to be a harmful force as much as a source of good, for its capacity to clean was seldom recognized at the time. Among elites attitudes differed somewhat. Upper-class opinion emphasized the cleansing power of underclothing much more than that of bathing. Meanwhile medical science saw a therapeutic value in the bath, even though cleaning the body was seldom the main goal.

During the second half of the eighteenth century a new concern for cleanliness began to emerge in middle-class circles everywhere. Initially it was as much a form of social identity as it was a cluster of practices, a means of distinguishing clean bourgeois bodies from the unclean ones of the lower ranks. Over time the middle classes began to wash themselves more often, no longer just for curative purposes but also simply to be clean. By the turn of the nineteenth century new, more regular bathing customs were beginning to take form, practices based on hygienic precepts that emphasized the intrinsic value of cleanliness. Though far from widespread at

the time, they marked a decisive turning point in the history of
personal hygiene. Half a century later, a new hygienic consensus
had taken root across the Western world and the future lay in ever
greater numbers of bodies washed with ever greater care.

I

BEFORE THE DELUGE

Louis XIV took two baths during his long royal lifetime. His doctors prescribed the first – in 1665, when he was twenty-seven – to help him recover from a bout of convulsions. But the presiding physician interrupted the process when Louis seemed not to hold up well under the strain. The king suffered severe headaches for the rest of the day. The experiment was repeated in the following year but with no greater success. From that point on Louis seems not to have immersed himself in water during his remaining forty-nine years. If so, it wasn't for lack of opportunity. He had had a bathroom with a large marble tub installed in his new palace at Versailles, but later it was renovated to provide living space for one of his illegitimate sons and the bath became a pool in the palace gardens. Nor did Louis neglect his skin. Each morning after he rose, his servants gave him a rubdown because he tended to sweat, and he changed his clothes often throughout the day, especially the linens next to his body. But as to washing, his only gestures were a ritual morning rinse of the hands in scented water and a wipe of the face every second day with a towel moistened with sprits of wine.[1]

At the same time, across the English Channel and several rungs down the social ladder, we encounter Samuel Pepys, the London naval administrator whose famous diary has long endeared him to historians. Pepys was an uninhibited record keeper with a deep interest in the minutia of his everyday life and social relations. So it should come as no great surprise to discover that he noted the lice in his hair (a trait he shared with many contemporaries) and the fact that either his wife or his servant combed him regularly to help him deal with the problem. Nor did he bathe, at least until coerced. In

February 1664 his wife Elisabeth went to a bathhouse for the first time and, so it seems, was converted to cleanliness. On returning home she insisted that her husband wash himself too, and when he demurred, she refused to accept him in the marital bed till he did. It took three days before Pepys gave in and submitted to a hot bath too.[2] But it's clear that his interest in bathing had much more to do with his conjugal pleasures than with any hygienic scruples.

Though highly atypical in most respects, Louis de Bourbon and Samuel Pepys represented much about the general state of personal hygiene in seventeenth-century Europe. When it came to bodily cleanliness they reflected the common practices of their contemporaries. Baths were taken infrequently, if at all, and when they were, it was often under some form of duress, such as a medical need. In the unlikely event of a bath, clean skin was seldom the primary goal. In this respect Elizabeth Pepys may have been something of an exception. Most of those who bathed did so for therapeutic reasons. Those who simply washed did little but rinse their hands and faces, and this they did infrequently. Whatever their discomforts, the unbathed endured them with little complaint, accepting them as part of everyday life.

Yet neither the French sovereign nor the British bureaucrat considered himself unclean. Nor did they ignore their personal hygiene. Concepts of cleanliness in seventeenth-century Europe were largely a matter of appearances. The water that cleansed washed clothing far more often than bodies. What mattered most was one's linen – the layer worn next to the skin – clean, white linen.[3] Writing in 1688, the wealthy bourgeois French writer Charles Perrault, best known to us as the author of some of our most beloved fairy tales, put the matter clearly: "we [the French] do not make great baths, but the cleanliness of our linen and its abundance, are worth more than all the baths in the world."[4] The whiteness of one's linen was the most visible sign of cleanliness and cleansing the body was mostly a matter of changing one's underclothes. While Louis XIV's frequent changes might seem the self-indulgence of a mighty monarch, he was following the hygienic precepts of his time – though admittedly his great wealth and prestige allowed him far more opportunities than virtually all of his subjects. In the seventeenth century clean bodies were those that looked clean and white linen was their principal sign.

Over the following century and more these practices slowly transformed, as did the knowledge on which they rested. While the changes were almost imperceptible at first, in time a new culture of personal cleanliness began to take form. It drew on emerging understandings of water: its properties and its meanings. It embraced differing views of the body: its needs and its nature. It appeared first in urban middle-class circles, articulated by self-conscious bourgeoisies keen to distinguish themselves from their social inferiors. It drew support from a nascent medical science of bodily hygiene. And it challenged long-established folkways and customs, beliefs and behaviours embedded in rural worlds from time beyond memory. Initially its reach was limited. But by the last decades of the eighteenth century – the age of so many revolutions – the cleanliness revolution had also begun and the notions held by Louis XIV and Samuel Pepys were beginning to appear outmoded. New concepts of personal hygiene, based on bathed bodies rather than well-laundered clothes, were finding a receptive audience.

MENTALITIES

A World of Custom and Tradition

Two kinds of knowledge marked eighteenth- and nineteenth-century Western thought about the care of the human body. One resided in the *ur*-memory of popular belief and custom, the other in intellectual traditions reaching back to ancient Greece. One drew most of its wisdom from the natural world and blended it with Christian understandings, the other from study of the body itself and reflections on these observations. One saw the body as embedded in nature, its welfare governed by natural and supernatural forces. The other placed it in the realm of human agency, its well-being guided – at least in part – by the rational mind. One was widely diffused in rural societies, where the great majority in the Western world lived at the dawn of the modern age. The other embraced learned understandings rooted in urban life and was largely the preserve of intellectuals.

Everyday wisdom about health was a vast and discursive body of knowledge: aphorisms and explanations, counsels and exhortations, preventatives and remedies. The other, more systematic, concept of hygiene embraced a wide range of understandings and practices about health and its preservation. Notions of personal cleanliness formed one small part of these varied beliefs, and in neither case were they more than peripheral. Clean bodies, at least as we know them today, had almost no place in how most people thought about their health before the end of the eighteenth century.

Yet it would be misleading to see these two ways of thinking as simply a confrontation between ancient superstitions and an emerging science of the body. On the contrary, early modern European medical thought mingled learned and popular traditions, ideas grounded in observations of a shared natural world reinforced by a common religious understanding.[5] With passing time medical wisdom advanced toward the dominance it established in the discourse on health, but it did not arrive at this point until the later nineteenth century. The Sicilian folklorist Giuseppe Pitrè, a prolific harvester and editor of popular beliefs, once commented that, although Sicilians knew nothing of hygiene, their aphorisms and practices clearly expressed concepts of health and its conservation.[6] While Pitrè, like many folklorists of his time, considered himself an enlightened modern man peering into a dark world of ignorance, confronting banal prejudices with undeniable truths, he wasn't quick to judge. As he put it, awareness of error was relatively recent, and it was certain that, not so long before, what he and his contemporaries now thought to be truth had been considered error too.

Knowing the popular mind in times past, however, is one of the historian's great challenges, a challenge all the greater in societies in which most were illiterate. Usually we learn about the inarticulate through the descriptions of others, both contemporaries and later generations, whose views inevitably are coloured by their own experience. Among the important sources of information about popular thought in past peasant societies are the vast collections gathered by nineteenth- and twentieth-century folklorists such as Pitrè, who, like their colleagues in the emerging field of anthropology, often believed they were salvaging fragments of vanishing lifeways. Proverbs, in particular, interested the folklore community, who collected them enthusiastically. These pithy observations about everyday matters, many with a touch of literary flair, are among the few places we can turn to for information about popular knowledge of the body in earlier times. And when we do we see "religion, magic, and medicine converging in popular culture, shaping everyday thought about the health of the body."[7]

A long list of French proverbs about sickness, health, and the body published in the 1970s included several hundred about personal hygiene.[8] A small sample reveals something of their range:

Cleanliness is the health of the body.
If we are poor, let's be clean.
Dirtiness is the companion of misery.
Who sleeps with dogs rises with fleas.
There's neither a man nor a woman who doesn't have vermin.
The devil hides under long nails.
Shirts washed often don't last long.
Those who bathed live short lives.
Lice help preserve good health.

As the list suggests, folklore's meanings are fragmentary, inconsistent, and sometimes contradictory. Occasionally proverbs may not even represent the authentic voice of the inarticulate. Over time one of the hygienic precepts of the medieval Salerno Medical School – *saepe manus, raro pedes, nunquam caput* (hands often, feet rarely, head never) – made its way into Mediterranean folk wisdom:[9]

Lave tes mains souvent, tes pieds rarement, et ta tête jamais
(Wash the hands often, the feet rarely, and the head never
– Provence)
Pri cunsirvarvi la saluti, nun ti lavari mai la testa, spissu li mani e raru li piedi. (To preserve health never wash the head, wash the hands often and the feet rarely – Sicily)[10]

The Sicilian version even connected this advice about bodily washing to the protection of good health. Yet aphorisms generally drew on common experience in early modern Europe, not on learned opinion. For the most part the world of academic understanding was disconnected from everyday knowledge of the body.

As some of these sayings hint, notions about the defensive qualities of filth and the dangers of too much cleanliness recurred in popular thought. In particular, young children, the most vulnerable of all beings, benefited from some dirtiness because it protected their health. One popular aphorism declared that the heads of newborn children shouldn't be washed often because dirt reinforced the fontanel – the vulnerable soft spot on the infant skull. Lice offered another protection for the young child because they cleaned the blood of its ill humours. Thus everyday opinion tolerated, and even encouraged, some dirtiness among children.[11] Another proverb from the Limousin – "the more children are dirty, the better they will be"

– underscores the point.[12] As to adults, one authority has suggested that behind the many practical reasons for the lack of attention to personal cleanliness in nineteenth-century France lay *obscures motivations psychologiques*, including the belief that the strong odour of peasants and workers expressed their vigour while excessive cleanliness would diminish it.[13] Nor should the sexual meanings of strong body smells be overlooked (the more the ram stinks, the more the ewe loves him).[14]

Wisdom about the protective and curative qualities of filth circulated in eighteenth- and early-nineteenth-century Germany too. The well-known *Heilsame Dreck-Apotheke* (*Healing Filth Pharmacy*), first published in 1696 by the physician Christian Franz Paullini and reprinted several times over the following decades, advocated animal and human feces and urine for their protective and curative value.[15] Published in German at a time when most medical texts were written in Latin, the book clearly was intended for a popular audience. These ideas formed part of an ancient medical tradition of manure therapies linked with rural societies and with the natural world, where human and animal body wastes had obvious life-sustaining functions, and where the medical aid offered by academically trained doctors was usually remote and always expensive. Admittedly it isn't possible to know how often the advice of the *Dreck-Apotheke* was actually followed – or even read. But as an indication of past understandings, the book resembles the folklorists' proverb collections: a record of beliefs circulating among an illiterate rural population in distant generations.

These notions lingered long into the nineteenth century and perhaps later still. According to Bavarian country doctors in the 1860s, the spirit of the *Dreck-Apotheke* still walked their land. Cow dung was used to treat burns while body dirt and lice were regarded as protective.[16] The French custom of not washing a newborn child's head was also known in southern Germany. According to common belief, the resulting dirt cap – which had its own distinctive name, *Kenuß* – safeguarded infant health. Some doctors feared that popular prohibitions about washing children, which they attributed to lay midwives, would create a lifelong prejudice against bathing. These notions corresponded to a deep and widespread fear of water used as a cleansing agent. Not only was it thought to promote disease – washing sick children should be avoided because it caused erysipelas – but bathing the elderly ill reinforced age-old associations between water and death. In some areas religious beliefs were linked with taboos about cleanliness. In the Upper Palatinate, for example, washing the genitals was considered sinful. Many country people avoided summer bathing in rivers and lakes out of a sense of modesty or shame.

These views of the body were tightly intertwined with a rich array of cosmological meanings attributed to water. In traditional Western thought water was both a hostile force and a source of renewal. Running water symbolized life, stagnant water death. In the legends of the Italian Romagna, swamps were home to dragons, the dwelling places of occult and adverse powers, sources of disease for humans and animals alike. But water was also the regenerator, the purifier, the healer. Holy water blessed the farmer's fields and animals, protecting them from calamity. Holy water countered Satan's demonic force with God's divine blessing.[17] Baptism cleansed the sinful man, both literally and symbolically, and transformed him in renewed Christian life. Sufferers sought relief from their ills by washing the afflicted parts of their bodies with holy water.[18] According to popular belief in the Abruzzo, the sea too had a purifying force.[19]

Protestant as well as Catholic teachings emphasized water's cleansing power: sins cleansed by water that had been blessed, bodies cleansed by water to reflect their inner purity. Water had a double meaning; it was linked with the sacred as well as the secular. Holy water was sanctified, offering God's protection; in nature still water meant danger while flowing water nurtured life. In an example drawn from late-eighteenth- or early-nineteenth-century Germany, Easter water was drawn against the river's current to protect against vermin as well as the threat of witches. In another from the same period, children from Osterode in the Harz Mountains of north-central Germany were washed with baptismal water to protect them from skin and head rashes.[20] Enlightened opinion at the time dismissed such practices as superstitious, and these views assumed greater force during the nineteenth century. By implication, too, the importance of such notions was not to be overestimated. But there's also compelling evidence from elsewhere in Western Europe of the broad and deep conviction that water possessed a magical force that cleansed and purified, protected and healed. Paul Sébillot's encyclopedic *Folklore de France* testifies to the endless variety of magical and supernatural meanings linked with the seas and shores, lakes and ponds, rivers and streams, fountains and wells of the Hexagon before the twentieth century.[21]

Of course, therapeutic powers had been attributed to water from time out of mind. Long before the beginning of the nineteenth century, healing pilgrimage sites were scattered across the face of Europe; the popular mind linked water sources to cures for specific diseases, and normally associated them with a particular saint or saints. For example, people sought relief from eye disorders at a cluster of them in lower Brittany dedicated to Sainte-Claire and Notre Dame de la Clarté; the waters of Saint-Méen in Ile-et-Vilaine were thought to heal skin diseases, and the church and fountain of Vitrac-Saint-Vincent in Charente were reputed to cure epilepsy as well as skin complaints.[22] In Protestant England and Scotland, too, believers sought out sacred wells for relief from a long list of ailments, among them female infertility. Some also hoped for knowledge of the future, cures for their animals, or fulfilment of their wishes. One Scottish fountain even promised mastery in marriage to the member of the bridal pair who took its waters first.[23]

Thus a strong undercurrent of ambivalence about water's relationship to the body ran through peasant culture. Despite its widely acknowledged medicinal powers, water's symbolic significance was essentially ambiguous, related as it also was to some of life's most important transitions. According to Jean-Pierre Goubert, "complete immersion of the body in water was associated with the major rites of passage, mainly with birth and death."[24] Therefore, whatever its remedial benefits, water was also a source of anxiety. It had the power to preserve life and to heal, but it also signified life's passing.

An Emerging Science of Personal Hygiene

We know much more of the second school of thought about the body's care because its exponents were literate and sometimes highly articulate. By the eighteenth century a science of the body had existed in Western thought since the time of Hippocrates, and over the millennia it had offered its wisdom – augmented by borrowings from Islamic medicine – to doctors and their patients throughout the European world. The Salerno and Montpellier medical schools played a leading role in diffusing understandings about health from the tenth century onward, and from that time as well, physicians were members of a profession with a corpus of special knowledge about the body. The Montpellier doctors, like those from Salerno, were skeptical about the benefits of bathing and held that excessive washing harmed the body's animal spirits.[25] But on this point opinion was divided; from at least the twelfth century, medical texts also endorsed curative and cleansing baths. The one prevented illness by reinforcing the normal organic functions of the body, thus maintaining equilibrium among the four humours that regulated health, while the other cleansed and beautified the skin. Because beauty was a visible sign of good health, some medical advisers counselled washing as a treatment.[26]

During and after the Renaissance, as direct observation rather than classical theory began to inform understandings of the body, medical curiosity focused most attention on its internal organs and functions. The skin masked the body's mechanics, and as countless illustrations in the great sixteenth- and seventeenth-century anatomies demonstrate, it had to be peeled back to reveal the secrets beneath. It was little studied as a subject in its own right. From a medical perspective, whatever concerns the skin raised had more to do with appearances than with health.

In the Germanic world medical authorities began to recommend bathing as a way to promote good health during the first half of the eighteenth century. While cleanliness *per se* was not the principle objective, some physicians saw healing properties in the body's total immersion. Then during the second half of the century cleanness itself became a leading goal of bathing. Theoreticians disputed the relative values of cold, tepid, and hot baths, but they shared a common view that the entire body should be washed. Toward the end of the century a rising tide of advice literature about the value of bathing spread the word among the literate population, though some of it was little more than thinly veiled advertising for spas and thermal baths.[27] Soon the advice became more prescriptive still. When the Viennese physician, musician, and polymath Peter Lichtenthal published a medical topography of the city in 1810 he prescribed regular washing of the head, whole body bathing two to three times weekly, and a change of underwear every three or four days.[28] By the early nineteenth century many German doctors shared similar views, some even describing a daily bath as the ideal.[29]

During the second half of the eighteenth century a reawakened interest in environmental influences on health began to circulate in other European medical circles, and this too raised sensitivities about the links between health and personal cleanliness. The new awareness directed fresh attention to the effects of climate on fitness, as well as the human factors – customs, diet, work and living conditions – that influenced well-being. An early expression of this interest surfaced in British military circles, where concern for high rates of fever and mortality among soldiers prompted John Pringle, the physician general of the British Army in the 1740s and 1750s, to look for ways of improving the health of troops. His investigations into infection and contagion convinced him that systematic programs promoting personal cleanliness yielded impressive results. James Cook implemented his findings on the first of his global voyages from 1768 to 1771, and with notable success, though the fact that he lost only one man during his circumnavigation was due to more than the simple fact of cleaner sailors' bodies. By the turn of the century the new awareness of hygiene was circulating widely in British military circles.[30] Over the coming decades European military medicine learned much about preserving the health of soldiers and sailors by improving their sanitary conditions. The high mortality rate among troops on imperial adventures, especially in tropical and subtropical climates, made the issue a priority.[31]

As to civilian life, the Scottish physician William Buchan's *Domestic Medicine,* first published in 1769, was the most widely sold English-language health guide during the second half of the eighteenth century. Addressed largely to practitioners, it went through nineteen British editions and 80,000 copies in his lifetime, as well as at least seventeen American editions adapted to the North American climate and disease environment, to say nothing of translations into most major European languages, which also took local circumstances into account.[32] Buchan was a staunch proponent of cleanliness, both personal and communal. As he put it, "few virtues are of more importance than general cleanliness. It ought to be carefully cultivated everywhere; but in populous cities it should be almost revered."[33] Lack of it was one of the great sources of human disease and misery. Worse still, the dirty were not only a threat to themselves but also a menace to the cleanly. "It is not sufficient that I be clean myself," he argued, "while the want of it in my neighbour affects my health as well as his. If dirty people cannot be removed as a common nuisance, they ought at least to be avoided as infectious. All who regard their health should keep a distance from their habitations."[34]

One expression of the new interest in the environmental determinants of well-being was a flourishing school of medical topography, which explored relationships between the health of humans and their immediate surroundings.[35] The new environmentalism also breathed fresh life into the old miasmatic theory of disease transmission – the belief that illnesses were caused by the noxious fumes of decomposing organic matter – which flourished during the first half of the nineteenth century, notably during the cholera epidemics that swept Europe and North America in the 1830s and 1840s. The renewed alarm about miasmas, in turn, heightened sensitivities to unpleasant odours, particularly those of the human body and particularly in bourgeois circles. Offensive smells not only offended but threatened.[36] This fear, in turn, led directly to the body and its hygiene. As Buchan had declared half a century earlier, unclean individuals were a menace to the collective health, and the surest sign of a threat was the stink of an unwashed body.

Toward the end of the eighteenth century, the vitalist impulse in medical thought also turned new attention to the care of the body, including the matter of bathing. Vitalism, with its roots in earlier beliefs about the physical existence of divine and supernatural forces, emphasized regimens drawn from nature. While most deeply rooted in Germany, these doctrines found adherents throughout Europe well into the nineteenth century.[37] Vitalists emphasized the value of bathing as the best means of cleansing the skin, which they recognized as one of the body's major organs. The need to purify the skin seemed particularly important in the period after 1830.[38] Washing opened the skin's pores (all too often obstructed by dirt) and allowed them to exhale the body's impurities. In turn the body functioned more effectively because, like the steam engine – an analogy the vitalists often employed – it used its energy sources more efficiently. Yet some also saw need for caution, fearing a possible loss of physical vitality. If overindulged, bathing might weaken the body by relaxing its fibres.[39] Obviously prudence was needed if the health-giving benefits of washing were to be won.

A further expression of new interest in the body's health was the revival of the spa. Medicinal waters had formed an important part of the culture of health in the classical world, and while thermal baths and bathing went into steep decline after the end of the Roman era, over the following centuries they never entirely lost their curative reputation. Seventeenth-century France saw a renewed interest in water cures and new spas opened, attracting new publics.[40] A parallel impulse surfaced in Great Britain during the same period.[41] Almost invariably the inspiration to found a spa came from an enterprising physician who promoted his establishment as a therapeutic site. The most successful among them developed reputations as important healing centres, but their success also relied on the social prominence of their physician promoters and the genteel clienteles they attracted. The best known English spa, Bath, developed during the same century, though its appeal was as much social as medicinal. In France and the Germanic lands spas for the wealthy flourished from the 1780s onward, their popularity continuing long into the following century.[42] But spa therapy was much more concerned with internal than with external cleanliness. While treatments varied from one establishment to the next, virtually all involved drinking waters for their purgative powers as well as their mineral content. The bathing therapies on offer – mineral baths, steam baths, and various types of showers – were intended to heal much more than to cleanse.

We see a further sign of growing medical awareness about cleanliness in an old word that gained new meaning: hygiene. A term with ancient Greek origins, and one uncommon in Western medical literature before the later eighteenth century, it referred specifically to health and its preservation. But thereafter the concept of hygiene broadened markedly, in time becoming a new discipline within the burgeoning medical sciences, a separate body of knowledge with its own authority and authorities. In 1793 a chair in hygiene was established in the Faculty of Medicine in Paris, creating an institutional foundation for the growth of a new discipline and establishing a model often reproduced during the following decades.[43] Over the course of the nineteenth century, chairs and schools of hygiene were founded in leading medical faculties across the Western world. Hygiene (English), hygiène (French), igiene (Italian), Hygiene (German), higiene (Spanish), hygiëne (Dutch), hygien (Swedish), hygienia (Finnish), higiena (Polish), hygiejne (Danish): the word diffused widely in obviously recognizable forms, at least among cultures using the Latin alphabet, and so did its underlying concepts. In its broadest forms the term referred to the entire branch of human understanding – principles as well as practices – that sustained the health of the individual and of the community. Personal hygiene formed a small but important subset of this new body of knowledge.

It's not entirely clear if the growing interest in bathing was due largely to an increasing acceptance of the physician's expert opinions or if it had other sources as well. But given the limited social reach of medical thought in pre- and early-industrial societies, we probably shouldn't attribute too much influence to the doctors. The emergence of sea bathing certainly owed something to medical sponsorship, but it also had popular and commercial origins. Once an environment with negative, even hostile associations, in the mid-eighteenth-century the seaside began to assume some of its modern meanings, with their strong accent on leisure and pleasure.[44] Naturally the long-standing traditions associating water with curative powers married medicine to the sea. The medicinal sea bath, with its prophets, its physicians, and its patients, became an institution on European coastlines in the second half of the eighteenth century, based on models provided by existing spas.[45] Brighton became a fashionable English seaside resort in the 1750s, the most popular of its kind in the British Isles and one much imitated over the coming decades. By the end of the century the coastlines of Europe were dotted with baths and spas, *bagni* and *kurorten* – Biarritz, Scheveningen, the shores of Campania – supervised by ambitious doctors and offering therapies that ranged from the vigorous to the brutal, the intention being to toughen the body. None held cleanliness as a primary objective.[46]

But sea bathing didn't always have medical associations. The pleasures of immersing the body in ocean water attracted some who felt no need for therapy. Several British coastal communities were offering summer bathing seasons well before Brighton's popularity, and by the end of the century, beaches thronged by thousands in the summer months could be found near many large European cities. Meanwhile, on the other side of the Atlantic, one busy Long Island site served as the fashionable seaside destination for New York residents.[47] Nor were bathers confined to these nascent resorts. While walking along the Welsh coast sands in the 1790s the English poet Coleridge met a group of local bathers, men and boys as well as women, all unselfconsciously – and in his eyes quite innocently – naked. What seems to have prompted his interest was not the bathing itself but rather the mixed-sex nudity of the bathers. By then recreational sea bathing was common enough that it didn't even require comment. After all, Coleridge himself was a swimmer.[48]

Class and the New Cleanliness

Middle class, *bourgeoisie, borghesia, Bürgertum*. The terms have long had many shades of meaning. But they all identify social groups or categories, collectivities that emerged in late-medieval Europe and

evolved slowly over time, occupying the social space between peas-
antries and aristocracies. The boundaries defining their member-
ships were mutable, the economies supporting them volatile. Their
customs and habits, their cultural beliefs and social aspirations,
expressed their wish to distance themselves from those who ranked
beneath them, as well as their equally clear hope to draw closer to
those who stood above them.

Of course, in the highly stratified societies of Western Europe,
social elites had distinguished themselves from others below them
since antiquity. The symbolic display of claims to higher status had
been a feature of social relations for millennia. Clothing expressed
these claims particularly forcefully, and by the seventeenth century
the cleanliness of clothing formed an important part of the message. The elaborate white lace collars we see in Frans Hals's portraits
from the Dutch Golden Age were triumphs of the launderer's art,
and they spoke of the place of spotless clothes in the display of bourgeois respectability.

The state of the skin beneath the clothes was quite another matter.
From the later eighteenth century onward doctors were far from alone
in revising the norms of hygiene. Across Western Europe as well as
in America, new attitudes toward the body and new understandings
about its cleanliness began to circulate in middle-class circles. Initially
these notions were mere germs of ideas, shared by only a few of "the
few." But slowly they gained much wider acceptance, in time becoming a defining characteristic of bourgeois life, one of the cultural pillars
of bourgeois self-awareness. In Germany from the mid-eighteenth-
century onward, cleanliness came to be one of a cluster of *bürgerlich*
attributes that, as an outward expression, spoke to the inner values
of good health, self-discipline, and personal responsibility.[49] A new
form of personal care for a new form of the bourgeois self. In Paris
from the 1780s onward, these aspirations were expressed more often
in material than personal terms, with the construction of public baths
for the rich and bathrooms in the homes of the richer.[50] In the rather
more egalitarian atmosphere of post-revolutionary America, bathing
was also associated with gentility, an impulse that mimicked contemporary British middle-class attitudes.[51]

If these class-based convictions were borne of introspection and
the wish to affirm a more self-confident bourgeois personality, they
also were nourished by comparisons the middle classes drew between
themselves and others. Cleanliness set the dirty apart from the clean,

the foul – to follow Alain Corbin – from the fragrant. For the most part too, the clean were rich and urban – or at least they aspired to be – while the dirty were poor and most often rural. It's a commonplace among Europe's historians to describe the nineteenth as the "bourgeois century," the years when middle-class cultural beliefs, social practices, and economic and political aspirations came to prevail. Bourgeois norms of deportment included views about personal cleanliness that were based on a searching critique of, and a profound disdain for, the unwashed state of the urban poor and the great mass of rural dwellers. A rising tide of condemnation marked the nineteenth-century middle-class hygienic revolution, each censure emphasizing the social chasm between the two groups.[52] And by disparaging lower-class habits, they flattered bourgeois self-perceptions.

The middle-class critique of the unclean lower orders took two contrasting forms. One spoke more of unease, the other more of charity, though both displayed deep concern. As noted earlier, the Scottish physician William Buchan suspected that his unclean neighbours might threaten his own health. Worries like these sharpened with passing time, especially during the great pandemics of the first half of the nineteenth century. Cholera, one of the most dramatic killers in modern history, roused deep-seated anxieties wherever it struck, anxieties about personal health as well as public sanitation. Great soul (and intellectual) searching followed the epidemics of the 1830s in particular. Without an adequate theory to account for the disease and its dramatic spread, physicians and public officials often looked to miasmatic explanations for the outbreaks. They quickly identified the filth of their communities as a primary source of their afflictions. From that perspective it took little imagination to see the connection between dirty bodies and cholera, especially given the disgusting nature of the disease. This was especially so because it tended to strike the poorer districts – and therefore the poor – in most of the communities it blighted. In the major cities of Austria, France, Germany, and Italy the stink of poverty not only offended but threatened. Bourgeois sensibilities about personal cleanliness fused with bourgeois fears about epidemic disease. And the unwashed poor were the source of the deepest anxieties of all.[53]

In Britain too, the combination of filth and epidemics provoked concern about the threat posed by the poor, but there more than elsewhere, middle- and upper-class opinion took a broader view of the matter. It interested itself in the welfare of the lower orders as well as the health of the upper. Beneath these opinions lay an optimistic Protestant evangelical belief in the possibility of a better society as well as a powerful philanthropic impulse. The issues may also have been more sharply etched there than elsewhere, for the first industrial nation displayed the grim living conditions of the working poor earlier and more nakedly than anywhere else in the Western world at the time. Charitable concern was one response. In 1842, when Edwin Chadwick reported on the sanitary state of the British working class, he offered several examples of poor personal hygiene and noted that "the promotion of civic, household, and personal cleanliness, are necessary to the improvement of the moral condition of the population; for that sound morality and refinement in manners and health are not long found co-existent with filthy habits amongst any class of the community."[54] Here Chadwick was merely repeating a commonplace in reform thought.

The Whitechapel Association for Promoting Habits Tending to the Cleanliness, Health and Comfort of the Industrious Classes offers another small but clear example of this charitable impulse. In 1849 a group of concerned residents of the Parish of St Mary in Whitechapel, one of the poorest parts of poor east London, set out to investigate the living conditions of the most wretched of their neighbours on a dwelling-by-dwelling basis and to promote the cause of cleanliness. Their primary goal was the improved welfare of the lower classes, whose health, they believed, was declining. They hired an agent who visited 7,600 residences over the year, recording facts, giving advice, and distributing a tract on the leading causes of disease. His report was a catalogue of distressed housing conditions: insufficient water supply, absent drainage, dilapidated and overcrowded dwellings, and inadequate light and ventilation. He also singled out for comment "the filthy habits of the people."[55] Whatever the practical results of his efforts – and he did report some modest achievements – the work itself was a sign of middle-class concern for the cleanliness of their social lessers, a blend of Christian charity and secular voluntarism combined with confidence that the working class would help itself once shown the right path by those who knew the way.

Cleanliness and the Body Beautiful

Another sign of the new bourgeois interest in bathing was the counsel offered by manuals on feminine beauty. A publishing tradition as old as the printed word, advice literature flourished from the later eighteenth century onward, spurred by the spread of literacy, the declining cost of book publishing, an expanding middle class seeking guidance on right conduct, and the increasing numbers of self-declared experts keen to profit from the market for advice. Self-help books circulated, and at the same time reflected, a wide variety of views about appropriate behaviour. Before the mid-eighteenth century they had little to say about how to accentuate feminine beauty and preserve it from time's certainties. Rather, they viewed a woman's attractions in relation to her conduct, placing them in a moral sphere rather than a physical setting.[56]

A curious novel by a Parisian doctor published in 1754, however, departed from the usual offerings of the loveliness literature. *Abdeker ou l'art de conserver la beauté*, by Antoine Le Camus, purported to be the translation of an Arabic manuscript from the time of Mahomet II, the Ottoman Sultan who conquered Constantinople in 1453. It was a tale of illicit love between Abdeker, a young physician to the women of the Sultan's harem, and Fatmé, an odalisque in his seraglio and a woman of unequalled sweetness and beauty. Time and again Abdeker gained access to the darkest mysteries of the harem, to say nothing of the forbidden charms of the lovely Fatmé, by teaching her the means of preserving her beauty while instructing her in the arts of love.

Le Camus wrote in the orientalist tradition of the erotic exotic. He was one among many Western observers of the Ottoman world fascinated by the image of the harem, with its imagined air of perfumed sensuality and sexual licence. His book was republished at least four times over the coming decades, was translated into English and Italian, and was still in circulation when Mozart's *Die Entführung aus dem Serail* and Rossini's *Il Turco in Italia* and *L'Italiana in Algeri* used the harem to comic effect. In the visual arts, Western painters – famously Ingres in his *Grande Odalisque* – returned time and again to the theme of the seraglio from the late eighteenth century onward.

The curiosity of the book, however, came neither from its romantic plot nor from its erotic overtones but from the fact that it offered feminine beauty tips on a broad range of subjects, bathing among them. Le Camus dotted his text with bits of practical wisdom about women's health, offering handy summaries of his major points at the end of each of the book's two parts. Here was a health care catechism with a difference! His advice on bathing was set in the context of Abdekar's visit to a bath in the harem, a luxurious setting rich with the promise of voluptuous delights. But the author's suggestions about bathing were quite prosaic. One bathed to preserve a white skin and to cleanse it of dirt, for pleasure and politeness as well as for health. Bathing offered a host of natural benefits, Le Camus declared, yet one should proceed with caution because inconsiderate use could be the cause of major ills.[57]

With its emphasis on a suggestive world of exquisite sensuality, Le Camus's advice left the idea of such a bath in the realm of his reader's imagination. For all but the most privileged Europeans of the time, even the remote possibility of actually bathing in this manner was utterly out of reach. In this respect the author's views on how to display and preserve feminine attractiveness were out of step with those offered by most other advisers of the later eighteenth century. The beauty counsellors of the period had little to say about washing the body and much to say about a host of other matters: cosmetics, perfumes, hair care, and dress, to name a few.[58]

But soon after the turn of the century, some of these self-appointed advisers – most of them male – began to pay more attention to the role of bathing in women's personal care. One of the first was Auguste Caron, whose *Toilette des dames ou Encyclopédie de la beauté*, published in 1806 and later translated into English and Italian, hymned the importance of cleanliness to women's beauty. As the English edition explained,

> there is in the toilette of women one very essential requisite, and which constitutes its greatest merit in the eyes of the delicate man; I mean cleanliness. Cleanliness alone, unaccompanied by any other recommendation, has a right to please, to attract the eye, to gratify the taste, to excite desire; the toilette, without cleanliness, fails in its object; it displays only idle pretentions, bad taste and low sentiments ... Cleanliness is that precious quality which nearly transforms a woman into a divinity, by removing from her every thing that might betray the imperfections of human nature.[59]

In Caron's view, careful attention to her personal hygiene, of her body and its clothing, was the primary means a woman had to display and preserve her beauty. He advocated frequent bathing in warm water – never cold, which injured feminine loveliness – and even suggested that scented soaps might be used to cleanse the skin more perfectly. The face, hands, and feet should be washed regularly if bathing was not possible. Hair, however, was quite another matter. While Caron advised the same high standards for its cleanliness, he strongly criticized washing the head with water, which produced aches of the head, ears, and teeth, as well as eye complaints. Regular combing and the occasional application of hair powders or bran would keep it clean.[60]

The nineteenth-century woman addressed by these authors could only be a lady of leisure. The frequent baths proposed by an anonymous Italian author in 1827 – at least once weekly and more often in the hot season – should take at least one and a half hours, an opinion shared by Mme Celnart, another mentor generous with her advice about matters feminine.[61] A generation later Auguste Debay, the prolific and widely published French author of guides to hygiene (clothes, diet, beards, vocal organs, marriage, hands and feet, to name only some), suggested that baths should probably last longer still.[62] Obviously the woman imagined by these authors had time on her hands. But of far greater significance, by the early decades of the nineteenth century the virtues of the bath had become indisputable, and from this point on it occupied a central place in the advice directed to women. As Debay claimed in 1846, the warm bath is essential to the cleanliness of the body, to the maintenance of its flexibility and freshness; one can consider it necessary for the general health of the individual.[63]

Modesty and Ambivalence

But whatever support bathing could muster from the health and beauty guides, it also had to contend with misgivings and restrictions, for modesty challenged the spread of the bath throughout much of its long history. The Greco-Roman myth of the huntress Artemis (or Diana) and Actaeon was one of its early expressions, most widely known from the Renaissance onward through Ovid's *Metamorphoses*.[64] Tired from her day's hunt, the chaste goddess Diana was surprised while bathing in a limpid forest pool, together with her attending nymphs. The male intruder was the mortal Actaeon, a hunter like herself, who blundered alone into her sacred grove at the end of his day's pursuits. The nymphs tried, but failed, to cover Diana's nakedness with their own and Actaeon saw her unclothed. In shame and anger she took revenge by depriving him of speech and turning him into a stag. Transformed, he took flight, but soon his hunting dogs took up the chase and, unable to cry out, he met his death at their jaws, avenging Diana's wronged modesty. The myth was a recurring theme in European painting from the sixteenth to the eighteenth centuries, with Titian, Rubens, and Rembrandt among the many artists drawn to various moments in the story. Some depicted Diana quietly bathing alone, others the goddess in her grotto surrounded by her attendants. Still others – notably Titian – portrayed the dramatic moment of Actaeon's fatal glimpse and Diana's chilling response.[65] But the thread running through them all was a sense of diffidence and reserve that surrounded the bathing female.

The association of nudity and shame also lies deep within the Judeo-Christian tradition. Adam and Eve lived naked and unembarrassed in the Garden of Eden. But when God banished them from Paradise, disgraced by their disobedience, they covered themselves as best they could with leaves until He gave them animal skins to wear. From that point on humankind was to be clothed, for nakedness revealed the shame of original sin.[66] Two Old Testament stories related to bathing – David and Bathsheba (2 Samuel 11) and Susanna and the Elders (Daniel 13) – depict the virtues of feminine modesty and the masculine threat to its violation.[67] From the roof of his palace, David, King of the Israelites, observed Bathsheba at her bath and desired her. He sent for her, lay with her, and, having later learned from her that she had conceived his child, instructed that her husband Uriah be exposed to death in battle so he could marry her. When her mourning was over she became one of David's wives and bore him a son. But David's conduct had displeased the Lord, who punished David by taking the life of the son conceived in adultery.

In the second tale the Elders, two lecherous voyeurs, observed the faithful wife Susanna while she was bathing in her garden, alone and unaware of their gaze. They desired her, approached her, confessed their lust, and threatened to accuse her of lying with another man unless she accepted each of them. Rather than commit a sin she refused their embraces. The following day they accused her of adultery before an assembly in her husband's house. Believing the Elders, the assembly condemned her, but before she could be put to death, the youthful Daniel defended her, declaring that she had been sentenced without the facts being determined. He questioned each of the accusers separately, revealed them as false witnesses, and the people put them to death instead of her. The assembled, including Susanna's family and children, then praised God that she had not been found guilty of a shameful deed.

From their central place in Judeo-Christian teaching, both stories offered rich opportunities for European artists from the seventeenth century onward. The tale of Susanna, in particular, attracted a great deal of painterly attention. Most of these canvases feature a demure young woman, nude or lightly draped, David in the distance observing Bathsheba, the Elders leering at Susanna from much closer quarters. The artists themselves often seem more absorbed with the loveliness of the female form than with the deeper meanings of the stories they depict. Yet their female subjects are invariably modest, engrossed in the mundane moments of their baths, their eyes averted from the gaze of their voyeurs as well as those of the paintings' viewers. The eroticism depicted is that of male lust, not feminine seductiveness. But these paintings involve two groups of observers, not one: David and the Elders within the pictures themselves, and the patrons, connoisseurs, and other observers who view them. The outside eye may well have been – and may well still be – as voyeuristic as those of the inside observers. In any case the message is clear enough. The women in these paintings have had their privacy invaded, their modesty assaulted. Their innocent nakedness has aroused illicit male desire. In spite of the ambiguities beneath the painters' intentions or the observers' perceptions, these are cautionary tales.

Turning from paintings to practices and from high culture to everyday life, we can readily see the challenges bathing posed to feminine modesty. Both spiritual and secular authority, to say nothing of respectable opinion, upheld decorous norms of deportment, and these were internalized at all levels of society. The intimate act of cleansing the body, or at least those parts of it not normally visible, could arouse the prospect of shame whether performed in public or in private. The nude Welsh bathers whom Coleridge met while walking the shores of the Irish Sea were anything but typical of the period. Public nakedness was highly uncommon in his time, and long afterwards as well, throughout the transatlantic world. Of course there were exceptions. Naked summer bathing in lakes and rivers was far from unknown, but the practice was mostly confined to adolescent males. And it often prompted rebuke. On at least three occasions during a summer journey in Germany and Switzerland in 1775, the youthful Goethe and two young aristocratic travelling companions went swimming in the nude, and each time they met a hostile reception. On the first they were forced to flee, on the second (in Switzerland) they earned a lecture on civic respect, and on the third they were pelted with stones.[68] Similarly, in Vienna during the 1820s, when two of the composer Franz Schubert's circle went skinny-dipping in the *Wienerkanal,* several women from the Imperial Court spotted them. Embarrassed and apologetic, they hurried into their clothes so quickly that they abandoned their underwear, hiding their damp nakedness beneath their frock coats. No sooner dressed than they met two policemen on patrol, who eyed them suspiciously but didn't press charges.[69]

Nude public bathing was prohibited virtually everywhere, condemned by custom, public opinion, and the law. Open nakedness was both a moral and a legal violation. Even when bathers were clothed, their costumes were carefully regulated by canons of respectable conduct and their ever-vigilant guardians.[70] The body was to be well covered, and covered in ways that avoided any hint of sensuality. Costumes that were too brief, too clinging, too loose, or too transparent were condemned where not prohibited. Here too, naturally, there were exceptions. As a tourist in Biarritz in 1843, Victor Hugo enjoyed the sight of the girls of the village and the pretty grisettes of Bayonne bathing in serge shirts, often with many holes, without much care for what the openings showed and the shirts hid.[71] But the fact of the remark itself suggests that what Hugo saw was unusual.

The claims of modesty were just as strong within the domestic circle. Once early childhood had passed, strong prohibitions against nudity formed part of household culture at all levels of society. The mid-eighteenth-century tale of the Marquise du Châtelet (Voltaire's mistress) and her bath seems to contradict this observation. Attended by a male servant while bathing in the nude, the marquise asked him to warm the water, opened her legs to allow him to add boiling water without harming her, and then reproved him for not watching what he was doing more carefully. The young man was deeply embarrassed though du Châtelet, it seems, was not.[72] According to the sociologist Norbert Elias, this incident was an indication that nakedness among social elites did not infringe the claims of modesty when it occurred in front of servants and others of lower social status.[73] He regarded it as an expression of greater openness in matters of bodily privacy, as well as a sign that social inferiors counted for little when it came to respect, and it marked a way station along the broad path to far greater nineteenth-century prudery.

But this episode can be set against others from the same period that clearly reveal modesty's face. Marie Antoinette normally bathed in the presence of two female servants, clothed in a flannel bathing dress buttoned from the neck to the ankles.[74] She demanded that they hold a sheet between them and her high enough that she could not be seen so that, when she emerged from her bath, they would not be able to catch sight of her wet dress clinging to her body. Admittedly these examples are anything but typical, taken as they are from the highest reaches of pre-revolutionary French society, and we cannot be certain which of them more closely approached the norm. But it seems more likely that Marie Antoinette's prudery lay nearer to common concerns, while the marquise committed an indecency by eighteenth-century standards, as her servant recognized all too well.

Moving down the social hierarchy and ahead in time, we find many other occasions when modesty's reticence placed restrictions on washing. In French upper-class circles throughout much of the nineteenth century, girls and women commonly wore a shirt when bathing whether or not the body was immersed, cleaning themselves beneath it. The practice remained customary in boarding schools for girls well into the twentieth century.[75] Presumably shirts were worn when individual privacy was unavailable. Yet the solitary bath also held perils. While the beauty literature promoted a vision of feminine languor in the bath, other advisers were ambivalent, cautioning against its sensual pleasures while approving its hygienic benefits for both sexes. Usually they voiced their concerns only by implication, but what they feared most was the stimulus to sexual desire offered by nudity, warm water, and privacy. Genital hygiene was an especially risky matter, to be approached with particular caution.[76] More generally, nudity seems to have been highly problematic for elites on both sides of the Atlantic throughout the nineteenth century and well into the twentieth. Writing in the 1950s, the Italian novelist Giuseppe Tomasi di Lampedusa recognized this fact in *Il Gattopardo,* set in Risorgimento Sicily. The protagonist, Prince Fabrizio Salina, a wealthy member of the traditional landowning aristocracy, remarks at one point that he had had seven children by his wife but had never seen her navel.[77] While the observation was a fiction, it reflects a pervasive truth about privacy, modesty, and the bourgeois-aristocratic body across the Western world from the *ancien régime* to the *fin de siècle.*

Modesty, if not prudery, left its mark on the great rural and urban masses of the period as well. One particularly powerful example, the sense of shame about genital cleansing that we noted in the mid-nineteenth-century German Palatinate, seems to have been broadly shared throughout European society. French country doctors complained about the matter until at least the end of the century, some condemning it as the consequence of rural ignorance and superstition, others – often anticlericals – attributing it to Catholic teachings. Their primary concern was neglect of feminine hygiene, especially involving menstruation, to which they attached a long list of vaginal disorders.[78] As one physician put it in 1900: "A ridiculous modesty condemns this mysterious and secret region, where every disease is easily classified as shameful and the slightest gesture of cleanliness is considered an immoral act, to a revolting neglect."[79]

Powerful taboos about nakedness also marked urban working-class life in the early industrial period. Whatever the city, the vast majority of labouring families in nineteenth-century Europe and America lived in small, crowded dwellings that offered little privacy. Parents commonly took great pains to conceal their nakedness from their children and also to shield their children's eyes from the bodies of their opposite-sex siblings.[80] In Vienna, and no doubt everywhere else, working-class people seldom undressed before bed; they slept in their clothes or underclothes. A late-nineteenth-century Viennese account makes the impulse toward modesty perfectly clear:

> Kate F., born in 1889. Coming from a working class family, as a child she never learned anything about sexual matters from her parents ... The physical differences between boys and girls long remained unclear. She was the oldest of 13 children. While bathing in the washtub the siblings were separated, and though she slept in a bed with three other siblings, she never saw anything "indecent," because no one was allowed to go to bed without pants.[81]

To respect the canons of right conduct, parents bathed when their children were asleep or in school, if they bathed at all.[82]

The idea of the clean body thus had to contend with ambivalence and equivocation, as well as some outright opposition, before the twentieth century. Much of it came from the challenges bathing posed to traditional notions about the meaning of nakedness. There can be no doubt about the long-standing cultural bias towards modesty in the Western tradition. For centuries, in virtually all public and private settings, the fully clothed body was the only acceptable one. Yet the precise meanings of modesty and the locations of its frontiers had shifted over time, and they were to move further still during the nineteenth and twentieth centuries. Some of the key issues concerned the cultural significance of nudity, particularly whether it was intended or viewed as an erotic gesture. Ambivalence about bathing stemmed in part from the latent eroticism of the naked body, especially the naked female body. With the growth of recreational public bathing came the concern to clothe it in ways that erased its sexual signals. The same seems to have been true of the private baths enjoyed by the highborn and the rich, attended as they were by their servants, and also by those who took indoor baths communally. Ambivalence came, too, from a distrust of the sensuality that a private warm-water bath seemed to offer. On one hand it might weaken the body through indulgence in debilitating excess. On the other it might lead to erotic self-pleasure, challenging one of the greatest sexual taboos of the period. A further concern, much darker still, came from the fact of proximity. Well into the twentieth century, domestic spaces were crowded spaces for all but the favoured few, the less the favour the more the crowding. The shame of nakedness between sexes and generations – one rooted in primal incest taboos – was itself a major obstacle to the progress of the bath.

PRACTICES

The Old Cleanliness and the New

Before the modern age, fleas and lice were the body's constant companions. They were generally viewed as a fact of nature, a circumstance shared with the animal world, so normal that their presence attracted only occasional comment.[83] The remarks themselves seldom expressed concern or disgust but merely annoyance or discomfort, and even then with an occasional touch of irony. According to Emmanuel LeRoy Ladurie, delousing was much more common than washing in early-fourteenth-century Montaillou; it was a task commonly shared among family members or lovers – those most likely familiar with one another's privacies.[84] The graphic arts suggest something of the state of European bodies before the end of the eighteenth century. Genre pictures of everyday life sometimes include delousing scenes, a further indication of how normal the practice was. From our perspective it seems more a matter of grooming than of personal hygiene; if the gesture expressed any emotion at all it likely was affection (Plate 1).

Whatever ideas were in circulation about bodily cleanliness, customs varied greatly across the transatlantic world. The gulf between theory and practice was wide. It was one thing for counsellors to advocate regular bathing and systematic body care, quite another for the counselled to accept the advice. Most of them didn't even receive it and likely wouldn't have accepted it if they had. In matters concerning body care, traditional beliefs and lifeways resisted modernization's persuasions. The new cleanliness also required new technologies and resources, which in turn demanded new ideas and investments, obstacles that took decades to overcome. As well, full-body washing implied opportunities for privacy, difficult to find in the crowded dwellings where most people spent their lives. The occasional bathing scene in early modern genre art reminds us that the practice wasn't completely unknown. Plate 2, a seventeenth-century landscape by the Italian baroque painter Guercino, offers one example. It also includes the customary male figures in the distance, in this case two approaching hunters, with the implied threat they offered to feminine modesty. But over time new hygienic routines gradually spread, touching the daily lives of greater and greater numbers. When it came to personal cleanliness, the habits of 1900 were a far cry from those of centuries before.

In a world where most people lived and worked on the land, however, the new cleanliness made slow progress. We have ample evidence to indicate that country dwellers seldom washed, and when they did they only cleaned the parts of their bodies that others could see. Much of what we know on the subject comes from the complaints of country doctors, a far from disinterested group, who routinely deplored the lack of cleanliness among the rural folk in their communities. But while their comments were coloured by class perspectives and professional interests, there can be little doubt about the conditions they described. "In our countryside bathing is alien to residents, who believe that sweat replaces it," commented one mid-nineteenth-century observer from a rural district east of Frankfurt am Main. The adults of the countryside, echoed a colleague from a neighbouring community, never washed their bodies with water apart from their faces and hands. Instead, "from time to time sweat frees them from their crust-like dirt."[85]

Nor was the situation much different elsewhere. A careful investigation of popular hygiene in the Nivernais of central France from the 1860s onward concluded that, at least before 1914, the local populace "virtually never wash themselves, they don't have the habit of washing." According to a late-nineteenth-century observer from neighbouring Morvan, the men "wash their faces a little when they shave, but the rest of the body has never felt a drop of water since their birth. Baths are unknown in the Morvan."[86] In the Nivernais these conditions persisted into the interwar years of the twentieth century, and perhaps later still.[87] The examples multiply. Alexandre Layet, professor of hygiene at the University of Bordeaux, considered the French peasantry extremely unclean. Quoting his colleague Jean-Marie-Placide Munaret, a physician much published from the 1850s through the 1870s, Layet claimed that "the peasant... only bathes or washes himself when he falls in the water." According to Munaret, "the feet, the armpits, the genitals of the peasant, exhale an odor in itself so foul and penetrating that it often forced me to ventilate my examination room, after a consultation which lasted only fifteen minutes."[88] Antonin Baratier, another late-nineteenth-century French hygienist, noted that children were no exception: "The village child is a hydrophobe in the strict sense of the term; he is afraid of contact with water and most often he passes a dry cloth, more or less stained, over his face before leaving for school in the morning. If, sometimes, on Sundays and holidays, the ablutions are less summary, during the rest of the time they are considered useless and superfluous."[89]

On those rare occasions when bodies or body parts were washed, usually there were unusual reasons. Often these moments marked a transition from everyday to festive life. Country folk in mid-nineteenth-century Germany sometimes washed their heads and necks on Sundays and holidays but otherwise avoided bodily contact with water.[90] Similarly, in later-nineteenth-century France, rural dwellers sometimes gave themselves a cursory wash on Saturday nights or Sunday mornings and on the eves of holidays. It was on these occasions, too, that men also shaved or frequented a local barber.[91] In the Italian province of Macerata during the later nineteenth century and the early decades of the twentieth, a bride-to-be was allowed a bath on the morning of her wedding. Or rather allowed to bathe. She washed in the kitchen, using as much water from the water jugs as she wished, in addition to a clean towel. After donning new underclothes she then withdrew to a room left free for her, where she dressed for her nuptials with the help of her female relations and close friends.[92] We need not linger over the symbolic meanings of these gestures, rich though they no doubt are. But from a practical point of view it could well have been a bride's sole opportunity to bathe like this throughout her entire lifetime.

Conditions were not much different among the first generations of workers during the early Industrial Age. In the later 1830s, when the English reformer Edwin Chadwick surveyed the sanitary condition of the British working class, he heard from a Lancashire collier who reported that none of the men and women he worked with ever bathed their bodies, though he and his sisters did clean their faces, necks, and ears. As he told the inquiry, "they never wash their bodies underneath; I know that; and their legs and bodies are as black as your hat." As to the poor, his report observed, when paupers were washed on admission to a Poor House, they often objected to the process. At the same time, Chadwick did find examples of regular working class bathing, noting a group of Welsh colliers who had a tub wash each evening after they returned home from the pits. Lack of personal cleanliness, he concluded, wasn't the consequence of any particular occupation or of poverty but of "neglect and indolence."[93] What the labouring classes needed, he suggested, was new and better habits.

The "Longue Durée" of the Bath

Still, bathing had its own deep history in Western civilization, and while practices varied over time and across cultural space, it had persisted in one form or another across the millennia. Once numbered among the Roman world's greatest glories, public thermal baths gradually disappeared after the empire collapsed in the fourth century. Without the political will, the architectural understanding, and the technical knowledge to maintain them, the great baths declined along with the entire fabric of antique urban civilization. Moreover, the convivial customs of the Roman baths found no equivalents in medieval Europe. As centres of everyday sociability, they simply ceased to be.

Nonetheless, the concept of bathing continued to receive at least theoretical support from two important medieval sources: the Christian Church and the physicians. While the church strongly condemned some older social practices associated with bathing

– especially the mixed bathing of the two sexes – it strongly supported the bath *per se*. Some church fathers thought that bathing
was as necessary for the maintenance of the body as was food, that
a clean body was an image of the purity of the soul. During the
high Middle Ages many of the existing public baths were associated
with the Church and its charitable institutions. It was during this
period, as well, that soap – not used as a cleansing agent in antiquity
– was introduced into the bath. One surviving sign of its early use
in Europe was the eighth-century gift of 30 libbre (about 10 kg) of
soap given by the Longobard king Liutprando to the cathedral in
Piacenza for washing the poor.[94]

As to the physicians, from at least the twelfth century onward
medical texts endorsed both curative and cleansing baths. The
former, they declared, prevented illness by reinforcing the normal
organic functions of the body, thus maintaining the four humours
in equilibrium. The latter, just as necessary for good health, cleansed
and beautified the skin. Because beauty was a visible sign of well-being, medical advisers counselled washing as a treatment.[95] But as far
as practices were concerned, we know almost nothing about how
many people bathed in medieval society, how often they washed, and
what parts of their bodies they cleaned when they did. The medieval-
ist Jacques Le Goff notes scattered bits of evidence suggesting that
bathing persisted throughout the Middle Ages, but he concludes that
the cleansing bath was largely an individual and domestic practice,
not a public one.[96]

Inevitably there were exceptions. While medieval churchmen established public baths because they saw religious meanings in bathing,
there were those among the laity who built them for much more
profane reasons. Many of the surviving images of medieval bathing customs illustrate brothel scenes, depicting a reality in at least
some European communities and one reason why Church authorities condemned most public baths apart from their own. A licentious
reputation clung to public bathing throughout the later Middle Ages.
At the same time, other illustrations portray the bath's therapeutic
and rejuvenating associations, two common themes in late medieval
painting. In this instance art reflected another underlying reality, for
the healing bath became widely diffused throughout Europe at the
time, particularly in Italy.[97] As public institutions, however, baths
went into steep decline after the end of the fifteenth century. Their ill
repute, combined with a virgin soil epidemic of syphilis that swept

Europe following Columbus's return from the Americas, discouraged communal bathing and led many local authorities to suppress it. While bathhouses never disappeared, they lived fitful lives for the next two centuries. In Germany they often offered only steam baths – a cheaper alternative than tub bathing – and they served only the popular classes. If the refined bathed at all, they did so at home.[98]

Defining a New Hygienic Consensus

Public baths saw the first signs of revival in the mid-eighteenth century. An ambitious English apothecary, John King, opened a river bath on the river Waveney in Suffolk, northeast of London, in 1737, and according to a contemporary account it seemed a garden of earthly delights.[99] By the end of the century commercial baths could be found in major British cities, some offering hot-water bathing, a few even promising the exotic delights of a Turkish bath or *hammam*. Among them presumably were long-established spas whose watery functions now embraced something beyond therapy.

In 1761 Jean-Jacques Poitevin, a pioneer bathhouse entrepreneur in Paris, established the first warm-water baths there on two boats anchored near the Pont Royale adjacent to the Palais du Louvre. In effect, what Poitevin opened was an urban spa for hydrotherapy, and he obviously had the luxury trade in mind. As he stated, it was necessary to "to give the rich the chance to be healed more quickly than if they had to seek the necessary help far from home."[100] For the next few decades Poitevin had the Paris bath trade to himself, but in the early 1790s Barthélemy Turquin established a floating cold-water bath on the Seine at the Pont de la Tournelle, some distance downstream from the Poitevin amenities. The Turquin facilities combined the pleasures of river bathing with the discretions of individual privacy. They consisted of a series of small baths in private compartments pierced with holes allowing the free flow of water, and suspended in a way that kept them immersed at a constant depth. Each bath could hold up to three persons.[101] The new Turquin baths – termed *bains chinois* – were part of a trend, for the number of public bathing facilities in Paris grew toward the end of the century. There were 150 public bathtubs in the city on the eve of the Revolution, 500 by 1816. At that time, according to the early-nineteenth-century hygienist Louis Benoiston de Châteauneuf, Paris offered a choice between 20 and 25 establishments in addition to four bathing ships on the river. He estimated that on average, each provided 25 baths a day, amounting to 22,500 monthly or 270,000 per year – admittedly a modest number for a city of more than 700,000 people.[102] For the most part they served a genteel clientele, a fact reflected in their prices. The cost of a bath in one of the new Parisian facilities ranged from two to five times the daily wage of a common labourer.[103] As well, like the public baths of old, they offered a mix of therapeutic and recreational opportunities. Their hygienic possibilities were only beginning to be recognized.

As the nineteenth century progressed, so the number of public baths in Paris increased. According to one report, by the early 1830s there were nearly 2,400 fixed public bathtubs in the city, as well as several hundred portable ones, the so-called *bains à domicile* or *baignoires mobiles*, which delivered baths to private residences – tub, hot water, and all – to say nothing of the services offered by the now five bathing ships anchored on the Seine. But as the number of public bathing facilities grew, so did Paris; its population almost doubled to more than 1 million during the first half of the nineteenth century. The average price of a bath fell somewhat but the cost remained prohibitive for most city residents. Not only that but the bath proprietors naturally located their facilities close to their markets, serving the wealthiest parts of the city while stinting the poorer *quartiers*. Only 4 of the 68 establishments operating in 1830 were located in Paris's burgeoning suburbs, and although the number of baths doubled over the next two decades, this pattern would change very little.[104] The rise of the public bath certainly marked a shift in bourgeois hygienic sensibilities and a growing interest in personal cleanliness, but these new attitudes were largely confined to the relatively privileged. The great mass of the city's poor either had no desire to bathe or little opportunity to do so if they wished.

Before long the Parisian innovations in public bathing cropped up elsewhere too. By the early decades of the nineteenth century both cold- and warm-water baths, on ship and shore, could be found in other large French cities.[105] Meanwhile similar developments appeared in Vienna, not in imitation of the Paris example so much as an expression of an emerging *bürgerlich* concern for personal cleanliness like that found in France. In 1781 Pascal Joseph Ferro, a Viennese physician, opened a floating bath – *Flußbadeschiff* – on a tributary of the Danube in suburban Leopoldstadt, a moment seen at the time as the dawn of a new hygienic era. Two decades later the Austrian government established a free public swimming area not far from Ferro's ship, a gesture that offered the recreational benefits of bathing to all Viennese. In succeeding years other facilities opened, including a military swimming school in the Prater (1811) – among the earliest of several founded in Austria-Hungary and Prussia during the early nineteenth century – as well as a special swimming school for women (1831). By the later 1820s there were at least eight private bathing areas in Vienna, some offering warm-water baths.

New baths and new bathing customs spread quickly in the German-speaking lands during the late eighteenth and early nineteenth centuries. Pierre Girard, author of an 1832 report on public baths in Paris, noted that the so-called *bains à domicile* had long been available in Berlin and other German cities.[106] The first German *Flußbadeanstalt* was opened in Mannheim on the Rhine in 1777, and by the early nineteenth century both river baths and urban spas could be found in Berlin, Hamburg, and many smaller German centres. The German bath industry soon developed in two directions, one decidedly bourgeois, the other emphatically plebian. The new urban spas were well appointed, often luxurious, and therefore costly. They were centres of *bürgerlich* social life as well as sites of therapy and relaxation, and they exuded a strong note of social exclusivity. A clean, well-groomed body was a sign of high social standing and it set the washed well apart from the unclean.[107]

Across the Atlantic, the first commercial bathhouses opened in Philadelphia and New York in the 1780s and 1790s. While the goal of cleanliness was more clearly acknowledged in the New World than in the Old, personal hygiene had much the same associations with social rank, even though the class structure of early America departed strikingly from European patterns.[108] Long before the mid-nineteenth century, American standards of cleanliness had taken on obvious class associations, just as they had in Western Europe. A strong sense of social and moral superiority tinged middle-class notions of hygiene. Cleanliness and refinement stood in contrast with filthiness and vulgarity, clean bodies and clothes with grime and offensive odours. The washed wore their spotlessness as a badge of their social standing, though it seems unlikely that the unwashed felt a similar sense of identity in their soiled selves. Here too, practices followed mentalities; while middle-class Americans gradually began to absorb the new rituals of personal hygiene, the lower ranks lagged well behind.[109]

Swimming, River Bathing, and Popular Hygiene

As to the lower social orders, the most obvious opportunities for bathing were those offered seasonally by rivers and ponds, lakes and oceans. Swimming was common across Europe throughout the early modern era. In Central Europe it had a history reaching back to at least the later Middle Ages, and from the late eighteenth century we find growing evidence of "wild bathing" or "free water swimming" in many European areas. For the most part the swimmers seem to have been young, male, and nude, as the example of Goethe and his friends suggests. It also hints that the custom had little to do with cleansing the body and much with recreation. Certainly the practice was widespread enough to provoke concerns and restrictions, for example, a French law from the *ancien régime* that confined sporting bathing in Paris to designated areas on the Seine.[110] River bathing in London also aroused unease during the second half of the eighteenth century, its middle-class opponents concerned with offences to public decency, the effects of dirty plebian bodies on water quality, and the generally oafish conduct of the lower-class bathers. In 1814 Parliament banned nude bathing in the Thames.[111]

In Vienna swimming fell under even earlier scrutiny. From the seventeenth century onward public officials placed restrictions on swimming in open nature for a variety of reasons, mainly to do with assumptions about its immorality and its dangers. Given the limited powers of governments, strict enforcement of prohibitions was difficult, but toward the end of the eighteenth century the Austrian state began to supervise swimming much more closely. Most of the outdoor baths established from the 1780s onward were enclosed spaces in open, free-running water and were licensed by public officials. They were intended to offer recreation and improve their users' physical culture much more than to promote clean bodies. Their establishment sharply inscribed the line between legal supervised bathing and illegal swimming in nature.[112] These new facilities were an early sign of the modern state's interest in population health, the relationship between water and the body in particular.

In Paris too, river bathing in summer became more common from the late eighteenth century onward, for the most part at commercial sites, though elsewhere French youths usually swam wherever and whenever they wished.[113] The popular classes visited the inexpensive *bains à quatr' sous* that sprouted along the Seine after the turn of the century, while the bourgeoisie could choose among the greater comforts promised by more costly establishments.[114] By the 1840s the Paris baths were still something of a novelty, yet familiar enough that the caricaturist Honoré Daumier could lampoon their habitués. In a series of tableaux drawn from Parisian bath life – *Les Baigneurs* (1839–41) and *Les Baigneuses* (1847) – he satirized the gracelessness of the human body and the shallowness of bourgeois manners.[115] As in Vienna, several swimming schools appeared on the Seine during the early decades of the nineteenth century.[116] Inevitably they served a male clientele, though the Bains Lambert at the eastern end of the Île-Saint-Louis were a feminine preserve.[117] But unlike the Viennese, some promoted cleanliness as well as recreation. Still, bathing lay beyond the financial reach of most Parisians, a fact that concerned hygienists of the period, worried as they were becoming about the moral degradation of uncleanliness.[118] In the early 1820s health authorities proposed that the city provide free baths for the poor, but, lacking wider support, the idea sank without a trace.

From the 1780s onward, however, local governments in many German cities provided baths for the poor. In doing so they honoured long-standing traditions of communal care for the unfortunate. In Mainz, for example, the elector issued certificates providing free warm baths for the indigent. The government of Württemberg oversaw a large *Flußbadeplatz* on the Neckar, near Stuttgart, that offered free supervised bathing. According to contemporaries, hundreds of swimmers, local residents as well as soldiers from nearby regiments, took their pleasures there daily during the warm summer months. In 1788 civic authorities in Würzburg required the concessionaire licensed to operate a bath on the Main River to allow the poor free entry. The Nuremberg police department established a makeshift bathhouse for artisans in 1807. Gestures like these were the origins of the late-nineteenth-century *Volksbad*, intended for the lower orders. But despite concern to provide bathing facilities for the disadvantaged public, here too cleanliness was never the primary goal. Recreation and refreshment topped the list for river bathing and, as for the hot bath, it was still considered medicinal and disciplinary.[119]

By the mid-nineteenth century, then, a new hygienic consensus had taken form across Western Europe and North America. Decidedly urban and middle class, it set the standards by which personal hygiene was measured. While cleanliness itself was not yet its primary focus, it accepted immersing the body in water as a positive good. Regular, full-body bathing offered benefits for health and recreation as well as feminine beauty. The leading advocates of the new hygiene included a miscellany of enterprising spa promoters and bathhouse operators, medical experts eager with health advice, and earnest middle-class do-gooders dispensing benevolent wisdom. Their audiences, however, were seldom as keen to accept these messages as their advocates were to deliver them. Practice followed precept, at least to some extent, but the social reach of bathing remained limited. Spas addressed the health concerns of the wealthy as they long had done, and the new baths of the late-eighteenth and early-nineteenth centuries supplemented them by introducing limited public bathing to the urban scene. When the first European indoor swimming pool, the Dianabad, opened in Vienna in 1843, it promised a new age of watery pleasures.[120] A light and airy glass, wood, and cast-iron construction, it was the very model of modern functionality. But by itself the luxury bath trade was not brisk enough to keep the building open; over the following decades it also served other cultural ends as a fashionable concert hall and ballroom. Always a site of upper-class sociability, the Dianabad and its kind priced bathing beyond the reach of all but the well-to-do few. For the great majority one alternative was a dip in a nearby body of water, a seasonal pleasure that in some places was illegal. The other was no bath at all.

PART TWO

Cleanliness as Habit

In concept as much as in practice the habits of routine body care began to assume new forms throughout the Western world during the nineteenth century. Traditional beliefs about body care slowly decayed and age-old customs eroded, leading to new understandings of hygiene and a heightened concern for cleanliness. These changes found expression in attempts to improve the ways of the masses and, later, in public policies intended to raise standards of personal conduct. The new convictions reflected upper-class views about cleanliness, views buttressed in time by the discovery of microbes and the elaboration of the germ theory. Bourgeois opinion then joined hands with medical science to fashion hygienic regimes that would define best behaviour, elevate deportment, and preserve good health. In time these ideas became the common currency of public discussion about body care.

Yet by themselves new beliefs were not enough to transform time-worn habits. If the new cleanliness was to become the norm it also required innovations: new technologies and new architectures. The challenges and costs of water use in the pre-modern city had to be overcome if water was to be a universal good, abundant, inexpensive, and shared readily by all. New infrastructures needed to ease water's movement in and out of the city. Housing needed to channel water's flow through the dwelling and support the privacy that full-body bathing demanded. Together these developments required change on a massive scale, investments involving great amounts of financial and human capital in addition to time.

Complementing these changes were those involving the body's wrapping: clean clothing. While the pre-modern meaning of clean underclothes had faded and underclothes were no longer deemed the main agent of cleanliness, clean garments remained a basic aspiration. In particular they had important associations with social status. Abundant amounts of clean clothing were marks of high standing, and the ability to appear in spotless dress set gentle-folk apart from their social lessers. These status associations were reinforced by the fact that the clothing worn by the favoured few was washed by the less favoured many. Even in rural and village life – where women did the family laundry and social distinctions might scarcely seem visible – clean clothes were evident signs of respectability. As to laundry work itself, it remained a female task, laborious and time-consuming. Yet, though traditional practices marked both the laundry trades and domestic washing customs, the industrial age began to transform commercial laundry work during these years. Meanwhile the soap industry embarked on a process of wholesale transformation and, through its advertising, left an indelible mark on the culture of personal hygiene.

2

PUBLIC PLACES, PRIVATE SPACES

The growing concern for clean bodies was just one of many hygienic anxieties troubling the transatlantic world during the early and mid-nineteenth century. The alarming cholera and typhus epidemics of the 1830s and 1840s, the human misery on daily view in growing industrial cities, the filth and stink of undrained urban streets, and the latent threat of underclass violence fed unease about the state of the physical environment as well as that of the poor. During the first half of the century the term "sanitary" gradually made its way into most Western European languages, providing a new vocabulary for shaping public awareness about health and cleanliness. The new sanitarians surveyed their communities closely, exposing their foul-ness and urging cleansing remedies. Streets and buildings, waters and airs, habits and customs all fell under their purifying gaze. The title of Edwin Chadwick's famous *Report on the Sanitary Condition of the Labouring Population of Great Britain* summarized their main concern in a single phrase. In Chadwick's Britain the hygienic state of the lower orders was a source of alarm, as it was across much of the Western world. All too often the poor lived in squalor, a distress to themselves and a threat to their more prosperous neighbours. Their homes, their surroundings, their very bodies were dirty, and their bodies needed cleansing as much as their dwellings and streets.

If the unclean bodies of the lower classes were cause for broad con-cern, the responses of the concerned varied broadly too. In France bourgeois reactions emphasized the stench of the poor.[1] A sensitivity to offensive smells flourished in upper-class circles during the early and mid-nineteenth century decades. Rag pickers, dung workers, knackers, sewer men, sailors, factory workers – all reeked of the filth they worked with and lived in. The stink of the masses might even cling to servants when they entered the bourgeois home. Odour inscribed sharp class lines in French society. The upper classes complained of the poor's foul airs; some malcontents even dreamed of an ideal odourless worker. Still, proletarian smells fascinated as well as repelled, a contradiction that left its mark on sanitary thought. Stenches were things to be understood, not simply deplored. Their dangers were to be numbered, their risks confronted. The reformer's main task was that of surveillance. After the cholera of 1832 a rising tide of inspection engulfed the plebian habitat: streets, courtyards and, above all, houses. The sanitizing task began with the physical environment. As Alain Corbin has noted, objective living conditions among the French masses probably had changed very little for decades, but how these settings were understood now changed dramatically. Bourgeois disgust and intolerance replaced bourgeois indifference and neglect.[2]

The French sanitarians were driven largely by environmental fears. But despite their anxieties about the fetid French poor, they had little to say about cleaning dirty bodies. Their British counterparts were far from immune to foul smells too, but they saw the need to bathe the lower classes as well. English reform rhetoric drew on common tropes about the impoverished: their misery and wretchedness, the links between their physical and moral degradation, and the pathway that cleanliness offered to improved habits, better health, higher levels of self-respect, and greater Christian observance.[3] Lying just beneath the surface was the assumption that regular bathing would direct the bather to more orderly ways: industry, thrift, sobriety, and personal responsibility – the self-help virtues promoted by bestselling author Samuel Smiles.[4] Working-class bathing, then, was both a form of social discipline and a life-enhancing personal choice, one strongly encouraged by reform-minded elites.

The mounting nineteenth-century concern for unclean bodies fostered growing attempts across the Western world to promote personal cleanliness. Some of these efforts strove to encourage new understandings and habits, others to create the infrastructures required by new practices. Promoting the new hygiene entailed a mix of persuasion and coercion, but such efforts weren't sufficient in themselves. Lacking ready access to the means of bathing, to water and privacy most of all, most people couldn't readily adopt new customs – and many still couldn't imagine why they should. Thus the slow transition in body care rested on changes to the physical environment as well as to ideas, to the evolution of housing and domestic space, to the development and diffusion of household plumbing, and, perhaps most of all, to the growth of urban water management systems. The vast scale of these changes meant that the process itself could only have been gradual, and gradual it was. By the end of the nineteenth century it remained a work in progress. To these changes we now turn.

THE PUBLIC BATH CRUSADE

At a practical level, cost was a major obstacle to widespread bathing. Even the wealthy usually lacked the necessary facilities in their own homes, but at least they could afford to patronize the public baths that, by the mid-nineteenth-century decades, could be found in many Western cities. Their charges, though, still priced bathing beyond the reach of most wage earners. The idea of providing cheap baths and laundries for the bathless masses coursed through British sanitary reform circles during the 1830s and early 1840s, the common assumption being that private philanthropy should supply the need. Chadwick's Report in 1842 suggested that industrialists whose factories used steam power might divert their surplus hot water to baths for working-class families. It also offered tales of public-minded businessmen who encouraged their employees to develop good bathing habits.[5]

Within a short time these ideas began to take concrete form. Inexpensive public baths and washhouses were established in several English cities, placing Britain in the forefront of popular bathing reform. The Liverpool city government founded the first public bath in 1842. Located in a working-class district, it offered individual warm baths for 2 pence (or two or three children in the same water for the same price) at a time when most spas charged at least a shilling to bathe. Showers or cold baths cost a penny, and all prices included a dry towel, though patrons had to bring their own soap. In its first year it provided 11,000 baths and in its second over 16,000 – impressive growth but still a small number for a city of more than 250,000.[6] The city's washhouse also attracted a growing clientele. Intended to serve the laundry needs of the poor, it gave preference to occupants of cellars or single rooms and to women with large families. It charged a penny to use laundry tubs, water, and drying facilities for up to six hours. Here too users provided their own soap. The experiment was successful enough that the city established a much larger facility later in the decade. But in order to limit financial losses it also raised its prices.[7]

The Liverpool experiment provided the model for the later development of the British public bath movement: a publicly financed institution offering low-cost bath and laundry services to the working classes. Soon a group of prominent Londoners seized the national initiative. At a public meeting at Mansion House in October 1844 an assortment of lords, MPs, city aldermen, and Anglican clergymen founded the Association for the Establishment of Baths and Washhouses for the Labouring Poor, proposing a series of them in London's poorer districts to promote working-class cleanliness. Over the next few years the association and other voluntary societies opened three facilities in north and east London, all financed through public donations – including gifts from the royal family.[8] Yet the limits of private philanthropy soon became clear, and in 1846 Parliament approved legislation allowing parish and town councils to support baths and washhouses from public funds. In effect, the law established the principle that the state shared some responsibility for the cleanliness of British bodies.

And it had an immediate effect. By 1853 London hosted ten public baths and washhouses, which together provided 380,000 baths during the first half of the year, a sign that new notions about personal cleanliness were reaching a broader audience.[9] Over the coming decades the public bath movement spread its blessings to the larger cities and towns across Britain. By the First World War civic authorities were supporting 340 bathhouses, including 50 in London alone.[10] All offered facilities for private bathing, with modest charges for a simple cold bath or shower and higher ones for warm baths and more elaborate fittings. Many also supplied the necessaries for doing laundry, and a growing number provided swimming pools as well.

The nineteenth-century supporters of the public bath movement shared the conviction that both rich and poor could enjoy clean bodies; the poor lacked only the opportunity, not the will, to bathe. Inexpensive public baths and laundries offered them possibilities that their living conditions denied them, promising a better future for all regardless of wealth or standing. Not only would the less favoured profit from cleansing themselves but, as one group of London advocates argued, "the moral effect of cleanliness on character, and its physical effect on the health of all, old as well as young, must tend to lessen the continually increasing burden of rates for the maintenance of the poor and for attendance on them during illness."[11] Such views were the common currency of bathing reform rhetoric, though they shouldn't just be taken at face value. While belief in the virtue of cleanliness was genuine, it reflected the reductive thinking of those who saw simple solutions to complex social problems. The social disparities on view in growing industrial cities challenged the humanitarian conscience and spurred the search for remedies. But in offering the proletariat the means to wash itself, the new sanitarians confused effects with causes. The material conditions of daily life made it difficult, if not impossible, for most city dwellers to keep themselves clean – perhaps even to imagine what cleanliness might be. If working-class hygiene was as poor as its critics believed, cheap public baths could only begin to address the problem, let alone the larger inequalities it denoted.

However limited the goals of the bathing reformers might have been, by the 1850s Great Britain had become a beacon of sanitary enlightenment across much of the Western world. The Chadwick report circulated widely in Britain and elsewhere, along with a companion study of the state of large towns in England published in 1844.[12] The British public bath movement attracted the attention of sanitarians abroad because it addressed a need they saw in their own communities. In France the government of the Second Republic, with the blessing of President Louis Napoléon himself, formed a commission to study the British experiment. The commissioners even crossed the Channel to learn more about it. And they were impressed by what they saw: "The information gathered in England demonstrates incontestably that the habits of cleanliness and exterior dignity introduced by the program of these new institutions exercises the most beneficial influence on the health of individuals, on the cleanliness of dwellings, and on the morality of families."[13]

Convinced by the British example, the French government planned a publicly funded bath and laundry facility in the Quartier du Temple, a Parisian working-class district in the Marais. When work began in 1853 the project was endorsed by the now emperor Napoléon III, who agreed to pay the design and construction costs out of his imperial purse. But the expense – some 200,000 francs at a time when the daily income of laundresses was only 1 franc – proved so high that the experiment was never repeated.[14] Worse was

to follow. While prices for users remained low, problems beset the
establishment from the day it opened in 1855: poor building materials, inadequate maintenance, negligent users, financial difficulties,
bankruptcy, and even public scandals involving the director's family.
Its troubles compounding, the Temple bath- and wash-house closed
its doors in ignominy in 1864.[15] Meanwhile, though the state offered
small subsidies to local governments across the country to support
similar projects, only one accepted.

A similar private venture in Mulhouse, however, had more success. During the 1850s a group of philanthropic factory owners
from the region included inexpensive *bains et lavoirs* in a series of
housing developments built for their workers.[16] Whether they took
their inspiration from the English experience or simply responded to
local conditions isn't clear. But Mulhouse was a manufacturing centre specializing in textiles, tools, and chemicals – sometimes called
the Manchester of mid-nineteenth-century France – where urban
conditions had many parallels with British industrial cities.

Municipal interest in personal hygiene did not revive in France
until the later nineteenth century.[17] Swimming pools and, later, public
showers – the so-called *bains-douches municipales* – gradually found
their way onto local government agendas. They seemed the cheapest,
most effective way to clean the populace. By the early twentieth century, after half a century of reluctance, the French firmly embraced
the idea of public responsibility for individual cleanliness. In time
these facilities became a symbol of democratic republican values, a
sign that the interventionist state had a stake in personal hygiene.

In Germany, Hamburg established a bath and washhouse on
the British model in 1855. The guiding light of the project was the
English engineer William Lindley, a disciple and acquaintance of
Chadwick, who spent much of his career designing water and sewer
systems for major European cities.[18] Berlin opened a similar service
in the same year, and it included an indoor swimming pool. But the
British bath and washhouse model didn't flourish on German soil.
It soon became apparent that German housewives had little interest
in public laundry facilities and that paid washerwomen patronized
the few that did exist.[19] Thus the early *Volksbäder* were intended to
wash bodies and nothing more, providing cheap, warm tub baths for
the popular classes.

According to one historian of the German public bath movement,
the 1879 assembly of the Verein für öffentliche Gesundheitspflege

was a turning point in the development of national bathing habits.[20] Experts addressing the conference proposed a new bathing facility for a new urban man: the indoor swimming pool. Its main promise was not bodily cleanliness but recreation – to offer relief from modern life's demands. The delegates caught the spirit of the times. During the early decades of the national era, as municipal leaders embellished the *Gründerzeit* city, they often placed opulent bathhouses on the lists of public buildings they hoped to build – along with theatres, museums, city halls, and other monuments to municipal dignity. For the most part the new baths were funded by public/ private partnerships, but when private support failed, as it often did, municipal control soon followed. Many of the buildings were elegantly decorated in the era's new architectural styles. Many also boasted private bathing cabinets and therapeutic services in addition to swimming facilities. By the turn of the century more than 150 German cities enjoyed public baths with pools.[21] Not surprisingly, with luxury came costs that placed these facilities well beyond the reach of most German families. Like their spa forebears, the new civic *Badeanstalten* were decidedly *bürgerlich* institutions.

Yet working-class cleanliness still had its champions. One was the Munich hygienist Friedrich Renk, who considered inexpensive baths a necessity and a right. As he noted in 1882, "everyone who belongs to a larger communal group should have the opportunity to use public baths, not without paying, but for a little bit of money, to enjoy the essential necessity of caring for their body's skin, which they cannot do at home."[22] The Berlin dermatologist Oscar Lassar was another. Concerned by the high cost of public bathing services, he demonstrated a model *Volksbad,* consisting only of showers, at the Berlin Public Health Exhibition in 1883. The idea itself was far from new. By then showers had long been installed in some German military barracks. They also had many advantages: cheap to build and operate, they used much less water than baths and were easier to clean. In addition, bathers needed less time to wash themselves than when taking tub baths.[23] Vienna was the earliest large city to follow Lassar's advice. In 1887 it opened the first of seventeen inexpensive municipal bathhouses equipped with showers, in all but one of its *Bezirke* – its wealthy central district the only exception.[24] Cities and towns in Germany soon followed, particularly when the Deutsche Gesellschaft für Volksbäder – with state support and that of the Kaiser – began to promote the concept after its founding in 1899.[25]

Lassar and his supporters shared the conviction that the *Volksbäder* would bring cleanliness to the masses and introduce them to the wider world of *bürgerlich* family values.

Italy remained largely untouched by *borghese* enthusiasm for cheap public baths until toward the end of the century. Lamenting the situation in the later 1850s, Francesco Freschi, professor of hygiene at the University of Genoa, could only recount the ancient glories of the Roman bath and point to the many contemporary nations that bathed while those in southern Europe did not.[26] Of course, Italy too provided baths for people of means, but as far as Freschi could see, only the rich enjoyed the privilege. Even the well-to-do did without. Like many sanitarians, he considered cheap baths for the poor a municipal obligation.

Yet the winds of change were blowing in Italy as well, at least in the north. In 1869 a public bath opened in central Florence between Santa Croce and the Arno, ending the long period when river bathing was the only possibility for all but the prosperous patrons of the city's *bagni privati*.[27] The following year a group of Milanese businessmen built a swimming complex on a plot of land donated by the municipal council; it provided a low-priced pool for men, another for women and children, and a more costly one for the comfortably off.[28] As elsewhere, their motives mixed cleanliness with recreation. Meanwhile a sense of the need for public baths was growing, and not just in philanthropic circles. In the 1880s the Bolognese physician Giuseppe Ravaglia promoted one for his city, though his efforts came to little at the time. Despite grants from the municipal and regional councils as well as funds raised by a local workingmen's society, the amount gathered fell far short of the sum needed to finish the project.[29] But attempts elsewhere succeeded. An inexpensive public bath opened in Turin in 1887; more followed in Rome, Milan, Padua, and Bologna toward the end of the 1890s.[30]

During the early part of the next century the public bath became a common feature of most large Italian cities, usually based on the northern European model of tub baths or showers at modest prices. And city governments were not the only providers. During the interwar years some of the larger Case del Popolo, cooperative and mutual aid societies that flourished in central Italy, offered baths for their members, along with medical, financial, social, and cultural services.[31] At the same time and at the upper end of the personal care market, the Bologna entrepreneur Cleopatro Cobianchi developed a chain of posh *alberghi diurni* (day hotels) in twelve large and mid-sized Italian cities that offered clients a collection of services in elegant Art Nouveau settings.[32] In addition to baths and showers, the Cobianchi *alberghi* met a broad range of hygienic needs, providing barbers and hairdressing, manicures and pedicures, shoe shines and hat repairs, as well as laundry and ironing services. The gesture was reminiscent of the glories of Rome's ancient baths as well as a reminder that many of the Italian *borghesia* could not meet these needs at home.

North Americans came late to the public bath movement. As in Europe, commercial bathhouses for the upper classes could be found in American cities in the later eighteenth century and by the mid-nineteenth century they were fairly common.[33] At least one offered its hospitality in early-nineteenth-century Quebec; it advertised choice wines, cordials, and liqueurs as well as meals prepared on short notice – on a cash-only basis.[34] The early New World bathhouse, like its Old World counterpart, was intended to refresh and relax much more than to clean. Cheap baths for the poor were almost non-existent. A New York charity opened one on the British pattern in 1852 but closed it a decade later for lack of enough patrons to make it self-supporting. From the 1860s through the 1880s municipal governments in several American cities, as well as Montreal, established low-cost floating river baths like those in France and Germany, but their main purpose was recreation and they were only open seasonally.[35]

During the 1890s, however, a number of eastern American cities opened municipal public baths. Much like Britain, the primary initiative came from concerns about the degraded conditions found in tenement housing. New York was the largest city, and also among the first, to identify the problem and propose solutions. In 1897 a Mayor's Committee on public baths and toilets reported that tenement dwellers very seldom had either the room or the privacy to bathe at home, despite signs of growing popular interest in bathing.[36] But if needs existed, opportunities did not. The committee recommended the construction of several public baths, and over the next few years the city established five, mostly equipped with showers. By 1904 year-round public baths were in operation in at least nineteen American cities, most of them municipal, many of them free, and some of them with pools and laundry facilities.[37] Montreal and Toronto, the two largest cities in Canada, also provided free indoor public bathing by this time.[38]

The civic bath movement continued to expand in the early decades of the new century. Public baths and swimming pools, inexpensive or free, gradually became standard municipal services across the urban Western world. Local authorities took the lead in building these facilities, and many cities created an extensive network of them. Amsterdam established a system of municipal baths during the 1910s and 1920s and promoted them through advertising campaigns.[39] By the 1920s some of the larger American cities had greatly extended their bathing systems: New York (20), Chicago (19), Boston (12), Philadelphia (5), and Baltimore (6).[40]

Before the end of the nineteenth century, then, the idea of regular bathing had come to be embedded in leading notions of hygiene. The German hygienic reformer Oscar Lassar established it as the defining goal of his crusade during the 1880s, and he was only one of many champions of cleanliness for whom it became a core objective. Public bath promoters like Lasser wished to imbue the lower classes with bourgeois standards of body care: the new hygiene would improve the habits of the poor, animate their sense of self-control, and uplift their physical and moral condition. Bathing was a discipline that, once accepted, would prompt them to embrace the duty of their own body care and, in turn, their own general welfare. Many proponents wrapped the cause in the rhetoric of advancing social progress. As the New York Mayor's Committee on Public Baths put it in 1897, "That several hundred thousand people in the city have no proper facilities for keeping their bodies clean is a disgrace to the city and to the civilization of the nineteenth century."[41]

By this time, too, the project had enjoyed some successes. The rising trend in public bath attendance revealed a growing acceptance of the new personal hygiene. Still, the reformers' successes fell well short of their hopes. When the numbers of public bath users are compared to the size of urban populations, it's clear that only a small fraction of city dwellers took advantage of the new bathing services. An early survey of London's public baths, published in 1853, indicated an attendance rate of 1 in 100 for the first six months of the year – that is, 1 percent of the city's population used a public bath once during that period.[42] More than half a century later, when something approaching a national system of public baths had become well established, a British survey found that only one third of those who lived near one used it regularly, though attendance was on the rise.[43] At about the same time, of the fourteen American cities with populations of over 100,000 and with year-round indoor public baths, all but two had annual rates of use below 1 percent. In the two largest, New York and Chicago, rates stood at 0.3 percent.[44] Most baths were busy during the warm months, with use dropping off sharply during the winter. Most also provided separate – and less frequent – access for women than for men, one reason why female bath attendance was usually much lower than male. Critics concerned about the cost of municipal services made much of the fact that bath attendance was far less than what it might be. An advocacy group for New York's poor noted that in 1911 the city bathhouse system functioned at only 16 percent of capacity.[45] Statistics like these suggest that the demand for public baths came from their middle-class promoters rather more than from those for whom they were intended.

The modesty of these results stemmed from several causes. One was that, even after extensive building programs, the numbers of bathhouses were small compared to the potential numbers of users. In Germany in 1887 there was one public bathhouse for every 30,000 inhabitants, in 1900 one for every 18,000.[46] Also, while the public baths in larger cities were located in working-class districts, they seldom were conveniently placed for most local residents. Another cause was their expense. The working poor invariably lived on tight family budgets and cleanliness was a discretionary item. A British worker might only take a bath if there was an extra 2p available once the family's weekly costs were met, and his wife might not take one even then.[47] More fundamental still, the concept of the clean body had not yet won broad acceptance. The underclasses of the Western world were slow to embrace the new hygiene urged on them by their social superiors. While some had accepted the new cleanliness, many others still had not. According to one early-twentieth-century account, British coal miners ignored the baths and change rooms provided by their employers though their German contemporaries used those intended for them.[48] This report is just a straw in the wind, and we have no explanation for either alternative. But it seems clear that cleanliness remained a matter of choice. The value of full body bathing had yet to become self-evident, a truth accepted by all.

FROM PERSUASION TO COERCION

Bourgeois supporters of the public bath assumed that opportunity and persuasion were the keys to working-class bathing. Given the chance and a bit of encouragement, people would gladly take a bath. But some promoted the new hygiene by more direct means. Those who ran the emerging mass institutions of the nineteenth century – the barracks, prisons, poorhouses, hospitals, orphanages, and schools – faced new challenges in an age of growing hygienic awareness. Though most of these institutions had long existed, during the first industrial century they expanded their social reach, embracing growing numbers of people, confining ever larger groups in small spaces, and raising new concerns about sanitary conditions. They also shared a custodial responsibility for their inmates and a commitment to moulding their inmates' behaviour through careful supervision and systematic coercion. While the specific changes sought varied from one institution to another – as did the firmness of the intent – all of them hoped to fashion the self-disciplined individual: sober, thrifty, hard-working, and God-fearing men and women who guided their lives by an inner compass governed by middle-class values. A clean body was a major prerequisite of the new persona.

Military institutions began to endorse systematic regimes of personal cleanliness during the early nineteenth century. Improved hygiene was one of several goals pursued by the first military swimming schools in Germany and Austria-Hungary, though by no means the leading one. Seen from a military perspective, swimming was a form of physical training, intended to improve the general health and martial skills of soldiers and potential recruits. From at least the 1820s, senior Austrian officers endorsed routine body cleansing as a form of discipline, while the swimming schools promoted higher standards of personal care.[49]

During the century after Waterloo, the European armies gathered much of their understanding about hygienic matters from their imperial adventures. With no major conflicts at home, their experience came largely from problems they encountered when sending troops abroad. The issues were especially challenging in tropical climes where, as newcomers, Europeans were particularly vulnerable to new diseases. The high mortality rates of the century's early decades gradually fell as, through trial and error, army doctors learned the lessons of sanitation. But even when learned, these were only gradually applied, and when change did occur it was by fits and starts.[50]

Although they occasionally marched to the drumbeat of hygienic advice, soldiers often seemed slow to absorb the lesson of routine bathing. The Crimean War revealed a host of British sanitary short-comings, not just in the hospitals where Florence Nightingale and her colleagues treated the battle-wounded, but also in the field camps of the expeditionary forces. Almost a decade later, at the beginning of the American Civil War, the Crimean example prompted medical advice that soldiers wash their face, hands, and feet daily and take a bath weekly.[51] During the early months of the war the US Sanitary Commission, a civilian relief organization that looked to the needs of sick and wounded Union Army troops, made similar suggestions and offered inspection regimes to promote enforcement.[52] But the results betrayed all hopes, discouraging even the most prominent military physicians. When serving as surgeon general in 1862 and 1863, W.A. Hammond noted,

> it is greatly to be regretted that so little attention is paid in the army to the requirements of health in the matter of frequent and systematic bathing ... It is to be hoped that greater attention will be paid to this matter by those who have the immediate charge of the men, and that in time bath-houses will be built at all permanent posts and encampments. Attention to this point could not fail to add not only to the comfort but the health and conse-quent efficiency of the forces.[53]

Meanwhile, military officials elsewhere were beginning to think of bathing their troops. The Prussian army introduced shower baths into some of their barracks during the mid-century decades.[54] At the same time, French military doctors were starting to recognize the value of routine bodily washing.[55] Toward the end of the 1850s French military health authorities reported a similar experiment in a Marseilles *caserne*; it accommodated 350 soldiers who, as a group, could be showered in a mere four hours. They washed in clusters of three or four, supervised by their corporals, each man allowed three minutes and a small piece of soap.[56] At around the same time a British parliamentary inquiry reported that "there was hardly a bar-rack in the United Kingdom provided with means of bathing. The occasional use of an old horse-trough or of an iron barrack coal-box as a bath, such as we have seen in two or three barracks, cannot be considered as an exception to the rule."[57]

Obviously a broad gulf separated sanitary rhetoric from hygienic reality. Part of the problem was poor or non-existent facilities. At the end of the nineteenth century French barracks were still ill-equipped to meet a soldier's basic sanitary needs, and French troops were still unfamiliar with sanitary regimens despite decades of discipline and indoctrination.[58] Rules and advice seem to have gone unheard, or may even have met resistance. Across the Channel, by the 1890s British barracks commonly had bathtubs, one for each hundred soldiers, but only cold water was on offer so the tubs were seldom used for most of the year. According to one critic, a military surgeon, "No one sees as we in the Medical Service do, the absolute filth of the soldier's person. A man comes up before me well dressed and well turned out, but he is a whited sepulchre; the condition of this person and the odour that comes from him are very unpleasant."[59]

Prisons and poorhouses imposed bathing as a specific form of discipline. The new penology of the early nineteenth century subjected prison inmates to an unprecedented degree of supervision and control. The primary goal was to reform the criminal personality using discipline as the teaching method. According to the current understanding, lessons imposed through drill and routine would gradually be internalized. The inmate would learn self-mastery and moral purpose. Among the most important of these lessons were the rituals of cleanliness, for a primary goal of the new penitentiary was to teach the poor – and virtually none but the poor passed through its gates – to be clean. Observing the French penal colony at Mettray, near Tours, founded in 1840 to rehabilitate young male delinquents, Michel Foucault noted the coercive nature of its hygienic regime, which involved routine cleanliness inspections of bodies and clothes, daily for the former and weekly for the latter.[60] When admitting new inmates, the penitentiaries of nineteenth century Britain disrobed them, bathed them, and outfitted them in prison uniforms, enforcing sanitary regimes on them throughout their imprisonment. As one historian of nineteenth-century British criminal justice noted, "cleanliness was regarded as the outward manifestation of inner order; dirtiness, on the other hand, was seen as a sign of feckless indiscipline ... If prisoners could be taught to be clean, they would learn the value of method and order in their lives."[61]

The poorhouses and workhouses of the English-speaking world – refuges for those who couldn't support themselves – shared much of this outlook, even though their inhabitants might be voluntary while prisoners were not. In particular they shared the penal system's intention to mould new behaviours. As in the penitentiary, workhouse goals emphasized self-discipline, self-reliance, and moral improvement, and cleanliness formed part of the program of enforced personality change. It was literally the first rule in the book when the small British colonial city of Toronto established a House of Refuge and Industry in 1837: "1. ... no inmate shall be permitted to sit down to breakfast, without having been properly washed, or to any other meal, without appearing as clean and tidy as possible."[62]

Workhouse residents might be excused for thinking they'd been imprisoned, for on admission, they received the same treatment as convicted criminals entering the penitentiary: denuding, washing, and dressing in workhouse uniforms. A regime of regular supervised bathing followed.[63] Whatever the institutional differences, the coercive intent was the same. As to the poor themselves, Chadwick's report noted that when paupers were washed on admission to a Poor House, "they usually manifest an extreme repugnance to the process. Their common feeling was expressed by one of them when he declared that it was 'equal to robbing him of a great coat which he had had for some years.'"[64] Like prisoners, the institutionalized poor were stripped of their pride, their dignity, their autonomy, even elements of their identity, in the name of cleanliness. This example also suggests that other views of body care, those that rejected bathing outright, had an enduring quality to them. If so, the brusque treatment given those in custody may even have stiffened their resistance to the new hygiene.

The French artist Théodule Ribot captured the feeling of hygienic discipline more powerfully than any written document possibly could in *The Morning Wash (The Children's Home)* (Plate 3), painted during the early 1860s. With its dark tones, severe home matron, and empty children's faces, it depicts a bleak world of institutionalized childcare. The six children in the foreground – are they merely timid or truly fearful? – perform their morning ablutions, learning the stern lessons of cleanliness under strict and watchful adult eyes. The others, sober-faced in the background, sense the message too, and no doubt the hint of reprimand in the air for those who fail to understand it.

THE BATHROOM

The few bathrooms found in seventeenth- and eighteenth-century Europe were aristocratic ostentations. Only sovereigns and the wealthiest of their subjects installed baths in their palaces, elegant fixtures and lavish settings that offered more to conspicuous display than to hygienic refinement. During the later eighteenth century the *grandes bourgeoisies* began to incorporate them into their sumptuous homes as well, but the domestic bathroom remained an unattainable luxury for all but the privileged few until well into the nineteenth century.[65] Even wealth and power offered no guarantees. Buckingham Palace lacked a bathroom when Queen Victoria ascended the throne in 1837, though one was soon placed in her bedroom – the only one in the palace at the time. The White House saw its first in 1851.[66]

In lieu of a separate place for body cleansing, the hygienically minded middle classes made do with simple equipment placed in other household spaces. Wash stands with water pitchers and basins graced a growing number of better British and American bedrooms from the early nineteenth century onward, the furnishings more elaborate with passing time.[67] Meanwhile the fashionable master bedrooms of bourgeois Paris sprouted corners or alcoves – sometimes even small adjoining rooms – for these intimacies. The *cabinet de toilette* was invariably a woman's preserve, the keeper of her beauty's secrets, a sanctum for her body care. Her husband might use it as well, but only before her own morning grooming and then as a sign of her grace.[68] Portable tubs in various forms made full-body washing possible too. Most often used in bedrooms and commonly made of zinc or tinned copper, they came in a wide range of shapes and sizes. We see some of them in the oils and pastels of the Belle Époque artist Edgar Degas, whose preoccupation with daily lives and mundane matters combined with his interest in the female nude. Bathing offered artists like Degas an opportunity to display the unclothed female body without making an overtly erotic gesture, despite an obvious subtext of desire. Occasionally his models were immersed in a long, narrow tub but more often they squatted in a shallow basin (*le tub*), washing themselves in a few centimetres of water.[69]

The bathroom entered the bourgeois home during the mid-nineteenth-century decades but for many years it made slow progress. One English observer of the time remarked that, though seldom seen in middle-class London homes at mid-century, bathrooms had become common by the 1880s, while "lavatories and sinks for various purposes are now provided almost without limit."[70] Older homes required expensive renovations to accommodate the plumbing revolution, although often the result was a spacious bathroom in a chamber that had once served other purposes. The gracious middle-class homes built during the later 1870s in Bedford Park, an early garden suburb just west of central London, all featured bathrooms on their bedroom floors.[71] More generally, the better homes constructed in London from the 1880s onward usually had an upstairs bathroom, as did all but the smallest houses built after 1900 and a growing number of larger dwellings elsewhere in England.[72] But almost invariably the homes of the working classes did without, nor did there seem to be any expectation that this would ever change.[73]

Toilets were commonly placed in another room, usually adjacent to the bathroom but separate from it. The anglophile German architect and author Hermann Muthesius offered a sympathetic appraisal of the later-nineteenth-century English dwelling from a foreign cultural perspective and he strongly approved of the separation. His observations, published in 1904, deserve repeating here:

> The lavatory naturally adjoins the bathroom. But we must stress the fact that in England a lavatory [toilet] is never actually in the bathroom. Fifty years ago it may still have been permissible to put both in one room, but today it would be considered barbarous and is, we repeat, totally inadmissible. It is to be hoped that we in Germany will also soon begin to question the rightness of the custom. Even in its most splendid form, a lavatory is an appliance that one would prefer to keep out of sight as far as possible, primarily for aesthetic reasons. It is therefore also entirely out of place in the bathroom. Even there its presence evokes unpleasant associations of ideas, even assuming that the closet is entirely odourless, which can never be taken for granted. The bathroom, however, is a room that should be as agreeably appointed as possible, for bathing is pleasurable and not a necessary evil. Hand in hand with the increasing importance that is being attached to hygiene in our time, there has been a growing tendency to furnish the bathroom handsomely, as a room. But it should be axiomatic that even the slightest hint of anything dirty or evil-smelling is out of place in such a room, and that it should

rather be an inviting place in which to linger, as befits its character of a room serving no purpose other than cleanliness.

It would hardly be necessary to underline such obvious matters
if we did not daily see, even in the best houses in Germany, how
lovingly and with what sang-froid the opportunity of combining
the refreshing bath and that necessary evil known as the water-
closet is seized. Apart from aesthetic considerations there are
also practical disadvantages in combining the bath and the wc,
for every time a bath is taken the wc is put out of action for a
longish period, which might have awkward and inconvenient
consequences.[74]

The American bathroom also made its debut during the mid-century
decades, as we learn by comparing two important nineteenth-century
builders' pattern books. Asher Benjamin's influential *American
Builder's Companion*, first published in 1806, made no mention at
all of spaces for bathing. Half a century later A.J. Downing's popular
Architecture of Country Houses called for a bathroom on the second
floor of his more expensive country villas, though his more modest
dwellings still made no provision for one.[75] While Downing was
better known for his influence on housing style (his books popular-
ized the gothic revival in domestic architecture), he was also an early
advocate of the comfortable middle-class home, its sanitary comforts
included. Nineteenth-century Americans, however, seemed no quicker
than any others to accept the idea.[76] In Canada too the separate bathroom made an appearance around mid-century, though as elsewhere,
its progress was leisurely.[77]

In Paris even the finest apartments of the mid-nineteenth century
lacked a room dedicated to bathing, though by then they were an
everyday luxury in the grand *hôtels particuliers* built at the same
time.[78] One estimate suggests that fewer than 1 percent of Parisian
homes included a bathroom in 1850, the proportion rising to somewhat under 3 percent by 1900.[79] Beyond the capital, conditions
differed little. Bathrooms were rare in the bourgeois homes of the
Nivernais before the First World War, an example that probably
speaks for most of France outside Paris.[80]

Other scattered statistics also suggest the bathroom's slow progress. An inquiry into the water supply of Newcastle, for example,
found them in 8 percent of city households during the mid-1880s.[81]
A few years later a survey of housing in Basel revealed that only 32

of the city's 13,377 residences had a bathroom; none of the city's smaller dwellings possessed one and only 1 percent of those with five or more rooms did.[82] Large German cities were somewhat better supplied. In 1880, 4 percent of Berlin houses boasted one, the proportion rising to 14 percent by 1910.[83] But averages always mask variation and in this case it was wide. Seven percent of Hamburg houses were furnished with bathrooms in 1885 but the proportion varied from 0.1 to 45 percent depending on the district. By 1910 the city average was 21 percent and the range 3 to 70 percent.[84] The geography of urban wealth and poverty could scarcely have been clearer. In the same year an Austrian census revealed bathrooms in 7 percent of Viennese dwellings, virtually none of them in smaller homes.[85] In Amsterdam the *Maatschappij voor Volkswoningen*, a large model working-class housing project from the later 1880s, provided no separate space for bathing, though each apartment had its own water tap and toilet. In fact, by the First World War the bathroom had not yet become a standard feature of even the city's middle-class homes.[86] At 28 percent in 1910, Zurich stood at the upper end of the European distribution during the prewar years.[87] The experience in larger American cities at this time differed little. In 1893, 3 percent of families in New York and Chicago had bathrooms, along with 7 percent in Baltimore and 17 percent in Philadelphia, as did a fortunate 26 percent of Boston tenement dwellers.[88] Obviously the bathroom's pleasures had only begun to extend from the privileged few to the less favoured many by the end of the nineteenth century.

Sometimes the housing that industrialists provided for their employees proved an exception to the rule. Building company housing for workers was a common practice of the period, and some businessmen used the opportunity to include basic comforts otherwise found only in bourgeois homes.[89] Often prompted by a mixture of motives, they combined a philanthropic desire to improve their employees' welfare with a pragmatic need for access to a reliable labour force. In some cases, they also intended to set an example for like-minded business colleagues. As a result, bathrooms were not uncommon in British and American workingmen's settlements during the late nineteenth and early twentieth centuries. The cottages William Hesketh Lever built for his soap workers at Port Sunlight near Liverpool after 1888 – some 800 in total – each had one, though it's not clear if initially they were served by hot and cold running water.[90] Curiously, they were placed on the ground floor next to the front entrance. In this location they were set well apart from the toilet, normally detached from the house and sited at the back of the lot. The confectioner Thomas Cadbury's industrial village Bournville, just south of Birmingham, also included baths in most of its dwellings, while employing some ingenious space-saving strategies. In one building style the tub was sunk into the kitchen floor and uncovered only when used, in another it stood in the scullery where its lid served as a table, while in a third it was stored on end in a closet.[91] Only the better homes had a small, dedicated bathroom fed by hot and cold water.

Across the Atlantic bathrooms were still more common in model industrial communities.[92] The village of Pullman, built just outside Chicago in the 1880s by the railroad car company of the same name, included 1,550 houses, most of them outfitted with a separate bathroom. (But whatever effect they had on their occupants' cleanliness, they did nothing to calm the discontent that led to the storied Pullman strike of 1894, one of the major labour conflicts in nineteenth-century America.) The Westinghouse Air Brake Company in Pennsylvania, the Maryland Steel Company near Baltimore, and the Ludlow Manufacturing Association in Massachusetts, to name only a few, established comparable settlements with similar housing features.

On the continent, however, the bathroom was almost unknown in the industrial villages of the time. Best known among them were the series of workingmen's colonies built by the philanthropically minded businessman Alfred Krupp for employees at his Essen steelworks. None included bathrooms for individual households, though a few apartment blocks for foremen provided shared basement bathing and laundry facilities – available to each family one day a week.[93] (In the sumptuous country villa Krupp built for his family in the early 1870s, however, he installed two bathrooms per floor, as well as toilets and washbasins with running water in the servants' quarters.[94]) Nor did any of the workers' housing erected in early-twentieth-century Lyon have a bathroom, apart from some larger homes intended for factory foremen and engineers.[95] The bathroom was also omitted from Crespi d'Adda, a small workingmen's community near Bergamo patterned on the English industrial village and built in the 1880s and 1890s by Italian cotton manufacturers Cristoforo and Silvio Crespi. Instead the Crespi, father and son, placed a public bath and laundry at the centre of their model town.[96]

THE WATERS THAT CLEANSED

The invention of the modern bathroom depended on running water. Full-body cleansing required large amounts of it, and this need linked the bathroom to the world beyond its walls, to the mains and sewers that supplied clean water and disposed of wastes. These were urban artifacts, two of the fundamental innovations that sustained the urbanization process during the nineteenth century. The pace of urban growth increased dramatically across the Western world after 1800, particularly from mid-century onward. Consequently the swelling industrial city demanded water on an unprecedented scale, and what it took in it discharged on an unprecedented scale as well.

Water had been scarce and expensive in the early modern city, a luxury for all but the wealthy. Most Parisians obtained their supplies either from wells and public fountains or from water sellers, the licensed vendors who sold filtered water or the unofficial ones who drew it from fountains or the Canal de l'Ourcq.[97] On the eve of the French Revolution a cubic metre cost the equivalent of three to four days of wage labour. Working families could only store small amounts at home, on average about 15 litres at a time, and this to be used over several days.[98] An estimate in 1802 placed the average daily per capita consumption in Paris at about 5 litres, well below the 7 the estimator thought necessary.[99] His was just one of many suggestions about the quantities of water urban centres needed and consumed, and while the estimates varied from one city to another, invariably they grew over time. Providing an adequate clean water supply was one of the great challenges facing urbanizing societies. Long lost to folk memory was the fact that the Western world had once known better ways: the aqueducts of ancient Rome had distributed some 200 litres per person per day.[100]

Although more than 25,000 wells served Paris by the early 1830s – almost one for every two houses in the city[101] – and public officials tapped new water sources for Paris during the first half of the century, the decisive increase occurred under Baron Haussmann's massive urban renewal during the 1860s. Once an adequate supply existed, the Compagnie générale des eaux, which held the water distribution monopoly for the city, expanded its system rapidly, from 2 percent of buildings served with running water in 1875 to over 80 percent by 1887. While per capita supply in the city had lagged London for many years, Paris now drew nearer its rival. But unlike

London, Paris did not distribute water directly to most dwellings. Most landlords were reluctant to pay the cost of connecting to the urban water system, a reluctance only slowly overcome toward the end of the century.[102] Instead, the Compagnie générale placed its taps and holding tanks in building courtyards. The subscribers themselves had to carry their water to their own apartments. In 1880 more than 1 million Parisians, half the city's residents, lacked running water inside their homes.[103]

. Elsewhere in Europe, distribution in some cities relied partly on underground mains, but until the latter part of the century most city dwellers either drew their water from fountains or wells, or bought it directly from water sellers, as in Paris. The small northern Italian city of Bologna offers one example. At mid-century, basement cisterns and courtyard wells met its watery needs while canals washed the residents' clothing and bodies. By the early 1880s the city had added a new water supply and some twenty public fountains, but they suffered from low water flow, a problem that found no easy remedy.[104] The private company with the monopoly for water distribution was as reluctant to provide free water for the public as the public was to pay for what they had long enjoyed at no cost. By the beginning of the new century fewer than 10 percent of Bologna's households had tapped into the urban network and it took several decades before all of them did.[105] Bologna may have lagged Italy's urban trends, but only by a little; a government inquiry into national sanitary conditions in 1886 found that wells, fountains, and cisterns provided the main water supply for most of the national population, and only two thirds of them enjoyed access to good-quality water.[106] During the 1860s and 1870s, larger cities – Naples, Milan, Turin, and Rome – had all begun to improve their urban services, developments that gradually introduced water inside the home, but progress was slow. Only Milan stood apart from the trend; one-fifth of its houses were attached to the city's piped water supply in 1897, four-fifths by the eve of the Great War, a growth rate more like that in northern Europe than anywhere else on the peninsula.[107]

The great metropolis London had long been the great exception as well. Direct water supply to some private homes there dated from the early 1600s, long before anywhere else in the Western world. Some 45 percent of city buildings enjoyed piped water in 1700, the share rising to 70 percent in 1800 and to 85 percent in 1820 – this during a time when the city's huge population more than doubled.[108] Perhaps one reason for the rapid expansion was that London water became more affordable in real terms during these years: while its cost remained largely unchanged throughout the eighteenth century, wages gradually rose. By the beginning of the nineteenth century only the London poor – who admittedly numbered in the hundreds of thousands – couldn't afford an annual water contract. Yet even those with a water connection often had cause to grumble, for service regularly fell well short of expectations. Water only flowed for two or three hours every day or two, and its quality prompted frequent complaint.[109] Meanwhile, other British cities shared the conditions common to most urban centres across the Western world. Liverpool's water supply was still delivered in carts in the early 1840s at the very moment its city fathers were promoting their new public baths.

The second half of the nineteenth century saw major investments in urban sanitary infrastructure throughout the Western world. All the great cities of Western Europe and North America, as well as many smaller ones, poured money into centralized water distribution and sewer systems, creating underground networks of pipes and tubes linking overground networks of buildings and rooms.[110] Whatever the limitations of its distribution infrastructure, Britain led the rest of Europe in bringing water into the home; at the end of the century household water connections were the norm in its urban places. By then most large and mid-sized German cities also had water distribution networks, but smaller communities still lacked them, and the proportion of households connected lagged behind that in Britain.[111] Italy, in turn, trailed well behind northern Europe. The 1886 survey revealed that, at best, 12 percent of Italians had direct access to running water, a finding that began to encourage major investments in urban water supply systems there as well.[112]

In mid-century North America some middle-class homeowners experimented with self-contained household supply and disposal systems of their own.[113] Water distribution networks also served a growing number of cities from the early years of the century, though commonly they were small, underfinanced, and plagued with technical problems. Rapid expansion replaced slow growth in the 1870s, however, and by the end of the century some 3,200 American urban centres had a municipal waterworks of sorts, as did well over 200 Canadian cities and towns.[114] Information on domestic connection rates is scant for both countries, but per capita consumption was substantially higher in the New World than in the Old.

The social gradient of piped water access was obvious every-where, with the rich and well-to-do invariably at the head of the queue. In central Vienna, home to much of the city's wealth, close to 90 percent of residential buildings were connected to the pub-lic water system in 1890, just before civic expansion embraced Hernals, Ottakring, and the other working-class suburbs that arced around the wealthy urban core. Virtually none of the build-ings in the newly annexed *Vororte* were connected to the grid at the time, and it took another decade before they were.[115] As in Paris, even when buildings had a water connection, the apartments within them usually did not. In Austria and Germany particularly, where the urban lower classes clustered in large *Mietskaserne*, run-ning water was available in courtyards or on individual floors long before it favoured each unit in a tenement complex. If 92 percent of buildings in Munich were connected to the city water supply by 1900, the proportion of dwellings with taps of their own was very much smaller.[116] Conflicts of interest between owners and tenants inevitably kept company with these innovations. The new infrastructure raised landlords' costs that they hoped to pass on to their renters, and the renters were inclined to resist.[117] Conditions were broadly similar in American tenement districts: taps might be found on each floor of a building, or piped water might be avail-able in its courtyard, but a faucet in an apartment was a luxury, not an expectation.

The logical consequence of growing supplies of clean water was a growing problem with wastewater. But the great sewer-building proj-ects of the later nineteenth century were prompted by still broader concerns. Hygienic alarms and frequent epidemics demanded new efforts to cleanse the urban environment, and sewers offered one obvious solution. All too often the streets of early- and mid-nineteenth-century cities were seas of filth. Solid human wastes were usually collected in cesspits beneath buildings, to be dug out and carted away from time to time; but most other rubbish found its way onto roadways. Hamburg provides an example. The city's residents dumped their refuse on the streets in front of their homes, where house slops, rainwater, and nameless solids sluiced down gutters that ran down the middle of the road.[118] From there the foul mess found its way into a latticework of shallow canals and open sewers that, in turn, poured their contents into the Elbe or one of its tribu-taries. Local regulations discouraged householders from swelling the stream with their own debris, but with few means of enforcement, rules like these had little effect.

From the sanitary perspective, the steady march of urbanization posed a great and growing challenge. At the beginning of the nineteenth century one European in ten was a city dweller; by the outbreak of the First World War the proportion was one in three.[119] While most urban places shared in this growth, the great cities expanded especially dramatically, with vastly larger populations in the early twentieth century than they'd had a hundred years before. London grew six-fold during the century, Paris five-, Vienna nine-, Berlin ten-, and Rome six-. Growth rates in North America were much higher still: Boston thirty-, Montreal thirty-six-, and New York fifty-seven. The task of transforming civic hygiene in the face of such expansion was formidable. One of the most pressing concerns was what to do with human excreta. Given the body's production of wastes – 1,250 grams of urine and up to 160 grams of fecal matter daily[120] – urban growth had created an urgent problem, and as the biggest city of its time, London confronted it on a uniquely grand scale. The 70,000 tons of feces Londoners produced in 1800 had grown to well over 400,000 tons annually a century later. Given London's huge population, the magnitude of the problem may have set it apart from that in smaller cities, but urban places of every size faced a similar dilemma.

Horses, cattle, and other animals added substantially to the task. In the 1840s the London journalist and reformer Henry Mayhew calculated that a horse produced 45 pounds (20 kg) of dung every day. By his estimate London was then home to 25,000 horses, and they produced an impressive yield.[121] Added to it were the droppings of the thousands of frightened cattle, pigs, and sheep driven daily to slaughter in the city's central markets. Not to forget the cows, pigs, and chickens that some city dwellers kept to garnish their dinner tables,[122] nor the city's many dairy herds that supplied fresh milk and cream to residents. In the Paris of 1885, the XIIIe Arrondissement alone was home to 35 of them, with close to 500 head of cattle.[123] According to Mayhew, some 40,000 tons of animal manure layered London's streets each year. The conditions in other mid-nineteenth-century cities may have differed in scale, but not in kind, and apart from sporadic attempts at scraping muck from the streets, the only effective cleansing came from heavy rains. To the sanitarian mind the sewer was the best, if not the only, way to deal with the challenge of urban filth.

Hygienists were just as concerned about the cesspits, *fosses d'aisances*, *Senkgruben*, and *pozzi neri* that lurked beneath urban buildings. Apart from their unpleasantness, they were considered a serious health hazard. Despite bylaws requiring them to be water-tight, they often leaked and polluted nearby cleaner water sources. As well, according to miasmatic theory their odours might be a source of disease. Also, the process of digging them out and removing their contents offended public sensibilities, itself a reason for local regulation. Sewers were the obvious solution to these problems too. But the cesspit also had its defenders, among them the cesspit cleaners themselves, whose livelihoods were at stake. They earned their living by carting off the most despised of all urban rejects and selling it to nearby farmers as fertilizer. Then, too, many landlords objected to the cost of sewer connections, just as they often opposed connections to main water lines, and for the same reason. The political contest in Paris was a prolonged and noisy one, beginning in the 1870s and lingering into the final years of the century, when the friends of the sewer finally triumphed. From that point on, owners were required to link their buildings to the urban network, though even then progress was slow. One third of Parisian buildings remained unconnected on the eve of the First World War.[124]

Thus, while some places had sewers before the nineteenth century, from the 1860s onward a new, more urgent awareness spurred construction on a far grander scale. Scores of cities on both sides of the Atlantic built sewer systems during the last four decades of the century and the early decades of the twentieth,[125] and usually they made more rapid progress than Paris. The statistics speak to the creation of a new city beneath the city, a subterranean world of tunnels and pipes, shafts and galleries. Berlin began to develop an underground system in the early 1870s and by the 1890s most buildings were connected to it.[126] At the end of the century the cesspit had largely vanished from Vienna as well, and those that remained lingered in the working-class suburbs rather than in the inner city.[127] The national investigation of the hygienic state of Italy in 1886 revealed a range of conditions,: some larger cities in the north compared favourably with those in northern Europe, but three quarters of Italy's municipalities lacked sewer systems of any type. Not surprisingly, over the next four decades Italian cities invested heavily in improved drainage networks.[128]

If anywhere seemed the promised land of the sewer it was North America. In the United States the proportion of the urban population served by a public sewage system grew from 50 percent in 1870 to 87 percent in 1920, impressive growth at a time when the national population was growing impressively too. (It increased by three times, and the urban populace by seven, during these years.)[129] Canadian systems developed in parallel with those south of the border.[130] But everywhere the sewer's progress was slower in small cities than in large, slower still in towns than in small cities, and almost non-existent in village and rural life. And as with water supply, the fact that a building was linked to a sewer network didn't mean that every apartment had a separate connection. Shared toilets remained common in European working-class tenements well into the twentieth century, though they disappeared more quickly on the other side of the Atlantic.

At the dawn of the twentieth century, then, the public infrastructure to support household bathing was still being built. The necessary apparatus – clean water supplies and waste water outlets – was widely available in major cities and many minor ones as well, though only wealthy and well-to-do Europeans could take them for granted. The same was true in North America, but diffusion there was broader, and often the merely better off could expect these benefits too. By then even town and village residents were entering the charmed circle of household sanitation. But indoor plumbing was mostly an urban phenomenon. In the French and British countrysides, only the wealthy could afford such costly installations on their estates, and by no means all of them chose to pay.[131] Most rural dwellers everywhere still did without, as they would for decades to come.

PLUMBING AND FIXTURES

The urban revolution in sanitary systems had its parallel inside the home. For water to reach the far corners of a dwelling, it required its own network of pipes and drains, a municipal system writ small. Old buildings needed refitting to adopt innovations, new buildings needed improved designs to incorporate novel demands. Once a dealer or worker in lead, the plumber became a fitter of water pipes and fixtures. Instead of working on roofs and gutters to keep water outside the dwelling, he now guided its safe passage through the building's interior.

The introduction of running water into the home created technical challenges. One of the first came from the fact that many early suppliers of piped water couldn't provide a continuous flow. As a result, houses needed cisterns to store water for later use. Their number and placement depended on the size of the house, the location of its taps, and the capacity of the main water system to maintain supply at an adequate pressure. In London homes cisterns usually were placed in the basement, one at the front of the house and, if the building was large, another at the back.[132] Over time smaller tanks were placed on the upper floors, usually above the toilets they served. When modest houses lacked their own reservoirs, these might be located in a common yard shared by several dwellings. At first water was simply drawn from a tap on the side of a cistern; later, pipes carried it to taps and sinks inside the house.

During the mid-century decades some Americans relied on other ways of supplying water to their homes, using rain, wells, streams, or lakes to fill their cisterns when other sources weren't available. At the same time they began to adopt the sanitary trinity of modern bathroom fixtures: sinks, tubs, and toilets. According to one historian of American plumbing, they did so in the name of convenience rather than from any health concerns.[133] But whatever the water's origins, the challenge of moving it inside the dwelling was the same in Europe and North America. One fundamental problem was how to raise water to the upper stories of the house.[134] Geography favoured some cities – for example New York, where the urban water system has long relied largely on gravity. Elsewhere, early solutions often involved attic cisterns and various types of pumps to fill them, but the problem wasn't resolved until water distributors deployed effective pumping equipment and pressure within main systems became adequate to the task; inevitably progress varied. London was not fully served by a continuous-pressure water supply until 1899.[135]

The second half of the nineteenth century saw much trial and error in the evolution of plumbing technology and bathroom fixtures. The need to heat water for washing and bathing was a fundamental challenge. Even if running water was provided in an upstairs bathroom, if hot water wasn't available there it had to be brought from the kitchen, and filling a large tub by hand was no small task. One solution was to heat water in or near the bathroom, but this too was a tedious chore in an age when homes were heated by coal or wood and rooms were warmed individually. The Marquis de Bonneval described the process he knew during the mid-nineteenth century: "When one wished to take a bath, two hours in advance one advised the valet responsible for lighting a wood stove with a pipe that opened into the tub; the hot water emptied into a zinc container painted in false marble on the exterior."[136] Experiments included bathtubs with heating elements beneath them, heaters placed in the bathroom (including gas-fuelled models that promised instant hot water), and boilers – free-standing or attached to the kitchen range.[137] Toward the end of the century, solutions began to converge on a central hot-water source for the dwelling, but as with so many other innovations in household plumbing, adoption rates were slow to trickle down from wealthy and well-to-do early adopters to the wider population.

At the same time mass manufacturing began to standardize bathroom equipment. The porcelain transformation of sanitary appliances replaced earthenware basins and metal tubs with enameled cast iron and vitreous china fixtures, while the industrial scale of production simplified styles, reduced costs, and quickened the pace of adoption. This new generation of conveniences was made for homes with water and sewer service and came equipped with the necessary connections. Hermann Muthesius considered England the model for all domestic sanitation and the English bathroom the finest of its kind. England had led Europe in the development of the bathroom and British sanitary fixtures were superior to all others; those made by Shanks and by Doulton, he believed, were celebrated worldwide. He also noted the unadorned, utilitarian nature of the English bathroom, in keeping with its modern fittings: "[It] is always the simple, plain room dictated by need. Everything is of the best, but the room is fundamentally modest and unpretentious. It is alien to the nature of an Englishman of standing to envelope himself in luxury; it is a role that would be painful to him."[138] Yet if England led in the quality of its bathroom appointments, the United States didn't lag far behind.[139] Rapid economic growth created an expanding national market for many domestic goods, sanitary equipment included, and by the end of the century American manufacturers were meeting the demand, often by following British standards.[140] The American bathroom too had a simple, utilitarian character, one befitting the nation of the common man. Elsewhere the common man did without while the bathrooms of the uncommon shared a lingering sense of luxury that spoke of lives lived graciously.[141]

The bidet is a fixture with a history all its own. While its national roots aren't entirely clear, the word itself was French and in time it became embedded in most Western languages. Originally the term meant small horse or pony, and the connection with a low, shallow basin to be straddled when washing the nether parts is obvious, as are its erotic intimations. Until fairly recently its long career as a sanitary device has been tied as closely to the Western world's tangled history of sexuality as to the history of hygiene. First noted in France in the early eighteenth century, bidets found a place among the aristocracy's fashionable furnishings during the pre-revolutionary years.[142] Often they were elaborately made – triumphs of the ceramic arts set in elegant wooden casings, their functions disguised by ornate lids, seat backs, and shelves.[143] Toward the end of the century the bidet began to enter the bourgeois world as well, but even there it remained exceptional.[144] Although used primarily by women, during the mid- and late eighteenth century occasionally men owned one as well. In 1808 the now emperor Napoléon – imperial in taste as in manner – acquired a sumptuous model: "A silver vermeil bidet, the syringe and its cannons, the bowl, the sponge box, all in gold silver, two crystal bottles trimmed with diamonds."[145] But whether he obtained it for his own use or simply as a piece of showy furniture isn't clear. During the Biedermeier period after 1815, Viennese furniture makers also began offering bidets and other furniture for the toilette, artfully concealing the uses of the more functional pieces.[146] Apart from its place in aristocratic and bourgeois life, the bidet occupied a niche in the lives of the demimonde, the courtesans of fame and infamy who fluttered around the rich. That, at least, was its reputation. Certainly its gradual adoption didn't echo any change in the hygiene advice offered by eighteenth-century health and beauty manuals.[147]

The bidet was above all a woman's device, and its highly sexualized overtones stemmed largely from this fact. From its earliest mention it wore an aura of feminine immodesty, licence, and sin. It also held associations with contraceptive washing and masturbation.[148] Sometimes it featured in eighteenth-century pornographic art, for conventional opinion linked it to forbidden sexual practices more than to any notions of cleanliness.[149] The dominant morality opposed it as an "object of abominations" and linked it with transgressive behaviours.[150] No doubt there was some truth in these views, for during the nineteenth century the bidet seems to have been widely used among prostitutes, to prevent conception, to preserve their seductive capital, to protect themselves against venereal disorders, and to disguise diseased conditions. Yet the bidet's erotic associations also reflected a deep ambivalence about sexuality and intimate hygiene that flowed through Western culture well into the twentieth century, anxieties explored at length by Freud, Havelock Ellis, and their many successors. The binaries of cleanliness versus impurity, decency versus indecency, innocence versus sin, and chastity versus wantonness lay at the heart of Western notions about the sexual self, and as an instrument of genital cleansing, the bidet stirred a host of misgivings about the libido and its disquiets.

Perhaps because of its connotations, the bidet never found broad acceptance before the twentieth century. Bidets were virtually unknown in England and North America, where, by one account, they were regarded as *una sconvenienza continentale*, a continental impropriety.[151] The one that the American heiress and newlywed Iris Origo found in her bedroom when visiting her aristocratic grandparents in London in 1924 was highly exceptional, though having lived much of her life in Italy, she probably didn't recognize it at the time.[152] The bidet's empire expanded most widely in France and Italy, where, whatever its licentious aura, its hygienic value also seemed clear. Yet even there it never gained wide adoption before the twentieth century, despite the best efforts of plumbing fixture manufacturers, whose catalogues promised bright porcelain futures to all who bought their wares.[153] By then, however, the bidet had found a place in the bathroom, linked by taps and drains to the household plumbing system.

On the subject of bidet ownership in the past, the few statistics we have come from France, and relying as they do on estate inventories, they provide insights only into the social circles of those with enough wealth to require a process of legal inheritance. Virtually all of them come from Paris, as well, and they vary surprisingly little: 7.5 percent of households in 1740, 10 percent during the 1760s, 7 percent in 1850, 4.8 percent in 1900, the decline likely due to the gradual spread of bathrooms and fixed tubs.[154] Elsewhere in France adoption was still more limited. Bidets made their appearance in bourgeois Nevers around the turn of the twentieth century, and in the neighbouring villages some two decades later.[155] In the French countryside they seem to have been unknown. One rural physician in the Auvergne at the time was utterly dismissive. "As for the bidet," he remarked, "women scarcely know what they mount to go to market." The good doctor deplored what he saw as the complete neglect of genital hygiene by the women in his community.[156] While his was the voice of a single witness, it spoke for rural France at the time.

THE BATHROOMLESS MASSES

Those who lived well back from the cutting edge of the new hygiene made do with what means came to hand, if and when they chose to bathe at all. In general, rural residents chose not to, or so the evidence seems to show, and by 1900 they still formed the substantial majority everywhere but in Great Britain. City dwellers enjoyed the first fruits of the sanitary revolution, and the wealthy and well-to-do enjoyed them sooner than everyone else. While the evidence is patchy, the picture is clear enough. Around the turn of the century most inhabitants of the major European cities lived in crowded quarters. During the mid-1880s, 80 percent of Viennese homes had three or fewer rooms, the proportion rising to well over 90 percent in the new industrial suburbs.[157] At the turn of the century some 70 percent of Milan residents lived in similar conditions.[158] In 1910 the same proportion of Berlin's 2 millions lived in one to three rooms while some 10 to 20 percent of them also hosted a *Bettgeher* or *Schlafgängern*, who rented by day a bed used by someone else at night; much the same conditions existed in Munich.[159] Plate 4 offers an example. The kitchen in a Berlin basement dwelling in 1905, it also served as a child's bedroom. Note the single tap and basin in the centre of the photo, a benefit then largely found in below-ground apartments, where easy access to the urban water supply network made installation fairly simple. In London at the same time, half of all dwellings had no more than three rooms, though the proportion was just one quarter for England and Wales as a whole.[160] Meanwhile two thirds of Glasgow residents lived in one or two rooms, as did half of all Scots.[161] Homes generally were larger in North America, though here the data are elusive. A survey of tenement life in Boston during the early 1890s revealed that only 16 percent of residents lived in three or fewer rooms; in Canada two decades later the proportion was 20 percent.[162] Whatever the specifics, small homes hadn't enough space to dedicate any part of it exclusively to bathing, and even when they enjoyed running water, toilets usually appeared before bathtubs. The water closet took up less space and met more immediate needs.

Some large tenement complexes included a bathhouse for residents. One was Meyer's-Hof, built in 1873–74, which consisted of more than 700 small apartments located in six parallel buildings on Ackerstraße in north-central Berlin.[163] But it was an exception at the time, as it was for some time to come. Working-class housing on either side of the Atlantic generally made no provision for bathing until after the turn of the century. When new Paris houses were connected to running water, for example, it serviced their toilets and sinks rather than tubs.[164] Thus if they bathed at home, the lower classes improvised as best they could: a washtub or basin, a pail, pot, or jug – things found in the most simply furnished homes – though in time purpose-made bathtubs also made their appearance.[165] Most often families bathed in the kitchen, the room where water could be heated. In circumstances like these privacy might not be possible but modesty could be respected.

The few accounts we have of prewar working-class domesticity tell much the same story: a weekly scrub, children washed in strict order (youngest to oldest), the family using the same water, at best occasionally refreshed. Adolescents enjoyed some privacy by bathing after their siblings, and parents bathed last if they had a chance at all. As one Viennese historian has noted, "great care was taken lest the children see their parents naked."[166] In 1913 the British Fabian Maude Pember Reeves's study of life among the London poor indicated that adults bathed less often than their children, mothers at home when an opportunity arose and fathers at a public bath when the family could afford it. One of her informants, a mother of four living in a single room, told Pember Reeves that she bathed when her elder children were at school while her husband couldn't afford 2 pence for a the public bath but sometimes got a "washdown" after their children were asleep. "A bath it ain't, not fer grownup people," she explained, "it's just a bit at a time like."[167] Hidden behind her account was the fact that the family bath was a major chore. Clean water had to be brought from the nearest source, then heated on the stove, and when the bath was over, the dirty water had to be carted away again. Like most household tasks involving water, cleanliness was women's work, and it was heavy labour.

Yet we shouldn't think that hygienic innovation simply trickled down from the rich to the poor, that the wealthy and privileged always were early adopters while the less favoured stood in line waiting their turn. More than a few French aristocrats resisted the new technology and clung to their older ways. Recalling her young life at the turn of the century, the Comtesse de Pange reminisced: "No one in my family took a bath! One washed in tubs, with 5 cm of water, or better one sponged in large washbasins, but the idea of immersing oneself in water up to the neck appeared pagan, almost guilty."[168] Later, when her parents decided to restore the family's country home, they introduced running water, a toilet, and a hot water heater but no bathroom. "That," she remembered, "seemed the luxury of a grand hotel, useless and even reprehensible among ordinary people."[169] According to one historian of the French country house, the dawn of modern plumbing came late to the chateaux of the old aristocracy, rather later than to those of the *nouveau riche*.[170] Did disdain for parvenu comforts lie at the heart of patrician stodginess?

We don't know how often people bathed by the early twentieth century and we probably never will. The few estimates available are simply straws in the wind. German studies of the period suggest that only 1 percent of the population took a weekly bath, and no city averaged more than five baths per person per year.[171] In Paris in 1911, the residents of a philanthropic tenement funded by the Rothschilds reportedly took an average of fifteen baths or showers yearly, which if anything seems high for the French working class at the time.[172] An American estimate from the same period placed the annual number of baths per year at no more than six.[173] The 1915 survey of the Britain's public bath system also concluded that only a minority of those with easy access to one used it often.[174] Together these facts leave the strong impression that before the First World War routine bathing was very far from widespread among the broader public. The supporters of regular bathing believed that those who could bathe would. But not all of those who could did, and far larger numbers could not. Even a bathroom in the home didn't mean that the occupants bathed. Occasional reports of poor working-class families storing coal in their bathtub might seem apocryphal but they recurred often enough to claim some truth. For families with low incomes and limited household space, bathrooms were costly in both respects. A bath required much more water than did a simple wash in a basin, and the price of heating it was much higher too. Meanwhile, in the crowded conditions of everyday working-class life, the space needed for bathing could be used for more immediate ends.[175]

For those who lived in circumstances like these – and they included the substantial majority no matter where they lived – partial washing was the main alternative: daily, weekly, or only occasionally; hands and faces, necks, and sometimes feet. Water was usually fetched from a source outside the home, tubs and basins were common household equipment, the water was heated on a stove, and soap was used sparingly if at all. The only other option was a public bath, available in a growing number of larger urban centres but seldom in smaller ones and almost never in country villages. Bath fees were a discretionary expense for working families so baths were discretionary too. And in a world that only permitted same sex bathing, public baths invariably favoured men over women. In short, at the end of the nineteenth century routine bathing remained a privilege of the privileged. The bourgeois social critics, the hygiene professionals, and the health and beauty advocates of bathing for the many shared a vision of personal cleanliness available only to the few.

CLOTHES AND THEIR CLEANING

As with clean bodies, so with clean clothes. During the seventeenth and eighteenth centuries freshly laundered clothing was valued throughout the Western world, prized much more than the cleanliness of the bodies it covered. Respectable society placed great store in well-washed garments and even the deeply disadvantaged aspired to them, though the cost and effort of laundry work might make the goal elusive. Whether done by laundresses for pay or by housewives out of family duty, washing was time-consuming and labour-intensive work. It also involved financial costs. In economies where mass consumer markets only existed in faint outline, soap for laundering was among the few commodities commonly purchased, an item in the household budgets of all but the very poor. Thus a hierarchy of clean clothes paralleled the social hierarchy, a visible reminder of the status distinctions layering all Western societies, from the cleanest at the top to the unclean at the bottom. Freshly laundered clothing distinguished the classes from the masses. At minimum it implied that one had more than a single suit of clothing. In the upper ranks it expressed substantial wealth and high standing.

THE LINEN THAT CLEANED

Before the nineteenth century, cleanliness was much more a matter of clothing than bodies. That great Renaissance guide to courtly manners Baldassare Castiglione had little to say about either, but his successors generally placed care of garments well above care of the skin on any list of cultivated refinements.[1] Because full body bathing was highly uncommon in the early modern world, the skin that most often felt water's touch was the skin that others could see. Yet upper-class Europeans, the only ones remotely concerned about such matters, never thought of themselves as unclean. Rather, their notions of cleanliness rested on the state of the clothing worn next to the skin – the whiteness of their linens. Clean clothes, especially clean underclothes, were the leading signs of good grooming.

Underwear holds a modest place in the history of clothing. As with so many parts of the everyday past, it was usually hidden from view. But we do catch occasional glimpses of underclothes in earlier times and the broad outlines of their history are clear enough, their relationships to the clean body included. By the seventeenth century, linen undergarments were commonly worn by the upper classes in Western Europe, as they had been since the later Middle Ages, though before then the inner layer had normally been concealed.[2] By then, as well, the term "linen" had come to mean underclothes as well as the cloth from which they were made. In an age when bodies were very seldom washed, cleanliness meant refreshing the hidden layer of clothing if it meant anything at all. Over time, as sensibilities sharpened, the regular change of underwear passed from a personal choice to a social rule, at least in refined circles. Linens themselves were regarded as the agents that cleansed. According to Georges Vigarello, they "became the sole criterion for cleanliness in classical France. Fresh, white linen removed dirt by its intimate contact with the body. Its effect was comparable to that of water."[3] The same was true in colonial America.[4]

Linen's whiteness advertised both its own cleanliness and that of the body it covered, and these facts yielded two important consequences. One was the need for frequent replacement. Lying next to the skin and absorbing its impurities, linen had to be renewed often. The Sun King's habit of several changes daily was simply an extravagant version of practices common among his wealthier subjects, and no doubt some of the less wealthy too. At the same time, underwear protected outerwear from the body's emanations and helped maintain its unsoiled appearance.

The other consequence was a matter of display. As the symbolic value of white linen grew, the wish to proclaim its meanings grew too. Once hidden beneath the outer garments, underwear gradually revealed itself in ever more impressive ways. White collars and cuffs crept out from beneath doublets, white linen undershirts burst forth at the neck and peered through openings in jackets and cloaks. In time ruffs and cuffs became separate articles of clothing, confections detached from their underwear origins. Best known today through the art of the Dutch Golden Age, the fashion embraced genteel society in Western Europe and America throughout the seventeenth and eighteenth centuries. As visible linen grew more ostentatious, as its whiteness became more highly prized, it proclaimed the wearer's refinement with an increasingly bold voice. It also proclaimed the unsoiled state of the body beneath the linen. Fresh white linen was a mark of personal cleanliness and a sign of respectability. Cleanliness had become a matter of appearances, not for the first time, nor for the last.

Because we know more about these matters in France than elsewhere, we turn to the French example here. According to the historian Daniel Roche, French dress habits changed markedly over the eighteenth century. As with so many transformations in material life, these innovations originated in the upper reaches of society and slowly diffused to the wider population, the lower ranks imitating their social superiors as time passed and growing wealth permitted. Among the changes Roche discovered were those involving underwear. Through a careful examination of estate inventories he found that both sexes usually wore shirts and stockings while petticoats and stays or corsets completed the feminine under layer. On the eve of the Revolution the former were almost universal among both sexes and all classes, as were petticoats among women. But the same was not true of underpants. They were seldom noted in women's estates, and while slightly more often owned by men, they remained far from common.[5]

Other evidence also indicates that women, in particular, seldom wore underpants until well into the nineteenth century. They are missing from eighteenth-century erotic illustrations, for example, their absence suggesting that they were optional.[6] Louis-Sébastien Mercier, a careful observer of Parisian life on the eve of the revolution, noted that only actresses wore *les caleçons* – and they were creatures of low repute.[7] The Italian historian of everyday life Raffaella Sarti also concluded that women of the popular classes did without, noting that victims of sexual violence failed to mention *mutande* when testifying before law courts.[8] Nor were they noted on Paris laundry lists before the mid-1840s.[9] And while men may have worn drawers somewhat more frequently, this didn't mean they changed them often. Roche tells the tale of a Baron Schomberg who, before his marriage in the early 1760s, replaced his shirt and collar daily, his handkerchief every second day, and his underpants once a month.[10] The central place of appearances in cleanliness couldn't be more clear. Once married, however, the good Baron changed his habits – and his briefs once a week.

By the middle decades of the nineteenth century, customs had started to change and French women of fashion began to wear *les pantalons*, a practice perhaps borrowed from their English sisters. According to Edmond Texier, another chatty observer of fashionable Parisian life, an earlier attempt to introduce them had failed: "Even in 1822, some of the elegant women of the Chaussée d'Antin had wanted to adopt the Turkish fashion of muslin leggings worn by children, but, strange to say, only the courtesans adopted this decent mode; it did not need more to discredit the practice."[11]

During the Second Empire, however, bourgeois women gradually adopted underpants, and the trend descended the social scale with passing time.[12] Judging by the fictional laundry lists in Zola's *L'Assommoir*, even working-class *Parisiennes* wore them by the 1870s.[13] Italian women of style followed the same path, led by French fashion.[14] In the German Rhineland women gradually adopted them toward the end of the nineteenth century too.[15] Drawers for men seem to have won wider acceptance at the same time – in Germany they sometimes were worn in winter – though here the evidence is elusive.[16] But whenever change came it came slowly. Long after mid-century, hygienic advisers were still urging both sexes to don drawers, a sign that adoption was lagging.[17] By the end of the century, the practice had become the urban norm, but in the countryside it remained an exception. In the Nivernais, the Limousin, and the Pyrenees, *les caleçons* and *les pantalons* were still seldom worn on the eve of the First World War.[18] And when they finally won the day, their victory had little to do with the bourgeois clothing reform movements that flourished from the mid-nineteenth century onward.[19] Rather it reflected a growing acceptance of the new hygiene.

How often people changed their clothes in former times is difficult to know. The past often speaks to us in whispers and this is one such occasion. The new sanitarian advice was clear and insistent, and it grew louder with passing time: clothes should be clean and changed frequently, the underclothes in particular.[20] But the gap between principle and practice was broad and persistent, or so it seems. According to one account, during the early nineteenth century shirts and stockings were changed weekly in the countryside surrounding Paris, a custom that persisted in the Nivernais at the turn of the twentieth. Nightclothes were almost unknown except among the bourgeoisie, and in France and Germany, most people slept in the shirts and shifts they wore during the day.[21] In Britain at mid-century the working-class custom was to wash shirts once a week; the middle classes might wear and wash four of them weekly.[22] Conditions in the eastern United States seem to have differed little.[23] At the end of the century Breton peasants wore their hemp shirts day and night till they were stiff with sweat and soil before throwing them in a pile to wait for the great wash.[24] Working families in Germany of the time seem to have washed their clothes weekly.[25] But the evidence is scanty and it offers no clear picture, apart from the strong impression that habits varied widely by nation, region, and class.

The rapid spread of cotton textiles during the Industrial Revolution affected laundry processes in two ways. Because cotton goods were easier to care for than the fabrics traditionally used for clothing, they reduced the effort needed for cleaning. Roche reminds us that during the *ancien régime*, many of the clothes worn by both sexes couldn't be washed at all because their fabrics wouldn't support it.[26] The fashionable woollen and linen garments worn by the wealthy often were difficult to clean: their delicate nature and elaborate construction challenged the launderer's arts. Spots and stains were removed with costly dry cleaning techniques or with dyes. Cotton was also easier to launder than hemp, the common fabric used for the rough clothing worn by country people, though hemp's greater durability easily offset this advantage.

Meanwhile the sharp fall in the price of cotton – the cost of a yard of plain-woven calico declined by more than 80 percent between 1780 and 1830 – greatly expanded the market for cotton goods.[27] The first half of the nineteenth century saw a dramatic increase in the quantities of cotton clothing and household draperies owned by families of modest means.[28] The historian Jules Michelet noted the phenomenon in France in the mid-1840s, calling it a great but little noticed "revolution in cleanliness and beautification experienced in the poor household: underwear, linen for beds, tables and windows; whole classes had these things which they had never owned since the origin of the world."[29] For Michelet the change was a clear sign of improved material welfare among the poor as well as of women's growing influence over the family budget.[30] Cotton use grew steadily throughout the century; in Germany, while homespun linens were worn until after the turn of the twentieth century, per capita cotton consumption increased twentyfold between 1840 and the First World War.[31] Yet these gains came at a cost, for while cottons were easier to clean, more clothes and higher standards of care meant more work for the laundress.

VILLAGE CUSTOMS

La grande lessive, the great wash, was the major laundry ritual of traditional rural France, an ancient practice that lingered well into the twentieth century. Once, twice, sometimes three times a year, normally in spring and fall, rural dwellers did the family washing. Invariably this was women's work. It also was communal: relatives, friends, and neighbours shared the labour and the camaraderie, the task spread over several days.[32] First, the dirty laundry was soaked in cold water for several hours, frequently overnight. Then it was layered in a tub, the largest and dirtiest items on the bottom, and covered with a coarse sheet folded over a thick layer of wood ash, often mixed with nettles, crushed egg shells, soapwort roots, or other natural products. Boiling water was poured over the cloth and the mixture till the tub overflowed; the excess liquid was then collected, reheated, and poured over the tub again and again in a process that might take ten, fifteen, or even twenty hours. The following day the laundry was taken to running water – a nearby washhouse, canal, pond, or river – to be soaped, rubbed, beaten, rinsed, and then wrung. Finally it was spread out to dry over hay or bushes, or hung on lines strung between trees. Ahead, of course, lay the ironing. The great wash was heavy labour, a woman's burden in a world in which both sexes knew hard physical work.

The public, communal aspect of doing the laundry had broad implications for feminine sociability. Cleaning apart, the great wash was a moment to display a woman's possessions, the trousseau of personal and household linens a bride had sewed for her new home, together with those she and her husband had acquired over the course of their marriage.[33] It revealed the quality of her handwork, the quantity of her household goods, the fineness of her possessions, and the care with which she kept her things, proclaiming her wealth and her housekeeping skills. As the sociologist Frédéric Le Play observed in the mid-1850s, linens were the wealth goods of the lower classes. The only storehouse of savings for most rural families, they were easy to keep and readily turned into cash if and when the need arose.[34] Thus *la grande lessive* was an occasion when household riches were on view, when prestige was claimed and tested, when women asserted their rank in the village social order, and when local hierarchies were affirmed or altered.

The great wash was also a moment of feminine solidarity, a time in the annual cycle when women shared domestic chores, along with some fun and a chance to gossip. Through the eyes of a child, the folklorist Pierre-Jakez Hélias recalled the importance of washday and female social space in Pouldreuzic, his native Breton village, soon after the turn of the twentieth century. Recounting his childhood he commented that the

> wash-trough was one of our most constant worries. It was there
> that the women held their own county-council, and the busi-
> ness of the day was often ourselves – either an enumeration
> of our good qualities (some of the time) or a discussion of our
> depraved behavior (most of the time). The place was called *ar
> prada* (the meadow), and the verb *prada* meant both paddling
> the laundry and giving spankings. The "meadow" was a water-
> hole surrounded by a clump of willow trees and was reserved for
> women. Never would a man dare to show his face there for fear
> of hearing some home truths about himself or, at the very least,
> of providing the gossips with a lot to talk about behind his back.
> It's so difficult to sing anyone's praises at a wash-trough.[35]

The village of Minot, north of Dijon, had five covered *lavoirs* by the later nineteenth century, and the washhouse was the only place where women met regularly, the equivalent of the local café for men.[36] Men were wholly excluded, and male passers-by were routinely heckled with obscene language and gestures to keep them at a distance. These were sites where women shared confidences and where a close examination of laundry – theirs and that of their friends and neighbours – revealed the intimate tales that only the washing can tell. As the ethnographer Yvonne Verdier put it, "From the body's dirt, one passes quickly to that of the soul. To wash all your dirty laundry, or wash the dirty laundry of others, is to put your nose in other people's business, into the secret of her misery, her thoughts, her desires, her soul – but at the same time to remove spots and stains, to whiten."[37]

While we know far less about laundering routines elsewhere, the great wash wasn't just a French practice. *Die großen Wäsche* was also common in pre-modern Austria and Germany, where it had the same seasonal cycles and socio-cultural meanings. Here too it was a communal event that took two or three days and displayed housewifely skills as well as valued possessions.[38] Similar customs persisted in the Italian Marche, and presumably in much of rural Italy, long into the twentieth century, though whether community work-sharing was as common as in France and Germany isn't clear.[39] In England, however, the term "great wash" held rather different meanings. From at least the eighteenth century it was linked to the homes of the well-to-do and to their large amounts of washing. The British rural wash lacked some of the communal and seasonal features of continental laundering customs; for all but the wealthy it was simply a routine household chore.[40] By the early nineteenth century, washdays commonly took place once a month.[41] Still, British women used similar methods to do their washing. The task involved a good deal of beating, scrubbing, and wringing, as well as some form of cleansing agent: lye leached from wood ash or sometimes animal dung or stale urine, valued for its ammonia content.[42] Soap, perhaps costlier in Britain than elsewhere because it was subject to an excise tax, was common during the first half of the nineteenth century, but even then it often was used together with lye.

As to settings, country women usually did the first phase of their wash at home, and the second on the banks of nearby pools, streams, rivers, or fountains, almost anywhere clean water was available. These practices continued in parts of rural Europe into the mid-twentieth-century decades. But new sites for washing also appeared in rural communities during the nineteenth century, used by women for their household laundry as well as by paid washerwomen. In France, local governments built public fountains and washhouses – *lavoirs* – to supply fresh water for the second stage of the laundering process: scrubbing and paddling, rinsing and wringing. Many were roofed and partly enclosed, while others offered little more than a source of running water and a rough work surface. In areas where water was scarce, the village washhouse provided a central source. It also extended the hope of keeping laundry wastes from polluting local fresh water supplies.[43] Toward the end of the century the village wash site became a common subject for postcard photos. Plate 5 is typical. Displaced to the realm of tourist curiosity, they consigned the *lavoir* to a vanishing world of colourful rustic practices. It's hard to imagine the laundresses in the photo sending this postcard to a friend but easy to assume that one of the well-dressed onlookers might.

In Italy even simpler structures, little more than stone ledges beside streams or rivers, often met the basic need. By the nineteenth century the ancient canals of Milan were lined with *lavatoi*, some covered but most of them simple platforms by the water. A recent count noted sixty-two sites along the 50-kilometre length of the Naviglio Grande and another twenty-nine on other canals radiating out of the city.[44]

Water's age-old associations with the magical and supernatural left their mark on laundering customs, particularly their timing. Most popular beliefs surrounding the great wash were related to death. Folk wisdom named many inauspicious days for laundry work: Fridays (especially Good Friday), Ascension, Corpus Christi, Holy Week, and the twelve days from Christmas to Epiphany, all moments of solemn religious observance. According to common belief, defying these prohibitions posed grave danger to the laundress or her near and dear. In Charente, Normandy, eastern Brittany, and Poitou, laundering during Holy Week invoked the threat of death during the year. In the Limousin, all men of the house were at risk, while in Savoy, only the head of the house was threatened. Washing on Good Friday was, if anything, even more ill-omened: in eastern Brittany, "one washed one's shroud," and in Valenciennes, "God damned those who washed."[45] Across the Channel, Devonshire folk wisdom held the same view: if clothes were washed on the holiest of Fridays, a family member would die before the year was out.[46] In many parts of France, local legends spoke of supernatural washerwomen who haunted *lavoirs*: witches, fairies, and phantom *lavandières* condemned to wash their laundry by night in penance for past misdeeds.[47] Yet not all infractions brought such severe punishments. In the German-speaking lands, washing on the prohibited days threatened little more than bad luck or a rebuke from one of the ghostly washerwomen rumoured to live near streams.[48] In the Italian Romagna, laundry cleaned during the full moon might be stained, and even some religious celebrations could be infringed with no greater punishment than linen that wouldn't whiten.[49] At the same time, while prohibitions greatly outnumbered permissions, some days were auspicious for doing the wash, among them St Thomas Day (21 December) in preparation for Christmas.[50]

Beneath these popular truths lay anxieties long associated with water's ambiguities. Its power to cleanse was universally acknowledged but its relationship to the body was fundamentally ambivalent, as we've seen. It could clean and cure, but it also was linked with evil spirits and death. The villagers of Minot believed that evil dwelt in their waters. Every year at Rogations the local priest blessed the village wells and fountains because they were the haunts of demons. Thus, washing had symbolic as well as practical meanings: the great wash was a laundering of spirits and souls as much as of clothes and household textiles.[51] Moreover, because linens absorbed the body's impurities, they were a physical form of its aura, an extension of the skin. In effect, washing the clothes that cleaned the body was a form of washing the body itself. When it came to water's supernatural qualities, clothing occupied the same sphere as the body, and the act of washing clothes might raise similar concerns. Underlying these proverbs about the appropriate days for washing lay the attempts of traditional rural peoples to reconcile the uncertainty and supernatural of their natural environments with the competing claims of their religious beliefs.

In housekeeping matters as in so many others, the rural upper classes lived lives remote from those of their less favoured neighbours, and their material conditions maintained the distance as much as their social pretensions did. Wealthy families needed help to care for the greater number of possessions they owned, and this invariably required servants, sometimes many of them. Cleaning clothes and other linens was one of their basic chores. During the 1820s and 1830s the du Tarn family, from a small village in southeastern France and recently raised to the noblesse, lived in the manner of the period's leading rural proprietors.[52] Rather than having their own servants wash their laundry, they hired local women to do it at their chateau, the pay rate fixed by local custom. The du Tarns cleaned their clothing six or seven times a year, though like the local peasants they did their kitchen, table, and bed linen only in spring and autumn. The seasonal rhythms of the *grande linge* implied that families held large stocks of textiles. But estate inventories reveal that even the wealthy seldom owned enough clothing to rely on the annual cycle for clean shirts and stockings. They normally washed them at home as the need arose. How frequently clothes were cleaned depended on how much was owned as well as how fastidious the wearers might be.[53]

Toward the end of the century, the British rural middle classes lived in much the same manner, or so the example of a Bedfordshire village parson and his family suggests. The household included the rector, his wife, their ten children, and seven live-in servants. Despite the large staff, the daily housework seems to have absorbed all their energies, for every Monday morning, a group of village women came to the rectory to do the household laundry.[54] In the heady heights above them stood the great British country houses, many with servants numbering in the scores and in some cases the hundreds. The larger among them had their own laundries, no doubt run according to Mrs Beeton's guide to domestic management.[55] Her view of the task spread the chores over the entire work week. Rural life in this form had virtually nothing in common with that lived by the great majority of country people. Britain's large country homes shared a dedication to conspicuous consumption and an institutional character that set them apart from other forms of domestic life on the Isles. One former laundry maid employed on a great estate in Yorkshire toward the end of the nineteenth century recalled that, together with two others, she was responsible for laundering a thousand table napkins weekly, and that only a small part of the regular wash. The house consumed a ton of soap and half a ton of soda annually.[56]

URBAN WAYS

By the standards of the countryside the nineteenth-century city was dirty, and urban conditions made bodies and clothes hard to keep clean. While the great industrial cities were by far the worst, most urban places shared the same broad features. Crowded, smoky, dusty, and gritty, they posed a major challenge to personal cleanliness. The muck of the streets stained the clothes of both rich and poor while the soot from open fires blackened bodies and buildings alike. According to one mid-nineteenth-century report, in the densely peopled parts of London clothing soiled in one third the time it would in a rural community.[57]

Compounding this problem, the urban environment raised two obstacles to doing the laundry: access to water and limited space. Before the later nineteenth century, water distribution in most large cities relied on peddlers or on public fountains, standpipes, and wells. The leading exception was London, a global city at mid-century, where almost 90 percent of private houses had water supplied on site, though only the wealthy and well-to-do were likely to have it piped inside their homes.[58] By contrast, Berlin, with a population of half a million at that point, had some nine hundred fountains, and perhaps nine thousand buildings had water available in a courtyard, but only 669 households had a water connection.[59]

Water from public sources might be free, but the cost of its use in time and effort was high. One British estimate of the period indicated that a family living on the third or fourth floor and using fifty gallons daily would require twenty pails carried from the nearest standpipe. The water alone would weigh five hundred pounds, in addition to the weight of the pail. Then, in the absence of drain pipes, the waste water had to be carried out again.[60] Considered on a weekly basis, the author suggested, "to fetch the water, and carry such a weight, would probably require the amount of two days' labour in the week." Like many similar guesses, this one stood some distance from everyday life, at least as lived by the British working classes. True, the poor tended to occupy the upper floors of houses because rents were lower there. But this assumption about the quantities of water used daily was much closer to upper- than to lower-class norms. Still, as one observer noted in rotund Victorian prose, "the labour of carriage [was] an insurmountable obstacle to the liberal use of water for household purposes," whatever the amount consumed.[61] Toward the end of the century, as more and more dwellings were directly connected to water distribution systems, the problem began to diminish. But long into the twentieth century many British working-class families continued to fetch their household water supplies by the pailful.[62]

The small size and crowded conditions of mass housing also hampered home laundry work. Rosmarie Beier, a historian of the German proletarian home at the turn of the century, reveals some of the challenges:

Washing the laundry became a new hardship in the tenement. It was mostly done in the apartment because laundry rooms were rare. The boiling water on the stove filled the room with hot steam and also moistened the walls ... On the eve of the washday the laundry was soaked in water and soda. The next morning the kitchen stove was fueled and the clothes packed in the washing pot. The boiling laundry was loosened and stirred with the help of a washing stick. Then it was lifted piece by piece from the wash. When it had cooled a little it was scrubbed clean

on the washboard and wrung out. Then collars and cuffs, table-
cloths, blouses and the like were stiffened. For this purpose a
piece of starch was dissolved in boiling water. The fabrics were
then rinsed in this solution and wrung out one last time. Cottons
were usually washed in the still-warm wash water. The washing
was hung either in the kitchen, where it took the last available
room, or on the drying ground.[63]

The laundry problem was general in the rapidly growing cities of
Continental Europe (where most families lived in very close quarters), challenging in those of the British Isles (where domestic space
was slightly more ample), and common among the urban poor
across the Atlantic as well. At times it was possible to move some
of the work outdoors. Certainly England's terraced housing offered
more open air access than the multi-storeyed tenements of France,
Germany, and Austria. But laundering out-of-doors was fair-weather
work and for much of the year washing could only be done inside.[64]
Given the length and tedium of the task, family life in the new industrial city must have revolved around the laundry cycle, for it regularly
monopolized household space and filled the air with its vapours. Big
tenement complexes like Meyer's-Hof sometimes provided washing
and drying spaces for their residents, and model housing developments for working-class families often included laundry facilities
too.[65] Some large low-rent buildings in Paris even offered communal
steam-powered laundry machinery by the end of the century. But
facilities like these were the exception, not the rule. American conditions were something of a contrast, at least if judged by the Boston example. According to a study of tenement life during the early
1890s, most residents lived in larger apartments and virtually all
families dried their washing out-of-doors.[66] While they still washed
their effects in the kitchen, at least they had more workspace, and
their homes were less often festooned with drying laundry.

Given the crowded conditions and limited comforts of working-class life, the room needed to wash was often shared, and when
it was, sharing itself might become a source of conflict. In 1913
Maude Pember Reeves sketched a common scenario in Britain – and
presumably elsewhere too:

Where two families share a six-room house the landlady of the
two probably chooses the ground-floor, with command over the

yard and washing arrangements. The upstairs people contract with her for use of the copper [the large kitchen basin used for heating water] and yard on one day of the week. The downstairs woman hates having the upstairs woman washing in her scullery, and the upstairs woman hates washing there. Differences which result in "not speaking" often begin over the copper.[67]

In some larger continental tenements with laundry facilities, building caretakers drew up work schedules and policed their observance.[68] But shared laundry facilities often were unsupervised, poorly maintained, and unsatisfactory.

The alternatives to home laundering varied from country to country. From its origins in the 1840s, the British public bath movement included laundries in its grand plan to cleanse the working classes. The Liverpool bath, founded in 1842, included laundry facilities for the poor, and many others established during the rest of the century also provided them. By the early twentieth century there were more than one hundred public baths with laundries in England and Scotland, mostly in the larger industrial cities.[69] In addition to limitless supplies of hot water, they offered facilities for washing, drying, and ironing at a low cost in time, labour, and money. Purportedly it took just two to three hours to complete a wash cycle. Yet Britain's public laundries did little to meet the needs they were intended to address. In London on the eve of the First World War, annual use in the city's thirty-six washhouses was the equivalent of regular weekly visits for 1 percent of all households.[70] Some institutions tried to distinguish between housewives and washerwomen, charging daily users more than those who came only once a week. Social attitudes may also have discouraged use. As the author of a comprehensive report on the British bath and wash house movement observed: "It is undoubtedly the case that a good wife and mother in every rank of society usually dislikes publicity, and prefers having a home which is self-contained, to any form of co-operation. Public Wash-houses involve mixed company and the exposure of the small family effects to the outer world."[71] The contrast between the sociable feminine world of the rural great wash and the urban working-class wife toiling alone at her family's laundry is striking. But perhaps here we also catch a glimpse of other cultural differences, those dividing British notions of individualism and privacy from continental views of communal solidarity.

Although the British "bath and wash house" model caught the attention of hygiene reformers abroad, it failed to win the affections of laundry patrons in other countries. Attempts to introduce public washhouses in Germany during the mid-1850s soon failed, as did the costly Paris experiment supported by Napoléon III, though at least two were established in French provincial towns.[72] In Italy the innovation appeared in Turin only after the city began to industrialize during the later nineteenth century.[73] A few of the public baths opened in eastern American cities toward the end of the century also offered laundry services, but their numbers were small and their histories brief.

Still, there were other possibilities for urban housewives to wash the family laundry outside their homes, especially in warmer climes. In Italian cities located along canals or rivers, *lavatoi* usually lined their banks, providing easy access to the water. Plate 6 depicts a popular washing site along a canal in Bologna around the turn of the twentieth century. The sunlight and freshly washed laundry in the photo speak of productive work in pleasant conditions, though the laundresses' wet feet, soaked skirts, and stooped backs tell quite a different tale.

The Bolognese physician Vittorio Puntoni came closer to the truth when, soon after the turn of the century, he wrote with alarm about the state of the water: "The conditions in laundries along the network of the Reno Canal are absolutely incredible. In them is real sewer water, in which all the human waste materials are unaltered or in full decomposition. I believe that we can hardly imagine worse conditions."[74] Good hygienist that he was, Puntoni urged a modern sewer system in the city and a prohibition on the use of canal water for all but industrial purposes.

In many French cities, most notably Paris, the laundry industry lay in private hands. Small proprietors owned the *lavoirs* where working-class housewives and washerwomen did their washing. The city possessed some ninety of them at mid-century, most reportedly in poor hygienic condition.[75] Users divided their laundry into small packets and, after a first soaking, left the initial stage of the washing process to employees of the *lavoir*, who poured a boiling solution of lye or soda over the packets and allowed them to drain overnight. Next day the clients reclaimed their packages, and those who wished to pay for additional services could soap, rinse, and hang their laundry to dry with the equipment provided.[76] The vice-president of the

Chambre syndicale des lavoirs estimated that 300,000 to 400,000 women used the system daily in the later 1860s.[77] Half of the places for washing were used by washerwomen working for pay, the other half by housewives.[78]

And the system kept pace with the city's growth. As the century drew to a close, an industrial census recorded 117 *lavoirs* in Paris with close to 35,000 wash stations, the smaller, traditional establishments in the city's inner *arrondissements*, the larger – some with more than 1,000 workplaces – in the proletarian suburbs.[79] The noted hygienist Octave du Mesnil continued to admire the English public washhouse system, which allowed the lower classes to do the family wash outside their homes at a modest cost. But given the entrenched interests of the laundry sector, he was far from certain that a public system would be supported, even by those it was intended to help.[80]

In France, Austria, and Germany, *bateaux-lavoirs* and *Waschschiffs* opened other opportunities for laundering outside the home. Boats or barges permanently moored to the bank of a river or canal, they offered water access in cities and towns where the foreshore might be occupied or contested. Like land-based *lavoirs*, most were small businesses, though local governments also operated some. The boats were divided into separate workspaces, available to users for a few hours for a small fee. Basic washing equipment and space for drying were also supplied. An institution with a history reaching back to at least the seventeenth century, they remained features of French riverine life well into the twentieth century, though their numbers were in decline long before then.[81] In 1849 Paris hosted eighty-one *bateaux-lavoirs* along the Seine and the Canal Saint-Martin.[82] They averaged thirty-five work sites each and together constituted one third of the city's public *lavoirs*. Though less well-documented than in France, *Waschschiffs* were commonplace in Austria and Germany too, sometimes depicted in period art.[83]

THE LAUNDRY TRADES

For centuries the laundry business coexisted with domestic washing across Europe. Communities often assigned specific locations for laundry work, public sites where paid laundresses pursued their humdrum tasks together with female servants and housewives.[84] From the eighteenth century onward, the increasing numbers of garments

worn and the rising standards of their care slowly expanded the
market for commercial laundry services. The demand was highest
in urban places, where the wealthy and well-to-do tended to gather,
for they owned the largest numbers of clothes and held the greatest
social investment in the symbolic value of cleanliness. But the popular classes often paid for laundry services too; cramped houses and
costly water made home laundering difficult if not impossible for
many. During the nineteenth century the laundry trades expanded
rapidly, more complex laundry systems replaced older ways, and
industrialization began to transform longstanding work patterns.
Meanwhile the time-honoured craft of hand-laundering lingered on,
the two systems working in parallel.

In the homes of the better-off, servants normally did the light,
routine washing while heavier tasks fell to laundresses. Those who
paid for laundry services either hired someone to do the work in
their households or sent their things out to a commercial laundry.
Employing a washerwoman at home allowed the mistress of the
house to supervise the process and keep an eye on her valued possessions, but it also took her time and, at least in smaller dwellings,
disrupted household life. Sending the washing to a laundry removed
the chore from the domestic scene but also increased the risk of poor
work and lost articles, besides exposing the laundry's secrets to the
public gaze. It may also have been more costly, though those unable
to wash at home had no alternative.

As a business, laundry work varied considerably. We know very
little about the women who regularly came to their employers'
homes to do their washing. They were part of the casual market
for female labour, workers who simply arrived, washed, pocketed
their small wages, and departed, to return for the next laundry
cycle. Laundry shops were the primary alternative, most of them
family affairs, the work normally organized by a proprietor – often
female – who hired a few assistants. The shop served a group of
customers, fetching their dirty laundry at the beginning of the week
and delivering it clean, ironed, and folded by week's end. In Britain,
poor laundry workers sometimes used the public washhouse to earn
their living, though the practice often irritated their competitors.[85] In
Paris, where *lavoirs* were private businesses, laundresses were regular clients alongside housewives, paying to use facilities they lacked
in their own shops.[86] Wherever done, laundry work was hard physical labour. It involved a great deal of heavy lifting (water for boiling

and rinsing as well as the wet laundry itself) in addition to beating or agitating the soiled articles in wash water.[87] Before mechanical wringers or mangles were common, wringing out the washing was an equally arduous task. Ironing involved a separate set of skills with their own taxing demands, long hours with hot, heavy irons in overheated rooms included.

Laundry work was among the most common forms of female wage labour throughout the Western world. It called on skills women learned in childhood, it could be fitted into the rhythms of domestic life, it required little investment capital, and it met a seemingly endless need. Men, too, worked in the trade, though greatly outnumbered by women – they were only one in ten in Paris in the 1870s, one in four in Milan at the turn of the century.[88] Most of them were either proprietors or employees in larger mechanized laundries. Because many laundry workers were casual labourers, census records under-estimate their numbers, but they still offer a sense of the scale of the sector: 167,000 in England and Wales in 1861, 205,000 by the end of the century; in Germany, 110,000 in 1882 rising to 165,000 by 1907.[89] In France, laundry work employed more than 100,000 in the Paris basin alone in the late 1870s.[90]

Despite the large numbers employed in the trade, the laundress remains an elusive figure in Western urban history. Today the best-known among them is fictional: Zola's Gervaise Macquart, whose short happiness and long decline through poverty, alcoholism, and despair to early death are sketched in *L'Assommoir*, his portrait of working-class life in mid-nineteenth-century Paris.[91] Young, abandoned, and an unmarried mother of two, she was a washerwoman of necessity. In the floodtide of her modest good fortune she opened her own laundry shop and enjoyed brief success, but in time she lost both her shop and her skills, as she lost all else in her life.

Though Gervaise was a fiction, Zola's novel captures something of the reality of a working life in laundry before the machine age. According to one well-placed observer of the time, the Paris *blanchisseuse* worked thirteen to fourteen hours a day, from 6 a.m. to 8 or 8:30 p.m., with an hour for dinner. The condition, it seems, was general; everywhere long workdays were the laundry worker's lot.[92] The various steps in the process governed the weekly rhythms of the trade: soaking, washing, soaping, bleaching, rinsing, bluing, starching, wringing, drying, and ironing, the tasks spread over several days. Seasonal cycles shaped laundry work as well; there was a

lull during the summer months that sometimes forced laundresses
to look for other employment. Wages varied according to tasks and
skills, with ironers (who did piecework) generally earning the most,
washerwomen in private homes the least, regular laundry workers
somewhere between the two. While the work was arduous, it paid
better than many other forms of women's employment. During
the mid-nineteenth century, German laundresses earned more than
women who worked in the textile trades.[93] Unlike many forms of
female wage labour, older women dominated the profession. At the
turn of the century over half of British female laundry workers and
70 percent of those in Milan were married or widowed.[94] Despite
the fragmented structure of the trades, laundresses shared bonds of
common interest. Nineteenth-century Vienna's *Wäschermadln* were
known for their fun-loving, independent ways, idealized in story and
song. The annual wash maid's ball celebrated their solidarity while
raising funds for needy colleagues.[95]

Though the mechanization of laundry work dates from at least
the later eighteenth century, the process began to intensify in the
1830s, and over time, it transformed the industry.[96] Technological
change first touched the tasks demanding the heaviest physical
work – soaking, washing, and wringing – after which the machines
themselves passed through a long and uneven technical evolution,
transforming different parts of the laundering process in discon-
tinuous phases. Soaking, the stage based on the cleansing power
of soap and soda dissolved in hot water, submitted early to steam
technology. The more complex mechanical processes, washing and
wringing, required more sophisticated machinery and a longer process of technological trial and error. By the late nineteenth century,
however, large-scale mechanized steam laundries were common in
urban centres across the Western world, and manufacturers offered
a range of laundry equipment for industrial and domestic use. But
given the size and cost of the new machinery, it was used almost
exclusively in big commercial laundries or in hotels, hospitals, and
other large institutions. .

Mechanization only touched the domestic hand laundry trade
lightly before the end of the century. Laundresses and *blanchisseuses*,
Wäschfrauen and *lavandaie*, continued to ply their trade as they
long had, though some also began to employ small labour-saving
innovations such as mangles. In other respects however the new
machines had a transformative impact. Industrialization drew the

machine laundry trade to the urban outskirts, especially around the great cities. In 1900 some thousand *blanchisseries* could be found in Boulogne, Rueil, and other towns south and west of Paris, while London's bigger laundries concentrated in Fulham, Hammersmith, and Acton.[97] By then Vienna, Berlin, Bonn, Hamburg, Dresden, and Frankfurt all had satellite laundry towns as well. In effect, the suburbs washed the city's laundry. Pushed by municipal bylaws aimed at ridding city centres of traditional washhouses, and drawn by the greater space and lower cost of suburban locations, owners moved their operations to the urban periphery. Even independent laundresses followed the same route. Toward the end of the century many in Paris were taking their fine articles to the suburbs instead of inner-city *lavoirs* where, the heaviest work now done by machines, the clean clothes were only ironed and folded before being returned to their customers.[98]

In the longer run washerwomen often became laundry workers, wage earners like so many others, their lives framed by capitalist labour relations. Their employers were factory owners, men with major investments in the capital stock of their businesses, socially and personally distant from the lives of their employees. The classic conflicts between labour and capital soon emerged: contests over wages, working conditions, worker safety, and union rights. By the late nineteenth century labour unrest had come to the industry in Europe and America, a common tale with a twist because most laundry workers were women and organized labour activity at the time was largely a male affair.[99] Laundries run by some Roman Catholic organizations were a variation on the theme. The first of the "Magdalene" laundries in Ireland were opened soon after the First World War. Operated by several sisterhoods, they were staffed by women inmates, many of them detained for unwed motherhood. They worked for no wages and served indeterminate sentences, doing the laundry for hotels, military organizations, and other large establishments.[100] Thus by the early twentieth century the laundry industry had two contrasting faces, one obviously artisanal and one decidedly industrial. Traditional washerwomen pursued their craft in ways little different from those of the distant past while their industrial colleagues laboured in the modern mechanical laundry. Both ways of working and earning were soon to change.

THE COST OF CLEAN CLOTHES

By now it should be obvious that whether laundry was done at home or sent out, clean clothes involved costs. Those who did their own washing normally had to purchase some of the materials they used, and the labour value of their work could be imputed though it wasn't paid. Thus even when no sums changed hands the time cost of domestic laundry work was substantial. As a result, washing clothes and domestic linens was an item in the family budget for most households. Estimates for London in the late eighteenth and early nineteenth centuries suggest that laundry charges made up 4 percent of annual household expenses for a genteel family of five with two servants – almost as much as they paid their servants and a bit more than half the cost of heat and lighting. Conditions in Paris at the time seem to have been broadly similar.[101] Over time, in London at least, laundry expenses gradually rose, surpassing those for heat and light in the middle-class household budget. Soap had long been a common household expenditure for working families too, and the outlays absorbed a substantial part of their incomes.[102]

By the mid-nineteenth-century decades the cost of clean laundry was important enough to attract interest during social inquiries. A study of working-class life in the French textile community of Rouen and environs during the later 1830s indicated that families spent between 4 and 7.5 percent of their annual income on laundry.[103] Most of the accounts of household expenses reported in Le Play's mid-nineteenth-century survey of European workers' welfare revealed outlays on soap ranging from 0.5 to 2 percent of household income. Even the poor rural families at the low end of the spectrum set aside a small sum for it.[104] Le Play was among the first to see that unpaid domestic labour should be valued in monetary terms, and in several of his budgets he attached a financial value to a housewife's family laundry work, a value double or even triple that of the washing products they used.[105] Two of his examples shed further light on the place of the laundry economy in daily life. In one, a Paris rag picker's household sent its laundry out to be washed at a cost of over 5 percent of its modest annual income.[106] The other was a *maître blanchisseur* from the Paris suburbs.[107] A successful small businessman, his annual household income was twice that of the next-highest family in the Le Play sample. Clearly there was money in dirty clothes.

By mid-century the French and British governments had begun to take an interest in the question of laundry care. The French national commission on public baths and washhouses deplored the existing condition of Paris *lavoirs* and upheld England's recent innovation as a better alternative. In passing, the commissioners noted the cost of laundry services for working-class families – 2 francs per person per month – an amount broadly in line with earlier French estimates.[108] At the same time, after investigating the condition of London's water supply, the British Board of Health concluded that middle-class families spent about 8 percent of their income on laundry expenses, an amount rarely less than one third of their rental costs. As for the working classes, the board estimated that the amount they should spend on washing likely equalled half their rents, well beyond the ability of many labourers' families. To put the matter in different terms, a working man's calico shirt might last nine or ten months, and if washed once a week, the cost of washing it over its lifetime would be five times its original price. In contrast, the middle classes might wear and wash four linen shirts weekly, and these could last up to eight years. In this case the expense of laundering them was less than double their original price.[109]

Thus clean clothes were expensive, and the ability to pay reflected the deep inequalities of nineteenth-century society. The wealthy could bear the cost of cleanliness when those of low incomes might not. A well-washed wardrobe was a form of conspicuous consumption, a sign that the wearer could afford to be clean.[110] It should come as no surprise, then, that the comfortable classes spent a larger fraction of their incomes on their laundry bills than did the less favoured, and that, when household incomes rose, family outlays for washing and ironing often rose disproportionately.[111] As for the desperately poor, clean clothes were beyond their means in the struggle to keep up appearances. Reduced to begging for a living, Jordan Fitzstephen – a fifty-seven-year-old widower and former labourer with three young children – told an inquiry into Irish poverty during the early 1830s, "We are sometimes short even of potatoes, and sometimes get as much above what we can eat as buys soap to wash my shirt. I must often wear my shirt two or three weeks without washing. I have but one."[112] Fitzstephen spoke from County Mayo on the northwestern European fringe, but he spoke for the countless poor of the Western world who shared the degradation of dirty clothes.

According to Le Play the social nuances of cleanliness were most evident in the city. Living in close contact with their bourgeois superiors, working people sensed the need for clean clothing but were much less able to meet it in their own domestic lives.[113] As for the laundered clothes themselves, the late-eighteenth-century Parisian observer Louis-Sébastien Mercier lamented the rough treatment they received at the hands of the city's *blanchisseuses*, for it shortened their lives. "Once they've been washed 5 or 6 times," he noted, "they're only good for making scraps."[114]

4

THE SOAP TRADE AND THE NEW HYGIENE

No single influence spread the word of the new hygiene more widely –
and more insistently – than the emerging modern soap industry. Soap
was one of the two basic elements needed to clean bodies and clothes,
and its manufacture expanded rapidly throughout the nineteenth and
early twentieth centuries. In turn, increased output required growing markets, legions of consumers to buy the growing mountains
of soap produced. The soap makers faced major challenges as they
searched for customers. In their highly competitive trade, the difference between success and failure was largely a matter of expanding
a firm's market base, and the task was far from simple. Of the many
who tried, a handful triumphed spectacularly while an added few
achieved more modestly, but the great majority failed. What distinguished the victors from the rest was less the quality of their product
than the success of their marketing. The most far-sighted business
leaders in soap saw boundless opportunity in the expanding consumer marketplace, and they grasped the most promising tool to connect with it: advertising. The advertising trade was new at the time,
growing hand in glove with other consumer goods industries, bringing prospective buyers the glad tidings of products old and new. The
great soap makers adopted the new persuasive arts with energy and
enthusiasm. Advertising became one of the basic building blocks of
their businesses, a tool to create a dependable market for their product lines. And as the soap makers promoted their goods, they became
some of hygiene's greatest educators, for their ads also instructed,
teaching regular habits and shaping cultural values. With messages
that came to reach millions of customers, existing and potential, they
had the power to influence on an unparalleled scale.

THE ART OF SOAP MAKING

Soap is reasonably simple to make. It is produced when fatty acids are mixed with a base and the mixture is heated. Combining animal or vegetable oils with an alkali yields soap and the by-product glycerine. Expressed in terms of a chemical reaction, saponification occurs as the glycerine molecules attached to fatty acids of triglycerides are replaced with a hydroxide. When combined with fats, salts of potassium yield soft soaps while those of sodium produce harder varieties.[1] The resulting product is soluble in water and therefore can serve as a cleaning agent.

While soap was known in antiquity, its early uses were cosmetic and medicinal, and when its cleansing properties became widely recognized isn't clear. Still, soap making was a well-established craft during the early Middle Ages, a sign that by then soap was being manufactured on an industrial basis, particularly on the Italian peninsula.[2] By the early seventeenth century, England and France had become the leading European producers, with the industry centred in London and Marseilles.[3] Tallow was the main fat used in northern European production while olive oil supplied the need in the Mediterranean world. The quantities manufactured must have been substantial, for some makers sold their goods on national and international as well as local markets. A large though unknown part of production was destined for the textile industry because wool was washed before being spun and woven. As well, soap was used to clean other fabrics during their manufacture. Most of the remainder was for general household use.

Over the following two centuries the industry changed substantially. New understandings about soap-making processes improved productivity while imperial expansion, transportation improvements, and increasing trade brought new vegetable fats to those practices.[4] Late-eighteenth- and early-nineteenth-century guides to the soap maker's art summarized the technical knowledge of the time and unveiled the wider range of products then available: soaps based on palm, rapeseed, and cotton seed oils as well as floral and nut sources; harsh soaps for industrial and household use, costly toilet soaps for delicate skins.[5] Commercial soap production was spread across Europe, but the industry came to be concentrated in a small number of centres, locations with ready access to basic ingredients and transportation services. By the eve of the French Revolution,

Marseille dominated the industry in France, exporting over 20 percent of its product to Europe, the Levant, and the Americas.[6] One result of this concentration was the development of regional specialties in soaps known for their distinctive properties. Those from Venice, Naples, Marseille, and Castile were especially prized. Yet at the end of the eighteenth century, soap making remained an artisanal activity, governed by craft knowledge and skills rather than by a scientific understanding of saponification. Although the study of soap's chemical properties had proceeded during the Enlightenment, in the great age of political revolutions the industry still awaited its revolutionary moment.

It arrived during the first half of the nineteenth century, when three developments altered soap manufacturing fundamentally.[7] In a typical example of the new machine age and its transformative force, industrialization brought steam power and mechanization to fabrication processes, increasing productivity while reducing production costs. In addition, during the late eighteenth century the French physician Nicolas Leblanc had invented a way to obtain alkali from salt. While the technique wasn't widely employed until the first decades of the following century, and then more extensively in England than in France, once adopted it reduced the industry's reliance on alkalis derived from wood or other plant ashes and introduced the large-scale manufacture of caustic soda, one of the principle ingredients in soap manufacturing. Finally, the French chemist Michel Eugène Chevreul's research on animal fatty acids and soap, published between 1813 and 1823, provided a scientific understanding of the chemistry underlying saponification. His discoveries offered a deeper knowledge of core industrial processes, giving them a precision and predictability they had formerly lacked. Together these developments created the capacity to manufacture soap on an unprecedented scale and signalled that soap's future lay with industrial chemistry.

Given the many manufacturers and their scattered distribution, the amounts of soap produced and consumed at this time are far from clear. According to one account, during the early nineteenth century French production averaged 62,000 tons a year, or a bit over 4 pounds (1.9 kg) per capita, some of it for export.[8] A contemporary estimate claimed that Paris alone bought at least 50,000 cases of Marseille soap annually, or about 16 pounds (6 kg) per capita.[9] If even remotely accurate, this figure must have reflected a high level of industrial use beyond household and personal consumption. Over the coming

decades the French soap industry expanded while Marseille struggled
to defend its leading role in the national trade.[10] At mid-century there
were about 50 manufacturers in the city with some 700 workers,
soap making remaining a main support of the local economy.[11] From
the early years of the century, however, imported vegetable oils had
challenged the olive's dominance and chemistry's progress had created new products. As a result, though Marseille managed to expand
its production and defend the prestige of its brand – the true "savon
de Marseille" – it gradually lost its national predominance. By the
later nineteenth century soap manufacturing had become widespread
throughout France, with a second concentration in the Paris basin and
lesser centres near major seaports.[12]

More reliable estimates come from Britain from the late eighteenth century onward, reliable because the British government
levied an excise duty on soap, creating a helpful paper trail.[13]
Even then the estimates vary, but all of them reveal a steady rise
in national soap production and consumption, the latter more than
doubling from 3.1 pounds (1.4 kg) per capita in 1791 to 8 pounds
(3.6 kg) in the 1860s, somewhat higher than in France.[14] In addition, before the excise tax on soap was repealed in 1853, unknown
quantities were smuggled from France and Ireland to evade the levy.
Some three quarters of all soap produced at the time was for household use rather than export or manufacturing. As the industry grew,
soap making came to be clustered around major ports – London,
Liverpool, Bristol, Plymouth, and Newcastle – with some makers
also at inland locations.[15]

Much has been said but little is known about home soap production in the North American colonies. Household soap making
is a common theme in the mythology of pioneer self-sufficiency, yet
with only anecdotes to inform us, we'll never know how extensive
the practice was. It may also have been common in Western Europe,
but because it didn't resonate with foundational myths as it did in
America, the subject has been ignored. In either case we shouldn't
assume that those who couldn't readily buy their soap therefore
made their own. Even on a small scale, soap making needed basic
equipment, a cost not everyone could afford. It also required supplies of fats and alkalis that home production couldn't always offer.
New World land clearing provided the first settlers with an abundant
harvest of wood ashes, often enough for sale as well as for domestic
use, but those who arrived later and those who had no land to clear

had to buy what they required. As to fats, the thrifty housewife who saved her kitchen scraps to make soap is a shining figure in frontier legend, but the by-products of her cooking had other claims on them as well. Most fats used in soap making were edible and, at least in poor households, as likely to feed families as soap boilers. Tallow was also used to make candles: the two products often came from the same factory during the artisanal stage of the industry's evolution. Thus the homemade soap of pioneer lore wasn't necessarily a ready alternative to the factory-produced article. It involved its own costs in time and money.

It should come as no surprise, then, that commercial soap making developed early in colonial America. According to Samuel Colgate – no historian to be sure, but a highly successful captain of the American soap industry – skilled soap makers were among the earliest arrivals to the Jamestown colony in Virginia, the first permanent English settlement in the United States.[16] From that point on the industry grew as colonial society expanded. By the early 1830s a survey of American manufacturing revealed soap works scattered among the cities, towns, and villages of the nation, especially in the northeast. Most were small factories with only a few employees using traditional handicraft production techniques.[17] While they relied heavily on local markets, some soap makers also sold part of their production abroad, principally to the West Indies and South America. According to one survey respondent, with more than a note of national pride, by then the United States was almost completely self-sufficient in soap as well as a significant force in export markets.[18] Still, the achievement failed to impress all observers. A French study published a generation later noted that "the United States produce great quantities of low cost soap; but it is badly made and mixed with so much foreign material that it has no parallel with European products."[19] The note of national pride was equally clear.

Even before the turn of the nineteenth century, then, soap was widely used across much of the Western world, one of a small group of household commodities more often purchased than made at home. It figured among the everyday expenses noted in reports on popular living conditions, included with food and fuel, candles and cloth. Estimates suggest that it accounted for 2 to 3 per cent of rural and working-class family expenses in late-eighteenth-century Britain, the proportion perhaps doubling by the 1840s.[20] It was also a standard item in the budgets of schools, almshouses, prisons, and military

forces. Of the 36 households examined in Frédéric Le Play's pioneering mid-nineteenth-century study of European working-class living
conditions, only one – a family of semi-nomadic herders in eastern
Russia – seems to have produced its own soap, and even they purchased the potassium carbonate they needed.[21] As a result, the cost
of soap mattered to the great majority, those whose cash incomes
were modest at best. In this sense, at least, their lot improved during
the long nineteenth century, for the price of soap fell substantially.
The data we have are patchy but they show a decline of close to two
thirds in England from the end of the Napoleonic Wars to 1870, one
fifth in Vienna and two thirds in Paris between 1840 and 1914. In
Italy wholesale soap prices fell by one third between the mid-1870s
and the outbreak of the First World War.[22] Meanwhile real wages
rose across Western Europe, gradually after 1815 and more rapidly
after 1850.[23] Thus, as the century progressed, soap was ever easier to
afford and consumption increased steadily. Per capita use in Britain
quintupled during the period, while the continental countries also
revealed impressive growth. By 1914 British consumers were buying
upwards of 15 pounds (6.8 kg) of soap a year, Americans slightly
more, French, Germans, and Italians somewhat less – a sign of the
broad rise in living standards everywhere.[24]

THE TRANSFORMATION OF SOAP PRODUCTION

From the later nineteenth century onward the soap industry grew
even more dramatically throughout the Western world, as did soap
consumption. Once used sparingly to wash clothes, and even more
sparingly to wash the bodies they covered, soap claimed ever more
importance in all but the poorest households. Soap manufacturing
rapidly evolved from an industry of small producers to an enterprise
dominated by a few large multinational corporations, able to link
their products to their customers' needs and to shape their habits as
well. The new soap makers had a presence that their predecessors
lacked, a capacity to enter the discussion about personal cleanliness
and to define it on terms that served their own business interests.
And they used this power to great effect.

Thousands of soap factories dotted the transatlantic world before
the turn of the twentieth century. Most were small businesses with
just a few employees, though some had workforces numbering in the
scores, a handful in the low hundreds. In Germany during the early

1880s there were more than two thousand soap works with five or fewer employees, six with more than fifty.[25] While productivity gains had driven some of the great increase in soap production since the early years of the century, most of the growth in output had come from adding new firms to the ranks of the producers. The one exception was Great Britain, where production grew more than tenfold during the century while the number of soap makers declined.[26]

As a business, soap making involved low entry costs. By the early nineteenth century knowledge of its processes was widely accessible and manufacturing technology was comparatively simple while the family firm or partnership provided the basic business model. Small producers everywhere often made candles as well as soap since the two products shared the same raw materials (natural fats and an alkali), and some larger firms evolved from these modest origins. Whatever their size, most soap makers supplied local and regional markets, and until transportation improvements encouraged national market integration, the industry's dispersed structure persisted. In addition, a few of the more entrepreneurially disposed added an export line to their business. Larger firms in their respective countries tended to locate near one another, in part for easy access to cheap transportation, in part for nearness to major markets, in part because they always had. Their demand for fats and oils having long outstripped local supplies, they depended on imports from distant sources, making easy access to harbour and shipping services a necessity.

Soap making everywhere was based on the batch system. While the details of processing varied with local practices, the raw materials used, the equipment employed, and the type of soap made, production employed a core set of methods. A mixture of oils and fats was added to an alkali solution and the combination boiled for several hours until saponification occurred. The soap was then separated from its by-products (mainly glycerine and water), further purified, dried, and prepared for sale. From beginning to end the process commonly took a week or so.[27] The finished soap was formed into large bars, generally weighing about 10 lbs. (4 kg), which shopkeepers cut, weighed, and wrapped at the point of sale.[28] Despite the wide range of soaps manufactured, the great bulk of production was for general household use.

Toward the end of the century, however, fundamental change began to reshape the industry, and within two decades a small number of market leaders dominated the soap trades throughout Europe and

North America. Two decades later still, the outlines of today's major multinational consumer goods conglomerates were clearly visible. Yet the industry followed more than one path as it transformed itself, and its modern structure differed from one country to another.

The United States and Britain were first to see these changes. In the former, Procter & Gamble, a soap and candle maker founded in 1837, took the lead as it faced a series of business challenges in the 1870s. The company had prospered during the Civil War years, thanks in part to government contracts, but as kerosene replaced candles for home lighting, the market for one of its principle products shrank quickly. The more than six hundred American soap and candle manufacturers in 1880 had to grapple with the same problem, and the agile among them looked to the soap trade for new opportunities.[29] Between 1870 and 1895 the American patent office recorded over one thousand trademarks for soaps of various descriptions.[30] Procter & Gamble met the challenge in 1879 by creating a new product: Ivory Soap. The reasons why P&G enjoyed greater success than its rivals aren't entirely clear. According to the firm's historians, the company combined a program of scientific product development with a strategic marketing plan, creating a new soap with a strong brand identity and promoting it aggressively.[31] Ivory was advertised as an all-purpose cleanser, suitable for laundry and personal use. P&G sold Ivory in individual 9 ounce (270 g) cakes, sealed in attractive wrappers that distinguished them from other bar soaps on the market.[32] While the firm was far from the first soap maker to adopt these techniques – some had been using them for more than two decades – it did so more effectively than its major rivals. Within a short time it had greatly expanded its manufacturing capacity to supply a growing demand. In a further sign of innovation it also led the industry in trademarking new products, with 10 percent of all American registrations by the mid-1890s.[33] Having seized the initiative at a defining moment, by the turn of the century P&G had become the largest soap maker in the United States, and while other firms followed its lead – some such as Colgate & Co. closely – none could overtake it.[34]

In Britain, soap production doubled and then doubled again during the second half of the nineteenth century.[35] Most of the growth occurred within existing companies as they invested in improved technology and greater capacity. By the 1880s several well-established firms dominated an industry that, despite a significant export trade, still largely served regional markets. Long one of the two lead-ing soap manufacturing nations in Western Europe, by then Britain produced more than France, and Britain's consumption per capita was more than double that of its cross-Channel neighbour.[36]

The arrival of a dynamic entrepreneurial force in the mid-1880s, however, soon transformed the British soap trade. William Hesketh Lever, son of a Bolton wholesale grocer and junior partner in the fam-ily business, saw possibilities in soap that none of his contemporaries recognized.[37] He entered the industry in 1884 with a trademarked brand name – Sunlight – and a limited range of soap products made by existing producers. Within a short time he had leased a small, unprof-itable soap works on the north bank of the Mersey River upstream from Liverpool and, funded by his own capital and family loans, begun manufacturing in his own right. Soon he moved operations to a vacant site, renamed Port Sunlight, across the river and closer to the city, with ample room to expand operations and build a model village for his employees. Production grew dramatically over the company's first decade, and by the end of the century, Lever Brothers was the industry leader in Britain, with over 20 percent of the national mar-ket for hard soap. During the first two decades of the new century the firm's lead continued to grow. The company acquired a dominant interest in most of its rivals when it did not buy them outright. By 1920 Lever Brothers controlled 70 to 75 percent of British soap pro-duction, leaving only one independent manufacturer of importance in the national marketplace. The resulting oligopoly allowed the Lever group to set prices with little regard for their competition.[38]

As business enterprises Procter & Gamble and Lever Brothers differed in important respects, but they shared a commitment to ambitious marketing strategies and, more than any other influence, owed their market leads to this fact.[39] Lever was well aware of the American industry's example and he followed it closely. Like Ivory, Sunlight was a hard, all-purpose household soap, sold in small, uni-form, appealingly wrapped cakes. Like Ivory, Sunlight was marketed as a distinctive brand. Like Ivory, Sunlight was promoted through extensive advertising and sales campaigns. Like Ivory, Sunlight became the most widely selling soap in its market. Like Procter & Gamble, Lever Brothers was a first mover in the industry, and like P&G, it enjoyed the success that followed from seizing the initiative.

Compared to their other European counterparts, Austrian and German soap makers shared a geographic disadvantage that complicated their activities and raised their costs. They were located farther than their international rivals from the tropical sources of the palm and coconut oils that most nineteenth-century manufacturers relied on. They also had access to fewer seaports, and these were more remote. Austria endured a double disadvantage because much of its productive capacity had been located in its Adriatic ports, Venice and Trieste, which it had lost after Italian unification.[40] One result was that the predominantly local, small-scale character of soap manufacturing lingered longer in Austria-Hungary and Germany than in Britain or America. But when growth did occur it took a familiar form. Georg Schicht, son of a late-eighteenth-century German soap and candle maker, established a small soap factory in a northern Bohemian village during the late 1840s. By the 1880s the growing business required easier access to vegetable oils, so the family firm relocated to a more favourable site in Aussig, on the Elbe River near the German border, drawing its raw materials through the distant port of Hamburg. Within a decade Georg's son Johann had expanded their scale of operations, integrating the basic processes of the oils and fats industries into his soap business and reducing production costs sharply. Like P&G and Lever Brothers before them, the Schichts sold branded household soaps in small bars – their wrappings decorated with swans and deer – and advertised them broadly. Small when compared to their largest contemporaries, even so they soon claimed a leading role in Austrian and German soap markets.[41]

Though soap consumption in Germany more than quadrupled between unification in 1871 and the eve of the First World War, organizational change came slowly to the industry.[42] Production remained concentrated in small or mid-sized firms until well after the turn of the century.[43] And when it finally did occur, the change was rooted in Germany's emerging chemical industries, not its older craft manufacturing traditions. Now the Düsseldorf businessman Fritz Henkel assumed the lead. He began his career in the later 1870s selling pulverized waterglass (the common name for sodium metasilicate) and bleaching soda, a washing agent and laundry whitener.[44] During the 1880s he launched a new wash powder combining soap, soda, and waterglass that promised to reduce the heavy labour of laundry work. No longer would dirty clothes and linens need to be rubbed with soap, Henkel announced; now they could be washed much more easily by soaking or boiling them in *Bleichsoda*. Then in 1907 Henkel launched a new laundry cleaner, Persil, which combined washing and bleaching actions in a single product. In keeping with best international practice in the industry, he adopted the marketing strategies pioneered by Lever and other soap trade leaders, promoting the Persil brand vigorously and advertising it extensively.

But no single industrial leader emerged in the Mediterranean world. The Italian soap industry had deep craft roots on the peninsula but it only began to grow during the early national era. A census in 1879 revealed more than five hundred factories scattered around the country, most of them in the primary olive-growing regions and most of them small-scale workshops.[45] The average workforce size was just under four employees. Half a century later the situation had changed little: the number of firms had doubled, but most of them were still small artisanal producers, though by then three large firms in Genoa accounted for one quarter of all production.[46] Reading between the lines of the data on imports, exports, and wholesale prices, by the later nineteenth century Italy was producing enough soap to meet national needs and sell substantial quantities abroad.[47] But it relied heavily on a craft production model and traditional sales techniques – even including itinerant vendors who peddled their wares in the streets.[48] A substantial manufacturing capacity also developed in Spain at the time, but after the Spanish American War, the country lost much of its West Indian export market and the national trade declined.[49]

The French industry also remained fragmented and decentralized during these years. By the early 1870s soap factories were located across much of the country, though Marseille remained the great centre of production and its dominance continued long into the new century.[50] On the eve of the First World War the city was home to some forty producers, with an average workforce of sixty. Twelve factories accounted for three quarters of local production.[51] At the time, Marseille produced half of all soap made in France. While national output had more than trebled since the mid-nineteenth century, growth didn't bring about restructuring as it had in Britain and the United States.[52] Instead, and particularly in Marseille, the industry was controlled by a group of family businesses, a few of which produced on the scale of their smaller international contemporaries, while handicraft manufacturing lingered as well.[53] On major points of strategy the Marseille soap makers differed sharply from the American and British business model. They rejected the concept of branding and continued to produce a generic product, its quality regulated by law rather than by marketplace reputation, and, though they advertised, they avoided major sales promotion campaigns.[54] Their business system consisted of a network of family firms that competed in the marketplace but were linked informally by social ties as well as strong connections to the wider local economic elite.

THE INDUSTRY DIVERSIFIES

While hard soaps for general household use remained the trade's staple well into the twentieth century, manufacturers started to broaden their product ranges toward the end of the nineteenth. They began selling soap powders and flakes that dissolved in water more easily, which meant that laundry could be soaked before being scrubbed. The new products offered substantial labour-saving possibilities, reducing the drudgery that had always been the laundress's lot. Some of these innovations came not from the industry's emerging leaders, who clung to the formulas of their early success, but from smaller firms seeking niche markets for their goods. In time the dominant players absorbed many of the latter through merger or purchase, adding their products to their own line of brands, often improving them in the process.[55] Packaged brightly and labelled with engaging names, the new laundry detergents were heavily promoted, by then the industry's common practice. After the First World War industry leaders continued to invest large sums in developing new laundry soaps, their most potent weapons in the long struggle for market dominance.[56]

As the leading soap makers broadened their product offerings they also widened their international reach. European soap makers had long served export customers in addition to home markets, as did those in colonial America.[57] But industrial-scale soap manufacturing called for new forms of internationalism, and toward the end of the nineteenth century the leading firms developed more ambitious programs. Some were technological: scientific, mechanical, and process innovations exchanged between non-competing producers, occasionally leading to business alliances.[58] Markets, however, were another matter, and competition was intense. By the later nineteenth century Britain had become the world's leading soap exporter, selling its wares abroad through a network of commission agents and export merchants.[59] The ever-aggressive Lever moved more quickly than his British competitors. Within five years of founding the company, he had established a substantial number of national sales agencies in Continental Europe, North America, and the Empire. He then began to move manufacturing processes abroad. By 1900 Lever Brothers had opened factories in Australia, Canada, the United States, Germany, and Switzerland, with others soon to follow, making it the first of the major soap producers to serve overseas markets with branch plants.[60] Manufacturing elsewhere offered two major advantages: it avoided import duties, and it provided better knowledge of local market conditions.

Though a latecomer to the trade, Henkel quickly extended its international reach as well. Initially the company served only the German market, reaching its foreign customers through commission agents and licensing agreements. Shortly after it placed Persil on the German market, Henkel sold its patent rights in Great Britain and parts of the British Empire to Crosfield's, a Lever rival.[61] According to the firm's historian, the sale was "the most profitable stroke of business Crosfield's ever made," and Henkel probably signed the agreement because it lacked the capacity or the confidence to enter the British market directly. At the same time the company reached a similar accord with the Viennese firm Gottlieb Voith for Austria-Hungary.[62] But like Lever Brothers, it soon began to expand in its own right, opening a factory in Switzerland in 1913. The Great War checked the company's growth plans temporarily, however. Expansion came to a halt, and after the war all of Henkel's foreign assets apart from its Swiss subsidiary were expropriated. In addition, the company permanently lost the British and French rights to its leading brand, Persil, and from that point on there were two Persils, one owned by Henkel and one by Lever Brothers (which had acquired the brand when it absorbed Crosfield's in 1919), each sold in different markets.[63] But Henkel soon refocused its energies, and over the next two decades it built a network of subsidiaries throughout northern and central Europe. In 1930 it held 80 percent of the German market for soap powders, and by the end of the decade it owned production facilities in eleven other countries.[64]

Still, Henkel's expansion was far from unopposed, for Lever Brothers also had ambitions in the European market. In 1914 it too had factories in Belgium, Germany, and Switzerland, and it met the Persil challenge with Rinso, its own improved soap powder.[65] Initially the Lever product prevailed in Britain, but after the war Persil's sales rose dramatically, a benefit to the new owner Lever Brothers in any case. Meanwhile it continued to produce Rinso

under its own name.[66] By the later 1930s, however, Persil's British
sales had overtaken those of its leading British competitor, both now
the products of Unilever, the company formed in 1929 through the
merger of Lever Brothers with the Dutch company Margarine Unie.
On the continent Lever/Unilever and Henkel were each other's chief
rivals. The former built a strong presence in Belgium, France, and the
Netherlands, but elsewhere Henkel had the upper hand, not least in
Germany itself, where it had the soap powder trade to itself.[67]

In North America too, Lever Brothers seized the initiative. The
Canadian soap industry, small-scale and dispersed, was already being
consolidated when Lever Brothers built its first factory in Toronto in
1900, and it quickly folded several small competitors into the company, extending its reach across the continent.[68] However, its entry
into the US market three years earlier had been a modest success at
best. Facing strong competition from the emerging American soap
giants as well as consumer preferences it struggled to understand, it
spent more than a decade in the business doldrums before an energetic
American-born manager, Francis Countway, assumed Lever's North
American leadership and led the subsidiary's expansion. Countway
enthusiastically promoted the company's main brands – Lifebuoy,
Lux Flakes, Rinso, and later Lux Toilet Soap – supported by an advertising budget that approached half the firm's worldwide publicity
outlays, and building a sales network that marketed the company's
products nationwide. By the early 1920s Lever Brothers ranked third
among the majors in the American soap trade, and on the eve of the
Second World War it was closing in on the leader, with 30 percent of
the national laundry soap market compared to P&G's 34 percent.[69]

In contrast, American soap makers were slower to invest abroad.
With a national population growth rate more than three times that
of Western Europe, they enjoyed compelling opportunities at home,
all the more attractive because this was known territory. When they
finally began to look over the horizon their first glances were ten-
tative: across the northern border to friendly, familiar Canada. The
B.J. Johnson Company, soon renamed the Palmolive Soap Company
after its leading product, was first, setting up in an existing Toronto
soap factory purchased in 1913. Two years later Procter & Gamble
opened a plant in nearby Hamilton, the company's first foreign
investment venture, built to protect its Canadian market share
from Lever Brothers' encroachments. Before their merger in the late
1920s, Colgate and Palmolive opened several plants in Europe, Latin

America, and Australia. P&G, however, made no more investments abroad until 1930, when it bought the British toilet soap maker Thomas Hedley & Company, one of the few significant English soap makers not already in the Unilever fold. It soon expanded operations by building new production facilities.[70] This was the first major challenge on home territory that Lever interests had faced since early in the century, and it eroded its monopoly position somewhat. Within a short time P&G had gained 15 percent of the British soap market.[71]

While relying on their established brands, the leading soap makers also grew by diversifying their product ranges, developing new lines of business that overlapped with their core activities in order to take advantage of available synergies. Again Lever Brothers took the lead. Heavily dependent on imported tropical vegetable oils, it developed palm and copra plantations and oil mills in Africa to reduce its vulnerability on international commodity markets. Initially Lever Brothers' goal was to integrate raw material production with soap manufacturing, but in time it grasped the advantage of running its oils subsidiaries separately. Later still it saw possibilities in the margarine business. As Lever later recalled, "Finding that these oils and fats were even superior for margarine than they were for soap, we naturally diverted to and developed margarine manufacture."[72] Ultimately the overlapping interests of Lever Brothers and Margarine Unie led to the Unilever merger in 1929, creating a multinational manufacturer of soaps and edible fat products. The Austrian firm Schicht followed a similar path, branching early into vegetable fats, a move that in the long run led to its absorption by Margarine Unie and, in turn, by the Unilever conglomerate.[73] Similarly, just before the First World War, P&G developed Crisco, a vegetable shortening based on cottonseed oil, drawing the company into new and profitable territory.[74] By the later 1930s vegetable oil products accounted for one third of P&G sales. Meanwhile Colgate-Palmolive-Peet reached out in another direction: toothpaste and toilet preparations, commodity siblings for its leading soaps and cleansers.[75] On the eve of the Great Depression the soap trade looked strikingly different from what it had been half a century before. Decades of growth and consolidation had transformed small-scale artisanal production into multinational industrial manufacturing. While many small producers continued in business, four large companies dominated the global soap trade: Procter & Gamble and Colgate-Palmolive-Peet in the United States, Unilever and Henkel in Europe. Together they accounted for more than half of all soap production in the Western world at the time.[76] American manufacturers produced almost twice as much as those in France, Britain, Germany, and Italy combined, though they exported little of what they made. The Europeans, or at least some of them, sold a substantial proportion of their production abroad: France, 13 percent, and Britain, 11 percent. A small cluster of soap brands now left an increasingly sharp imprint on consumer markets across the Western world, and their impact elsewhere was beginning to grow as well.[77]

By the early decades of the twentieth century, soap had become such a basic commodity that governments began to take a greater interest in the industry too. No longer was the soap trade simply a source of tax revenue; it made products now considered essential for everyone's well-being, a fact that justified greater government involvement in the soap trade when events seemed to require it. In 1921 the dominant role of Lever interests in the British soap industry prompted a parliamentary inquiry into the high level of ownership concentration in the trade. The investigating committee concluded that the Lever group alone had enough market power to determine the price of soap in Britain without any regard for its competitors' actions. The only effective check on price increases was fear of reduced demand. Given the current conditions, it suggested, household soap was overpriced by close to 20 percent.[78] Though nothing concrete came from the inquiry, the investigation itself was an early indication of the British government's growing concern about the industry and, more generally, the related problems of monopolies and consumer protection.

During the two world wars all Western governments faced serious challenges in meeting basic consumer needs. Through administrative procedures and rationing programs, they directed the production and distribution of domestic staples, though the specific contents of these baskets of goods varied from one country to another. In Europe, though not in North America, most governments regulated soap consumption as part of this process, and some attempted to control production as well.

With four fifths of its oil and fat supplies imported from abroad at the outbreak of the First World War the German soap industry was particularly vulnerable. The war administration centralized all industrial procurement in the sector and allocated the soap makers a small fraction of their former supply, favouring only a few larger enterprises. At the same time they imposed rationing on soap, one among many consumer items whose distribution was restricted.[79] During the economic recovery after the War, the industry again came to rely as heavily as it formerly had on basic supplies from foreign markets, and this led the National Socialist government to intervene directly once it took office in 1933. As part of a broad program to promote national economic self-sufficiency, it monitored industrial oil and fat supplies, reduced the fatty acid content of household soaps, and encouraged farmers to cultivate oil seeds, meanwhile extending state control over the soaps and detergents industry. When war broke out in 1939 and the rationing of consumer goods resumed, the list of controlled articles once more included soap.[80] Highly dependent on foreign vegetable oils, and embarked on its own pursuit of autarky, the Italian government acted similarly.[81] Elsewhere in wartime Europe rationing differed more in detail than in kind. The Allies didn't regulate soap manufacturing centrally, but early in the conflict most of them placed soap on their growing lists of restricted consumer products. Britain rationed soap from 1942 to 1950, France from the early days of the conflict. Even non-belligerents like Sweden and Switzerland adopted the practice.[82] The motives for wartime soap rationing were complex and they varied somewhat from one country to another. But beneath these decisions lay the understanding that soap was a household necessity, as essential to daily life as basic foods, and governments had to ensure its distribution.

ADVERTISING, MARKETING, AND BUSINESS STRATEGY

The transformation of the soap trade unfolded during the nascent years of the age of mass consumption. Increasing production and declining prices, rising incomes and growing demand framed the emerging world of late-nineteenth-century consumer goods industries, providing their leaders with rich business opportunities and serious market challenges. One leading response was to centralize production and distribution, thus creating organizations of unprecedented "scale and scope."[83] The industrial giants of the age controlled their supply chains, their production processes, and their markets in ways that had few precedents in Western economies. Building a broad customer base was a formidable challenge for major producers in the new consumer economy, for they had to match their expanding productive capacity with expanding markets. Among the tools they used were a cluster of innovations in branding, packaging, and advertising, techniques that attempted to create a new and closer relationship between manufacturers and consumers.[84] The companies most committed to this strategy were those making goods for home and personal use – foods and beverages, pharmaceuticals, tobacco products, and soap – all of them mass-produced articles with low profit margins and little to distinguish them from rival commodities.[85]

The soap industry was poised on the leading edge of these innovations. Two of its most important advances involved treating old products in new ways. Instead of making large pieces for grocers to cut, weigh, and wrap to a customer's order, they produced small, uniform bars with identical weights wrapped in appealing packages. And instead of manufacturing a generic product similar to those of their competitors, they gave it a cheerful name, a brand identity, and a catchy logo, stamping and wrapping each bar with a distinctive label. These two innovations were tightly entwined with a third: intense publicity campaigns. The soap makers were among the earliest firms to use inventive promotional strategies, ranging from straightforward print advertising to sophisticated marketing schemes. They were also among those with the highest ratios of advertising expenses to sales incomes.[86]

To attract new customers and retain existing ones, all the leading soap manufacturers invested large sums in ambitious marketing schemes. The American B.T. Babbitt – maker of Babbitt's Best Soap – was one of the early innovators during the mid-nineteenth-century decades.[87] Probably the most flamboyant, though, was Thomas Barratt, initially an employee of the London toilet soap maker Francis Pears, then his son-in-law and general manager, and in time full owner of the Pears Soap Company. Barratt had a flair for publicity, and from the later 1860s onward, he pursued an imaginative and costly marketing strategy, first in Britain and later in the United States, that brought his product widespread fame and his methods some notoriety.[88] Similarly, after dipping a gingerly toe into advertising during the early 1880s, P&G began to invest heavily in print-based product promotions, using the new American mass circulation magazines to spread the happy news of Ivory Soap across the nation.[89] Lever, ever alert to the American example, quickly followed in Britain, promoting Sunlight through posters, railway hoardings, and newspaper advertising.[90] As competitive market pressures grew, both industry leaders and their challengers adopted still more engaging ways of selling their products. Lever Brothers and P&G published pamphlets hymning the virtues of their wares and explaining their useful features.[91] They also used free samples, prize schemes, and direct mail campaigns. Crosfield's, one of Lever's chief rivals and a reluctant convert to the new marketing techniques, resorted to street theatre in 1886 when it hired four llamas ("beautiful and highly trained animals ... lately the property of the King of Italy") to draw a carriage promoting its wares from Liverpool to Glasgow.[92] Soon after the turn of the century Henkel adopted equally ambitious programs to advertise Persil in Germany.[93]

Marketing on this scale was costly, and industry leaders spent lavishly. Before the 1880s most soap makers had relied almost entirely on their own sales forces, their reputations occasionally burnished by prizes won at national fairs and international exhibitions.[94] But at that point the major firms began to direct large sums toward product promotion. At Pears, Barratt was spending £100,000 annually by the later 1880s, an amount that continued to grow over time.[95] From relatively modest beginnings P&G's advertising budget increased fivefold to $223,000 between 1884 and 1889, most of it devoted to Ivory.[96] For its part Lever Brothers spent some £2 million on marketing during the company's first two decades. The sum amounted to 12 or 13 percent of the factory gate sales value of Sunlight, a much higher ratio than other industries devoted to advertising at the time.[97] Henkel followed the same pattern, investing between 800,000 and 1,000,000 marks in 1907 alone to introduce Persil to the German market.[98]

While these outlays were far from aimless, the early soap advertisers had a less than perfect sense of how their advertising budgets could best be spent. Lever reputedly once remarked that half of his advertising expenses were wasted but he didn't know which half – a comment attributed to several American business leaders at the time as well.[99] Whether apocryphal or not, it reflects a deeper truth about the central role of advertising in the growth of the soap trade. Mass marketing was a fundamental tool of the emerging soap industry. The soap makers were creating not only new businesses and new goods but also new consumers. Where buyers once sought products, producers now sought customers, and customers had to be courted, informed, and convinced. Advertising mattered deeply to the industry's leaders, and over time their activities moulded habits and mentalities across the Western world.[100]

MESSAGES AND MEANINGS

The soap manufacturers made two kinds of soap, all-purpose soap and toilet soap, and they directed their products toward two different markets, working class and middle class. It should come as no surprise, then, that they adopted two different strategies when promoting their products. Household soap was marketed for everyday use: suitable for all cleaning needs, tough enough for dirty laundry yet gentle enough for sensitive skins. Toilet soap was refined and subtle, an aid to enhance feminine beauty, an indulgence to pamper the bourgeois body. Soap advertising created brand identities, product personalities that spoke to distinctive audiences and fostered new desires. The most successful marketing programs singled out a few leading themes and repeated them endlessly. Often they identified their products with enduring human needs and values, linking a particular brand of soap to matters well above the mundane and the material.

Publicity for household soaps emphasized their labour-saving qualities above all else. The new general-purpose cleaners promised an end to laundry's drudgery. A well-known Lever ad from the late 1880s asked, "Why does a woman look old sooner than a man?," and replied that the heavy work of the household wash took its toll on a housewife's health. But Sunlight cleaned the dirtiest laundry with ease. "The work is so light," the ad declared, "that a girl of 12 or 13 can do a large wash without being tired."[101] Not only that but Sunlight produced the finest results, with whiter whites, brighter colours, and softer flannels. Two decades later Henkel named its new product, Persil, the first "selbsttätige Waschmittel" (self-acting detergent).[102] Persil did the hard work of the weekly wash, freeing the *hausfrau* from the toil of the ages.

Other branding strategies gave some soaps a more nuanced identity. The leading theme in Ivory's advertising spoke to its purity; two of its slogans – "the soap that floats," and "99 44/100ths % pure" – were so well known that they became everyday catchphrases. Ivory ads stressed its value as a versatile, economical, high-quality soap.[103] They offered portraits of happy soap-using households and families, and healthy soap-loving women and children, linking Ivory to idealized notions of conventional home life. By emphasizing its pureness and utility, and by aligning it with leading values in middle-class domesticity, the ads strove to make Ivory a staple in the American home. More broadly, the industry's publicity commonly featured images of flowers, gentle animals, tropical landscapes, and happy laundresses, as advertisers associated the natural, the exotic, and the easeful with their soaps.

Because toilet soaps were intended for the well-to-do, their advertising used a different pictorial language, one depending heavily on associational images. The innovative Pears Soap campaigns created by Thomas Barratt appealed to bourgeois self-awareness by speaking to cultivated interests and linking Pears Soap with the refinements of life. Barratt's well-known use of the painting *A Child's World* was characteristic. A picture by the celebrated mid-Victorian artist John Everett Millais, it depicted a seated young boy blowing bubbles, his eyes fixed on one as it floats above him, the bubbles an obvious reference to childhood's fleeting innocence. A potted plant rests on the boy's left while a broken pot lies on his right – other symbols of life's transience. A work of marzipan sentimentality, it stands in the long European artistic tradition of "vanitas" paintings that express the impermanence of earthly life and the inevitability of its end.

Sir William Ingram, publisher of the *Illustrated London News*, bought the painting from the artist in 1886 and the following year reproduced it in the paper's Christmas issue.[104] Yet even before then, Barratt had bought the painting from Ingram, together with its copyright. In 1888 Barratt reproduced it again, surrounded by a printed gold frame and this time with a bar of Pears Soap added to the foreground (Plate 7). Now renamed "Bubbles," Millais's painting had become a soap ad. Though he owned its publication rights, Barratt evidently consulted the painter himself, seeking permission to use a work of art for commercial ends, and after some misgivings Millais apparently agreed, a decision that brought him stinging criticism for prostituting art to commerce.[105] But Barratt, at least, saw no contradiction in the union of art and business. He recognized the advertising value of the alliance and it proved highly successful. He continued to promote Pears Soap using serious art, and others quickly followed his lead, notably William Hesketh Lever.[106] As for "Bubbles," Pears used the image for years to come, and it remains an icon of Victorian advertising to this day.

In Europe as well as America, toilet soap manufacturers directed most of their advertising toward women, their principle market. The leading themes in their messaging focused on beauty, health, and luxury, refrains that came to dominate their marketing rhetoric over time.[107] In the background, as well, lay idealized images of bourgeois family life, centred mostly on women and children. Marketing campaigns often depicted women as romantic or erotic objects, sensuous or languid when they weren't coquettish or alluring, and emphasized soap's benefits for beauty's major asset: the complexion.[108] Barratt was one of the first to use this approach as well. An 1887 ad featured five noted European beauties, all draped in classical dress, collectively endorsing Pears Soap for its cosmetic benefits.[109] The children portrayed in soap advertising clearly lived happy, comfortable middle-class lives.[110] Occasionally they were discreetly nude, their tender skins a testament to the mild and gentle benefits of a particular brand of soap.[111]

According to Juliann Sivulka, over time soap advertising in the United States came to rely heavily on emotional appeals. Before the turn of the twentieth century, she observes, it commonly offered rational accounts of a soap's virtues, but from that point onward it relied increasingly on suggestion and promise.[112] In the process some soaps changed their brand identities, though the soap itself may not have changed much, if at all. Palmolive, a toilet soap formulated from palm and olive oils in 1898, was initially sold as a skin cleanser, but soon after the turn of the century its manufacturer began to advertise it as a skin care treatment. The makers of Woodbury's Facial Soap, another leading American label of the later nineteenth century, first advertised the health benefits of their product. But in 1910 they rebranded it, appealing to romantic and sexual interests and directing it toward middle- and upper-class American women aged sixteen to sixty.[113] Their new advertising "borrowed beauty culture techniques to transform use of Woodbury's Facial Soap into a daily beauty ritual."[114]

The interlaced rhetoric of nation, empire, and race also wove its way through soap advertising of the period. British soap makers traded heavily on wartime patriotism during the South African War, as did British and North American firms during the First World War, a widely used marketing strategy in both conflicts. In peacetime as well, they deployed common national symbols – flags, colours, and popular landmarks – to connect their products with national images.[115] In doing so they associated individual brands with symbols of national identity. Lever's ads for Sunlight traded heavily on John Bull, the Royal Family, and the Union Jack; the promoters of Sapolio described it as "an American product that has won the patronage of the civilized world."[116] The British soap makers, led by Barratt and Lever, also exploited the nation's imperial associations, an especially potent symbol during the flood tide of Empire. The overt racism embedded in Britain's many imperial adventures was a conspicuous theme in their advertising. Soap was presented as a civilizing force, a tool of cultural uplift, a means to cleanse the unclean, even a way to whiten dark skins.[117] Although American views of the period opposed Britain's imperial claims, they shared the same fundamental racist assumptions, as the soap advertisers made clear. A late-nineteenth-century Babbitt's ad declared that "cleanliness is the scale of civilization" and marketed their soap as a civilizing force. What distinguished America from Britain, the advertisements implied, was that those who most needed their product's civilizing touch weren't faraway subjects in a distant empire. Blacks, Native Americans, and non-Anglo-Saxon immigrants, they already lived in the United States.[118]

Slow to appear in the ad campaigns were claims about soap's health benefits. The soap makers had surprisingly little to say about the matter despite growing public awareness of the germ theory. None of them made much of disinfection and disease protection until Lever Brothers introduced Lifebuoy, a household soap with carbolic acid content and a distinctive hospital smell, in the mid-1890s.[119] Only then did antibacterial products begin to appear on merchants' shelves. Zam-Buk Medicinal Soap and Nubolic Soap, launched in Britain around 1910, were specialized toilet bars that purported to defend the body against dangerous microbes.[120] But by then shop shelves were crowded with other soap products, each with its own compelling claims. The promise of good health never seemed enough to promote the bestselling soaps. Instead they offered far richer life possibilities.

Well before the Industrial Age, soap had become a staple commodity in homes across the Western world, an item in the family budget or a product of the family kitchen. Most often used for washing clothes, it ranked with fuel and candles as a household necessity. But whether bought or made at home, soap was relatively costly in money or time, so it was used sparingly. Only the affluent could afford delicate toilet soaps for personal use, and since they washed themselves infrequently, they used little enough of it too. As the nineteenth century progressed, however, soap gradually became more

affordable and consumption rose steadily. New manufacturing processes reduced production costs while rising real wages provided
higher disposable incomes. One of the first "goods" consumers purchased more and more often was better personal hygiene, an unmis-
takable sign of rising living standards. Still, Great Britain apart, soap
making everywhere remained an artisanal affair until the later years
of the century. Then the transformative force of industrial capitalism
combined with the business opportunities offered by budding mass
consumerism to fashion a dramatically new soap industry. In little
more than a generation it grew from a trade pursued by thousands
of small producers to one dominated by a handful of large manufacturers, each with a leading role in its national markets, which it then
enhanced with ambitious international expansion programs.

The new soap industry was an early adopter of the innovative
merchandising methods then emerging in the flourishing consumer
goods sectors of most Western economies. In particular, each of the
leading soap makers relied on aggressive advertising to promote
business growth. Advertisements allowed them to speak directly
to growing numbers of customers by tailoring their messages to
specific social groups. Over time their claims grew less direct and
more sophisticated, moving from basic descriptions of their product's functions and virtues to emotional and associative appeals.
Some soap ads even tried to reach undercurrents deep within the
self, appealing to personal values or understandings, aspirations or a
sense of identity. Among the most powerful of these messages were
those linking cleanliness with purity and whiteness, concepts with
deep symbolic meaning in Western culture. Indeed, the links between
soap and whiteness became the dominant trope in soap marketing, a
powerful image that the industry would exploit long into the future.

THE EDUCATORS

By the mid-nineteenth century the upper ranks in Western societies had come to define new norms of personal cleanliness for themselves. They also believed that their standards should apply to all, rich and poor alike. Their minimum guidelines included a daily wash of the hands and face, a weekly bath, and routinely changed and laundered clothes, especially the underclothes. Yet the same could not be said of their social lessers. At best the lower-class body knew water's touch only through occasional encounters and often there were no encounters at all. In the past, washing and bathing had had their champions, and from time to time they'd been outspoken. But after mid-century, the hygienists spoke with new force and urgency, and with a new assertiveness too. They accepted bourgeois understandings of cleanliness and promoted them as the benchmark for all. They also took advantage of new instruments at their disposal: a new scientific understanding of the nature of disease and new means of bringing their message to the wider public, which they did with growing insistency. In short, the clean body's promoters performed on a larger stage, with a more compelling message to deliver and more powerful tools to deliver it with. This chapter explores their message and how they delivered it.

More often than not their beliefs and aspirations challenged those of the rural and urban lower classes, whose views about care of the body often conflicted with theirs. Country people clung to habits and understandings worn smooth as river stones by the running waters of time. Among them were age-old notions of health and body care, and the wider cosmology that enveloped them. When they moved to the city, as they did in countless thousands during the new urban age, they brought their rural lifeworlds with them. Those who moved between cities, in numbers of similar scale, came from places where rural ideas about the physical self had already been tested, refined, and adapted to the realities of a harsh new setting. They too shared views about their own well-being and how best to preserve it, ideas that helped fashion working-class mentalities then in the making. Some of these views were lingering shreds of traditional rural understandings; others reflected the challenges of the urban Industrial Age. In either case, whether urban migrants were newly arrived from the countryside or from another city or nation, their ways of understanding the body, its needs and its care, set them well apart from the upper social ranks. It was they who became the objects of the sanitarians' concern, whose habits the hygienists sought to change, and whose understandings they hoped to educate.

THE SANITARY MOVEMENT

If you stroll down the narrow via del Collegio Capranica near the Pantheon in central Rome today you'll find a civic decree dated 11 May 1740, carved on a stone plaque fastened to one of the walls overlooking the street.[1] It prohibits the throwing of rubbish or manure in the road on pain of a fine of 10 scudi, a reminder that cities and towns in the Western world have regulated their thoroughfares for centuries. Drainage and street cleaning have long been public responsibilities, and civic administrations have commonly assumed them, though before 1800 public health measures usually didn't extend much further. Then over the coming decades, as urban populations grew, governments created boards of health and councils of hygiene, assigning them new responsibilities for the sanitary state of their communities. Some of these bodies were temporary, intended for an emergency, while others became permanent. Some were a response to one of the many epidemics that scourged the first half of the century. Others grew out of concern for the dangers to health lurking in the growing city itself.[2]

Until late in the nineteenth century, however, common infectious diseases and their means of transmission were poorly understood. Medical knowledge offered conflicting theories to explain them and practising physicians relied on a host of assumptions when treating them. The miasmatic theory dominated medical thought during the first half of the century and most etiologies were vague, diffuse, and mutable. They seldom offered an understanding that met the needs of the moment. To choose just one example, recurring cholera pandemics were the most alarming public health crises in the Western world for much of the century, confronting communities and their doctors with widespread threats to life. We now know that the disease is caused by a bacterial infection of the intestinal tract that prevents the body from reabsorbing the water and electrolytes entering it from the blood-stream. Victims suffer from acute diarrhea, the attacks often sudden and massive. The body endures extensive dehydration followed by shock and frequently – at least in the past – death. Rehydration ther-apy, now used to treat the disease successfully, was unknown before the twentieth century. Thus, with little understanding of cholera's origins and diffusion, and a troubling awareness of its dramatic symp-toms, nineteenth-century physicians could do little to prevent it, let alone offer a cure. Their primary tools were basic and crude: quaran-tine and isolation, cleansing towns and burying the dead.

During the mid-century decades a new public health movement took form, built on foundations laid earlier in the century. The new sanitary crusade and the new sanitarians were products of the dawn-ing Industrial Age. Even the term "sanitation" was novel, a new word for a new understanding. Though older anxieties still preoccu-pied the sanitary reformers, much broader concerns now animated them: rising mortality, spreading poverty, air and water pollution, child labour, occupational safety, poor housing and degraded living conditions in particular. In response they created new tools to study these problems: broad inquiries into social conditions, statistical approaches to investigation, and public reports of their findings. And they sought new ways of making improvements, first and foremost through greater government engagement. They saw public authority as the primary agent of change and regulation as its principal instru-ment. Governments everywhere used the authority of the state to define new standards of public health and enforce their observance.[3]

The new personal hygiene of the nineteenth century extended its reach at a time of major advances in medical understandings of health and sickness, changes that discarded older conceptions of ill-ness, described and classified diseases more accurately, and clarified some of their causes. For much of the period competing theories of causation absorbed physicians in debate over fundamental concepts. But toward the end of the century a professional consensus formed around the germ theory of disease, a hypothesis supported by

empirical research based on the most accurate scientific techniques
then available. This in turn laid the foundations for modern medical research, knowledge, and practice. As well, the new sanitarians
promoted ambitious strategies to check the spread of disease and
improve population health. At first, and for a considerable period,
these innovations left almost no visible imprint on individual cleanliness. But by the end of the century the sanitarian message had come
to embrace the body as well as its environment. From that time on
personal health and personal cleanliness became one.

The new sanitary movement was no respecter of national frontiers.
Signs of alarm about the urban condition appeared across much of
Western Europe during the 1840s. Cholera had stirred fears about the
unclean state of affected communities and these often combined with
concerns for health in the new Industrial Age. Sanitarians everywhere
looked to the English example, to Edwin Chadwick most of all. They
read his *Report on the Sanitary State of the Labouring Population
of Great Britain* closely, and it cast a long shadow across the great
cities of the West. Wherever the transforming power of industrialization appeared, the sanitary movement soon followed, eagerly offering
solutions to the many ills of the industrializing city. Interestingly, the
impetus to reform came more from outside the medical profession
than from within it, even though many physicians supported the
cause. Chadwick himself was a lawyer by training and an essayist by
calling before he found his place in the sanitarians' first ranks. At that
point medical knowledge could offer little enough to understanding
the problems that concerned the sanitarians most deeply.[4]

If the fundamental task of the movement could be summed up
in a single word it would be "cleansing." Sanitarians were alarmed
by filth and they saw it at every turn. Uncleanness, they believed,
posed the great threat to health because it was the source of disease. Thus cleansing became the great sanitarian objective. It was
a broad goal that had many meanings: washing streets, providing
safe water, installing drains and sewers, eliminating noxious industries, clearing slums, scrubbing homes, ventilating rooms – in short,
a wholesale cleaning of the urban environment. And in themselves
these programs had significant health benefits. In Britain, at least,
they played an important role in the mortality decline between the
1870s and 1914.[5] But before the early 1880s they also lacked clear
theoretical foundations, foundations that the germ theory would
soon provide.

GERMS AND THEORIES

In 1889 Dean Paul Brouardel told the incoming students of the Paris Medical Faculty: "Under the influence of the doctrines of Mr. Pasteur medical science has undergone, in the past several years, a revolution without equal since the beginning of the world."[6] The good dean was referring, of course, to the germ theory of disease and the French chemist Louis Pasteur's fundamental contribution to its formulation. For Brouardel and many of his contemporaries this was a truly revolutionary moment. And so it has seemed ever since. The conventional history of the microbe theory is one of progress from ignorance to understanding, of a journey from error to truth.[7] It is a tale of great men, great ideas, and great discoveries, centred on the careers of two brilliant scientists.

Between the later 1870s and the mid-1880s, after previous work on the causes of spoilage in beer and wines, Pasteur investigated a series of infectious diseases – anthrax, puerperal fever, and rabies – revealing their microbial origins and discovering vaccines to protect against some of them. Pasteur shared his position in the pantheon of medicine's nineteenth-century giants with the German physician Robert Koch, who identified the tuberculosis bacillus and the bacteria causing cholera during these same years. The belief that microbes caused many diseases had long guided both researchers, and their findings offered irrefutable proof of this scientific truth. The story of the germ theory also included earlier figures whose understandings pointed the way: the American and Hungarian doctors Oliver Wendell Holmes and Ignàz Semmelweis, who believed that puerperal fever was caused by infections transmitted to maternity patients by their medical attendants, and the English epidemiologist John Snow, who offered proof that cholera was a waterborne disease.[8] Later, influenced by Pasteur's initial work, the British surgeon Joseph Lister accepted the theory that microbial life caused wound infections, and towards the end of the 1860s he introduced antiseptic procedures to surgical practice.[9] Of particular interest to us here, Holmes, Semmelweis, and Lister were concerned with one of the basic elements of personal hygiene: clean hands. Semmelweis was something of a martyr to the cause. His work on maternal mortality in the obstetric clinics of Vienna's Algemeines Krankenhaus during the later 1840s indicated that hand washing by clinical attendants lowered postpartum death rates. But his views didn't prevail against

opposition from his colleagues and superiors, who considered them
without scientific basis; his clinical appointment not renewed, in
1850 he left the hospital – and Vienna – in embittered defeat.[10]

Dramatic narratives like these make fine theatre but in many cases
– and this is one – they don't serve historical understanding particularly well. The microbe theory of disease has a rather longer, less
sensational history than these accounts indicate, though its importance to the making of modern medicine remains just as significant.
The belief that infectious diseases could be spread by invisible organ-
isms had substantial support in the mid-nineteenth-century decades,
when a wide range of germ theories each had their proponents.[11]
Yet uncertainties about the nature of germs and their relationships
to disease persisted. Were germs independent life forms or were they
not? Were they a cause or a consequence of disease – or perhaps
simply an accessory to it? Differing views divided the germ theorists
of the time though, by the early 1880s, medical thought had begun
to converge on a dominant bacterial model.[12] Still, many practitioners remained unconvinced, for much medical opinion rejected
the microbe hypothesis outright prior to Pasteur's and Koch's discoveries, and doubt persisted long afterwards as well.

Thus, despite the myth of the bacterial revolution, the germ theory
had no revolutionary moment. Rather it gradually permeated medical
thinking and practice, promoted by committed advocates, opposed
by critics clinging to other theories and evidence. Its influence began
to penetrate public health thinking during the 1870s at a time when
its ecological emphasis was pronounced. From the early days of their
movement the sanitarians' basic goal had been to cleanse the environment. But the new awareness of germs shifted public health concerns
from places to people. Once infectious diseases could be traced to
human agents as well as their surroundings, the defenders of the
public's health began to direct their concern toward individuals and
their illnesses.[13] With passing years the scientific agendas of the older
hygienists and the new bacteriologists converged, and by the dawn
of the new century the microbial theory of disease was fast becoming
medical orthodoxy on both sides of the Atlantic.[14]

Until then the sanitarians had had much to say about clean cities but little about clean bodies. The public health movement had
always concerned itself far more with sanitary conditions than with
personal hygiene. Even the public bath and washhouse campaigns,
more ambitious in Britain than anywhere else, had no goal beyond

providing new opportunities for those who couldn't bathe and wash their laundry at home. As the microbe theory redirected the sanitarian gaze toward the human body, however, the issue of changing individual behaviour came into sharper focus. The first generation of public health textbooks from the germ theory era reflected the new awareness. They inserted advice about body care into discussions about the new bacteriology and more traditional prescriptions for public health.[15] A French manual published in 1893 offers an early example. Lack of cleanliness, it stated, caused a great many illnesses because the unclean skin didn't function normally. It had to be cared for assiduously to prevent microbes from entering the body through wounds. Bathing offered the best defence: the ears and eyes as well as the face, hands, and feet should all be washed frequently. A hot bath for half an hour once a month was indispensable as well.[16]

Apart from public health, surgery was the branch of medicine most caught up in debates about germs and cleanliness. Lister's antisepsis was an early innovation that over time led to fundamental changes in surgical practice, and in health care more generally. Like all of his surgeon contemporaries, Lister was concerned about wound management. His initial procedures were intended for lesions that had already been infected and entailed daubing them with a cloth soaked in carbolic acid. Having accepted Pasteur's view that putrefaction was caused by airborne microorganisms, Lister sought to destroy them by chemical means.[17] But surgical practice in the 1860s offered other approaches to wound care, each with its own theoretical and empirical basis, and Lister's views didn't win out immediately despite his early bedside successes. The debate between his supporters and his critics persisted over the next two decades. Then, during the 1890s, the principles of "Listerism" were extended further through the development of aseptic (germ-free) surgery. On the assumption that prevention was better than cure, its advocates prescribed a comprehensively sterile environment for surgical practice. The operating theatre and its furnishings, the surgeon's hands and his instruments, the patient's skin and its wound dressings, were all to be germ free.[18] While this acute sensitivity about cleanliness was specific to the unique setting of the operating room, it also began to penetrate other aspects of medical thinking. In 1882 a young American medical student, on the threshold of his professional life, even termed it "a fundamental law of practice."[19] From that point onward concern for ever more scrupulous hygienic standards tinged health care routines as the germ theory came to dominate thinking about infectious diseases. In a more general sense, it reached beyond the boundaries of health care as well, where it fed popular fears of contamination and contagion as well as calls for improved personal cleanliness.[20]

THE STATE AND PERSONAL CLEANLINESS

In the course of expanding their powers during the nineteenth century, governments in Western nations assumed new responsibilities for what had long been private matters. Though the extent of this process varied from country to country, the common thread was growing state authority in areas that once had only concerned the individual or the family. These changes were central processes in modern state formation, unfolding in republics as well as monarchies, colonies as well as nations. Among the most important of them were basic initiatives in health and education. As a result, by the last quarter of the nineteenth century, core public institutions in both spheres were in place across most of the Western world.

With new powers in hand governments embarked on ambitious social programs based on their understandings of the common good. They passed laws, created institutions, appointed officials, raised taxes, and spent large sums in the name of better lives for their citizens. Sometimes they sought to create better citizens as well, and as part of this pursuit they attempted to mould personal conduct. Sharp class distinctions invariably marked these attempts. Governing elites defined behavioural standards based on their own beliefs and experience, pursuing them with their new-found legal instruments. Whether we see their activities as paternalistic philanthropy or as authoritarian repression – both views have their advocates – their primary goal was reform through education.[21] Much of their effort involved sanitary matters, and the standards in question commonly rested on bourgeois norms of personal hygiene; modernizing Western governments promoted new habits of cleanliness in order to create "civically hygienic citizens."[22] The institutions of public health and schooling gave them ready access to those they hoped to educate, and under state guidance, health services and schools became tools of behaviour change.

Yet these were blunt instruments at best and their effectiveness varied widely. The influence of the public health movement in the West differed substantially from country to country. Distinctive national constitutions created an array of bureaucratic cultures and institutions, and the political history of each nation left unique marks on its public services, including those concerned with health. As the first industrial nation Britain took the lead in developing a national public health infrastructure, the process simplified by its centralized governance structure. In contrast, as a federation shaped by entrenched regional interests, the United States failed to establish a strong national public health presence until well into the twentieth century, though many programs functioned at state and local levels. Much the same was true of the new Canadian federation to the north. In France and Germany the authority of centralized public health organizations developed slowly before the First World War, and local or regional diversity persisted in both countries long afterwards.[23] Italy laid the legislative foundations for a public health infrastructure in the later nineteenth century but there too the law's influence was limited: financial constraints combined with local resistance to curb its effectiveness.[24] As a result, the state's capacity to promote the new hygiene ranged widely across the *fin de siècle* West.

We can see its longest reach in the British example. On several occasions from the 1840s onward the British government surveyed the health of the nation and, piecemeal, fashioned the institutions needed for a public health administration. Key to their functioning was the medical officer of health, the official who carried out policy at the local level. The first such officers were appointed during the mid-century decades though it took another fifty years before virtually all health districts did so, even though the law had required the office to be filled since the early 1870s. Once named, the MOH faced a multitude of responsibilities, foremost among them sanitary inspections and the promotion of sanitary improvements.[25] As most officers were part-time appointees with uncertain job tenure, their duties usually outstripped their resources, and it seems almost certain that teaching the lessons of personal hygiene would have been a low priority for most. But at least some MOHs took up the cause by giving public lectures and publishing pamphlets on the need for bodily cleanliness.

During the second half of the nineteenth century volunteer groups of middle-class women came together in a number of British industrial cities in support of the state's efforts, promoting sanitary improvement, temperance, and healthy family life.[26] The Ladies Sanitary

Associations borrowed two common proselytizing techniques from Protestant evangelicals – a background shared by many of them – using home visits and pamphlets to publicize the new hygiene. Their work involved two primary activities, inspection and promotion, though the latter was the task they acknowledged most freely. They directed most of their efforts toward women in lower-middle-class and artisanal households, though the greater need lay in the still lower ranks of the urban poor. Recognizing the social gulf between themselves and the objects of their concern, they hired working-class women to visit homes, distribute tracts, and offer friendly advice. The advice itself ranged widely, as one set of rules suggests:

> They [the visitors] must carry with them the carbolic powder, explain its use, and leave it where it is accepted; direct the attention of those they visit to the evils of bad smells, want of fresh air, impurities of all kinds; give hints to mothers on feeding and clothing their children – where they find sickness assist in promoting the comfort of the invalid by personal help, and report such cases to their superintendent. They must urge the importance of cleanliness, thrift, and temperance on all possible occasions.[27]

Obviously their concern for personal hygiene was embedded in broader anxieties about housing and domestic management. Still, the lady sanitarians centred their campaigns on cleanliness – clean homes, clean clothes, and clean bodies. Nor did they merely advise. When the moment was opportune they provided the tools of sanitation too: brooms, whitewash, and disinfectants to cleanse dwellings, and soaps to cleanse their occupants.

In time the British government recruited growing numbers of women into the paid public health workforce. Job opportunities emerged for sanitary inspectors, home visitors, and school nurses, positions that brought the new hygiene into the homes of the nation's lower ranks.[28] These supposedly feminine callings were concentrated heavily in the social services, in health care most of all, for such tasks were often thought suited to women's unique interests and attributes. Some of these occupations were new; others, such as sanitary inspector, were carved out of what till then had been men's work. The public health nurse, in particular, was an innovation linking schools and local health services with families and households, another sign of government's new presence in family life. Plate 8, a photo of two stern women bathing a group of solemn working-class boys in a London cleansing station on the eve of the First World War, offers a compelling glimpse of the British state's new interest in personal hygiene.

Public health bureaux in Massachusetts and New York City were among the movement's American leaders and their efforts often paralleled – in some cases even exceeded – those of their British counterparts.[29] Meanwhile feminine philanthropy and voluntarism supported the movement in the United States, with a concern for cleanliness and efficient domestic management that also found expression in the home economics movement. Blended into the Old World mix of motives behind these initiatives were American concerns about the apparent threat raised by millions of diseased and dirty immigrants.[30] In the minds of their many supporters, public health programs became tools for assimilating dangerous foreigners into American society. From the late nineteenth century onward, the visiting nurse was a fixture in many parts of America. The northeastern cities in particular established agencies to provide home nursing care for the poor, and while these nurses ministered to the ill, they also offered advice on personal hygiene and daily health habits.[31] Within a short time public health nursing arrived in Canada as well, promoting similar programs and pursuing similar ends.[32]

Developments in France paralleled those in Great Britain. During the later nineteenth century maternal charities sent volunteer visitors to assist married women, offering advice on childcare and household management. Their stock in trade was hygienic counsel based on the traditional feminine knowledge they were expected to possess rather than on any professional competence they might have.[33] From the later 1870s, however, while voluntary associations continued to promote the hygienist agenda, formal training for nurses became available, an important step toward establishing public health nursing on professional foundations. By the turn of the century the community nurse had become a feature of the French hygiene landscape too, performing much the same functions as her counterparts did elsewhere.[34]

THE PUBLIC SCHOOL AND THE NEW HYGIENE

Schools offered a compelling opportunity to promote personal hygiene. Their task was to educate the young, and fostering the habits of cleanliness was part of the process. By the later nineteenth

century the boarding schools patronized by wealthy and well-to-do
families had long subjected their pupils to body care regimens.
Some of our most useful information about these conditions comes
from a curious 1892 study comparing hygienic practices in Britain's
fee-paying secondary schools (the "public schools") with a number
of residential *lycées* in France. The primary goal of the author – an
English physician and member of the Paris medical faculty – seems
to have been to expose French backwardness in these matters.[35]
Good social scientist that he sought to be, he sent a questionnaire
to some five hundred school headmasters, mostly in the British Isles,
asking for information about students' washing and bathing habits
as well as routines for changing their clothes. While practices varied
somewhat, the virtues of British over French schooling seemed clear.
In Britain,

> Immediately after rising, the schoolboy performs his toilet. He is
> not content to pass a little water over his hands and face, as this
> is done in France, but he intends to be clean and spares neither
> water nor soap. He is left, moreover, sufficient time to indulge
> in these treatments: half an hour to three quarters of an hour, or
> rather, it is for him to take the time he needs.[36]

Here was a little paradise of daily ablutions: a weekly hot bath, and
shirts, shoes, and underwear changed once, twice, or sometimes
even three times a week – standards it seems French schools seldom
equalled or perhaps even aspired to.

But these schools taught the children of the truly privileged, a class
whose commitment to cleanliness was never in doubt. In trying to
improve mass personal hygiene the state relied heavily on its public
schools instead. The tangled history of compulsory free public education need not detain us here. It's enough to note that developments
varied widely among Western nations and that decades separated
first decisions from final accomplishments.[37] Though laws might pre-
scribe compulsory universal basic schooling, a host of impediments
– social, economic, religious, and political – delayed its full attain-
ment everywhere until well into the twentieth century. Still, by the
turn of the century, free or inexpensive public elementary schooling
in some form existed across the Western world, touching the lives of
greater and greater numbers of children over time. It was the state's
primary tool for fashioning responsible adults, willing workers, and

loyal citizens, and governments used it tenaciously to promote their social agendas, clean bodies and clean clothes among them.

When France established a universal, free, and secular primary school system in the early 1880s, the government of the day placed personal hygiene on the list of compulsory subjects for study.[38] At the same time it reviewed hygienic conditions in the nation's primary schools and found them seriously wanting.[39] The reviewers noted a general lag in matters of personal care, as well as the relative absence of private and public bathing facilities in French homes and cities. Worse still were the habits and conditions found in rural communities. In light of these findings the next steps seemed clear: the public school should teach the virtues and techniques of cleanliness to the coming generations. And if schools were to teach these lessons, the teachers themselves had to be clean. After all, many came from the same social backgrounds as their pupils and therefore needed the same instruction. As a result, the reviewers insisted that normal school students be taught the fundamentals of personal hygiene too so that they could set an example when they became teachers in turn.[40]

Elsewhere reforming voices were equally firm. Soon after Italian unification in 1871 the Associazione Medica Italiana called on schools to teach the principles of hygiene and personal cleanliness. The appeal echoed time and again before the turn of the century.[41] One example among many was the entreaty of a leading Italian hygienist and founder of the Pasteur Institute in Italy, Angelo Celli, who called for a national government commitment to improve hygienic conditions and teaching throughout the Italian education system, from the *asili d'infanzia* to the *scuola normale*.[42] If children in elementary schools had the opportunity to wash themselves, he insisted, it would improve their health and reduce the incidence of disease. In the same vein Arthur Newsholme, a leading English public health authority and author of a basic textbook on school hygiene, remarked, "No school education is complete which does not teach children the necessity for a clean skin. A dirty condition of the person strongly favours the incidence of infectious disease, as well as helps to produce that unpleasant odour which commonly belongs to the air of a school-room full of scholars."[43]

Schools used the complementary tools of instruction and inspection to pursue the cause of cleanliness. Primary school programs usually blended physiology and hygiene into their mix of instruction on arithmetic and literacy skills, and schoolbooks offer a clear picture of the content of these lessons. Mass schooling created a flourishing market for textbooks, and from the later nineteenth century onward, numerous works on hygiene and physiology appeared. Initially hygienists wrote many of these books, and often they were too difficult for young children to master, even when approved for school use. The German physician Carl Ernst Bock's widely used *Bau, Leben und Pflege des menschlichen Körpers in Wort und Bild* (*Structure, Life, and Care of the Human Body in Words and Pictures*) – a book of many words and few pictures – now seems quite unsuitable for elementary school use. Yet it went through nineteen editions between 1869 and 1916 and enjoyed a further life during the 1920s in a revised edition under new authorship.[44] Over time, however, age-graded books replaced works like Bock's, bringing the lessons of hygiene to all ages, including the very young. In a health primer for schoolchildren from the same period, Alfred Baur reduced the message to ten rules for living, the second being "keep your house, your clothes, and yourself clean" – to which he then added ten prohibitions.[45]

These German examples had scores of parallels in public education systems throughout the Western world. There were textbooks for children, textbooks for adolescents, textbooks for their teachers as well, and everywhere they spelled out much the same message. The skin that showed – hands, face, neck, and ears – should be washed daily, and the skin that was hidden bathed weekly. Clothes should be changed once or twice a week and laundered regularly too. Those worn during the day should never be worn to bed. There wasn't the same consensus, however, around cleaning some other parts of the body: the hair, the mouth, and the feet. Some authorities showed more concern for their condition than others. But the message was clear enough. The body should know the regular touch of water and, if possible, soap as well. An Italian manual for teachers put it bluntly. Poor children might still be admitted to school barefoot, but "the teacher should not allow even the little children of the peasants, the blacksmiths, the tinkers, the charcoal burners, to come to school dirty, without having washed their face and hands, with disgusting nails, with tousled hair, with a greasy blackened shirt."[46]

We know much less, however, about what actually occurred in the classroom and how important it may have been in bringing the young to cleanliness. In Germany, we are told, schools played only a limited role in teaching hygiene, though home visiting by physicians and health workers may have had some influence.[47] The authorized curriculum in France, however, was outlined in some detail, and it gives us an idea of what might have been taught elsewhere. When the national public school system was first established, instruction in hygiene was left to the teacher's discretion. But in 1897 the Conseil supérieur de l'instruction publique created a coordinated series of programs for students at all levels.[48] Children in the écoles maternelles publiques were to be given "petits conseils d'hygiène" in simple, concrete terms, to rouse their awareness of cleanliness. The older ones in elementary school were inspected on arrival, when "une absolue propreté" was demanded; in class these pupils received practical lessons on personal habits and bodily care. Senior students in *lycées* and *collèges* heard the message of cleanliness again (and again!), combined with a growing list of topics and cautions about health and well-being. The secondary school curriculum required twelve one-hour lectures that taught personal hygiene in the context of core hygienic understandings about water, air, contagious diseases, vaccination, housing conditions, and animal care – with a separate program adapted to female students' needs.[49] In any event, the formal curriculum may have been less instructive than the teacher herself or himself. Jean-Pierre Goubert notes that the French primary schoolteacher was "a living model of ... hygienic puritanism" whose well-scrubbed presence was a powerful lesson in itself.[50]

In Britain, too, cleanliness took priority over virtually every other issue in primary schooling and teachers routinely checked their pupils' hands and faces at the beginning of the school day, sending delinquents home to their mothers.[51] How to teach hygiene to the very young, however, was not entirely clear: was it better to teach by precept or by practice? The first approach used lessons and textbooks to inform; the second used practical drills to train. The national Board of Education, advised by its chief medical officer, had no doubt about the answer. It considered practice far more important than theory. As it noted in 1910, "the Hygiene reader [textbook] should seldom if ever be used, but the children should actually learn to carry out many ordinary habits of cleanliness ... as part of their school routine."[52] The teaching "should be above all things practical and direct. Children should be made to do things ... not once, but regularly until the habit of doing them is formed to a greater or lesser degree." The Board reported that a substantial number of schools were using these methods, though the decision to adopt them depended on the school's head teacher.

But since neither precept nor practice was usually enough to change the behaviours of the ages, inspection took up the task where instruction let off. As bureaucratic institutions, schools ran according to rules and regulations, and rules defined the school's responsibilities for the cleanliness of their charges. As the Italian Ministry of Public Instruction decreed in 1908, "The teacher and the director shall see that the pupils ... are clean personally and have clean clothing, and shall teach them the indispensible norms of hygiene."[53] From the early 1880s the French Ministry of Public Instruction required the teachers of the very young to inspect them daily, not forgetting their ears and teeth.[54] In many settings the ultimate responsibility fell on the shoulders of school medical inspectors, whose remit included the hygienic condition of the entire school environment – the building, its facilities, and its occupants. France began to organize systematic school medical inspections in 1879, though once again the periphery was slow to do what the centre decreed, and it was many years before a fully functioning program extended across the nation.[55] By the late nineteenth century similar practices had been adopted across the Western world.[56]

At first school doctors were more concerned about infectious disease outbreaks and the sanitary condition of school facilities than about the health of individual pupils. But after the turn of the century, as public health services redirected their gaze from communities to individuals, schoolchildren themselves received more attention.[57] Underlying this shift in Britain lay a concern, widely shared in military, medical, and government circles, about racial deterioration.[58] The poor health and stature of army volunteers during the Boer War, combined with a series of military humiliations in the South African conflict, had convinced many that the nation's vigour was in decline. Although these views weren't universally shared, they prompted a series of government inquiries into British well-being, that of children in particular.[59] Out of these concerns came a new national school medical service, responsible for inspecting the health of the nation's pupils and promoting their welfare.[60]

The evidence seemed to support the case for the state's use of the public school as a tool for improving children's health. Poverty, child neglect, and ill health were widespread in urban Britain, and washing less fortunate children was one obvious response. The introduction of compulsory elementary education more than trebled the British school population between 1870 and 1890, for the first time revealing the extent of poor child health.[61] The original English school medical officer (SMO), appointed in the industrial city of Bradford in 1893, noted that more than one third of the first three hundred children he inspected hadn't removed their clothes for at least six months.[62] A turn-of-the-century survey of Scottish schoolchildren from Edinburgh and Aberdeen deemed 20 to 30 percent either unclean or moderately clean and the clothing of 20 percent in the same condition.[63] Environments like these were also linked with common skin diseases: school health officials, as well as children and parents, struggled with ringworm, scabies, and impetigo in addition to infestations of lice and fleas.[64] Notification and exclusion were their first line of defence. The affected children were identified, their parents informed, and in serious cases the children were sent home from school until they could pass a second inspection. And the problems seemed widespread. One in five of those examined in an early-twentieth-century London examination fell short of the mark and their parents were duly informed of the failure.

Americans adopted similar solutions to similar problems around the same time. Public health officials in Boston, New York, and Chicago introduced school medical inspections in the 1890s and other centres soon followed their example.[65] Here, too, contagious diseases were a leading concern, and notification and exclusion the routine responses, but cleanliness was the clearest sign of a child's well-being and it attracted close attention. Conditions in the New World seemed as troubling as in the Old, especially among tenement dwellers. In her autobiography the pioneer New York public health physician Sara Josephine Baker estimated that 80 percent of the children she saw had head lice and close to 20 percent suffered from infectious skin diseases. Her memory may have misled her, for these rates are rather higher than others published at the time, but even then a sizable majority of notified cases involved child cleanliness.[66] The subject was an ongoing concern for the progressively minded. The social reformer and photojournalist Jacob Riis once overheard a Lower East Side New York elementary schoolteacher ask her class "what must I do to be healthy" and the pupils' chant in response:

I must keep my skin clean,
Wear clean clothes,
Breathe pure air,
And live in the sunlight.

Riis understood all too well that many of them had never known such things.[67]

By its very nature inspection was a form of surveillance, and surveillance could lead to resistance. The poor often resented public intrusions into their private lives and the violation was all the more offensive if it came from their social superiors.[68] In working-class circles particularly, inspections roused the shame of being singled out for lapses in personal hygiene. The resulting stigma touched schoolchildren as well as their parents, particularly their mothers, whose struggles to keep their offspring clean were closely tied to their family's strivings for respectability.[69] In itself, then, the higher status of teachers and inspectors fed ill feeling that hindered the spread of the sanitarian message. Excluding pupils from classrooms because they weren't clean was another sensitive matter. One early-twentieth-century New York social worker observed that school inspectors used verbal codes when identifying pupils' hygienic shortcomings to save them from embarrassment.[70] A note sent home about a child's health problems, let alone an excluded child herself or himself, was usually far from welcome. The gesture could easily be regarded as a rebuke to parents, an invasion of family privacy, a challenge to alternative notions of disease, or a failure to understand life on the social margins.

In some parts of Italy, hygiene's basic teachings denied deep-rooted religious beliefs. As a professor of medicine at the University of Naples put it soon after the turn of the twentieth century, "for many hygienists and educators this explains the insurmountable obstacle that meets the rules of hygiene in popular consciousness and the result is often absolutely negative for their existence." It was thought that most of the time "religions, made of stupid beliefs and harmful penances, of contempt for all that concerns the health and enjoyment of the body, deifying the soul" became "incentives for moral and physical ruin and an inevitable cause of death."[71] Here, and by extension in much of Catholic Europe, Church doctrine conflicted with progressive, science-based understandings. If anything, however, the hygienists' derision slowed acceptance of hygiene's principles even further.

Resistance itself might take many forms and mean many things. Probably the most common reaction was to do little or nothing when school authorities drew a child's unclean condition to its parents' attention. But at least in some places, ignoring a school health notice risked the next step: coercion. In serious cases stubborn parents courted the chance that the state would lean on them heavily, as it did from time to time. In extreme cases British parents who ignored school health notices were prosecuted for child neglect. Punishments varied from fines of 6s. and court costs (roughly two to three days' pay for a common labourer) to a short prison sentence.[72] In France the broader hygiene movement faced criticism from liberals and outright condemnation from the political left; both groups were concerned about growing state power and the invasion of private family life.[73]

What came of these prodigious efforts to improve schoolchildren's cleanliness is anything but clear. One contemporary in a northern British industrial city, who directed an Anglican institute for work among the poor, observed that schools taught hygiene scientifically, but "I do not think it sinks in at all."[74] The turn-of-the-century French physician Antonin Baratier, a close observer of child health, had similar views. Village schools, he claimed, hosted a festival of childhood diseases, which thrived among their dirty, unkempt pupils.[75] Lion Murard and Patrick Zylberman, historians of the public health movement in France, noted dismissively that French schools in the later nineteenth century revealed a "perfect inconsideration" for teaching hygiene.[76] Teachers may have dealt with the subject in passing at a theoretical level but their pupils showed great ignorance of the subject. In fact, Murard and Zylberman believed that schooling in hygiene had had no effect at all, and if anything, schoolmasters' impressions of student cleanliness in interwar France strongly supported this conclusion.[77] Italian circumstances stirred much the same pessimism. At the end of the nineteenth century, after a generation of broadly based public instruction, it seemed to one observer that the great mass of people still lived in fatalism and superstition and hadn't yet achieved any basic hygienic awareness.[78] The American public health movement's efforts to improve personal health and hygiene appeared to enjoy little more success.[79]

Admittedly it would have been difficult to quantify improvement at the time, and the task is still more difficult in retrospect. Apart from the problem of selecting what to measure, the amount of change itself must often have been subtle, if evident at all. The state had chosen schools to perform a demanding task: to transform pervasive daily practices, the unspoken customs of generations, which lay at the heart of family life. Installing showers, baths, or swimming pools in schools was just a small step in this process. Though proposed much more often than actually built, they began to appear in schools around the turn of the century, in larger cities more commonly than elsewhere.[80] In their absence, teachers sometimes escorted their charges to nearby public baths, fleeting signs of schooling's role in forming new habits. Goubert notes that the great transformation of personal hygiene began in the primary school, and others share his view.[81] But in the short run at least, any change that did occur must have been modest at best.

MOULDING THE YOUNG

While physicians, nurses, and teachers staffed the front ranks of the new model hygiene army, others walked in step with them a pace or two behind. Though they often lacked the professional standing that would justify claims to leadership, they were just as determined to extend the social frontiers of the clean body. Their ranks included a broad assortment of the well-intentioned – public officials, professionals, volunteers, self-selected advisers – united most of all by their desire to improve the conduct of others. Prominent among them were the leaders of youth movements, moulders of the young, heirs to the sanitarians' core beliefs and propagators of their message.

Though associations for young people had a long history in Western societies, they assumed new forms during the late nineteenth and early twentieth centuries.[82] The urban industrial age transformed both the setting and the experience of growing up and even altered basic understandings of young life. Adolescence itself was "discovered" during the later 1800s, a theory made real through experience, rather like the European discovery of the Americas had once made imagined lands a reality. Regardless of their great variety, the new youth movements shared one basic feature. Created and directed by adults, they were meant to guide youths toward mature life in society. Their shared techniques were instructional, their goals educational.

The best known among them, the Scout movement, had a foundational history with the ring of myth, for it seemed to spring from the soil overnight. Within months of its creation in England in 1908 its youthful membership numbered some 60,000, and it immediately developed a broad international following. Within two or three years scout groups in the thousands had been formed across the English-speaking world and throughout Western Europe. Its distinctive British ethos was conservative and middle class, but it quickly adapted to the local environment wherever it took root, the broader organization held together by little more than a loose international structure. Its immediate popularity owed much to a single book, *Scouting for Boys,* whose publication early in 1908 seems to have sparked the movement. It was written and illustrated by the Boy Scouts' founder, Robert Baden-Powell, a retired British general and South African War hero, who declared his objective in the book's subtitle: "a handbook for instruction in good citizenship."[83] In English or in translation – and except in the United States – the book was the master text of the international scout movement, and so it remained for the next half century and more.[84] *Scouting for Boys* became one of the bestselling English-language books of the twentieth century. According to one account, only the Bible exceeded its publishing figures in the English-speaking world until after the Second World War.[85] Whether widely read or merely widely owned we'll never know, but here was a book with the potential to influence.

Scouting for Boys is a primer on growing up and it underscores a boy's need to grow up strong. Baden-Powell emphasized that boys were personally responsible for their own health and strength, and he advised them on care of the nose, ears, eyes, and teeth, all essential for scouts in the wilderness.[86] He stressed the need for cleanliness in particular: "it may not be always possible for you to get a bath every day, but you can at any rate rub yourself over with a wet towel, or scrub yourself with a dry one, and you ought not to miss a single day in doing this if you want to keep fit and well."[87] In addition, he encouraged, boys should wash their hands and nails before every meal. Then he added clothes to the list. "You should also keep clean in your clothing, both your underclothing as well as that which shows. Beat it out with a stick every day before putting it on," he recommended. Failure to do so courted danger, for diseases lurked everywhere, "carried about in the air and in water by tiny invisible insects called 'germs' or 'microbes,'" threatening illness to those who weren't vigilant and clean. The teeth, too, needed regular cleaning. He recommended brushing twice a day, after rising and before bed, with a toothbrush and tooth powder; even American cowboys did so, he solemnly assured his readers. Good teacher that he was, Baden-Powell concluded his lesson with some suggestions for further reading: three recent books on fitness and health. In later years he included similar advice in parallel texts for the Girl Guide movement and the leadership manuals he addressed to scoutmasters.[88] From that point on the message of cleanliness in *Scouting for*

Boys assumed a life of its own. The 26th edition, issued in 1951, repeated it word for word.[89]

The many translations of *Scouting for Boys* spread Baden-Powell's message throughout Western Europe and beyond.[90] But scouting never enjoyed quite the same success abroad that it did in Britain, the settler Dominions, and the United States. Other youth movements in Continental European countries, better able to express the cultural aspirations of their young, were more popular or important. The *Jungdeutschlandbund,* with its strong military and nationalist associations, was the largest youth group in prewar Germany, while the *Wandervögel,* individualistic, unconventional, and committed to outdoor life and folkloric romanticism, became the most influential.[91] Despite their ideological differences, they shared a concern for physical exercise and body care that differed little from that endorsed by the Boy Scouts. They also provided a link with the more politicized German youth movements of the interwar years, culminating in the *Hitlerjugend,* a training ground for future soldiers, whose summer camps were places where "cleanliness, discipline, obedience and manliness were the fundamental values of what was called the 'cultural labor.'"[92]

The vacation colony movement also concerned itself with the health of the coming generation, in this case that of still younger children. During the mid-1870s a Zurich pastor organized a three-week summer mountain holiday for a group of poor youths from his parish, and his example launched a pan-European movement: vacation camps providing summer retreats for working-class children aged six to thirteen. The colonies flourished in France and Italy into the 1960s; a parallel movement lasted in Germany until 1933. The numbers of children involved are elusive but they appear to have been substantial. As many as 250,000 attended the German *Ferienkolonie* from 1912 to 1914.[93] The colonies' programs invariably emphasized basic hygiene, personal cleanliness in particular, and their approach was vigorously didactic. Even the poorest children were expected to arrive equipped with brushes for teeth, clothes, and shoes, though those who appeared without the necessaries might be supplied with them.[94] The campers' daily routines included bathing and brushing their clothes as well as cleaning their dormitories. According to an early leader in the French movement, "the *Colonies de Vacances* ... were first conceived as a school of cleanliness."[95] During the interwar years the Mussolini government used the pre-existing Italian *colonie estive* to promote its own political program, redoubling earlier efforts to impart proper hygienic habits and underscoring fascist concern for individual cleanliness.[96] National directives prescribed a daily schedule for colonists that included four periods for personal care: half an hour after waking, fifteen minutes before lunch and supper, and another fifteen minutes before bed (when special attention was directed to the hands and feet). Plate 9 captures a moment in the daily hygiene routines of a *colonia* during the later 1920s. The caption beneath the photo when first published – "Igiene innanzi tutto" (hygiene first of all) – sums up the main message.

In the United States, summer camp programs grew out of similar concerns for poor children from the urban core, but to a greater extent than elsewhere, they also directed their programs toward middle-class children. The American movement too began to take form in the 1880s and 1890s, and it flourished after the turn of the century.[97] Best known among them were the Boy Scouts and the YMCA, but these were just the tip of the summer camp iceberg. By the early 1920s there were more than seven hundred private camps in the United States, as well as more than five hundred others linked to various organizations. Some of their sponsors had religious and philanthropic goals; others intended only to teach life skills and provide recreation. One way or another, though, all of them hoped to mould the young personality. Camping offered them a special opportunity because it withdrew children from their families for days or even weeks at a time and placed them under the supervision of the camp's leadership. Inevitably this raised the issue of personal hygiene, and the camps themselves confronted the question in various ways. The earliest among them were simple affairs with few facilities so campers swam in a nearby lake or river if they bathed at all.[98] As the movement expanded, however, many camps built more substantial sanitary infrastructures, complete with baths or showers and furnished with hot and cold running water. Some camps for girls even provided laundry facilities, a less than subtle hint that the standards for campers varied according to gender. Girl campers usually faced higher hygienic expectations than boys. While at this point it is difficult to be certain, American summer camps don't appear to have offered the same degree of formal instruction in personal cleanliness or enforced the same rigid cleansing regimes so common among European youth movements. But through their daily routines and their up-to-date facilities, they reinforced the norms of personal cleanliness that most of the middle-class campers surely followed at home. In some cases a week or two at summer camp may even have offered children a chance to relax family standards a bit.

Needless to say, the list of the persuaders was longer still. As volunteers and philanthropists, many middle- and upper-class women became strong advocates for the new cleanliness.[99] The scribbling army of self-help counsellors continued to advise regular bathing, as they had for decades. A rising tide of popular medical publications also fed the growing public appetite for information about sanitary health.[100] Army and navy doctors took a fresh interest in cleanliness, declaring it even more necessary in military than in civilian life.[101] Even the new moving picture technology was harnessed to the cause. A short film from the Edison Company's Spanish American War series made in 1898 depicted a group of cheerful American soldiers at their morning wash.[102] Equipped with basins of water and towels (though with no soap in sight) their efforts seem rather cursory, a simple hands-and-face affair. A few even wore their hats in the process.

Still, the new personal hygiene remained largely a middle-and upper-class concern. By the early twentieth century most of those in the loftier ranks of Western societies had long since absorbed the lessons of modern cleanliness, practices that had only begun to make inroads in rural communities and urban working-class circles. Armed with an emerging scientific rationale, Western elites spread the new hygienic culture among the socially less advantaged.[103] They expected the lower ranks to accept cleanliness as a first step on the path toward good health and social respectability. Practised regularly, washing and bathing would become personal habits; shared universally, they would form the basis of a hygienic mode of life. What was needed was a transformation of lower-class mentalities replacing folk beliefs and traditional ways with those endorsed by contemporary medical science. For assistance the cleanliness advocates turned to the state, leaning on its authority to encourage, to require, and in some cases to compel the lower orders to accept the new norms. They also enlisted youth leaders and others committed to the young. What they failed to consider carefully was the enormity of the task, since for a large proportion of the Western world's peoples, the modern tools of cleanliness still lay beyond reach.

PART THREE

Cleanliness as Commodity

One of the nineteenth-century West's greatest legacies to the twentieth was a technology of water management. It supplied great cities and small dwellings alike, making fresh water more readily available – and foul water more easily disposable – than at any point since Roman times. Expanding these systems was still a work in progress when the Victorian era came to an end, and at that time its blessings were far from universally available. But within half a century most residents of the Western world could claim them as an entitlement and those who couldn't soon would. The major building block of modern personal hygiene was then in place. Others took form during the same years as well. Once enjoyed only by the well-to-do, the bathroom gradually extended its domain as the century progressed; by the 1980s the great majority of Western dwellings included at least one and often two or more. Meanwhile hot running water had become so commonplace that it ceased to be cause for comment. Together these changes created the basic infrastructure of modern body care, found everywhere in the late-twentieth-century home.

From the nineteenth century the twentieth also inherited an ideology of personal cleanliness. The lessons of the educators and the messages of the physicians became platitudes as the new century progressed. They underscored the need to avoid harmful germs by developing healthy habits. Many public institutions, especially those that cared for children, preached the gospel of cleanliness as a matter of course. But voices from another quarter joined them, and they proved still more pervasive – and persuasive – over ·

time. These were the claims of the makers of products: the soaps, the detergents, and the beauty aids that commercialized personal hygiene as the century progressed. Advertising came to dominate the discourse on cleanliness, transforming it from a habit into a commodity. Rather than representing it as a worthy end in itself, publicity emphasized its central place in an individual's social relationships, its importance to self-presentation and social acceptance, its role in making oneself attractive to others. Success in public and private life came not from being clean *per se* but from consuming goods that represented the individual as clean, sometimes even masking its absence in the process.

One of the greatest of these commercial campaigns involved one of life's most mundane tasks: the laundry. Over the course of the twentieth century household laundry chores were mechanized and automated, their physical burdens eased, their demands on a housewife's time greatly reduced. An onerous duty that took a very full workday at the beginning of the century, the family wash had become a light and simple task by its end. These changes unfolded at a time when shifting fashions, rising living standards, and new forms of work greatly increased the consumption of clothing. In particular, the steady growth of the service sector fostered a demand for larger wardrobes, more frequently changed clothes, and – inevitably – more clothing to be washed. The makers of automatic washing machines promoted their wares energetically, and by the century's later decades, they had succeeded in placing their products in most family homes. But their advertising efforts paled when compared with those of the laundry detergent manufacturers, who peddled their products with unmatched energy. They became great teachers, defining the new terms of cleanness, promoting them relentlessly, and convincing consumers that their products offered the cleanest clothes of all.

During the middle and late years of the century the body's surfaces also became sites for intense publicity campaigns, and given the competitive nature of the personal hygiene marketplace, they were contested terrain. The personal care industries promoted wares that offered cleanliness – or its likeness – to all who used their products. Along the way the merchants taught new hygienic routines and promoted new personal habits. The regular use of toilet soaps, shampoos, dental creams, shaving supplies, and other related commodities spread across the Western world, gradually after the First World War, rapidly from mid-century onward. The business strategies behind these developments rested on a well-known relationship between cleanliness and beauty that the beauty trades redefined in pursuit of their business interests. The new personal hygiene products promised not just cleaner bodies but more attractive ones too. Their consumption was not only, and perhaps not even primarily, the pathway to better health but also the route to a more beautiful self and a better life. By the later twentieth century beauty had replaced health as the primary goal of personal hygiene and hygiene had been reconceived in terms of beauty. In the process cleanliness, like beauty, had become a product for sale, yet another commodity on the market in the age of mass consumption.

BATHROOMS AND BATHING

Regular bathing became democratized during the twentieth century. Habits only common among the upper classes at its outset were common to all by its end. Though the rate of change varied from one country to another, the experience was broadly shared through-out the Western world. Over time, millions learned the lessons of the new cleanliness and put them into practice, transforming popular hygiene dramatically. Formal instruction on washing and bathing left an imprint on this development, but by itself it was not enough to fashion cultural change on this scale. Regular full body bathing, in particular, also needed privacy and convenience, a room of its own, one furnished for the task. The diffusion of both the bathroom and hot and cold running water were central to the process. These innovations demanded continent-wide changes in housing design and technology, investments as great as any in the maturing Indus-trial Age and a time frame measured in decades rather than years. The English-speaking world – the United States in particular – stood in the front ranks of innovation while Continental Europe lagged somewhat behind. But by the eve of the twenty-first century the rev-olution in personal cleanliness was complete and the very concept of the clean body had been redefined in the process.

THE BATHROOM TRIUMPHANT

At the beginning of the twentieth century a separate room for bathing had found a permanent place in the homes of the affluent throughout the Western world. In some areas it had even embarked on its slow journey from luxury to common utility. By the end of the century it had become an indispensable part of the dwelling, the one room with a door that could always be closed in the name of privacy. Indeed, we can no longer imagine house and home without one. The transition from the exclusive to the universal bathroom was a long, drawn-out affair. Basic understandings of the dwelling had to be reconsidered, building technologies revised, fixtures invented, regulations reviewed, infrastructures created, and all of this on a monumental scale. For the bathroom to be available to all, existing buildings by the millions needed renovation and still greater numbers had to be built. These processes also required major capital investments, which some could afford more easily than others. So the empire of the bathroom expanded fitfully, at differing rates in different places according to local circumstances.

As to statistics, unfortunately we've been left with meagre rations, at least before the mid-century decades. In Chapter 2 we caught fleeting glimpses of the share of dwellings with bathrooms between the mid-nineteenth century and the First World War in a few large cities, but we can only begin to map the bathroom's diffusion more precisely in the 1940s, when census takers and survey directors began a deeper exploration of national housing standards (Figure 6.1). At that point roughly half of all dwellings in North America – slightly more in the United States, slightly less in Canada – had a room with a tub or shower and hot and cold running water, a fact that gives us a benchmark from which to measure the bathroom's progress.[1] Naturally there was variation. In the United States in 1940 only one in six California homes lacked a fully equipped bathroom while in Mississippi only one in seven possessed one. California apart, those states with the highest levels of full household plumbing facilities were concentrated in the northeast while those with the lowest were found in the old South. But over the next twenty years national living standards rose quickly and these differences were largely erased; by 1970 well over 90 percent of American homes had a full-function bathroom, and virtually all of those that didn't were soon to acquire one. By the end of the century close to half of all dwellings included two or more of them.[2] Meanwhile the American bathroom had long since assumed its standard form: a basin, tub, and toilet placed in a five- by seven-foot room.[3] The Canadian experience closely paralleled the American one; there too, by the 1990s, bathrooms dignified all but a small fraction of houses, and almost half boasted more than one.

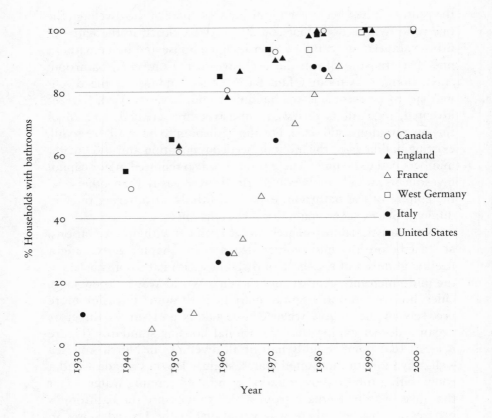

Figure 6.1 | Households with bathrooms

Note: For England and Wales the data record the presence of a fixed bath or
shower, not necessarily that of a private bathroom.
Sources: See Appendix.

In England, long considered the vanguard of modern home
plumbing in Europe, the growth rate was similar. Nearly two thirds
of English households included a fixed bath by mid-century, roughly
the same proportion as in North America, though one in eight were
shared with other families.[4] Here, though, we compare apples with
oranges. The British census generously defined the term "bath" to
include all tubs installed and permanently attached to a drainpipe
whether or not they had a piped water supply or were located in a
room used only for bathing, a description that masked some curious

domestic arrangements. But by the end of the twentieth century, the English home was as likely to include a bathroom as the North American dwelling.[5]

Elsewhere conditions varied greatly. The well-known public housing program of interwar "Red" Vienna was something of a special case, if only for its reputation as an enlightened social democratic plan to meet working-class housing needs. But of the more than 60,000 units built between 1920 and 1933, virtually none included a separate room for a bath, though running water was installed in all and private toilets were common.[6] In larger building complexes, bathing and laundry facilities were relegated to a basement if they existed at all. Similarly, the *Mietskaserne* that housed working-class families in German industrial cities sometimes provided residents with communal baths but bathrooms in their own cramped apartments were utterly unknown. The idea that there might be an alternative didn't even enter discussions about workers' dwellings until the 1920s, when architects and planners first introduced the concept into the discourse on popular housing.[7]

Unfortunately, for lack of national-level data, the state of the German bathroom isn't clear until the later twentieth century.[8] The disruptions and destructions of the 1930s and 1940s must have discouraged even the thought of gathering this information. Still, at the end of the war, with almost half of Germany's building stock either destroyed or heavily damaged, reconstruction offered an opportunity to introduce up-to-date comforts into the German dwelling, and during the 1960s and 1970s the proportion of homes with a bathroom rose sharply.[9] A comparative survey of European family budgets at the end of the 1970s revealed that 93 percent of West German households had a bathroom, ranking them just below the United Kingdom, the Netherlands, and North America in sanitary comforts.[10] According to a national survey a decade later, one eighth of homes had multiple bathrooms, one for every one or two residents, and the standard bathroom now came equipped with a minimum of a washbasin and tub or shower.[11] The diffusion of the bathroom in East Germany, however, was quite another matter; low investment in housing after the war retarded its progress. There it long remained a benefit only for the minority; two thirds of homes in the DDR lacked a bathroom or toilet in 1971, and almost one third had no running water.[12] In most other East Bloc countries during the 1960s the proportion of bathroomless homes ranged between 50 and 80 percent.[13]

With slower rates of adoption over the first half of the twentieth century, the bathroom in France and Italy had a still different history. During the first decade after the Second World War the proportion of French homes with a bath or shower was at best 10 percent and perhaps even lower – a level well below even the poorest state in America at the time.[14] Across the nation the urban/rural divide was particularly wide. By 1964 government programs to build low-cost housing had substantially increased the proportion of dwellings with bathrooms, but the greater part of the increase had occurred in towns and cities. City dwellers were two to three times more likely to have one than their country cousins.[15] In interwar Italy even urban planners ignored the private bathroom. The Roman suburb of Garbatella, designed after the First World War along English garden city principles, seems not to have included them in its apartments, though it did offer public baths for the community.[16] In Bologna the bathroom delayed its debut in popular housing until well into the fascist era. An early complex of seventy-eight modest homes built in 1937 included a room with a toilet, tub, sink, and bidet in each apartment, fittings that became standard equipment in less expensive postwar housing.[17] Yet at mid-century only 36 percent of all Italian dwellings had piped water and only 11 percent a bath or shower, conditions unchanged over the previous two decades.[18] As with so much else in Italy, living standards varied markedly along the length of the peninsula. Even at these low rates, housing in the north was three to four times more likely to a have bathing facilities. Over the next three decades, however, French and Italian dwellings eagerly adopted the bathroom. By the 1980s at least 85 percent of households in both countries included one, and by the end of the century the standards in both countries were those of the Western world.[19]

Timing apart, the other distinguishing feature of French and Italian bathrooms was the presence of the bidet. While elsewhere it was seldom found – and then more often as a symbol of worldly refinement than a device for routine use – it was widely adopted in both countries during the postwar years. Shorn of its older associations with sexual indecorum, it now was valued for its ease of use and its frugal water consumption. By the 1970s over 90 percent of new homes in France and Italy included one, and though the fascination waned toward the end of the century – particularly in France – they remained much more common in French and Italian bathrooms than those found elsewhere.[20]

Everywhere in the transatlantic world, class and social status directed the bathroom's diffusion. Labouring families waited longer for one than those who were better off, while the urban poor and rural dwellers waited longer still.[21] Even when simply equipped, bathrooms increased housing costs, and as long as one could choose between a home with no bathroom and another with one, affordability remained a common concern on the lower economic margins. The expense of building the urban infrastructure that the bathroom required also shaped its distribution. Usually the water mains and sewer systems that made the bathroom possible arrived first in a city's more gracious neighbourhoods and only later – sometimes much later – in its working-class suburbs. By the time city building codes began to require bathrooms in new dwellings, the utilities needed to support them were already in place. Meanwhile, rural residents faced unique disadvantages when addressing the need for a bathroom. With no access to a system that supplied fresh water and disposed of its wastes, they had to create their own, a costly process that competed with the rural householder's many other financial needs. In the light of these barriers it's not surprising that the countryside was last to know the bathroom's delights.

HOT AND COLD RUNNING WATER

Of course cleanliness required more than privacy. Bathrooms depended on running water, and large amounts of it too. But it took decades before water was available in all homes at the turn of a tap. Once more cities led the process of change, while towns and villages followed step and rural communities trailed well behind. Growth rates also varied from country to country, higher in North America and lower in Western Europe, notably (again) in France and Italy. The French example is telling. In 1954 fewer than two thirds of dwellings had access to running water. Three decades later virtually all French homes did.[22] Meanwhile, if statistics tell us of quantities, anecdotes offer us glimpses of the small human dramas behind the numbers – in this case the story of Giacomo Rossi and his wife Maria Tassoni, a poor Italian family in Lazio, on that banner day in 1963 when their modest village house was finally connected to running water: "The first time Maria turned on the faucet in the kitchen sink, the water gushed out and sprayed her. Giacomo laughed as she wiped herself off. 'No matter,' she said, 'I only have to think of all those years I sacrificed myself carrying water. Now I can just stand here and the water carries itself. What a miracle.'"[23] The new house they began to plan the following year would have a bathtub too. No one in the family had ever taken a tub bath before. Like so many others they had always washed themselves in the kitchen sink.[24]

The provision of hot water in the home lagged still further behind. An American survey toward the end of the First World War indicated that, while over 90 percent of homes in the sample had running water, it only ran hot in only 40 percent of them.[25] A British study during the depths of the Second World War revealed that almost two thirds of families earning less than £300 a year (i.e., some three quarters of the British population) lacked hot running water.[26] If anything Italy and France were still less well served. A small Italian survey in 1957 found that only one quarter of the respondents – workers with incomes above those in the general population – had hot water on tap in their homes while, poignantly, a slightly larger group wanted to have it but didn't expect they ever would.[27] Three years later a national survey yielded even bleaker results, indicating that less than one home in five had a water heater of any sort.[28] A similar French family budget survey in the early 1960s indicated that two fifths of homes enjoyed hot water, a lower proportion than found in more favoured nations at the time.[29] Yet by the end of the century, the laggards had caught up with the leaders and most houses everywhere offered hot water at several points in the dwelling. The postwar economic miracle had worked its magic inside the home, and one of its many benefits was hot and cold water for everyone, a condition known only by a happy minority not all that long before.

The leisurely pace of hot water's domestication was due in large measure to the long delay in solving a technological problem: how could water best be heated for household use? At its simplest the question had two parts. Should water be heated on demand or heated and stored until needed? Should it be heated where it was used or warmed centrally and distributed throughout the house? Answers to these questions emerged slowly from the mid-nineteenth century onward, and this time Britain took the lead in exploring the possibilities. One was the geyser, a water heater in the bathroom. Later, heating from a central source – usually the kitchen range – emerged as the preferred solution.[30] Similar experiments were made abroad but most didn't produce enduring results.[31]

Water heaters located in bathrooms were more than merely bothersome since they had to be fuelled there too, usually with coal, compromising cleanliness and posing added risks. The main alternative, hot water drawn from reservoirs on kitchen stoves or fireplaces, needed a fire throughout the day in summer and winter alike, a seasonal discomfort and an added expense. One alternative was the independent heater with its own storage tank and thermostat, developed in Britain and the United States at the end of the nineteenth century, though its initial acceptance was slow. The same survey during the First World War that found piped hot water in 40 percent of American homes also found that only 2 percent of them had a freestanding hot water heater.[32] Over the interwar years, however, the storage heater became the system of choice across North America.[33]

Herman Muthesius greatly admired the English domestic hot water system, as he did so much else about the nation's plumbing. His enthusiasm for turn-of-the-century British bourgeois comforts was palpable:

Hand in hand with the general introduction of the bath at an early date went the general introduction of a hot-water system into the house. Without this, of course, a perfect bath is unthinkable, since it is the only means of installing a bath without irksome devices for heating the water. With the disappearance of the geyser we have seen the last of a piece of bathroom furniture that was difficult to use, sometimes dangerous, and always unwelcome and the bathroom will become more hygienic, spacious and pleasanter in general appearance.[34]

Awed by the vision of hot water at the turn of a tap – then only seen in the homes of the favoured few – Muthesius overlooked the great British masses, who could scarcely imagine such luxury. In this respect developments in England were comparatively slow. On the eve of the Second World War, fewer than 4 percent of British homes included an electric hot water heater.[35] The British working class continued to warm its bath and laundry water on stoves well into the 1950s, and most of the minority with hot water on tap heated it in boilers attached to a fireplace or kitchen range fed by solid fuel. Gas and electric heaters were more costly to buy and use but they offered greater convenience.

It's no surprise, then, that these devices were more common in the homes of the better off. As well, North Americans viewed the hot water heater rather differently than the English. In the United States and Canada, its adoption was largely a matter of convenience, while in England, public health concerns left a sharp imprint on thoughts about the subject. Medical opinion considered hot water an essential element in everyday life and many physicians thought existing arrangements inadequate. In the eyes of the public health community, the high proportion of schoolchildren treated for vermin and skin diseases revealed their uncleanliness, and easy access to warm water for bathing was a large part of the remedy. As one report commented during the dark days of the Second World War, "an adequate supply of hot water is considered to be a necessity for any house. No other factor is so important for the encouragement of decent standards of cleanliness in the house and person."[36]

Several influences fostered the diffusion of the bathroom. Obviously it had its commercial sponsors: homebuilders promoting innovative housing features to attract prospective buyers. The British builders of better-quality speculative housing began to offer bathrooms in the 1880s, a practice that quickly developed on the continent and in North America too.[37] Consumer demand also entered the equation. As the new personal cleanliness gradually deepened its social penetration, changing beliefs and personal habits brought new aspirations to the housing market. A growing proportion of Western populations came to expect the bathroom's comforts, and the gradual rise in incomes meant that this aspiration became a realistic goal for ever greater numbers.[38] During the interwar years, building codes in Britain and America began to require bathrooms in new residential construction, though similar regulations didn't often appear elsewhere until after the Second World War.[39] Inevitably housing bylaws had to balance buyers' preferences with their ability to pay, conditions that varied widely.

The bathroom's spread was also linked to broader forces that reorganized space within Western homes. One was the prolonged decline in household size, a product of lower fertility rates and the rise of the nuclear family. From the mid-nineteenth century to the late twentieth century the average number of residents per dwelling fell by half across the Western world.[40] Smaller families and simpler household structures transformed the relationships between family members and the spaces they inhabited, though the changes may have been almost imperceptible at the time. Another was the growing physical size of the house itself, particularly from the Depression decade onward.

Though the numbers of rooms in dwellings varied greatly at any time, the proportion of smaller homes gradually decreased while that of mid- and larger-sized ones grew, at least in North America.[41] Together these changes created greater opportunities for privacy within the home than Western societies had ever known. Innovations in household technology and the design and use of interior spaces reinforced this trend. Electric lighting and central heating allowed individuals to place greater distance between themselves and other family members when at home. The spread of open planning also sharpened the line between public and private zones in home interiors, placing the bathroom firmly in the latter. This subdivision of household space reached its height in the last third of the twentieth century with the development of en suite bathrooms for parents and separate bedrooms for each child, small islands where domestic privacy reigned supreme.[42]

The progress of the bathroom also depended on ready access to water and the bathroom needed a plentiful supply. In this respect the dwelling's growing thirst mirrored that of the city at large, for an abundant water supply was one of the main pillars of modern urban life. In towns and cities most everywhere the need for water increased steadily throughout much of the twentieth century, as it had during the nineteenth. In Chicago demand quadrupled between 1860 and 1900, then grew by a further third over the next four decades.[43] Per capita water use in Munich more than doubled from 1890 to 1950, though from that point on it began to decline.[44] In Turin during the shorter interval between 1939 and 1959 it grew by more than half.[45] Daily consumption rates varied widely at any given time, though they generally were much higher in American than in European cities.[46] At the end of the nineteenth century the Viennese used twice as much water per capita as Londoners and Parisians, who in turn used three to four times as much as those in Berlin, Brussels, and Naples.[47] In the United States use rates in major urban centres also varied widely well into the twentieth century.[48]

Reports like these simply indicate the gross amounts of water consumed by a city for all its many needs; the smaller quantities used by households are more difficult to determine. The data on water consumption published by urban authorities often don't distinguish between domestic and other purposes and as a result rates of home use can't easily be established, let alone compared. One estimate of household water consumption, for the entire United States in 1965, indicated that Americans used 157 gallons (about 600 litres) of

water per person daily. Residential use accounted for slightly less
than half of this amount, 80 percent of which was used – more or
less equally – either for washing and bathing or for flushing toilets. Over the next two decades, though, American consumption
rates changed little.[49] In comparison, late-twentieth-century Western
Europeans averaged 150 litres per person for all household uses, one
fourth of what Americans consumed.[50]

Happily, information on water use within the home is available for
the Netherlands during the last quarter of the century, and it offers
at least a suggestion of broader Western European patterns. Dutch
domestic consumption increased gradually until the early 1990s
before declining slightly. The largest increase by far was in water used
for personal hygiene, which grew by three quarters during the final
decades of the century. By 1998 it accounted for over 40 percent of
water consumed in the home. The amounts used to wash laundry,
however, remained much the same over time. Still, we shouldn't make
too much of this information. Statistics on urban water utilization
are often incomplete, widely scattered, and frequently misleading;
they also employ differing measures and reflect a wide range of local
circumstances. But whatever their limitations they clearly reveal the
steady growth of dependence on water that marked the urban age.

The water that entered the modern home had also been transformed. Once an element of nature, it had become a commodity,
an engineered product of the industrial economy.[51] Science had
domesticated water, subjected it to analysis, filtered it to make it
limpid, chlorinated it to eliminate germs. As the twentieth century
progressed, water became as commonplace as it was ubiquitous, its
purity assumed, its quality reliable, its safety assured – and its presence in everyday life taken utterly for granted. Behind these changes
everywhere lay the steady growth of an immense infrastructure dedicated to securing, cleansing, and distributing water throughout entire
nations. The scale of these developments itself was remarkable, all
the more for being so little noticed. During the mid-1980s, after
more than a century of expansion, there were more than 58,000
community water supplies serving residential areas in the United
States (though admittedly most were small, as were the groups they
served).[52] By this time similar arrangements met most water needs in
all western nations, alongside parallel systems to treat wastewater, a
vast infrastructure created by one of the major social and financial
investments of the modern era.

As to costs and prices, there's little that can safely be said about water as a commodity. The subject defies generalizations except of the broadest kind. One is that water was much cheaper once new urban supply systems developed. The cost of water in the eighteenth century city was far higher than it became in the twentieth. Another is that once modern systems were in place, water prices tended to increase only slowly.[53] But water was too basic a commodity to be priced by market forces alone. Virtually everywhere public authorities influenced what consumers paid for their water, through taxes, subsidies, and regulations, and often government ownership, trying to balance the public benefit with the cost of building, financing, and operating a water distribution system. Thus the price of water to users has always been a local matter and the variation has been great. In late-nineteenth-century France the range from the lowest to highest prices was 1 to 561; by the early 1980s it had shrunk substantially but still remained at a striking 1 to 120.[54] In circumstances like these, those hoping to understand the history of water need to begin at the local level.

FROM THE WEEKLY BATH TO THE DAILY SHOWER

The twentieth century saw a wholesale transformation in popular hygiene throughout the Western world. The very concept of cleanliness itself was redefined. Routine washing and bathing habits replaced older, more intermittent practices, and customs once shared only by the few were adopted by the many. At the *fin de siècle* frequent bathing had primarily been an upper-class affair; the rest took a full bath a few times a year at best. Otherwise they merely washed those parts in greatest need whenever the need arose, and in an age of few hygienic sensibilities those moments were few as well. Half a century later the importance of personal cleanliness had become widely accepted, a truth beyond questioning. More people than ever bathed regularly and often, and their numbers continued to grow. The Saturday bath had become a commonplace ritual and daytime hand washing – before meals and after using the toilet, after rising and before bedtime – was routine. Those who hadn't yet adopted these customs were a vanishing species, soon to disappear. The new cleanliness had become a mass phenomenon.

The bathroom left an indelible mark on the spread of these habits for it made regular washing and bathing simple tasks. Yet those who lacked its benefits didn't necessarily neglect their hygiene. Even without permanent fixtures and private spaces, they made do in kitchens and sculleries with buckets and basins or whatever else was available. The new concepts of cleanliness were widely accepted long before everyone could practise them in their own bathroom, furnished with up-to-date fixtures and hot water at the turn of a tap. Bathrooms changed the ease, more than the fact, of washing and bathing. As much as the bathroom fostered cleanliness, the new hygiene promoted the diffusion of the bathroom by creating a demand for its advantages.

Still, changes like these in everyday practices are difficult to document. However remarkable they may have seemed at the time, such commonplace matters are scarcely visible in retrospect. One early study, a 1937 survey in North London, found that 80 percent of adults took a weekly bath, while another 10 percent bathed twice or more; rates were higher still for children and adolescents.[55] After a wartime inquiry into British housing conditions, the British social research organization Mass Observation noted that "broadly speaking, the pattern of washing bodies is a daily washing of the face and neck and a weekly washing of the whole body."[56] Informed by a later postwar survey, it reported:

> Among the middle classes, women wash more frequently than men. In frequency of handwashing they outnumber men by three to two, in bathing by two to one. The daily bath is more likely to be a feminine ritual – 12 women in every 100 bathe daily compared with only one man in 100. In fact, the majority of men have only one bath weekly.
>
> Men and women alike wash their faces on average between once and twice daily, but their hands at least five times during the same period.[57]

Not knowing how these surveys were conducted, we shouldn't assume that they reflected British practices in general, but they do suggest that national habits had changed markedly since the beginning of the century.

The French evidence is even more limited. In 1951 the fashion magazine *Elle* asked a group of women about their personal care practices. Having recently returned from New York and been impressed by American ways, its feminist editor Françoise Giroud was concerned about her countrywomen's seeming hygienic neglect. Unfortunately the report mentioned nothing at all about how those surveyed were selected, nor even their numbers, so its findings are little more than straws in the wind. Half of those interviewed replied that they performed a daily "toilette complète," while another third did so at least once a week. Giroud didn't specify the elements of a *toilette complète* and it almost certainly included some body washing, though given the scarcity of bathrooms in France at the time, the number of immersion baths must have been small.[58] This, at least, was the meaning accepted by Jean Maudit, who revisited the original survey in 1986 in a review of French womanhood's hygienic progress during the intervening thirty-five years.[59] His methods, alas, were no more clear than Giroud's, but by then three quarters of those asked performed a *toilette complète* daily and most of the remainder did so two or three times a week. In a much broader inquiry, three enterprising journalists mounted an ambitious survey during the early 1970s, seeking to describe the *moeurs* of the entire French nation at home and at work. While their interests were as broad as their survey techniques were unsound, they too gathered information on French cleanliness, finding that 13 percent took a daily bath or shower and 23 percent (most of them country dwellers) never took one at all.[60] The latter statistic seemed to confirm long-standing views that the French paid little heed to their personal care.

The *Elle* inquiries, like those in England, seem to have relied largely on urban middle-class informants. But whatever their shortcomings and our methodological misgivings, they point to an obvious fact: some daily routines of personal cleanliness were already widely practised in France by the 1950s and their acceptance continued to grow during the second half of the century. What Giroud overlooked in her concern for French hygienic standards was the fact that, though her countrywomen fell well short of the postwar New York example, they took greater care of their bodies than their mothers and grandmothers ever had. Like the British, the French were changing their hygienic ways. The range of habits varied in both countries and, especially in France, rural people still clung to older customs. But new hygiene routines were on the ascendant and in time would conquer all.

Despite their long-standing reputation for cleanliness, Americans have been strangely uncurious about their own bathing behaviour. One of the very few exceptions is a 1960 study of personal hygiene in California, the state with the highest proportion of homes with full bathrooms (95 percent) in the nation at the time. This survey of one thousand middle-class households in Los Angeles and district found that three quarters of family members bathed daily while almost all the remainder did so two or three times a week. Slightly more than half of them took baths rather than showers.[61] But urban California was not the nation and middle-class California's habits were not those of all Americans. This study surely reflected America at its cleanest.

Elsewhere routine bathing made further progress over time. Yet another study of hygiene habits, this one in Germany during the later 1960s, revealed bathing rates higher than those in France and England but well below those in California. Half the German respondents then took a weekly bath while another third did so at least two or three times a week.[62] The great majority also washed their hands, faces, and necks every morning.[63] Yet one in ten never bathed at all, though most of them must have scrubbed themselves regularly, for virtually all those surveyed washed their bodies, partly or fully, every day.[64] Over the next two decades, German habits changed still more dramatically. By the later 1980s more than half now showered daily and over 10 percent did so more than once a day, all this in addition to a weekly bath.[65] Small surveys done in France and Spain at the same time revealed an even more intense devotion to clean bodies. Three quarters of French respondents took a bath at least once a week as well as a shower once daily – at minimum. The Spanish took to the tub less often but made up the difference in their commitment to a daily shower, taken by seven in eight of them.

Apart from a few surveys, we have little more than anecdotes to tell us about the changing customs of cleanliness, and they usually offer mere glimpses of personal experience. Overall they paint a picture much like the one we've just seen, of growing concern for personal hygiene, and of gradually spreading bathing and washing routines. The United States led the change but there too standards and practices varied across the continent. Western European communities soon followed the American example, with France and Italy at the far end of the queue. Slower to adopt the bathroom and the new sanitary technologies, they were slower to embrace the new culture of cleanliness as well. But by the end of the twentieth century the very concept of bodily cleanliness had been transformed everywhere in the transatlantic world. A survey by the French newspaper *Le Figaro* in 1998 made the point abundantly clear. It found that fewer than half of French adults took a daily bath or shower at a time when 70 to 80 percent of northern Europeans already did so.[66] Leaving aside the discrepancies between this and earlier studies, the importance of the comment lay in how the newspaper defined cleanliness. When condemning its countrymen as hygienic laggards it used a late-twentieth-century measure. In a climate of ever more exacting standards, the only truly clean body had become one that was fully washed once a day.

THE LAUNDRY REVOLUTION

Sometime in the early 1970s, in the small *abruzzese* town of Pacentro, a woman rinsed her laundry in the public *lavatoio* for the final time, the last village woman to do so. It's not too much to imagine that she finished her work in the gathering dark of a cold autumn day. She probably was elderly, quite possibly widowed, and almost certainly poor. A large stone basin, the *lavatoio* stood at the upper end of the town near the old medieval castle, fed by the chilly stream that rushed down from the Majella Massif looming above (Plate 10). For generations the women of Pacentro had done their laundry there, carrying their soiled loads uphill to wash, soaping and rinsing them in the cold mountain water, wringing them out with their work-worn hands and lugging them home again, damp and heavier still. Like many moments of great change, this one was unremarked and unrecorded – and far from únique. But for all that it was momentous. Everywhere in Europe, in small places like Pacentro lately brushed by modernity's hand, the village washhouse was being abandoned, the end of an ancient era of women's work. From this point on all who lived in the Western world did their laundry with machines.

No form of housework knew more remarkable change in the twentieth century than did laundry cleaning. Mechanization dramatically reduced the time and effort it demanded while new soaps and detergents improved the results it produced. The development of the automatic washing machine did more to transform the housewife's lot than any other domestic appliance. And once that goal was largely accomplished, it even encouraged the occasional husband to share what traditionally had been a woman's task. Beneath these changes lay a long history of technological development as washing machines evolved, along with the vast infrastructure on which they depended. The automatic washer also developed in tandem with a wide variety of soaps and detergents, cleaning agents adapted to both the demands of the new machines and the requirements of their users. The detergent makers themselves tutored these needs through advertising programs that promoted their products relentlessly. And in the process they became a leading influence on the idea of personal cleanliness, its meanings and its authority.

MECHANIZATION COMES TO LAUNDRY WORK

Washing machines were among a small group of household appliances that altered women's work in the home from the late nineteenth century onward. Together with refrigerators, stoves, dryers, and dishwashers, they formed the white goods revolution that mechanized housework in the second half of the twentieth century. As a far-sighted French report observed in the mid-1950s while the revolution was gathering force, "the washing machine and, to a lesser extent, the refrigerator greatly contribute to easing the burden on housewives, which given the changing customs of our time, create a significant demand in all countries from the public. The sale of these devices does not require any special effort on the part of retail organizations."[1]

By the mid-1980s, when the white goods revolution had largely run it course, the refrigerator had proved even more desirable than the washer. By then it was the most common household appliance of all.[2] But the washing machine ran a close second, a fixture in most households everywhere.

The history of the mechanical washer reaches back well into the eighteenth century, when a few inventive minds began looking for ways to reduce the laundress's toil.[3] What followed were decades of trial, error, and intermittent patenting that produced a few designs and devices. In 1840 Carl Christian Schäfer published descriptions of six, British as well as German, though whether some simply remained drawings isn't clear. But by mid-century several mechanical washers had made their way into homes on both sides of the Atlantic.[4] During the second half of the century, as industrial-scale methods and machinery emerged to meet the laundry needs of large institutions, interest in improving household equipment moved in parallel. The advertisement in Plate 11 placed by a New

York manufacturer in 1869 provides one example: a hand-powered washer with an attached wringer. The basic design persisted into the mid-twentieth century. But these first generation machines left little imprint on home laundry practices.[5] As an American guide to household management observed in 1878, "The success of Washing Machines for clothes is at yet doubtful, none having as yet been found to furnish a perfectly satisfactory substitute for washing by hand; but *clothes-wringers* perform their work far more perfectly than it can be done even by the strongest laundress."[6] Still, the manual washer had its supporters. The German company Miele, makers of cream separators and butter churns, extended its rotary technology by introducing its first mechanical washer, the Meteor, at the turn of the century. Anticipating countless washing machine testimonials to come, a satisfied owner told the family magazine *Daheim* (At Home) that she had used hers for a year and wouldn't do without it.

> Formerly, in addition to my girl I also had a washerwoman and they took almost a whole day to do the laundry together. Today it takes just my girl half a day. In 8 to 10 minutes half a machine full of laundry is really clean. Formerly I only washed the coarse linen with the washing machine since I assumed the fine linen would tear, but this is not the case because I have even washed curtains and other things in it lately.[7]

Yet several factors slowed the manual home washer's acceptance. The basic steps in laundry work were enduring: soaking, leaching, soaping, rinsing, wringing, drying, and ironing.[8] But though promoted as labour-saving devices, early models mechanized only some of the laundress's tasks. The nineteenth-century hand-powered washing machine saved a modest amount of labour at best and much of it that of servants, as the advertisement in Plate 11 and the Meteor testimonial indicate. The high cost of washers also limited their market. In addition, some of the same conditions that impeded the spread of the bathroom – lack of a running water supply, sewer connections, and easy access to hot water – also retarded their progress. Without these there might be little to choose between doing the wash with a tub and washboard or using a hand-cranked apparatus. And if these obstacles weren't enough, the problem of household space added a further deterrent. The great majority of families on both sides of the Atlantic lived in homes too small for a large piece of permanent laundry equipment. Thus, as the twentieth century dawned, the washing machine for mass consumption still lay in the distant future.

The development of the electric washer was the decisive next step. Miele was among the first to fit an electric motor to the hand-powered machine, offering various models in 1904 priced from 100 to 177 marks. Costing substantially more than the monthly food budget of a Berlin working-class household, the least expensive among them was well out of reach for most.[9] The cheapest model advertised in the American Sears and Roebuck Catalogue for 1912 equalled the monthly income of a New York unskilled worker, which put it beyond the means of most American labouring families.[10] Nevertheless, over the next two decades manufacturers placed a wide variety of electric washing machines on the household equipment market. The first Salon des arts ménagers, held in Paris in 1923, showed a dozen, the second, a year later, more than thirty.[11] For the rest of the decade the Salon annually offered displays that outlined an array of variations in washing machine design: with and without motors, with and without agitators, with and without water heaters, and with tubs on a horizontal or a vertical axis. But in spite of strong public interest, buyers lay thin on the ground. The early electric washers were costly as well as plagued with technical problems that took many years to resolve.[12] In 1928, 0.3 percent of Berlin households had an electric washing machine.[13] Two small German urban surveys a decade later revealed ownership rates under 2 percent.[14] Meanwhile in Great Britain, where sales were higher than anywhere else in Europe, fewer than 4 percent of households had a washing machine of any sort on the eve of the Second World War, and just one third of them were electric.[15] Once again the United States was the great exception (see Figure 7.1). Electric-powered washing machines found eager American buyers by the thousands in the years after their introduction just prior to the First World War. By 1929 one quarter of American households with electricity had a washing machine of some sort and over 80 percent of them were electric models.[16] Even the troubled years of depression and war failed to suppress consumer demand; by mid-century three quarters of the families in both the United States and Canada owned one, or similar models powered by small gasoline engines for communities without electricity. Levels like these weren't reached in Western Europe for

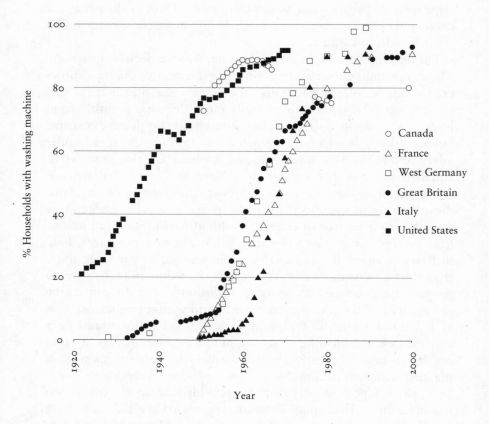

Figure 7.1 ┤ Diffusion of the washing machine
Sources: See Appendix.

another generation. A later study of American washing machine ownership by income level discovered a suggestive pattern.[17] During the mid-1930s the highest rates were found in the middle quartiles of the income distribution, the lowest at the bottom and an intermediate level at the top. By 1950, however, ownership rates were rising consistently from the bottom quartile, though they were virtually identical in the two highest groups. It seems likely that upper-income Depression families used washing machines less often because many employed servants to do their laundry, while those in the middle-income streams relied more heavily on machines because housewives themselves did the washing. But by mid-century the paid laundress was fast disappearing from the American scene and the better off washed their laundry at home like everyone else.

What accounted for the leisurely pace of the electric washing machine's acceptance, and the substantial time lag in its adoption between Western Europe and North America? The leading factor was the ability of consumers to pay for the new device. The purchasing power of European earnings lagged those in North America by two or three decades during the first half of the twentieth century.[18] As a result more Americans and Canadians could afford home appliances than Europeans. But from the 1950s onward rising incomes across the Western world made consumer durables more affordable everywhere, just as large-scale manufacturing began to reduce the cost of white goods. In Britain the price of washing machines fell by one quarter during the mid- and late 1950s alone, a prelude to further declines over the decades ahead.[19]

Still another limitation was the pace of electrification. More than a decade after Miele introduced its first electric-powered washer, at best 7 percent of households in Germany's larger cities were served by electricity, and the service remained uneven.[20] As with so many innovations that transformed domestic life, electric power arrived first in the city and in the homes of the affluent, its influence trickling down the urban hierarchy over time. Internationally the United States took the lead, with one third of households wired by the early 1920s, though by the mid-1930s the wealthier countries of Western Europe had all overtaken North America, where bringing electricity to the scattered communities and open spaces of the West was a costly challenge.[21] Still, by mid-century virtually all dwellings in northwestern Europe, the United States, and even war-damaged Germany were connected to an electrical grid, and while Italy lagged somewhat, it soon closed the gap.[22]

Electricity also took decades to transform the home.[23] Its first major use was for lighting, in part because the wiring and fixtures were easily installed. Other household applications appeared in time, but older homes often needed remodelling to include electrical wiring while new ones had to be designed to exploit its opportunities. As a result home appliances only appeared gradually.[24] Old or new, houses often had fewer receptacles for plugs than sockets for light bulbs, which meant that extension cords screwed into sockets were the easiest way to add outlets, a further inconvenience. Clearly, the dwelling itself offered electric appliances a tepid welcome well into the twentieth century. Invention offered householders new opportunities, but adoption might easily involve more than making a purchase, bringing it home, and plugging it in. Sometimes new appliances involved the added expense of home improvements.

AUTOMATION ARRIVES IN THE LAUNDRY ROOM

The first electric washers mechanized some, but only some, of the laundress's chores. Most devices included an agitator to beat the laundry in soapy water and a wringer to squeeze the rinse water out before it was hung to dry. But the remaining tasks were still done by hand. The automatic washer transformed home laundry work by embracing all of the steps of laundry work that involved water, replacing the wringer with a centrifuge. Here too the technology evolved gradually, but when it reached its maturity the automatic machine performed the full range of laundering functions, from soaking to water extraction, with little effort from the operator. Only the drying and ironing remained. The Bendix Corporation introduced the first automatic washer to the American market in 1937, but production was soon suspended to divert scarce resources to the national war effort. Peacetime manufacturing resumed in the later 1940s, an ever larger proportion of it dedicated to automatic machines. By the mid-1950s, some 40 percent of all washers in the United States were automatic models.[25] A decade later two thirds of American households had adopted them, though despite smooth talk from the appliance makers, most Canadians at the time still clung thriftily to their wringer machines.[26] Soon the automatic overtook wringer models there as well, though, and by the mid-1970s, they accounted for the great majority of washers in Canadian homes.[27]

In North America the automatic washer superseded the earlier, simpler and widely owned wringer machine. Throughout Continental Europe, however, only a small minority had adopted the first generation of electric wringers, so previous ownership didn't slow the advance of the automatics. At mid-century an electric washer of any kind could be found in fewer than 5 percent of Western Europe's homes, but less than three decades later the automatic washer honoured the great majority of households. The debut of the Bendix automatic at the Salon des arts ménagers in 1949 must have been one of the great moments in washing machine history. "The highlight of the show," wrote one observer,

> is undoubtedly an amazing American machine that soaks, washes, rinses and removes most of the water from four kilos of laundry in fifty minutes ... This efficient washing, without manual intervention, is the cinema of the Salon. All the female visitors fight for a front row seat before the bull's-eye of the machine to follow the stained color pieces in an infernal saraband that promises effortless cleaning. The spectacle is an irresistible comedy. The "ohs!," the "ahs!" burst forth from all sides when the machine starts rotating at a demonic pace, as if we were witnessing the best gags of Charlot.

The machine sold for 700 francs, the equivalent of $260 – on presentation of an import licence.[28]

The earliest automatic washer marketed in Germany, the Constructa, was built in 1951. Costing well over 2,000 DM – six times the average monthly income of a working-class family of four – it was far beyond the financial grasp of most German households, as the first automatics were everywhere in Europe.[29] Because it included a centrifuge, it needed stable foundations, and installation often required home improvements as well. During the 1960s, however, as technological problems were mastered and production increased, machine prices declined. They fell first and furthest in Italy, where a new white goods manufacturing industry seemed to appear out of thin air during the postwar *miracolo economico*, but by the middle years of the decade they were falling everywhere.[30] In 1975 the retail price of a washing machine in France was half what it had been at mid-century.[31] The number of hours an electrician had to work to buy one fell by two thirds between the early 1960s and the later 1970s.[32] More dramatically still, in 1950 a *femme de ménage* – who earned her living cleaning others' homes – would have had to work the better part of half a year to purchase an automatic washer if she could even have imagined the possibility. By 1990 she could earn the purchase price in less than two weeks. The automatic washing machine was now within the reach of all. And the moment of change could be dramatic. When Giacomo and Maria bought a new washing machine on credit in 1969 she crossed the threshold from tradition to modernity. Till then she'd done the family's wash in the canal beside their home.[33] By that time the machine had become a household fixture across Western Europe, and those who lacked one could find them in the neighbourhood laundromat, the urban small business that appeared in many communities during the 1960s. The automatic washing machine had become a common household appliance in just two decades, half the time the process had taken in Britain and North America.

THE TRANSFORMATIVE FORCE OF
THE WASHING MACHINE

The electric washing machine brought more far-reaching change to most women's lives than any other twentieth-century device. We tend to use the term "revolutionary" rather freely, but it seems appropriate here. Over time, and everywhere in the Western world, electric washers replaced physical labour with mechanical effort in laundry work, initially for the happy few and gradually for the grateful many. By the end of the century all but the deeply poor could claim the benefits of the automatic washer. Before the machine age embraced laundry work, the wealthy paid others to do their washing and sometimes those of modest means did so too. But invariably it was women who did the work: paid laundresses and unpaid housewives, old and young, frail and robust alike. The work itself was arduous. A gallon of water weighs 10 pounds (4.5 kg), and a laundry session used many of them, carried from pumps or fountains or wells, lifted onto stoves, transferred to tubs, and carted off for disposal. Wet laundry was burdensome too, and wringing it required strength. An English survey done by the Manchester City Council in 1918 concluded that washing the laundry for a family of five required ten hours a week, much of it heavy labour.[34] While washday practices varied from one place to another, in the pre-machine age, long hours and hard work were common to them all.

The electric wringer washer promised to ease this burden, the automatic washer to abolish it. And in some respects they did – or nearly so. The first generation of washers rested on earlier developments in household water supply, heating, and disposal, combining them with mechanical processes that reduced the physical demands of laundry work. But their effect on the amount of time it took to perform these tasks is less clear. Older descriptions of traditional

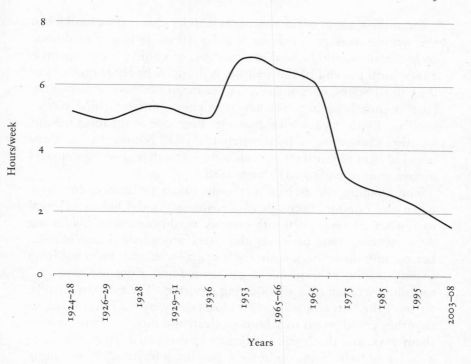

Figure 7.2 | Time spent on laundry work in the United States
Sources: See Appendix.

laundering measured work in days more often than hours. The development of time-use surveys in the 1920s and 1930s, however, made it possible to analyze daily life more precisely and explore how families spent their hours. One pioneering investigation of housework found that, if anything, the amount of time it took to do the weekly wash rose during the washing machine's first decades. American women, it indicated, spent just under six hours weekly on laundry chores in the later 1920s, when the electric wringer washer was winning broad acceptance, and slightly more than six hours in the mid-1960s, when automatic machines had begun to dominate markets[35] (Figure 7.2). This finding, in turn, informed a generation of inquiry into the history of women and housework which argued that mechanization actually increased the time and effort women spent on household chores by raising housekeeping standards – the irony of "more work for mother."[36]

But if the amount of time spent on laundry chores didn't fall when the wringer washer ruled the laundry room, it began to decline once the automatic became the machine of choice. From the mid-1960s until the end of the century, it dropped by three quarters in the United States, part of the great decline in housework during the later twentieth century. Studies in other countries yielded similar results.[37] By the 1980s what had once been one of the most tedious and time-consuming of housewifely tasks had become two or three hours of light physical effort each week – one that growing numbers of men seemed willing to share as well.

The changes themselves met only token resistance. In 1974, when the London Borough of Kensington and Chelsea planned to replace its late-nineteenth-century washhouse with a housing development, some of its regular users protested. "I can remember coming down here with my four children and queueing from five o'clock in the morning to get a tub when it opened at seven," one older woman told an inquiring reporter. "Then we'd go inside, strip off the kids and wash their clothes, dry, air and iron them, so that they could go off to school all clean and tidy. We were clean in them days, and that's still the beauty of this place. You can't scrub a collar or boil things up in these new laundryettes." It was more economical too, she added. "I can get a pramload done for less than you'd pay for a carrier bag full at the laundryettes, and they don't have the ironers and horses." "It's a right home-from-home," her friend chimed in. "You could never replace the atmosphere or the facilities. We're ever so happy."[38] But they were whistling up the wind. By the time the Kensington washerwomen raised their voices in protest their battle had long been lost. The automatic washer had become an unstoppable force.

THE METAMORPHOSIS OF CLEAN CLOTHES

The automation of home laundry work was tightly intertwined with major changes in everyday clothing, its care, its uses, and its social meanings. Long before the twentieth century clean garments held great symbolic value, as we've seen. Freshly washed clothing was prized in itself: it represented the cleanliness of the body it covered and it proclaimed the wearer's respectability. By the time mechanical washers arrived in home laundry rooms, these notions were widely shared. The upper classes enjoyed clean clothes because they paid others to do their laundry for them. But the great majority – or rather the great majority of women – faced a lifetime of toil keeping the family's clothing spotless. The history of working-class home life is filled with tales of women's washday labour, of the constant struggle to send children to school unsoiled, of the need for husbands and children to wear clean garments to preserve the family's social standing.[39] Those with low incomes usually had few clothes and even then keeping them clean demanded constant effort, the larger the family the greater the effort. The French ethnographer Yvonne Verdier noted the early-twentieth-century example of a woodcutter's daughter who wore her pinafore to school right side out for one week and inside out for the next in order to reduce her mother's laundry work.[40] Small though it was, the girl's gesture expressed an ideal that crossed all class lines. Clean clothes were the gateway to social acceptance, valued whatever the effort it took to achieve them.

At the upper end of the social ladder the symbolic meaning of clean laundry was no less important. There, frequently changed clothes and liberal use of household linens were forms of conspicuous consumption. Extravagant use of the fabrics that touched the skin – clothes, towels, serviettes, and bed linens – was commonplace in the homes of the wealthy, and it produced substantial quantities of lightly soiled laundry. The "great wash" in the great houses was great in large part because of the great amount of work these patterns of use generated: shirts and underclothes worn only once, bed clothes changed daily, table linens replaced after each meal, delicate materials demanding special care, and all this laundered weekly.[41] Generous with their use of clean clothes, the wealthy were just as generous with the labour of those who kept them clean. This prodigal consumption of well-laundered apparel had much less to do with hygiene and comfort than with display. In the highly stratified societies of the Victorian era it distinguished those who were clean through little effort of their own from those who worked hard to gain the same ends.

Toward the end of the nineteenth century, growing purchasing power, mass-produced clothing, and new forms of merchandising began to erode this pattern of status meanings in clothes and their cleaning.[42] Department stores led the way, selling inexpensive, ready-to-wear, and more easily cared-for variations of stylish clothes to lower-middle- and working-class customers. Mechanization – especially the sewing machine – launched standardized, mass-produced, inexpensive clothing based on designs that trickled down from bespoke tailors and dressmakers. The garment trades became major industries in major cities across the Western world, a sign of the growing market everywhere for popular fashions at popular prices.

Then the second half of the twentieth century saw a full-blown revolution in textiles and everyday dress, a change closely linked to the new personal cleanliness. One early development was the creation of easy-care fabrics. Garments made from these new materials needed less elaborate laundering and often required no ironing, innovations paralleled by improvements in synthetic laundry detergents.[43] From the standpoint of personal hygiene, however, still more important changes lay elsewhere. Once the preserve of the comfortable classes, fashion was gradually democratized. During the 1960s, popular clothing designs began to upset older dress conventions. These had long shared two leading characteristics: they were based on lower-class emulations of upper-class styles, and they expressed broad class identities. The emerging fashion system inverted both of these features. The centre of design innovation shifted from elite couturiers to trendy stylists who created cheap, popular, ready-to-wear, and ever-changing fashions.[44] The new clothing aesthetic emphasized youth, informality, and simplicity; its visual language was individualistic and playful. It offered buyers choices among alternative social identities and allowed them to express their individuality. Inexpensive and ephemeral, these clothes played a central role in the burgeoning consumer economy of the second half of the twentieth century. The same growth in real incomes that enabled shoppers to buy automatic washing machines also encouraged them to buy more clothing to wear – and to wash.

The new fashions were relatively trouble-free as well. Compared to those of earlier generations, designs as well as fabrics required little effort to clean. With the decline of manual labour and the growth of the service economy during the postwar decades, these new fashions met the clothing needs of the time.[45] The rapid expansion of professional, office, and clerical occupations called for lighter, more comfortable clothes, things that could be changed and laundered frequently. The growing role of women in the workforce offered an added stimulus since women often were more conscious of their dress and more aware of fashion's meanings. In many workplaces unspoken convention required a woman to change her outer clothing every day. Failure to do so might even raise idle questions about whether she'd been home the night before. As well, for both sexes dress made visual statements about an individual's professional status and ambitions. Thus, given the importance of self-presentation in professional circles, the cleanliness of garments was a deeply important matter. Workplace custom required female employees to arrive each morning in a freshly laundered blouse. And though the male business suit could be worn for many days running, the crisp white shirt had to be renewed daily too.

The transformation of undergarments was just as dramatic. By now underwear had long been universal for both sexes and only the occasional saucy actress confessed to (or boasted of) not wearing panties.[46] While underclothing had its own long design history, during the second half of the twentieth century fashion ruled lingerie as never before. Elaborate, sensual, often erotic and usually expensive underthings became everyday wear for young women as well as for the young at heart. Men's underwear never achieved the same design sophistication, but in time fashionable male briefs also came to suggest rather more than comfort and hygiene. At a time when frequent full body bathing was increasingly popular, the garments worn next to the skin claimed equal attention. The growing concern for clean outer clothing extended inward to the hidden layer, and the postwar decades saw the custom of changing underwear utterly transformed. The 1951 survey taken by *Elle* revealed that only 17 percent of Frenchwomen changed their *petites culottes* [underpants] daily.[47] As to their other dainties, 56 percent changed their bras and garter belts once a month and the remainder less often, many of them much less often. In Germany at the same time, 27 percent of women changed their *Schlüpfer* (knickers) every day.[48] But by the mid-1980s over 80 percent of French respondents changed their panties daily, and three quarters changed their brassieres at least two or three times a week, if not every day. Meanwhile three in four German women now changed their underpants daily while Spanish women were more scrupulous still.[49] By then the German male, too, had begun to alter his ways. In the later 1960s only 5 percent of them had been daily changers while two decades later the proportion had risen to almost half, slightly lower than among their French and Spanish counterparts.

During the late twentieth century, then, spotless clothes remained signs that the wearer was taking care of appearances, as people long had done. But aesthetics had replaced older notions of hygiene as the leading force behind grooming behaviour. The cleanliness of surfaces was much more important than any symbolic meanings they might have. A clean shirt or blouse expressed nothing about the state of what lay underneath. Clean bodies and underwear now spoke for themselves. Given the ease with which most clothes could be laundered and the abundance of clothes most people owned, even lightly soiled clothing was no longer acceptable for wear outside the home. What's more, for many the main goal of washing clothes had become the removal of any body odours that might lurk in their folds. Since work and play produced fewer soiled garments than ever, cleanliness now emphasized the attractive scent of fresh-smelling clothes; those with a whiff of anti-social aromas failed to meet the new criteria. Thus the heightened sensitivities of the later twentieth century invoked more demanding hygienic standards, more frequently changed clothing, and more regular laundering. Ironically, the new norms of wearing, changing, and washing clothes were not really new at all. Customs once confined to the wealthy, they'd become the common habits of the age.

THE WARS OF THE DETERGENTS

Traditional laundry soaps, the other variable in the clean clothes equation, were superseded during the 1950s and 1960s. Demand for the natural oils used to make them had strained against existing supplies for some time, encouraging manufacturers to create new formulas for their laundry cleaners. In addition, the automatic washer and the innovative textiles that they washed called for new cleaning agents. The industry met the challenge with synthetic detergents that replaced animal and vegetable fat sources with petrochemical by-products. And as these innovations emerged, the detergents industry itself was transformed. The major firms that had dominated the soap trade since the early twentieth century now deepened their research programs, broadened their product ranges, extended their global reach, and heightened their competition, promoting their products with greater vigour than ever. Their marketing campaigns were more intense as well, reinforcing accepted views about personal cleanliness and enriching public awareness of intimate hygiene.

Synthetic detergents helped solve a problem created by growing populations and rising living standards. As ever larger numbers of people owned ever greater numbers of clothes, and as ever more demanding customs required ever cleaner garments, laundry soap consumption grew decade by decade. In turn, securing the raw materials needed to manufacture soap became one of the industry's ongoing challenges. Well before the end of the nineteenth century soap makers met much of their need for natural fats from abroad, and their dependence on foreign sources grew over time. German reliance on overseas supplies was particularly high. Before the First World War its soap industry imported four fifths of its oils and fats, a need that created acute supply difficulties in wartime, and the problem persisted throughout the 1920s and 1930s.[50] Not surprisingly, then, it was German chemists who launched the search for alternative cleaning agents during the war, with British and American soap makers later joining the quest.[51] In the short run, however, their efforts yielded only modest results: chemical compounds that replaced some soaps used in textile production. The one synthetic product introduced to American and British households during the 1930s was *Dreft*, a powder used for dishes as well as delicate fabrics.

The outbreak of war in 1939 stalled efforts to find a chemically based substitute for laundry soap, but the peace that followed offered renewed opportunities. Procter & Gamble had spent the war years devising a formula for an all-purpose soapless washing product, and early in 1947 the company launched *Tide*, the first of many synthetic cleaning agents that replaced most laundry soaps over the next two decades. Following P&G's lead, Unilever and Colgate Palmolive quickly developed their own synthetic brands. Henkel, however, lagged well behind, introducing its first soapless agent only in 1959.[52] Like *Tide* these were powdered detergents with engaging names sold in colourful cardboard boxes. The packaging itself was well adapted to the new supermarket, an American postwar innovation in grocery marketing, where customers served themselves from shelves stocked with goods and paid for them at the exit. Brand name recognition and visual appeal had never been more important for sales, and the leading detergent manufacturers rose to the challenge, marketing their new wares determinedly. During the mid-1950s synthetics accounted for more than half of the American market for laundry washing agents and one third of the British as well, proportions that continued to grow over the rest of the decade. By the mid-1960s synthetic detergents had all but replaced soap powders everywhere in Europe except Britain.[53]

The four leading multinational soap makers of the interwar years dominated the synthetic detergent industry from the outset. They had access to the financial and human capital needed to develop new products, as well as the capacity to manufacture, improve, promote, and distribute them locally, regionally, and globally. Yet no single firm dominated everywhere. In 1960 P&G controlled well over half of the American laundry detergent market, with all but 10 percent of the remainder shared between its two major rivals.[54] At the same time 90 percent of the British trade was split almost evenly between Unilever and P&G. During the later 1970s in the major continental markets, Henkel controlled 40 percent of German sales, while Unilever and C-P shared 20 percent and 10 percent respectively. The Italian trade was rather more fragmented, with several smaller national firms sharing almost half of the detergent business then dominated by Henkel and P&G, while in France the big international companies controlled 90 percent of the sector. Overall the four major firms controlled over 80 percent of detergent sales in the European Community by the later 1970s, and Unilever had become the leading vendor of detergents worldwide, with more than 20 percent of the global trade.

The new synthetic detergents offered three main advantages over soap-based cleaning agents. Because they were produced from petroleum derivatives or coal tar fractions instead of natural fats, they were manufactured from a wider range of raw materials.[55] Synthetics also worked more effectively in hard water. Soaps used in hard water produce a deposit that clings to laundry items, and over time it accumulates, leaving unsightly stains and unhappy consumers. Synthetic detergents yield a cleaner hard water wash. In addition, the soap deposits themselves were signs of inefficiency in the laundering process, a waste that didn't occur when synthetics were used. For this reason a given amount of synthetic detergent could clean a larger amount of laundry than an equivalent quantity of soap, and the efficiency increased with the hardness of the water. In Britain, where the hard water problem had long existed, the average washing power of 1 pound of synthetic detergent was the same as that of 1.5 pounds of laundry soap.[56] Thus synthetics solved one of the laundress's chronic problems and saved her money in the process. Ironically, while they cleaned the laundry, synthetic detergents also dirtied the environment. First-generation synthetics contained ingredients that didn't fully degrade after use, leaving residues that created sewage treatment problems and even caused rivers and tap water to foam. More serious still, the phosphates included in synthetic formulas encouraged the rapid growth of algae in waters fed by sewage effluents, creating major environmental problems. Government regulation ultimately addressed the problem by forcing the detergent makers to change their product formulas.[57]

If the soap trade had been intensely competitive since the late nineteenth century, the emerging detergents industry was more competitive still. The industry itself remained highly concentrated, with each of the big multinational firms commanding the substantial resources needed to do battle with their major rivals. Detergent manufacturing produced high volumes of low-cost goods for a broad, stable market demand, and competition in the industry reflected these circumstances. Selling price itself was often not the determining factor in consumer choice. A British government study from the mid-1960s concluded that customers weren't notably price conscious and that small price variations had little impact on consumption patterns.[58] For the most part competition rested instead on product innovation and sales promotion, the two main tools used by the industry giants to encourage brand loyalty and increase their market share.

The first generation of mass-marketed washing products consisted of heavy-duty synthetic detergents for general household laundry chores. But before long each of the dominant firms offered a cluster of cleaning products for various washing needs, developed in competition with rivals and sometimes to complement – or even overtake – one of their own brands. P&G's Tide soon begot C-P's Fab and Unilever's Surf, as well as a second P&G product, Cheer.[59] In their quest for market leadership the major companies used new products as a vehicle for innovation, some of them successful, some of them not. They also innovated by improving their existing brands, usually with great fanfare. After Unilever turned its leading soap-based laundry agent Persil into a synthetic detergent, it introduced eight major improvements to the brand between the early 1960s and the mid-1970s.[60]

Cultural and technological factors also drove the dynamic of product development during the first decades of the synthetics. Laundering customs differed from one country to another and the detergent makers responded by developing formulations adapted to various national demands.[61] The normal temperature of wash water offers an example. North American washing machines used water heated to 60 degrees Centigrade by the home water heating system, and detergents had to function optimally at that temperature. Meanwhile Europeans commonly washed their laundry at 90 degrees and their machines usually included a heating element, calling for detergents that worked best at high temperatures. In time grocers' shelves everywhere offered detergents for delicate fabrics, low-sudsing detergents for front-loading washers, high- and low-temperature detergents, hard and soft water detergents, all adapted to consumer preferences. The industry leaders continued to place their greatest emphasis on their heavy-duty detergents, however. These were "the heart of the soap business," accounting for more than 60 percent of the trade.[62] As well they were the industry's most hotly contested terrain, the ground on which they fought their major advertising battles and defined popular views about cleanliness.

SELLING LAUNDRY CLEANERS

Advertising was the weapon of choice in the wars of the detergents. Each of the big manufacturers spent huge sums promoting its products, and they ranked among the leading advertisers everywhere in the postwar world. In this respect they simply followed the well-worn path trod by their forefathers. P&G, Lever Brothers, and Colgate had been aggressive publicists during the later nineteenth century, and Henkel had joined their ranks soon after 1900. From that point onward mass advertising campaigns remained a defining characteristic of the industry, a basic element in the business strategy of every firm, as each committed itself to the struggle for supremacy in laundry cleaners. Their primary goals were clear and simple: to persuade consumers to buy their products and to protect and strengthen their brands.[63]

Advertising expenses in the soap and detergent trades were higher than those in most other manufacturing industries. According to one estimate, from 1950 to 1955 the leading British firms annually spent between 5 percent and 11 percent of receipts to promote their new household detergents.[64] Another British study during the mid-1960s suggested that advertising alone cost Unilever and P&G 12 percent of the net selling price of their cleaning products while other promotional expenses added a further 6 percent.[65] Though these amounts fell somewhat in the 1970s, they remained high by British manufacturing standards.[66] More than a few critics argued that such expenses were extravagant, that prices would be lower if the makers reduced their advertising outlays. The detergent makers, however, claimed that the expenditures were needed given the intense competition in retail markets and in addition they offered value to economic life more generally. As the chairman of Unilever put it in 1951, by sustaining the demand needed to reduce production costs, advertising made the benefits of mass production possible.[67] It also helped producers recoup the high cost of developing new products and bringing them to market.

Everywhere in the Western world before the Second World War most advertising appeared in print, mainly in newspapers and mass circulation magazines, and the soap makers relied heavily on them.[68] P&G was the soap trade's largest magazine advertiser in the United States during the 1920s, and its major competitors were active publicists too.[69]

Between the wars the big firms also dabbled in radio and cinema advertising, testing the commercial possibilities of the new media. P&G took the American lead by sponsoring radio dramas, a new form of entertainment borne of commercial broadcasting. The term "soap opera" soon attached itself to these programs, sponsored as they were by the major soap makers. Hugely popular from their inception, they became icons of American mass culture during the Depression. Meanwhile some European manufacturers invested in cinema advertising. From 1927 to 1939 Henkel produced ten films about Persil, including one in 1931 that included an early soundtrack (*Drei Minuten für die Hausfrau*; 3 Minutes for the Housewife), and another, a feature-length film from the same period, that starred two prominent German actors (*Wäsche, Wasche, Wohlergehen*; Laundry, Washing, Well-being).[70]

Still, nothing in the interwar years approached the intense campaigns that the detergent makers launched in the early television age. The detergent wars were at their peak when the new medium's transformative power was also at its height. TV offered advertisers broader coverage than they had ever known at cost efficiencies they could only have imagined, and they seized these opportunities eagerly. The rapid growth of the laundry detergent market went hand in hand with the rapid spread of television, the two locked in a synergetic relationship. The detergent makers wanted access to the consuming masses that the broadcasters offered and the broadcasters wanted the high fees that the detergent makers paid. It was a marriage made in marketing heaven.

From the advertisers' perspective, the impact of television depended primarily on audience size. Size was mostly a matter of the number of homes with television sets, and television spread more quickly than any other home appliance throughout the modern Western world. Yet substantial national differences also marked the process. In North America the 1950s were television's decade. By mid-century a TV set graced 1 American household in 4, up from 1 in 200 at the war's end, and by 1960, 9 out of 10 homes possessed one. Dissemination was almost as rapid in Canada at the time. By the early 1960s the television set was the most common consumer durable in the North American home.[71] In Western Europe mass ownership lagged by a decade and more, though the pace of diffusion picked up during the 1960s, and by the early 1970s the great majority of families from the North Sea to the Mediterranean also possessed one.[72] Once a luxury good, the TV set, like the washing machine, had become just another household appliance.

Access to this growing forest of screens also depended on national broadcast policies, and these varied widely. In the English-speaking world, private commercial broadcasting dominated the American airwaves from the outset. Advertising fees paid for programming costs, and daily broadcast schedules invariably included a rich harvest of commercials. The investment itself was immense. In 1966 P&G, C-P, and Lever Brothers ranked first, sixth, and eleventh among the top 125 advertisers in America with a combined outlay of $430 million, most of it spent on television.[73] As one business journalist noted at the time, "from early morning until late evening there is scarcely a moment when some viewers somewhere – usually a great many of them – are not being exposed to a Colgate, Lever Brothers, or Procter & Gamble commercial."[74] In Britain the state broadcaster (BBC) accepted no advertisements, so prospective advertisers had to await the new Independent Television Network (ITV), established in 1955. From the outset the soap and detergent makers were major program sponsors. Unilever bought advertising time on ITV's opening night, and the company remained its leading advertiser for the next thirty years, promoting its full range of consumer goods, among them its washing products.[75]

Elsewhere in Europe the state took the early lead in the television industry, creating public broadcasting agencies supported by user fees and government subsidies. Initially advertising played only a small role, if any at all, in their daily programming, leaving the makers of things to promote their goods in print. In time, however, governments relaxed their rules and permitted state broadcasters to accept limited advertising. They also allowed commercial broadcasting companies into TV's charmed circle, yielding to pressure from potential advertisers eager for access to its vast markets. Still, on the continent commercial television arrived a generation later than it did in Britain.

Before 1968 television advertising was unknown in France except in those areas close to international borders reached by signals from foreign commercial broadcasters.[76] Then, in that tumultuous year of popular unrest, public TV was opened to limited advertising – a gesture that surely owed nothing to student protests. Initially, it was confined to seven minutes a day and programming restrictions barred many goods. Detergents, soaps, and beauty products were authorized a year later. But the publicity floodgates didn't open until 1984, when France finally permitted commercial broadcasting. German television offered an equally uninviting environment for advertising until private broadcasting arrived in 1980s.[77] Similarly, when national television transmission began in Italy in 1954 commercial announcements were prohibited. Three years later the Italian broadcasting authority began to air *Carosello*, a ten-minute advertising program broadcast every evening but governed by highly restrictive policies. The regulations reflected the conservatism of Italy's postwar political elites and the deep suspicion of consumerism embedded in Catholic thought of the time. Even so, *Carosello* quickly proved a huge success, and in time it became one of the most widely viewed programs in Italian television history. But despite its popularity, advertisers didn't gain broad access to national viewing audiences until Silvio Berlusconi established Italy's first private television network in 1980.[78]

MESSAGES AND CONSEQUENCES

The wars of the detergents were at their height throughout the 1950s and 1960s, the years when commercial television became a mass phenomenon in North America and Britain. By the early 1960s the big American detergent makers were spending 90 percent of their advertising budgets on television. With much less opportunity to exploit its possibilities, however, their European counterparts still relied heavily on print.[79] Newspapers and periodicals accounted for over 60 percent of all advertising expenses in Italy throughout the 1960s and early 1970s.[80] Despite the differing media, however, the battles weren't any less strenuous. A steady barrage of publicity for Tide and Fab, Omo and Dash, Bold and Rinso, All and Cheer confronted viewers and readers at every turn.

In fact there was little to distinguish the many detergents from one another, though their publicists claimed that each was unique. The typical ad singled out a brand's leading features and praised its exclusive merits. This was the foundation on which brand loyalty was built. Creating an exclusive product image was a universal marketing practice and advertisers crafted a distinct identity for each of the leading laundry detergents. As the products changed over time their images evolved as well, highlighting innovations and improvements that supposedly made fine detergents even better. At best these strategies underscored the subtle distinctions that distinguished washing agents from one another. Some emphasized their labour-saving features, others their scientific advances, still others their fresh clean odour or their whiter whites and brighter brights, while all laid claim to their superior cleaning power.

Whatever features set one apart from the others, the leitmotif "white" ran through laundry detergent advertising. A detergent's ability to produce a pure, white wash was the universal measure of its value. For millennia white had had deep symbolic meanings in Western culture, with associations ranging from truth and innocence to chastity and death. In the realm of laundry work white evoked purity and cleanliness, clean clothing most of all. By the television age white had held a long and continuous place in the history of personal cleanliness. The seventeenth-century concern for well-laundered white linen underclothes, and the related notion that personal hygiene was largely a matter of changing one's linen, still occupied an important place in the great chain of beliefs about the wider meaning of freshly washed garments. So did the work of the women who laboured to keep their family linens white – and preserve their own reputations as good housekeepers – before the washing machine transformed home laundry work in the twentieth century. P&G's all-purpose Ivory Soap, introduced in 1879, was one of the earliest brands to trade on white's associations with cleanliness and purity.[81] A generation later Henkel used it extensively to advertise Persil through its *Weiße Dame* (white lady) promotions

(Plate 12).[82] The woman in question was young and middle-class, simply but stylishly dressed in white and holding a package of Persil. Among Henkel's most enduring campaign icons, she appeared in various forms on posters and in print from the early 1920s to the later 1950s. While she always reflected the latest in feminine fashions, her youth and freshness remained intact, and over time her appearance changed little. The one thing she never seemed to touch, though, was the laundry itself.

During the postwar years, print-based detergent campaigns abandoned feminine elegance and gentility in favour of down-to-earth personalities and domestic scenes. Advertisements featured the housewife as laundress, a role she invariably played with common sense and good humour.[83] Detergent commercials on television used the same devices and redoubled claims about the whiteness produced by the brand being advertised. An early Carosello ad featured Bianco and Bianchissimo, two attractive young women dressed in identical frilly white dresses, who introduced a promotion for P&G's Olà that declared "OLÀ fa il bucato bianco ... bianchissimo!" (OLÀ makes the laundry white ... whitest!).[84] By the later 1970s whiteness by itself had come to identify some detergent brands. As one historian of British advertising noted, "'Persil whiteness,' thanks to what television had invested it with, had become what advertising people began to call 'a property' ... a totality by which a brand's values are communicated."[85] In every language competing products promised to make laundry not only white but whiter than ever, the whitest possible, even whiter than white, and certainly a whiter white than any competitor could produce.[86] But as for proof, viewers had to rely on a manufacturer's claims and advertising rhetoric. Technological limitations made it impossible to display small differences in shades of white on most television sets. Accepting claims about a detergent's cleaning power remained an act of faith.

Televised detergent ads often consisted of short domestic dramas in which a knowledgeable woman told a naive relative or friend about the superior merits of a particular brand. When the latter was presented with visible evidence, she was immediately convinced. Many commercials also featured an authority figure, an "expert" – usually male and dressed in a lab coat or a suit and tie – to affirm the truth of the claim.[87] On the whole, detergent advertisements were simple, repetitive, and unimaginative. Winston Fletcher, a prominent British advertising executive during the last third of the twentieth century, frankly admitted that they were "archetypes of distasteful advertising: brazen, patronizing, charmless, employing seemingly specious science, often comparing their brands with an apparently bogus 'Brand X,' always derided, always good for a comic joke."[88] Many in Britain shared Fletcher's distaste. In 1960 antagonized viewers prevailed on the Independent Television Authority, the agency responsible for supervising the ITV network, to limit the number of commercials for laundry cleaning products to one per hour.[89]

Yet TV became the great teacher of the twentieth century. As the Italian critic Aldo Grasso noted, "television is the most formidable instrument of the modernization of society and culture. Thanks to it we learn to communicate, to monitor personal hygiene, to dress, to furnish [our homes] and to conserve food better."[90] *Carosello*'s great popularity speaks to the powerful attractions of the medium, notably in Italy but elsewhere more generally. The program had a particular effect on women, revealing not just a world of labour-saving devices but also one of health and beauty and femininity.[91] It became an authoritative guide to the new consumerism as Italy passed from postwar privation to fast-rising living standards.[92] The impact of television on material life may have been more sharply etched in Italy than elsewhere because the transformation occurred quickly and in a context of relative deprivation. Consumerism emerged earlier and more gradually in North America and most of northern Europe. But the pedagogical function of television was broadly similar everywhere. TV taught the lessons of consumption – personal hygiene among them – and its students proved highly receptive.

More probing analysis revealed still deeper meanings. In 1954 the French literary theoretician Roland Barthes cut his semiotic teeth on publicity for laundry cleaners. In one of a series of short comments on French popular culture he explored the significance of terms used to describe the cleansing actions of two popular washing agents, probing the meanings and uses of language intended to sell products. Barthes rested his analysis on two Unilever brands: Omo, a synthetic detergent, and Persil, at that point still a laundry soap, at a moment when synthetics were fast overtaking soap powders in France. He drew no distinction between the two on these grounds, nor was he concerned with how they actually functioned. His sole interest was in the language used to describe the two products. "In the *Omo* imagery," he noted, "dirt is a diminutive enemy, stunted and black, which takes to its heels from the fine immaculate linen at the sole threat of the judgement of *Omo*." "'*Persil* whiteness,'" on the other hand,

> bases its prestige on the evidence of a result; it calls into play vanity, a social concern with appearances, by offering for comparison two objects, one of which is *whiter than* the other. Advertisements for *Omo* also indicate the effect of the product (and in superlative fashion, incidentally), but they chiefly reveal its mode of action; in doing so they involve the consumer in a kind of direct experience of the substance, make him the accomplice of a liberation rather than the mere beneficiary of a result.[93]

The language promoting Omo, Barthes continued, included two value-laden terms: deep and foamy. Deep referred to recesses in the laundered objects where dirt presumably lurked and, by extension, to associations with luxuriant fabrics possessing enough depth that they could enfold and caress the body. Foam held intimations of comfort, abundance, happiness, and even "a certain spirituality." The various overtones detected by Barthes thus transformed detergents from mere agents of cleanliness to pathways toward life-enriching experiences. Most likely, few homemakers would have followed Barthes's reasoning even if they had read it. The millions addressed by detergent advertising were far more concerned with a laundry cleaner's results than its abstruse cultural meanings. Yet Barthes's comments fell close to the tree. Though he did not mention it, beneath the surface of detergent advertising lay powerful symbolic meanings about femininity, domesticity, family life, and social status. Clean clothing expressed a housewife's home management skills, it spoke to the well-ordered life of her house, and it established her family's claims to respectability. All of these would be enhanced, a detergent commercial implied, if she used the brand it promoted.

Ever more ubiquitous, ever more insistent, advertising became ever more persuasive throughout the twentieth century. The central purpose of publicity was to inform prospective consumers about a product or service and encourage them to buy it. An educational tool, it sought to instruct as well as persuade. Laundry detergent advertising informed housekeepers about the need for regular washing, the routines to be followed, and the standards they should expect of the results. It encouraged them to use the best available washing

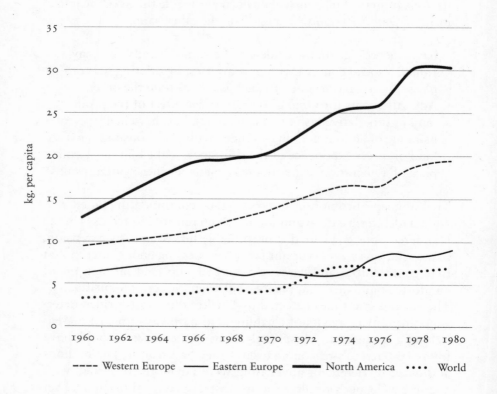

Figure 7.3 | Global soap and detergent consumption
Source: See Appendix.

products and to judge for themselves which products those might
be. And it sought to convince them that one product was better than
all the rest. Thus, beyond their commercial persuasions, detergent
advertisements shaped common beliefs about cleanliness and personal hygiene.

The relationship between advertising and consumer behaviour is
a thorny issue. No simple causal link between them seems to exist
though the question has long been debated.[94] On their part, though,
the detergent makers considered advertising a key to their success,
and they poured vast sums of money into publicity campaigns year
after year. The evidence of the time seemed to support them, as well,
because year after year their sales increased. Still, we shouldn't assume
that ambitious promotions alone sold more soap and detergent with

every passing year. By the mid-twentieth century the soap merchants were preaching to the converted. Long before the detergent wars, the value of clean clothing and bodies had won broad acceptance across the Western world. Addressing these embedded notions with their messages, the detergent makers refashioned older understandings to suit the circumstances of the age. By this time too, the commercial stakes were high, for their potential markets now numbered in the hundreds of millions. The only broad, comparative data on consumption we have are summarized in Figure 7.3, which groups soaps and detergents together with other cleaning agents. By 1980 laundry detergents alone amounted to over 80 percent of the total in most places, and therefore they dominated the consumption curves in the graph. During the 1960s and 1970s per capita soap and detergent consumption doubled in Western Europe and grew two-and-a-half-fold in North America, though it rose little elsewhere. Globally the rich world pulled away from the rest at that time. From the 1980s onward the growth of consumption began to slow. But by then the industry, its institutions, practices, and educational force, had assumed something close to worldwide dominance.[95] And Westerners, by far the greatest consumers of soaps and laundry cleaners, had come to enjoy a culture of cleanliness that bordered on luxury.

CLEANLINESS AND THE BEAUTY BUSINESS

What sense is brushing your teeth, or bathing, or using deodorant in a peasant society? But in the new society it makes sense because the dirty person, the stink, provokes revulsion in others, because being dirty and smelling bad are experienced as aggressive behaviours, as an escape from the duties of living together, of mutual respect, of civil self-restraint, and therefore as an indignity. The young women of peasant society in transition, at home or as immigrants, immediately grasped this meaning of consumption and they did it by skipping over virile feminism ...

Almost all modern hygiene products (toothpaste, razors, shaving cream, underwear, etc.) lie in the same area, and in many respects the outer clothing does as well. The use of soap, toothpaste, and hygienic equipment (the bathtub or the shower, for example) are never accepted without inner conflict and the voluntary overcoming of resistance. More than emulation, their acceptance in the new society involves the awareness that whoever does not use them is not as "a civil man should be."[1]

Writing in 1964, the sociologist Francesco Alberoni surveyed the postwar Italian world of personal hygiene, with its endless array of consumer goods. Many of the products he noted were new, at least in their commercial forms. While toilet soaps and dental cleaners had long histories of their own, they only became items of mass consumption in Italy during the 1950s and 1960s. As to practices, those Alberoni observed no longer drew their authority from the conviction that cleanliness was an inherent good, or from the belief that it offered the route to better health. Nor did they distinguish the respectable from the rest as they'd done in earlier times. What now encouraged cleanliness was the quality of an individual's personal relations. In order to attain full membership in society one must look, smell, and *be* clean, and in order to do so one had to buy and use the products that promised cleanliness.

Alberoni wrote with Italians in mind, and in matters concerning the clean body, Italy lagged a little behind other Western nations in some important respects. It remained rural longer, and its rural population poorer, than most of northern Europe and North America. This was one reason why, in the century after unification, it also endured one of the largest outflows of emigrants in modern European history. In addition, its service and manufacturing sectors developed slower and later than in most of the Western world; as a result, a flourishing consumer economy emerged in Italy only after the Second World War.[2] When it did, however, change occurred quickly and habits that had appeared more gradually in other countries spread rapidly there. The swiftness of this transition etched Italian "before and after" contrasts particularly clearly, sharpening the differences Alberoni noted as he watched these developments spread. Still, the Italian example was anything but unique. The reinvention of the clean body as a commodity was unfolding everywhere in the Western world, though elsewhere the process occurred in a more leisurely fashion.

This latest version of cleanliness emphasized products more than practices. As hygiene became largely a matter of self-presentation it quickly linked itself with the expanding world of toiletries and cosmetics. The beauty trades had had a long history in the Western world and an equally long association with wealth and rank. But they too began to feel democratic impulses toward the end of the nineteenth century and from that point on their consumer base expanded. Now beauty could be had by all and it could be purchased too; in the words of the American makeup magnate Charles Revson cosmetics offered "hope in a jar."[3] Hope to women most of all. A growing profusion of soaps and creams, colourants and sprays, lotions and perfumes all promised to enhance their natural beauty and suspend the aging process. New products and marketing strategies enticed new buyers, and retail receipts grew briskly, first and foremost in the United States. In 1950 American sales of toiletries and cosmetics were almost twenty times what they had been at the beginning of the First World War, and the industry continued to expand quickly from that point onward. Between 1950 and 1976 the global beauty trade increased sixfold, though North America and Western Europe remained by far the largest markets.[4]

The sustained growth of the beauty business was tightly intertwined with the metamorphosis of notions about beauty itself. Throughout the twentieth century, shifting ideas of beauty – largely feminine, though far from exclusively so – transformed personal habits and consumer behaviour. The new personal care industry (as the toiletries and cosmetics sector came to be known) was based on ideal conceptions of human physical form – body shape and line, facial type, and standards of grooming most of all – but the fact that few could attain these goals lost much of its significance over time. Films, television, and mass circulation magazines proposed the dominant standards of beauty, standards drawn from the world of commercial consumption, and they proposed them to all. As Umberto Eco observed, "the mass media are totally democratic, they offer the model of beauty for those whom nature has already provided with aristocratic grace and for the proletarian girl of shapely form … for those who cannot possess the beauty of a Maserati, there is the suitable beauty of the Mini Morris."[5]

By the later twentieth century popular opinion eagerly embraced male and female forms of beauty and expressed them in highly personal forms. Each individual had their own unique beauty, to accent and embellish as they wished. Beauty had become a universal attribute and a matter of personal choice. It articulated a deep aestheticization of everyday life, one that emphasized the value of beauty in, of, and for itself: beauty as an intrinsic good.[6] And it could be enhanced by the bounty of soaps, shampoos, and toothpastes that the modern consumer economy offered so generously to all.

BEAUTY SOAPS

Toilet soaps offer us a window on the links between cleanliness and beauty – or, to put it more precisely, on the growing certainty that cleanliness was the pathway to beauty. The beauty trades offered costly soaps long before the Industrial Age, products of the perfumer's arts created for women of wealth and standing. But from the mid-nineteenth century onward a growing number of manufacturers began to make refined soaps for a growing middle-class market.[7] During the later 1860s the pioneer British and Austrian dermatologists Erasmus Wilson and Heinrich Auspitz warmly endorsed their benefits.[8] As Wilson put it, "Soap is to the skin what wine is to the stomach, a generous stimulant; and a solvent to boot of the surface which holds the dirt." Soaps like these remained much too costly for the ordinary consumer, however. At two francs, the small Turkish tablet on display at the Paris Universal Exhibition of 1867 cost well over half a day's wage for a city laundress, someone who spent long working hours up to her elbows in soapy water.[9] Still, as bourgeois living standards rose everywhere during the second half of the century, toilet soaps began to find a broader public. They offered a milder, gentler alternative to the all-purpose household soaps sold by the big industrial producers.

Before the end of the century, small and mid-sized firms in perfumes and cosmetics manufactured most toilet soaps. Rather than making their own, many bought a prepared base soap from a larger supplier and refined it further before adding their own perfumes and colourings.[10] For the most part toilet soap manufacturing remained small-scale and decentralized, though a few labels were mass produced and commanded larger markets. Pears Soap was one, made and distributed in Britain and North America from the 1880s onward. Another was Palmolive, introduced by the American B.J. Johnson Soap Company in 1898, whose sales increased so dramatically after a successful advertising campaign in 1911 that the company renamed itself after its leading product.[11] In time it too became a bestselling toilet soap on both sides of the Atlantic. Meanwhile many small and mid-sized firms in France, Germany, and Italy made similar soaps for their home markets and occasionally for export as well, though none on the same scale as the largest British and American firms of the time.[12] In Germany alone by the end of the nineteenth century, middle-class consumers could choose from more than one hundred fine soaps, with charming floral names like Rose or Violet or Lilac.[13] Some of the emerging soap giants with wider product ranges also entered the trade, but the quantities they produced were small compared to the volumes of household soap they sold. Toilet soaps accounted for only a small fraction of total soap production everywhere until well into the twentieth century.[14] On the eve of the Depression they made up less than 4 percent of Lever's production and only 5 percent of all soaps manufactured in Britain. In the United States at the same time they amounted to 10 percent of national soap output.[15]

Still, Lever Brothers, Procter & Gamble, and Colgate sold a variety of toilet soaps, brands often acquired while absorbing smaller business rivals, though initially none were market leaders. Profit margins on refined soaps were much higher than on all-purpose soaps, and for that reason if no other, the larger manufacturers were drawn to the business.[16] According to the memoirs of a retired Unilever executive,

> one of the most prominent operators in this field at the time was Vinolia which the Old Man [W.H. Lever] bought in 1906. Vinolia had an enormous range of products, soundly based for the luxury trade at which it aimed, on really good perfumes and splendid packaging. At the peak of its toilet soap range was Vinolia Vestal Soap, believed to be used by the Queen, retailing at 15/- (75p) per tablet (bath size) which was cradled in white satin in a gold lettered, hand-made, oval box. The second step down was a mere 12/6 (62½p) per tablet – Otto of Roses, supplies of which certainly did go to the Palace. In this bath soap range, but at a more modest price, was Boracic and Cold Cream Soap which ... in my recollection shared with Lifebuoy and Pears Soap the distinction of providing the pervading smell of respectable Edwardian bathrooms.[17]

On its hundredth anniversary in 1906 the Colgate Company alone sold 160 different toilet soap varieties.[18] But consumed by their rivalry in laundry soaps and domestic cleaners, none of the major firms paid much attention to the body care market at the time, and the situation remained largely unchanged until the mid-1920s, when all three began to mass-market a scented toilet soap bar. Lever introduced Lux to Americans in 1925 and to the British public three years later; P&G followed with Camay in 1926; Colgate acquired Palmolive through a corporate merger in 1928.[19] Each company then owned a major toilet soap brand, another weapon in their ongoing struggle for supremacy in soaps and detergents. Meanwhile Henkel, its business disrupted by the Depression and the National Socialist and early postwar years, trailed its international rivals by a quarter century, introducing its first toilet soap Fa only in 1954.[20] As a latecomer it lagged badly in market share, except in its home territory.

The three titans' entry into the fine soap trade greatly intensified competition in the field. The major firms were formidable opponents, already well established in most national markets, with long experience in product promotion and far greater financial resources than the small toilet soap makers. Over time they came to dominate the international fine soap business as they already did in household soaps and soon would do in synthetic detergents. Here too advertising was key to their growth. But by the 1920s the early leaders in toilet soaps also had years of experience in innovative product promotion, and they offered spirited competition.

Whatever the specific claims advertisers made about their products' merits, the ongoing industry dialogue focused on toilet soap's role in enhancing feminine beauty. From the outset the industry directed its message to middle-class women – not the affluent and well placed, who could well afford costly cosmetics – but those who aspired to such luxuries. It promoted toilet soap as an inexpensive beauty aid, a fitting alternative for those who found more exclusive products beyond their reach. When using formal works of art in their advertisements Pears made this claim indirectly, associating their product with cultivated middle-class interests.[21] More commonly, early ads for toilet soap – Pears included – appealed directly to feminine sensibilities, to concerns about beauty and self-representation. The attractive woman quickly became the leading motif in toilet soap advertising, though the specific nature of her attractions varied widely.[22] Some depictions revealed a pretty woman in a domestic setting, absorbed in her toilette. Others represented her as an erotic object: nearly nude or thinly veiled, bathing or reclining provocatively: languid and sensuous, remote but accessible. Art Nouveau, the prevailing graphic design language of the period, clothed femininity in curvilinear forms that muted the aggressive sensuality of nudity and near nudity while still proposing suggestiveness. Images like these probably appealed to male and female tastes in different ways, men drawn by allusions to sensual pleasures, women by hints of their empowerment as seductresses.

The American advertising campaign for Woodbury's Facial Soap embodied an important next step in toilet soap marketing.[23] Druggist and self-proclaimed dermatologist John H. Woodbury introduced the soap in 1885, offering it as a treatment for skin complaints. After some initial success, however, sales began to falter and Woodbury sold the brand to the Andrew Jergens Company in 1900. Jergens tried to breathe new commercial life into the product, again with some short-term success, but before the decade was out its sales had slumped once more. The company then responded by increasing its advertising outlay for the brand, but without a clear promotional strategy, the gesture had little effect. Then in 1910 it placed the Woodbury's account with the advertising agency J. Walter Thompson.

Thompson assigned the account to its Women's Editorial Department, which surveyed the soap's retail distribution, analyzed its healing properties, recruited experts to endorse the product, and interviewed its main customer: the female consumer. They then devised a sales campaign that combined cleansing therapies recommended by prominent dermatologists with emotional enticements that emphasized beauty, romance, and sex. The soap was packaged and sold with instructions about its use in skin treatments and marketed with the slogan "A Skin You Love To Touch." Placed in mass circulation American women's magazines, its ads usually featured a handsome romantic couple, touching, caressing, or embracing.

Though the slogan itself implied male desire, the ads were intended for the female reader, encouraging her to enhance her beauty in order to invite male attention. They were based on a curious reciprocity of wants: a man's active desire for a woman and a woman's more passive desire to be desired by a man.[24] In developing this campaign the Thompson agency used new market research techniques to support established advertising practices, employing tools from the social sciences to revive the fortunes of Woodbury's Facial Soap. The results exceeded all expectations. From a low in 1910, Woodbury sales increased steadily over the next decade. By 1921 they had grown more than twentyfold.[25] According to a Thompson agency historian, the Woodbury campaign was one of the firm's ten greatest achievements, no small feat in a company that then was – as it remains today – the largest advertising agency in the United States.[26]

Though clear differences marked the Palmolive, Lux, and Camay advertising campaigns, the publicity for them featured the same broad themes. The three brands placed a heavy accent on luxury, sophistication, and beauty, each in its own way. Well before Lux and Camay joined the contest in the mid-1920s, Palmolive's marketing stressed its value as a refined aid to beauty, and the narratives created for the newcomers told much the same story – again and again.[27] Each was a mild and gentle soap, each beneficial for the skin, each not just a soap but an effective beauty treatment. The three firms also relied on testimonials from specialists and luminaries to promote their products. Other soap makers had long since pioneered the technique, and by the early twentieth century, celebrity endorsements had become a well-established advertising practice.[28]

But they achieved new heights in the age of mass celebrity created by Hollywood and the American film industry. Films reached far larger audiences than any previous entertainments, and film stars enjoyed a far wider fame than any previous entertainers. As a result their value as product advocates was far greater too. And although many soap makers used public figures to endorse their products, none did so more ambitiously, or with greater success, than Lever Brothers did with its new toilet soap, Lux.

Lever Brothers created Lux bar soap in 1923 to follow the success of its laundry soap flakes of the same name, introduced two decades earlier.[29] Lux was a white, lightly perfumed soap cake wrapped in a simple, attractive package. It was first sold in the United States in 1925 and introduced across the Western world and beyond over the next decade. In time it became a global brand, the bestselling bar soap worldwide, offered as a luxury but sold at a popular price. Well before the product launch, Lever turned to the Thompson agency to develop a marketing strategy. At first Thompson devised themes that drew on the same features ascribed to its main competing brands: gentleness and elegance, subtlety and beauty. They also emphasized Lux's inspiration – based on the finest French perfumed soaps, refined products of Parisian *haute couture*, and far more expensive than Lux. But while early sales figures were promising, these were easily surpassed when Thompson introduced a celebrity endorsement campaign featuring female Hollywood stars. Between 1925 and 1928 Thompson sent cases of Lux to 425 prominent actresses and received statements from 414, leading the agency to boast that "9 out of 10 screen stars use Lux soap."[30] Their testimonials all emphasized that a beautiful skin was a woman's greatest asset and that Lux soap would keep her skin fresh, young, and lovely. And the slogan proved durable. Decades later it was still in use across the Unilever empire.

Through their energetic sales campaigns the leading toilet soap makers thus used feminine beauty, real and aspirational, to sell their products. In turn they used soap and cleanliness to define ideal feminine beauty.[31] Cleanliness was no longer just a matter of health and appearance. It had come to distinguish one of the fundamentals of femininity. The two concepts – soap and beauty – became so tightly intertwined that Unilever relabelled Lux a "beauty soap" during the mid-1950s, and over the coming decades the term crept into everyday speech, largely replacing "toilet soap." Meanwhile, though the fame of Hollywood actresses seemed to know no borders and though they carried the reputations of the brands they endorsed wherever they were known, the soap makers sought endorsements from other nations' beauties too, actresses with whom their countrywomen might identify more closely. In the new age of the cinema each country had created its own star system and local heroines everywhere lent their allure to Lux.[32] Through them all women could glimpse beauty's promise in a bar of soap.

Toilet soap ads spoke to no single ideal; instead they offered endless variations on the theme of loveliness. Toward the end of the century, however, the soap–glamour–beauty nexus began to weaken and, as Umberto Eco suggests, beauty became democratized. No longer the preserve of the cinema goddesses (and a few gods as well) it became common property. All women now had a claim on beauty and all could see themselves as beautiful in their own way. Then, because the glamour queens no longer held a monopoly on loveliness, advertisers began to seek product testimonials from women whose only starring role was in their own lives. By the late twentieth century Lux's well-worn marketing formula had passed its time, and its sales and profits declined across the Western world. Unilever withdrew it from supermarket shelves in the 1990s (though they continued to sell it in more than one hundred countries in the developing world) and Lux beauty soap faded away, just as surely as the aging stars themselves. From that point on, the company placed its marketing emphasis on Dove, yet another beauty cleansing bar, once more emphasizing its benefits for the skin and now featuring women from all walks of life.

HAIR CARE

During the eighteenth and nineteenth centuries hair care practices varied greatly, as did views about what constituted clean hair and how hair should be cleaned. The loveliness literature brimmed with suggestions about hair management, most of it intended for the bourgeois woman with enough wealth and leisure to spend on her appearance – but perhaps not quite enough to pay a fashionable hairdresser. Early- and mid-nineteenth-century authorities urged caution about washing one's hair with water, cold water in particular. Some thought it harmed the ears, eyes, and teeth as well as the hair, though others offered cautious support if the hair was washed infrequently.[33] They also proposed other forms of treatment in the name of cleanliness: most often simple combing and brushing, but hair powders, bran, and even egg yolks were occasionally recommended as cleaning agents too. With support from the emerging medical science of dermatology, the soap and water wash gained more favour over time, but even then unease about its potential to damage the hair lingered into the twentieth century.[34] Thus, while the nineteenth-century beauty advisers allowed that clean hair enhanced a woman's appeal, they seldom agreed on how cleanliness could best be achieved. As a result they offer us few trustworthy signs of daily practices. How clean were bourgeois female heads during the nineteenth century? We'll never know. By themselves beauty tips tell us nothing about who followed their advice and how often they did so. We can only assume that, as a theme running through the self-help literature of the time, their guidance won a measure of acceptance in middle- and upper-class circles.

The state of lower-class hair and scalps of the time is almost as obscure. Apart from the critical comments of a few observers we have little to inform us. One was the French physician Antonin Baratier, a professional whose social standing and medical training had taught him the virtues of clean bodies. Baratier deplored the hygienic state and grooming practices of the rural French young at the end of the nineteenth century – as he probably deplored the young themselves. He reported that "no care for cleanliness is taken, the complete bath is unknown; the child, girl or boy, almost never combs herself; the long hair is oiled or pomaded every holiday and Sunday without being combed beforehand, and in a short time, under this thick and sticky layer, lice swarm to infinity, deposit eggs without number and spread everywhere."[35]

The urban poor lived in similar conditions. To choose a British example, in 1904, when the London County Council mounted a campaign to cleanse schoolchildren in the city's poorer boroughs, it discovered that close to half of them had head lice, a common sign of uncleanliness and a close companion of poverty. Through determined, even draconian efforts they reduced the problem somewhat but it persisted long into the century. More than a generation later, when London's young were evacuated to the countryside at the outbreak of the Second World War, the proportion of lousy heads varied across the city's boroughs from 4 to 45 percent.[36] As a public health issue the problem had obvious links to the British class

structure. In the northern industrial city of Bradford in 1913, only
2 percent of children with scholarships to the local grammar school
– virtually all from middle-class families – had head lice. Nor was
this just a childhood affliction. One fifth of the women who reported
to the recruiting centres of the British Auxiliary Territorial Service
(the women's branch of the British Army) in the early 1940s were
infested as well. Years later, the historian Guy Thuillier observed
that hair washing had been almost unknown among women in the
Nivernais before 1925; the British evidence strongly suggests that
the French were far from unique.[37]

Still, over time the efforts of educators may have reaped some
rewards. Schools directed much of their personal hygiene teaching
toward girls, emphasizing hair care and exploiting a feminine sense
of beauty.[38] In some respects this was a practical strategy because,
with their longer hair, girls were more vulnerable to head lice than
boys. It also formed part of a broader attempt to emphasize cleanliness and neatness as distinctly female attributes. But well into the
twentieth century, concern for attractive hair was far from universal.
As with clean bodies, the prospect was elusive for those of modest
means. The same social boundaries dividing rich from poor, urban
from rural, and schooled from unschooled, separated those who
could care more – or less – for their hair.

The gradual spread of inexpensive shampoos simplified hair
washing, improved results, and encouraged new personal habits.[39] The Berlin druggist Hans Schwartzkopf introduced the first
cleaning agent specifically intended for hair in 1903. His shampoo
came in powdered form and sold for 20 *pfennig* a packet. It proved
such a success that he soon abandoned his drugstore and devoted
himself to the hair care business, building a major enterprise over
time.[40] He promoted his *Schaumpon* as an improvement on soap,
which left an unsightly film on newly washed hair. Over the next
three decades competing brands found their way onto transatlantic
markets, others from Schwartzkopf among them, offering various
formulas that promised to clean and beautify hair.[41] Despite their
long-standing commitment to personal hygiene, the household
soap giants left most of the early product development challenges
to more specialized firms. During the 1930s, however, Procter &
Gamble and Colgate-Palmolive exploited their recent research on
synthetic detergents and introduced the first non-soapy shampoos
– Drene and Halo – to the American public. Both promised to do

away with the dulling effect soap based cleansers had on newly washed hair, Halo even backing its claims with a "double your money back" guarantee.[42] Both also worked well in the hard water conditions common across North America that checked soap's sudsing action. Meanwhile Unilever, more intent on its core soap business, continued to market the conventional shampoo brands it had purchased over the years.[43]

The outbreak of war delayed the transition to synthetic-based hair care products, but when change came after the war it was dramatic. The greatest drama occurred in the United States, where by 1945 three quarters of American women already washed their hair at least once a week and more than four in five used a shampoo.[44] Between 1935 and 1951 the American shampoo market expanded more than twenty times, mostly after 1945.[45] In time synthetic-based shampoos became the most widely used personal care products in the United States apart from toilet soaps.[46] The industry itself was volatile and highly competitive. Of the five leading American hair cleaners on the market in 1934, none were among the top eight in 1951, and only one of the latter was on the list of bestselling brands three decades later.[47] Though P&G and C-P by then owned some of the major labels, other entrants – makers of cosmetics, hair treatments, and other personal care goods – played leading roles as the industry matured. Of the ten top-selling American shampoos in 1980, two were P&G products while five came from independent cosmetics firms and the remaining three from pharmaceutical and consumer chemicals conglomerates. By the last quarter of the century, P&G, C-P, and Unilever together commanded no more than one quarter of any national shampoo market in Western Europe and North America, a far cry from their dominance in laundry detergents.[48]

In Britain the Second John Bull Census, an early consumer products survey from the mid-1930s, found that one third of households regularly purchased a shampoo. By then routine hair washing had clearly become a well-established practice in some British social circles, where shampoos had found a ready market.[49] But during the immediate postwar years most Europeans embraced soapless shampoos far more cautiously than Americans, one obvious reason being that they washed their hair less often. The review carried out by Françoise Giroud of *Elle* in 1951 suggested that only 11 percent of Frenchwomen were weekly washers – whether with soap or shampoo she didn't say – while two thirds cleaned their hair less than every

two weeks.[50] A decade later an Italian inquiry found that 43 percent
of those surveyed shampooed their hair at least once a month, with
women more fastidious than men by a fairly wide margin (50 to 36
percent).[51] Here too the somewhat patchy evidence reveals striking
national differences. It also indicates that at mid-century, regular
hair washing was becoming more common everywhere in the West.

The great change in Western European hair care habits occurred
during the 1960s and 1970s as part of the wholesale transformation
of body care during the new age of mass consumption. A thorough
investigation of personal cleanliness in West Germany during the
late 1960s and early 1970s found that almost 90 percent of Germans
washed their hair weekly, half of them twice a week or more.[52] In
1986, when *Elle* surveyed the hygienic state of the French female
body again, they triumphantly announced that French womanhood had been converted to cleanliness since mid-century. Among
other things *les françaises* bathed much more frequently, changed
their underclothes far more regularly, and washed their hair at least
as often as women everywhere else in the Western world: 41 percent once a week, 38 percent two or three times weekly, and 10
percent daily.[53] Meanwhile, per capita shampoo consumption rose
sharply across Europe; by the early 1980s it was approaching (and
in Germany exceeding) American levels.[54]

As the hair care industry grew, it quickly became a dominant force
in shaping new habits, an influence that grew out of the industry's
own business needs. Developing new shampoos and bringing them to
market was a long and costly process. The usual path involved extensive market and laboratory research followed by consumer testing
and the development of a marketing strategy, all prior to the product's introduction. Each product required major investments, none
of which guaranteed success.[55] A new shampoo, Agree, launched in
the later 1970s, offers one example. The American company S.C.
Johnson, best known for its household cleaning supplies, created
the shampoo hoping to establish a market presence in personal care
products. It spent $30 million to introduce Agree, advertising it as
a shampoo that cleaned hair but left no oily residue. The launch
included the distribution of 40 million free samples.[56] Initially the
strategy seemed to work. In 1980 Agree enjoyed a moment of commercial glory as America's leading shampoo. But over the next few
years, rival brands overtook it, and it languished for a decade before
Johnson admitted defeat and sold the brand in 1993. The victor in

this contest was P&G. In the mid-1980s it introduced a series of new products that combined a shampoo with a hair conditioner, based on a new formula it had developed during several years of research.[57] The innovation revived two of its flagging brands (Pert and Pantene) as well as the company's growth more broadly. According to John Pepper, a senior P&G executive during the 1980s and 1990s, by the mid-1990s Pantene had become the leading global hair care brand. In his memoirs Pepper noted that "with this new development, hair care became one of the company's great growth engines during the 1990s. Annual sales increased tenfold. Proportionately, profits grew even more. From a position of relative insignificance in the mid-1980s, hair care has grown to rank among P&G's top four largest categories today. Why? We had delivered on the total experience that hundreds of millions of consumers wanted for their hair."

In an intensely competitive business environment such as this, mass-marketing strategies were essential to a brand's success. The shampoo makers used saturation advertising to place their labels before the public eye and keep them there. Initially the American shampoo makers used mass circulation magazines and radio sponsorships to deliver their message, but from the 1950s onward, they too relied primarily on television, filling the nation's screens each evening with attractive young women sporting perfectly groomed tresses. Often these ads featured a short before-and-after drama to display the transformative power of their brand. Regardless of the specific product, however, a single theme ran through these messages: attractive hair enhanced a woman's beauty and promised success in personal relationships, especially those with men. It seemed as though the main purpose of clean hair was to get your man and keep him.

By the 1960s most shampoos sold in the Western world washed hair adequately. Yet the business remained highly innovative and competitive. In 1980 one industry observer noted that all the leading shampoos in the United States were effective but beyond that they had little in common.[58] Each claimed unique properties, each addressed different conditions, each remedied distinctive problems. And problems there seemed to be. When the makers of Breck, a popular American shampoo, surveyed four thousand women about their hair needs in 1962, 84 percent of the respondents complained of at least one hair dilemma, "hard to manage" the most common.[59] It was Breck's fifteenth annual attempt to learn more about its market, and this year it found the same problems it had heard about in the past. By then market studies had become standard practice in consumer goods industries; Breck's competitors no doubt conducted them too. Whatever they taught the shampoo makers about their products and customers, the surveys and results also formed part of an ongoing dialogue about the nature of female beauty. Through them the makers proposed ideal standards of feminine attractiveness and, in response, their consumers asked for products that would help them achieve these goals. What the makers proposed were visions of loveliness that all could realize if they used the maker's shampoo. Here too concepts of cleanliness were now subsumed within much wider notions of femininity, beauty, and social acceptance.

BEAUTIFUL TEETH

The nineteenth-century self-help literature also had a good deal to say about teeth and their care, most of it also more concerned with good looks than good health. At the beginning of the century one French authority on feminine beauty declared that "nothing is more pleasing than clean, white teeth, and gums of the colour of the rose," a view that then seemed a universal truth.[60] But ideals like these were hard to achieve. According to a British dentist some three decades later, "the most general point of defection in the personal economy is the mouth and teeth," a condition he deeply deplored.[61] Throughout the century and long into the next, the self-help counsellors belaboured the subject, endorsing oral hygiene as an essential part of beauty care. Some were just as concerned about dental health, urging regular cleaning to preserve sound teeth and avoid toothaches. Still, appearances seemed to matter more, and in any case only healthy teeth could be truly beautiful. Usually the advisers encouraged hygienic routines that involved frequent rinsing and liberal use of a toothpick, as well as cleansing with some form of brush and cleaning agent.[62] Many also cautioned, though, that abrasive tooth powders and polishes might destroy the enamel, leaving the teeth lustreless and the inner tooth vulnerable. Still, if the advice literature is any indication, well before the end of the nineteenth century frequent tooth brushing and other oral hygiene practices were winning broader acceptance.

To learn more about the state of teeth in the past, however, we have to look elsewhere, beginning with the archaeological record. Studies of dental caries over the very long term reveal a sharply rising trend in tooth decay from the eighteenth century onward. One recent English survey indicates that adults in the later eighteenth and early nineteenth centuries had twice as many cavities in their molars as did those in the seventeenth, while adults from the mid-nineteenth century onward had three times as many. The proportions among juveniles were higher still, six and eight times respectively.[63] As the teeth most susceptible to decay, molars are a particularly revealing index of dental problems. In this case they indicate that the modern decline in dental health paralleled the rise of the urban Industrial Age. It began in childhood and adolescence and it produced life-long consequences. Its origins lay in dietary changes that spanned the nineteenth-century Western world, mainly the growing amounts of refined sugar consumed at all levels of society.[64] In this respect Britain led the league. Per capita sugar consumption there quadrupled between 1840 and 1900 and it continued to grow over the coming decades. By the mid-Depression years it stood at 110 pounds a year.[65] Americans lagged the British trend but only by a little. Their personal consumption grew by 60 percent to 80 pounds during the 1880s alone, and the increase persisted for decades, reaching 100 pounds by the mid-twentieth century.

The problems of dental health in childhood and adolescence became a public health concern during the later nineteenth century. In part this unease expressed the growing scientific authority of the dentists themselves, then engaged in professional self-definition.[66] But for the most part it simply revealed conditions that public health officials encountered on their daily rounds, and it stoked their apprehensions about population health more generally. At a moment when fears about physical deterioration and racial degeneration were circulating widely in Western Europe, the state of a nation's teeth was unsettling. In 1906 British dentists told a national commission on the health of schoolchildren that only a small minority enjoyed sound dentition while a substantial majority suffered from serious tooth decay. The problem began to affect the permanent teeth soon after they sprouted and became progressively worse as children grew older. One study of over eight thousand children revealed that more than half of those aged sixteen to eighteen had at least five defective teeth and nearly one quarter had nine or more, while only 6 percent had none.[67] Though the problem was more acute among the poor, tooth decay was no respecter of social class; the children of wealth and comfort suffered from dental caries almost as much as their poorer schoolmates. American conditions must have been similar, at least if military recruitment records are any indication. During the early twentieth century the minimum army fitness standard required men who had "'six serviceable double (bicuspid or molar) teeth' with at least two sets of opposing teeth on one side of the mouth and one at minimum on the other." Soldiers had to chew the tough meats included in standard army rations if they were to be properly nourished. In 1916, fully one third of potential recruits, young men in their late teens and early twenties, fell short of the standard.[68]

Having deplored what they saw in the mouths of the young, investigators concluded that the best place to promote good oral hygiene was the public school.[69] After all, dental problems were rooted in childhood, the school's main tasks included moulding young habits, and universal primary schooling was becoming the norm throughout the Western world. Educational authorities almost everywhere added oral hygiene to school curricula and in some cases even placed dental clinics in elementary schools.[70] In 1909 the German government established a national committee to oversee dental care and teaching in schools as well as among the wider public.[71] At about the same time the American National Dental Association launched a major program of oral hygiene education, intended to buttress public school initiatives and to emphasize the need for regular dental care.[72] In time most school health programs came to offer care of the teeth as a core topic.

If dentists and public health physicians saw dental problems as a health issue, the makers of toothpastes harboured larger aspirations. Before the later nineteenth century, pharmacists created most dental pastes and powders, preparations that only the better off could afford to use regularly. At the time a container of toothpaste in the United States might cost a labourer half a day's wage.[73] Searching for new products and markets, the soap maker Colgate introduced its first toothpaste in 1877, initially sold in jars but offered in collapsible tin tubes from 1896 onward.[74] The new packaging enabled mass production and prompted a sharp decline in prices. Following Colgate, other firms soon brought their own brands to the American market, but Colgate Dental Cream, having seized the initiative, remained the most popular toothpaste in the United States into the 1960s. Similar tales unfolded in Britain and Continental Europe. In 1907 the Dresden pharmacist Ottomar von Mayenburg developed Chlorodont, a paste made from tooth powder and mouthwash, and sold it in a metal tube as well.[75] Its commercial sails filled by brisk advertising breezes, Chlorodont became the German market leader within a decade. Soon many choices confronted users everywhere when they shopped for dental products. The 1937 John Bull Census of household goods noted eighteen leading dentifrices then on the British market, though the top four controlled 80 percent of the trade.[76]

Once again, heavy advertising was the main tool used to market toothpaste. Early dentifrices had little if any therapeutic value, so apart from possibly whitening the teeth or refreshing the breath, effective cleansing action came largely from the mechanical act of brushing.[77] For this reason alone the toothpaste promoters faced a major challenge in selling their wares. They needed to encourage new habits, but they also had to create a mass market for products that by themselves offered little to dental health. While toothpastes and powders had been publicized throughout the nineteenth century, product advertising increased markedly after the First World War. In the United States it grew sixtyfold between 1914 and 1939.[78] During the interwar years in particular, toothpaste became one of the most heavily advertised consumer products across the Western world. The cost of publicizing dentifrices in America and the United Kingdom at the time amounted to at least one quarter of the retail price.[79] The industry's first ads promoted them as health care products, reflecting concerns broadly shared in the public health movement.[80] But during the 1920s and 1930s, once more publicity began to emphasize appeals to beauty, personal attractiveness, and romance. As toothpaste advertising's most persuasive historian put it, "consumers were urged to buy brands like Listerine and Pepsodent, not to protect their teeth and gums against decay, but to avoid social exclusion or romantic rejection caused by 'halitosis.'"[81]

The advertising industry of the time seems to have been highly impressed by its impact on consumer habits. In the mid-1920s the well-known British advertiser Charles Higham wrote (with more than a note of self-congratulation):

What is now common hygienic knowledge – particularly the hygienic care of the teeth – is, despite all their efforts, in no way traceable to the warnings of dentists, or even to the magnificent work of the doctors in school clinics, but is almost entirely due to the advertisements of manufacturers who sell dental goods. What doctors and dentists have known and preached for many

years is now universally accepted because the public have
absorbed an impression, registered it, remembered it, acted upon
it almost unconsciously, impelled thereto by what they have seen
in the advertising columns of the Press.[82]

All advertisers hope to produce behaviour change, the more widespread the better, and Higham was clearly a true believer. But despite
his pitchman confidence, daily teeth care remained a far more common practice in urban places and in the upper ranks than in other
social circles. Early estimates of personal tooth brushing rested on
the presence or absence of toothpastes, powders, and brushes in
household inventories of consumer goods. By the later 1930s some
90 percent of American homes possessed these dental products, as
did a similar proportion of British families.[83] But possession doesn't
necessarily mean use. At the time, on average American households bought slightly more than a tube of toothpaste or a can of
tooth powder a year, far less than they would need for regular daily
brushing.[84] Perhaps consumers used them sparingly because of their
limited health benefits. Perhaps they usually brushed their teeth with
other common household products like baking soda or soap. Yet
despite this uncertainty, the broad diffusion of toothpaste still points
to the gradual spread of new personal dental care habits in Britain
and America after the First World War, as regular brushing grew
more common while growing numbers used a commercial dentifrice.

The second half of the century saw a steady increase in toothpaste
consumption. It also narrowed the gaps – once only suspected but
now revealed – between different national oral hygiene habits. By
the mid 1970s at least 95 percent of Germans used a commercial
toothpaste; a survey some years later revealed near universal daily
brushing – usually two or more times per day.[85] During these same
years the laggards – France and Italy – made up much of the lost
ground that divided them from the leading countries. Tooth brushing had been rare in the French countryside before mid-century and
probably uncommon among the urban multitudes too. But during
the mid-1960s alone the sale of toothpastes in France increased by
60 percent, a clear sign of changing habits. By the end of the 1980s
only 6 percent of Frenchmen were merely occasional brushers and
more than half cleaned their teeth at least twice a day.[86] In Italy 70
percent of families were using a dentifrice by 1960, and per capita consumption there increased steadily from that point onward as

well.[87] By the late years of the century high standards of personal oral care existed everywhere in the West.

Still, restless commercial energies flowed beneath the surface of these changes. From the mid-1940s onward the three great multinationals in soaps and detergents focused new attention on the dental care business. Colgate-Palmolive had sold toothpaste for more than half a century and at that point enjoyed a comfortable lead in the American market. Unilever also had a modest profile in the toothpaste trade though Procter & Gamble had none to speak of. At mid-century, however, the three companies began to develop strategies for global growth, and each used dental care products as instruments to realize their ambitions. C-P shifted from toilet soap to toothpaste as its primary tool of international expansion, Unilever followed long-standing corporate practice by buying a well-established American brand (Pepsodent), and P&G developed new products in-house. By 1959 the three firms shared 70 percent of the toothpaste market in the United States, the United Kingdom, and France, though a new label in Germany (Blendax) held one third of dentifrice sales there, forcing the three big multinationals to accept smaller market shares.[88]

In many respects, though, the toothpaste universe of the 1950s differed little from what it had been since the beginnings of mass marketing in the early 1920s, even if the markets themselves were larger and large-scale enterprises now dominated the trade. A few brands led sales in every country, by themselves none contributed dramatically to dental health, and heavy advertising emphasized toothpaste's cosmetic benefits: shining white teeth and attractive smiles. In 1955, however, P&G introduced a new product, Crest, which for the first time offered true therapeutic value. After several years of research and product development the company devised a dentifrice that included stannous fluoride, which offered some protection against tooth decay. The new toothpaste made its commercial debut with the usual corporate fanfare, but its early sales were modest. In 1960, however, when the American Dental Association endorsed Crest as a preventative against dental caries, its sales increased dramatically. Within two years it had become the American market leader with one third of national sales, and it retained its lead well into the 1990s.[89] Competitors soon introduced their own brands with fluoride content, and from the mid-1960s to the mid-1980s more than half of all toothpastes sold in America were marketed primarily for their therapeutic value, while the sales of so-called cosmetic dentifrices plummeted. Thus, like the toilet soap and shampoo manufacturers, the toothpaste makers had linked cleanliness to the beauty business throughout much of the century. But from the 1960s onward most of them framed their wares as health care products. Only in the last years of the century, when virtually all leading brands could promise health benefits, did older claims about toothpaste as a beauty aid creep back into their advertising.[90]

THE MANLY CHIN

For most of the nineteenth century beards were a leading male fashion across the Western world.[91] Often men shaved some parts of the face, giving their tastes a personal accent, but the clean-shaven face was uncommon. Frequently those who shaved employed a barber rather than attempting the chore themselves, commonly once or twice a week and before special occasions.[92] Saturdays and Sunday mornings were busy times for barbers, as men looked to their appearance before attending holy service. In the world of traditional practices shaving, like bathing, cleansed the body to prepare for sacred rites.

After 1900, however, beards and moustaches began to fall out of favour, and the decline continued for most of the century. The clean-shaven look became the face of the modern man. The new personal hygiene supported shaving and condemned facial hair as unclean.[93] Even before the end of the nineteenth century medical men began to abandon long beards, honoured symbols of masculinity, in favour of smooth cheeks and chins. The new look was also linked with changing concepts of manliness, notions paired with the emerging business culture of an expanding white-collar economy that emphasized intellectual talents, collaboration, polite manners, and good grooming.[94] Employers in these settings expected their male employees to arrive for work clean-shaven. In contrast, military men often clung to nineteenth century traditions of facial adornment that expressed martial values. In many instances beards or moustaches were obligatory. But opposition from within the ranks and trench warfare during the First World War forced a hasty revision. Surviving a mustard gas attack required a mask that fit the face tightly, and soldiers on both sides of the conflict chose survival over custom.[95]

The safety razor enabled the new clean-shaven look and also gave men the ability to shave themselves. Straight razors, consisting of a single blade that folded into an attached handle, had been the instrument of choice throughout the nineteenth century. Made of high-quality steel, they needed regular stropping to maintain a sharp edge and occasional honing when they became too dull to sharpen with a strop. Costly to buy and difficult to maintain, they required some skill to use, and even then the shaver sometimes nicked his client (or himself) while plying his art. The search for a better razor produced various improvements toward the end of the century, but the breakthrough product – a double-sided disposable razor blade – only reached western shavers in the early twentieth century.[96]

The inventor was King Gillette, an American travelling salesman and inveterate tinkerer.[97] He devised a blade that fitted into a hoe-shaped holder and could shave the face without cutting the skin. The Gillette Safety Razor made shaving easier than ever, easy enough for a man to shave himself. Similar razors were already available but Gillette's new blade offered three advantages over past improvements. It had two cutting edges instead of one, it was made of less costly material, and, most importantly, it could be discarded once it was dull. Introduced in 1903, Gillette razors and blades sold well in the United States before the First World War, and the company lost no time in extending its reach abroad. But its great leap forward didn't occur until 1918, when the American War Department bought 3.5 million Gillette shaving kits for standard issue to its servicemen – the equivalent of the company's total razor sales for the previous six years. From that point on sales grew dramatically, increasing sixfold by the mid-1920s alone.[98] Toward the end of the war the British government also bought kits for its military personnel, boosting the fortunes of Gillette's UK branch. When demobilized after the war, ex-servicemen returned home with their safety razors, along with the habit of regular shaving that they'd acquired – a large and promising market for blades that were discarded after a week or two's use.

Even before the war, though, the disposable bladed safety razor had made inroads across the Western world, and Gillette soon faced many rivals.[99] The company held the advantage, however, and its sales continued to grow. With his usual braggadocio King Gillette himself estimated that by 1926 its razor blade production could circle the globe at the equator.[100] At the time hyperbole was more abundant than reliable statistics, but the company's market share grew substantially, even in Britain and Germany, where the steel industry had long produced high-quality straight razors. British consumers could choose from among more than one hundred razor blade brands during the 1930s, but at mid-century Gillette Industries held three quarters of all UK sales.[101] By then Gillette claimed more than one quarter of the global market for men's shaving products.[102]

Here too marketing was key to the company's growth. The Gillette Safety Razor Company advertised widely from the outset.[103] Some early ads stressed the ease and economy of using its razor. But the central theme in the company's marketing program, one that it maintained for decades, was the masculinity of the smoothly shaved male face.[104] The message itself was simple: the Gillette user was manly and attractive, he was clean-shaven, and he shaved every day. Thus the company joined the beauty care chorus while promoting new daily hygienic routines. Like the makers of toilet soaps, shampoos, and toothpastes, it framed the product in terms of personal appearance, in this case the virile appeal of the well-shaved male face.

Unfortunately, we know little enough about how shaving habits actually developed in daily life a century ago. One exception is a survey done by Mass-Observation, the social research group founded in the Britain during the later 1930s that was intended to record everyday experience in British society. On the eve of the Second World War it issued a report that explored men's shaving practices. The survey discovered that three quarters of their sample shaved at least every second day, though the proportion of daily shavers was much higher among the over-thirties than among those who were younger.[105] And it also detected a strain of ambivalence about the practice itself. As one respondent, a thirty-two-year-old insurance employee, put it, "personally, I regard moustaches and beards as most frequently signs of affectation, though I rather hanker after a beard as relief from the boaring [sic] and arduous business of shaving."[106] For some the electric razor, introduced in America during the later 1920s and in Western Europe soon after, offered relief by eliminating soap and water and reducing shaving time. But the initial cost of an electric shaver was high – the better part of a British worker's weekly wage at the time – and the new device didn't gain broad adoption until after the Second World War.[107] Then, however, it assumed the same identity that the safety razor had long since enjoyed, becoming a tool of masculinity and allowing a man to present his male self at its clean-shaven best.

Razors in whatever form were the major competitive focus for shaving products throughout most of the twentieth century. The shaving soaps and creams business lacked the commercial dynamism of the razor products sector, as well as that of the soap and shampoo trades. The industry remained decentralized until after the Second World War, and consumers faced a wide range of choices. The John Bull Census in mid-Depression Britain noted twenty-seven shaving soaps and twenty-one shaving creams then on the market, only one of them a market leader.[108] Some of the titans in soaps and detergents, Unilever in particular, also sold shaving supplies, but these remained a small part of their business. It wasn't until the postwar era, when C-P, P&G, and Unilever refashioned themselves as consumer products firms and the beauty business developed globalizing ambitions, that the big multinationals saw opportunities in other products to enhance manliness.[109] At that point they folded men's shaving goods into their product ranges, marketing them worldwide as one of their many personal care goods. By then decades of salesmanship had realized their goals. All thought of a relationship between shaving and cleanliness had disappeared from view, and the clean-shaven face had become simply an expression of male beauty.

OVERCOMING BARRIERS TO BEAUTY

In marketing toilet soaps, shampoos, toothpastes, and shaving goods, the beauty care business appealed to hopes that their consumption would improve the user's appearance. The body also produced two barriers to beauty that weren't so easily overcome: perspiration and menstruation. While their odours and discomforts had long offended some, these concerns intensified during the first half of the twentieth century. Disquiets once limited to the medically informed and the hygienically minded became more widely shared. Here, too, the hygiene crusade shaped popular views, raising awareness and redefining perceptions. And once more the consumer goods industries became the main architects of popular understandings. New product offerings soon addressed growing apprehensions about perspiration and menstruation even as advertising fostered unease about them. The body itself had become a source of shame.

Antiperspirants and deodorants addressed one of these anxieties. By the early twentieth century upper-class distaste for the body's unpleasing odours knew a long history.[110] The wish to cleanse the poor had always rested in major part on their offensive smells – offensive at least to those who judged the malodorous masses by their own perfumed standards. During the 1920s and 1930s, however, unease over disagreeable body aromas began to spread, and it spread more rapidly still after the Second World War. In part the increase reflected the changed work conditions of the growing white-collar economy, the decline of physical labour, and the expansion of middle-class grooming standards. It also supported the ambitions of the antiperspirant and deodorant makers, who in turn fed popular concerns through their marketing programs. They offered products to reduce underarm perspiration and mask its odours, promoting them with the consumer goods sector's energetic marketing strategies.[111] Initially they directed their advertising to women, evoking fears of romantic or social rejection. The early campaigns for Odorono, the first nationally advertised American antiperspirant during the 1920s, stressed the need to avoid offending others in order to prosper in business and personal life.[112] From that point onward success in social relations remained the leading theme of deodorant publicity.

Before the 1950s deodorants were only one among many modestly selling personal care products, but at that point the industry began to expand rapidly. Once again advertising, on television in particular, played the dominant role in defining a hygienic problem, offering a solution, attracting new consumers, and maintaining brand loyalty. Sales increased briskly throughout the early postwar decades, and by the 1980s deodorants had become one of the leading cosmetic products sold in most Western markets, used regularly by the majority of older adolescents and adults. Yet national differences in deodorant consumption also persisted. Over 90 percent of Americans used a deodorant in the 1990s, followed closely by the British at 85 percent. The Germans and French, by contrast, seemed dawdlers at 70 percent and 63 percent.[113] Disparities within nations also varied widely over time by sex, age, occupation, and social class.[114]

The development and sale of menstruation products raised even more complex concerns. For centuries popular superstitions about menstruation had mingled with medical misundersandings on the subject, shrouding women in a haze of prescriptions and prohibitions about their monthly cycles. Folk knowledge long conferred special powers on menstruating women, occasionally for good but much more commonly for ill. Because of their impurity they were often considered a danger to the people and objects whom they touched.[115] In contrast, at least one strain of French medical understanding viewed menses positively, as a powerful force in human reproduction. According to Alain Corbin, "the woman at that point in her cycle was conveying the vitality of nature; she was emitting the products of a strong animality; she was making an appeal for fertilization, dispersing seductive effluvia."[116] Physicians drew their views from many sources, ancient medical knowledge and popular wisdom among them, but medical science only took its first steps toward an accurate understanding of human reproduction during the second half of the nineteenth century. Before then, and for some time afterwards as well, ideas about the physiology of reproduction lacked solid empirical foundations, and in the absence of evidence, doctors tended to emphasize women's "menstrual disability" – yet another explanation for their seemingly innate inferiority.[117]

As to practices, the past is largely silent about how women managed these monthly privacies. It seems likely, though, that before women wore underpants – and in Western Europe, at least, the great majority did not until after the mid-nineteenth century – most lower-class women did little more than allow their menstrual flows to collect on their petticoats and skirts.[118] The scathing comments of turn-of-the-century country physicians about feminine hygiene underscore the inference.[119] Once worn, however, underpants allowed women to use home-made pads that absorbed their menstrual discharges and avoid staining their clothes. As well, before the end of the century, menstrual belts and pads, and patterns for women who made their own, were commercially available on both sides of the Atlantic.[120] But whatever the chosen solution, menstruation inevitably involved concealed practices that mingled discomfort, inconvenience, awkwardness, and embarrassment, all elements of a confidential feminine world, and these customs and beliefs cast long shadows across the twentieth century. Though medical knowledge could provide an increasingly accurate account of ovulation and menstruation, traditions lived on, especially in rural areas and within the lower urban social ranks, where change came later to all forms of personal hygiene. What proved especially durable was the cloak of privacy that enveloped women's menstrual experience, an aspect of femininity that was seldom discussed and then only in the intimacy shared by mothers and daughters or close friends.

Disposable menstrual pads first appeared in the United States and Germany at the end of the nineteenth century, but though they enjoyed some early popularity, they failed to find a broad market at the time.[121] In 1919, however, the American paper company Kimberly-Clark produced an improved disposable sanitary napkin

based on cellucotton, a highly absorbent material developed for
wound dressings during the First World War, and sold it under
the brand name Kotex. It consisted of a cellulose core wrapped in
gauze, held in place by a belt. Soon other brands became available,
but by the later 1920s Kotex had established itself as the American
leader with 70 percent of the national sanitary napkin market, even
though its pads cost almost twice as much as those of their competitors.[122] During the mid-1920s a similar product, Camelia, arrived in
German shops.[123] The new disposables offered women greater convenience but at a cost that hindered widespread adoption. At five
cents a pad (the equivalent of a loaf of bread at the time) Kotex must
have forced many women to choose between their family's needs
and their own comfort. America apart, acceptance was slow everywhere. In Britain and Germany home-made napkins remained most
common until after the Second World War.[124] Intended for internal
use, tampons were first sold nationally in the United States during
the mid-1930s, though widespread adoption did not begin until the
1950s. By the 1970s, however, they held over one third of the market
for menstrual care products in the United States and were widely
sold in Western Europe as well.[125]

The commercialization of menstrual hygiene followed the pattern
for other personal care goods. After a period of trial and error a
company developed an innovative product and presented it to consumers through an ambitious marketing program. Competitors
soon introduced similar versions, but the originating company dominated the trade for an extended period before their rivals developed
superior alternatives and challenged its lead. What distinguished
the makers of menstrual care goods from those who sold soaps
and shampoos was the cultural context of their wares: a feminine
world of privacy and embarrassment. For centuries a measure of
repugnance and shame had clung to most of the body's excretions,
women's menses among them, but menstruation also had powerful associations with female sexuality and women's power to give
life. Its surrounding atmosphere had long been infused with some of
life's deepest mysteries, and although a scientific view of the repro-
ductive cycle gradually spread after the First World War, strands of
traditional understandings continued to cling to the new knowledge.
They clung, as well, to the new technologies of menstrual management, reinforcing the persistent sense of self-consciousness linked to
such intimate matters.

Because of these sensitivities, the marketing of menstrual products faced distinctive challenges. The initial publicity for sanitary pads framed them in a medical context and promoted them as hygienic aids. An early Kotex advertisement introduced the subject with the headline "Woman's Greatest Hygienic Handicap, As Your Daughter's Doctor Views It," and the advice that followed purportedly came from a "Registered Nurse."[126] In Germany, meanwhile, an authoritative Schwester (Sister) Thekla, a nurse as well, endorsed Camelia napkins in that company's early ads.[127] Over time, however, the leading theme in product advertising became a woman's need to manage a handicap and live a normal daily life. With the help of her chosen product she could work or play in perfect confidence that she alone would know of her circumstances. The promise of all menstrual aids was cleanliness with discretion: their use would allow women to hide their condition, avoiding any hint of embarrassment.[128] The embarrassment also extended to shopping for feminine hygiene goods, and manufacturers as well as shopkeepers went to great lengths to provide discreet packaging. The German makers of Camelia products even provided shopkeepers with plain white paper to wrap their blue boxes, allowing customers to make a purchase without betraying their menstrual status.[129]

This powerful sensitivity prevailed well into the postwar era. Before the 1970s, publicity for menstrual hygiene products in the United States was confined to the print media, but at the beginning of that decade, the National Association of Broadcasters reversed its long-standing policy and permitted their promotion on television. Even then some manufacturers were reluctant to seize the opportunity, the makers of Kotex among them. According to the head of the advertising agency with the brand account, the company took "a stand in opposition to the lifting of the television ban despite the clear advantage it would have given them ... This was a decision based on good taste and respect for consumer attitudes, rather than on sales and profits alone."[130] But soon enough concern for sales and profits carried the day, and in time canons of good taste came to accept the fact that women had menstrual cycles, even though the fact itself remained disguised.

By the mid-twentieth century decades personal hygiene had become a matter of comportment and a commodity to be bought. Soaps, shampoos, and toothpastes cleansed the body to make it acceptable in public while deodorants and menstrual aids concealed its secretions with the same goal in mind. Cleanliness had become an act of courtesy, one that prepared the body for its civic role. Washing, deodorizing, and shaving made it agreeable to others: family, friends, and strangers alike. These daily rituals still expressed concerns for good health, but as a motivating force, well-being placed a distant second to the wish to live comfortably in society, to be attractive, perhaps even beautiful. Behind this development lay the weight of commerce, the mass-marketing of products for body care, a force that had redefined cleanliness and steadily raised standards of personal grooming throughout most of the twentieth century. Advertising now served as hygiene's great teacher, endlessly rehearsing claims that beckoned shoppers to buy and consume. Where once advertisements had endorsed luxury cosmetics for the wealthy, they now promoted personal care goods for everyday use by all.[131] In doing so they tutored the broad public on the routine gestures of cleanliness. By the late-twentieth-century decades, hygiene and beauty had even come to assume abstract meanings as symbols of western modernity.[132] The freshly cleansed and deodorized body had become a global aspiration.

MAKING THE MODERN CLEAN BODY

The history of the clean body, then, is the sum of many histories. Of changing beliefs and habits, of new technologies and infrastructures, of growing economies and rising living standards, of class relations and clothing fashions, of lingering inequalities and slow convergences. No single influence formed the hygienic customs of our time. Rather there were many determinants whose pathways ranged across cultural settings and social circumstances, each with its own itinerary.

Still, some influences shaped the customs of cleanliness more powerfully than others, and of these, water was the most fundamental. Water was difficult to obtain almost everywhere in the eighteenth-century Western world, and often costly too. All but the wealthy few used it frugally and sometimes even they were constrained. Two centuries later water was abundant, cheap, and easily accessible throughout Europe and North America, conditions we now take for granted. Among the greatest engineering achievements of the age, urban systems of water provision and disposal steadily broadened their benefits from the second half of the nineteenth century onward, refreshing and cleansing cities everywhere, in time bringing water to all. Western modernity conquered water, subduing it to its needs, just as water conquered the Western world by creating new forms of dependency.[1]

As water transformed the urban landscape it also refashioned the dwelling. Once linked to civic water and sewer systems, domestic plumbing gave homes ready access to the one element essential for personal cleanliness. In turn water and cleanliness claimed a new space inside the home: the bathroom. Bathing's intimacies insisted on privacy and privacy called for a room of its own. The bathroom demanded a fundamental change in how home interiors were organized, a change as basic to cleanliness as was ready access to water. At first a novelty enjoyed only by the wealthy – and even then far from all of them – its long winding journey led in time to the egalitarian bathroom, a private space within each dwelling that offered everyone the opportunity to bathe.

Technological change also supported the new personal hygiene. Washing bodies and clothes were labour intensive activities before the twentieth century. Cleaning the household's laundry and organizing the family bath night required time and effort. By degrees, however, a host of innovations reduced the burdens of cleanliness. The freestanding water heater supplied hot water on demand instead of by the bucket from a stovetop, a boon to bathers and laundresses alike. Industrial manufacturing reduced the price of soap and created cleaning products for specific needs, easing the toil of laundry care. From a labour-saving perspective, however, the most important step by far was the long evolution of the washing machine, which progressively reduced the work required to clean the laundry. Once among the most onerous of female chores – whether done for money or for love – by the end of the twentieth century it had become a short and simple task.

The budding consumer economy of the later nineteenth century embraced the clean body project with enthusiasm and, as the twentieth progressed, with something close to fervour. Soap makers took the early lead, using novel methods to manufacture a common staple and sell it with newfound energy. Over time a few large multinational firms came to dominate the soap and detergent trades, and later still the body care products industries. Laundry cleaners and toilet soaps remained their core business for decades, but commercial ambition gradually brought new personal hygiene goods to market. Mass-merchandized wares for specific hygienic needs – shampoos, toothpastes, shaving supplies, deodorants, and menstrual hygiene products among them – filled growing amounts of shelf space in supermarkets and pharmacies. These developments had two important consequences for personal cleanliness. On one hand they extended the scope of hygiene by enlarging the range of consumer goods dedicated to the task. On the other they broadened existing concepts of clean and unclean, publicizing them widely through endless advertising campaigns. In the process cleanliness became a commodity, a product in itself. From the mid-twentieth century onward it also linked arms with the growing popular desire for personal attractiveness, and over time, cleanliness became auxiliary to beauty.

Within the framework of these changes, the idea of cleanliness itself evolved dramatically. Before the end of the eighteenth century it rested largely on clothing and appearances rather than the actual state of the skin. Visibly clean underclothes distinguished those who were clean from those who were not. From that point onward, however, the idea of full-body bathing slowly won acceptance and a new understanding of cleanliness gradually evolved. Its initial progress was largely confined to urban social elites, and the resistance it faced grew not so much from mere ignorance as from traditional beliefs about health and cleanliness deeply engrained in plebian cultures. With passing time, however, bourgeois views came to dominate. They blended a belief in cleanliness as a sign of higher social status with disdain for the lower classes and their seeming squalor, implying that the clean possessed greater merit while the unclean deserved little more than correction.[2] The philanthropically minded, however, were more optimistic. They became the public advocates of universal bathing, convinced that even the poor would wash if they could. All they lacked was opportunity.

From the 1880s onward the germ theory of disease causation added a scientific rationale to the discussion, giving the exponents of cleanliness a new tool to advance their cause. At a time when scientific knowledge was assuming greater authority, science itself could now be invoked to improve the human body. At the same time, the modern state was assembling new powers to better the human condition and the germ theory offered it a useful implement. The state used schools, public health departments, and other agencies to promote better personal hygiene, and even enforce it when faced with resistance. A cluster of voluntary organizations, most of them intent on moulding young lives, also joined the cleanliness crusade around the turn of the twentieth century. By now advocates of the new personal hygiene were the dominant force in these dialogues. They possessed a compelling ideology and powerful instruments to advance their goals. By this time too, core beliefs about body care – the need for daily topical washing and regular full-body bathing – were widely held, though not yet universal. In the lower social ranks, meanwhile, the will to wash remained greater than the occasion to do so, or at least do so with ease.

As the twentieth century advanced, the personal care industry came to play the dominant role in defining cleanliness and broadcasting its meanings. Through persistent marketing campaigns it reached deep into the homes and thoughts of consumers. Advertising displayed models of conduct and motives for behaviour that, more than any other influence, defined the norms of body care of the age. The norms themselves emphasized ever-higher standards of cleanliness: frequent hand washing, daily full-body cleansing, the morning shave, regular shampooing, and freshly laundered clothes in particular. And this in the search for social approval. In the age of Louis XIV and Samuel Pepys cleanliness had been concerned most of all with appearances, and it emphasized forms of exclusion, distinctions that set the upper classes apart from all others. The link between being clean and looking attractive persisted in the later twentieth century but by then it expressed new meanings. Careful grooming, using commercial personal hygiene products, and respecting the unspoken rules of cleanliness formed part of the search for social inclusion. Being clean had become a matter of comportment, valued much less for its own sake than for its central role in the endless search for self-esteem and acceptance – in short, for belonging.

The changes embedded in the Western cleanliness revolution were complex, slow, and uneven. Their patterns varied – sometimes widely – by nation and region, culture and class. In addition, from the standpoint of daily life, diffusion mattered much more than invention. While novelty played a leading role in promoting change, dissemination exerted by far the greater influence on the evolving culture of cleanliness. New ideas and techniques put innovation in motion but their rate and scale determined the reach of its influence. Of the many pathways to change three were particularly significant. Most important of all, the understandings and habits of cleanliness trickled down the social structure. The core meanings of personal hygiene developed in privileged circles during the eighteenth and nineteenth centuries and from there spread slowly to all levels of society. A second pathway led from the city to the countryside. The new cleanliness was an urban phenomenon that gradually made its way into village and rural life as the Western world urbanized during the nineteenth and twentieth centuries. The third proceeded from America to Western Europe after 1900, and it was largely commercial. More than any other single nation the United States created the twentieth-century economy of mass consumption, and it proved especially inventive at producing and promoting consumer goods, those for body care among them. In the process American enterprise commercialized cleanliness and established new imperatives for personal hygiene. Yet whatever the pathways followed, by the later twentieth century Western customs had converged on a new shared sense of cleanliness, one based on common understandings, common techniques, and common products, things available to all.

Europe's twentieth-century lag in hygienic practices, technologies, and facilities was among the many conditions generated by the grave economic shocks that ensued from two devastating wars, the Great Depression and postwar decolonization. Together these developments destroyed much of Europe's private and public wealth, delaying broad improvements to well-being by a generation or more. In North America, however, they had no similar effects. Only during the third quarter of the century, when economic growth rates in recovering Europe surpassed those of the United States and Canada, did living standards on the two sides of the Atlantic begin to approach each other again, a development with important consequences for the new cleanliness.[3] In the Old World as well as the New, hot and cold water became plentiful everywhere, the bathroom and its privacies ceased to be exceptional, and the automatic washing machine became ubiquitous, one of the many appliances now enhancing the modern home. At that point the new norms of personal hygiene became an element of a universal culture, an identity shared by all.

By the second half of the twentieth century most Westerners paid more attention to their intimate hygiene than at any time in the past. During the 1960s Europeans and North Americans set aside five or six hours a week for their personal care, and from then on the amounts of time they spent on the task grew steadily.[4] Some two decades later American women allotted ten hours weekly to these activities, American men seven. Meanwhile the French and Italians devoted similar amounts of time to their hygiene.[5] Of course these pursuits included more than washing and bathing, but cleanliness lay at their core. The increasing time dedicated to personal care expressed a concern for the body that continued to grow throughout the last half of the twentieth century, and both sexes shared the trend. Men generally spent almost as much time as women on their grooming, if not an equal amount, and more striking still, these patterns crossed national and cultural boundaries. Well before the end of the century all could enjoy the languid bath that the beauty counsellors of former times had advised for the favoured few.

Yet in spite of all there were – and still are – sceptics, and if anything their numbers are growing. There have always been doubters who questioned the deeper meanings of cleanliness and faulted its apparent excesses. In the early 1930s the Austrian novelist Robert Musil viewed the quest for the clean body in a moral, not a hygienic context. Quite apart from anything soap sales might say about cleanliness, he noted wryly, "a strong compulsion to wash suggests a dubious state of inner hygiene."[6] Roland Barthes's suspicions about laundry cleaners shine through his solemn analysis of meaning in detergent advertising; indeed his essay can easily be read as a satire on the industry's extravagant claims.[7] Still more recent concerns have raised the possibility that we've become too clean for our own good, that our immune systems don't develop as they should because they lack exposure to the bacteria that strengthen them, leaving us vulnerable to allergies and disease.[8] A growing scientific literature has explored the microbial implications of contemporary skin care practices, raising questions about the desirable limits of washing and bathing. According to one overview, too much hand washing may damage the skin and increase the risk of infection. As to full-body cleansing, "frequent bathing has aesthetic and stress-relieving benefits but serves little microbiologic purpose."[9] We bathe because it feels good, not because it protects our health. More isn't better and in some cases may well be worse. Meanwhile new challenges confront the beauty trades and their many claims about their skin care preparations. Lately dermatology has raised searching questions about the hygienic value of soap.[10] Media reports now suggest a growing popular skepticism of scrupulous body care customs – bathing and shampooing in particular.[11] And so the discussion continues. Has our sense of what cleanliness means become an open question once more?

ACKNOWLEDGMENTS

The historian's task is usually a solitary one and so it's been for me, not only during this project but throughout my entire career. As a result, those who've helped and encouraged me have left a lasting mark on my life as much as on my labour. First among them is my wife, Patricia Ward, my first reader, my firm critic, my generous partisan, and my steadfast support; for all that she has given me I'm profoundly grateful. In truth, if I write for anyone at all I write for her. I'm beholden to my library colleague Keith Bunnell as well. Over the years he's aided and abetted my interests and enthusiasms, opening windows for me on the world of historical scholarship throughout Europe and North America. Three of my former students also came to my aid when my time and attention were taken up by administrative chores. Maija Fenger, David Meola, and Chris Parsons were my eyes when my own were fixed on minutes and memos, and they left me a rich record of their inquiries. In return, I hope the experience gave them a strong sense of the historian's enterprise. Finally I'm deeply indebted to my publisher, editor, and good friend Philip Cercone. He has long been, and he remains, one of our country's greatest champions of the book, and our association has been one of the true pleasures of my life in history.

SOURCES TO FIGURES

FIGURE 6.1

Canada

1941–71. John R. Miron, *Housing in Postwar Canada: Demographic Change, Household Formation, and Housing Demand* (Kingston and Montreal: McGill-Queen's University Press, 1988), 187.

1981. Canada, "Census of Canada" (1981).

2000. Canada. Statistics Canada, "Survey of Household Spending and Household Equipment" (2000).

England and Wales

1951–91. Great Britain, Census of England and Wales.

1966. Great Britain, *Sample Census 1966. England and Wales, Housing Tables*. Part I, Table 11 (1966).

1972. "Better Homes: The Next Priorities," ed. House of Commons (London: HMSO, 1973).

1979. European Communities Commission, *Family Budgets: Comparative Tables: Germany, France, Italy, United Kingdom* (Luxembourg: Office des publications officielles des Communautés européennes, 1984).

France

1946. Nicole C. Rudolph, *At Home in Postwar France: Modern Mass Housing and the Right to Comfort* (New York: Berghahn, 2015), 18.

1954–84. Jacques Méraud, *Les Besoins des Français* (Paris: Economica, 1990), 46.

1964. Institut national de la statistique et des études économiques, "Enquête sur les budgets familiaux 1963–64: Résultats relatifs à l'ensemble des ménages" (Paris: Imprimerie nationale, 1968).

1979. European Communities Commission, *Family Budgets: Comparative Tables: Germany, France, Italy, United Kingdom.*

West Germany

1979. European Communities Commission, *Family Budgets: Comparative Tables: Germany, France, Italy, United Kingdom.*

1989. Alphons Silbermann and Michael Brüning, *Der Deutschen Badezimmer. Eine soziologische Studie* (Cologne: Wissenschaft und Politik, 1991), 37.

Italy

1931. Luciano Bergonzini, *Un'indagine sulle condizioni igieniche delle abitazioni in Italia* (Bologna: L. Cappelli, 1957), 29.

1951, 1959. Istituto nazionale di statistica, *Indagine speciale su alcuni aspetti delle condizioni igieniche e sanitarie della popolazione*, notes and reports 1960/10 (Rome: ISTAT, 1960), 30.

1961–81. Paolo Quirino, "I consumi in Italia dall'Unità ad oggi," in *Storia dell'economia italiana. III. L'età contemporanea: un paese nuovo*, ed. Ruggiero Romano (Turin: Einaudi, 1991), 225.

1979. Commission, *Family Budgets: Comparative Tables: Germany, France, Italy, United Kingdom.*

1991–2001. Italy. Censimento generale della popolazione e delle abitazioni.

United States

1940–90. Bureau, "Historical Census of Housing Tables, Plumbing Facilities."

2000. "American Housing Survey for the United States: 2001."

FIGURE 7.1

Canada

1951–68. Joy Parr, *Domestic Goods: The Material, the Moral, and the Economic in the Postwar Years* (Toronto: University of Toronto Press, 1999), 271.

1977–81. Canada. Statistics Canada, *Household Facilities and Equipment, 1977–1981* (Ottawa: Information Canada).

2000. Canada. Statistics Canada, "Survey of Household Spending and Household Equipment" (2000), CANSIM Table 203-0020.

France

1950–59. Union pour l'étude du marché de l'électricité, "Évolution des applications domestiques de l'électricité en France et dans quelques pays d'Europe" (Paris: Union pour l'étude du marché de l'électricité 1961), 20.
1960–73. Fernand Pascaud, "La consommation des ménages de 1959 à 1972" (Paris: Institut national de la statistique et des études économiques, 1974), 25.
1974–84. Sergio Paba, *Reputazione ed efficienza. Crescita e concentrazione nell'industria europea degli elettrodomestici bianchi* (Bologna: il Mulino, 1991), 112.
1985–1990. Jacques Méraud, *Les Besoins des Français* (Paris: Economica, 1990), 48.
1991–2000. Quynh Delaunay, *La machine à laver en France. Un objet technique qui parle des femmes* (Paris: L'Harmattan, 2003), 57.

West Germany

1928. Barbara Orland, *Wäsche waschen. Technik- und Sozialgeschichte der häuslichen Wäschepflege.* (Reinbek bei Hamburg: Rowohlt, 1991), 206.
1938. Jennifer Ann Loehlin, *From Rugs to Riches: Housework, Consumption and Modernity in Germany* (Oxford: Berg, 1999), 61.
1955–56. Union pour l'étude du marché de l'électricité, "Évolution des applications domestiques de l'électricité en France et dans quelques pays d'Europe" (Paris: Union pour l'étude du marché de l'électricité, 1961), 20.
1962. Arne Andersen, *Der Traum vom guten Leben. Alltags- und Konsumgeschichte vom Wirtschaftswunder bis heute* (Frankfurt am Main: Campus, 1997), 108.
1964–84, Paba, *Reputazione ed efficienza*, 112.
1986, 1988, 2000. "Statistisches Jahrbuch für die Bundesrepublik Deutschland."

Great Britain

1933–79. Sue Bowden and Avner Offer, "Household Appliances and the Use of Time: The United States and Britain since the 1920s." *Economic History Review* 47, no. 4 (1994): 729.
1980–2000. Allison Walker et al., "Living in Britain: Results from the 2000/01 General Household Survey" (London: HMSO, 2001), 45.

Italy

1950–59. Union pour l'étude du marché de l'électricité, "Évolution des applications domestiques de l'électricité en France et dans quelques pays d'Europe," 20.

1960–65. Bollettino della Doxa XIX, 23–24, 31 dec. 1965.

1966–87. Paba, *Reputazione ed efficienza*, 112.

1988–90. Massimiliano Pittau, "Da privilegio a intrattenimento. Consumi e pubblicità in Italia dal dopoguerra ad oggi," in *La scatola nera della pubblicità*, ed. Aldo Grasso (Turin: Silvana, 2000), 54.

United States

Bowden and Offer, "Household Appliances and the Use of Time," 729.

FIGURE 7.2

Joann Vanek, "Keeping Busy: Time Spent in Housework, United States, 1920–1970" (PhD diss., University of Wisconsin, 1973), 94; Suzanne M. Bianchi et al., "Is Anyone Doing the Housework? Trends in the Gender Division of Household Labor," *Social Forces* 79, no. 1 (2000), 208; Bureau of Labor Statistics United States Department of Labor, "American Time Use Survey (ATUS), 2003–2008. Multi-Year Data" (2008), T020102.

FIGURE 7.3

Edgar Woollatt, *The Manufacture of Soaps, Other Detergents, and Glycerine* (Chichester: E. Horwood, 1985), 106.

NOTES

In order to allow the past its own voice I've included quotations from many of the works I've relied on. A few short phrases apart, in quoting these passages the main text provides translations from those sources written in languages other than English. The endnotes include references to the original language materials themselves.

EPIGRAPH

Federico Fellini and Tonino Guerra, *Amarcord* (Milano: Rizzoli, 1973), 7.

IO MI RICORDO

Lo so, lo so, lo so,
Che un uomo a cinquant'anni
ha sempre le mani pulite
e io me le lavo due o tre volte al giorno,
Ma è soltanto se mi vedo le mani sporche
che io mi ricordo
di quando ero ragazzo.

I REMEMBER

I know, I know, I know,
that a man of 50 years
always has clean hands
and I wash mine two or three times a day,
But it's only when I see dirty hands
that I recall
when I was a boy.

PREFACE

1 Alexander Peter Hanley, *Interview with Alexander Peter Hanley* (Edmonton: Provincial Archives of Alberta, 1972), phonotape acc.71.6.

CHAPTER ONE

1 Georges Vigarello, *Concepts of Cleanliness: Changing Attitudes in France since the Middle Ages* (Cambridge: Cambridge University Press, 1988), 13, 18, 25, 68.

2 Lawrence Stone, *The Family, Sex, and Marriage in England, 1500–1800* (New York: Harper and Row, 1977), 485.

3 Vigarello, *Concepts of Cleanliness*, 39–89.

4 Quoted in ibid., 60–1.

5 Roy Porter and Georges Vigarello, "Corps, santé et maladies," in *Histoire du corps*, vol. 1: *De la Renaissance aux Lumières*, ed. Alain Corbin, Jean-Jacques Courtine, and Georges Vigarello (Paris: Seuil, 2005), 358.

6 Giuseppe Pitrè, *Medicina popolare siciliana* (Bologna: Forni, 1969), 151–71.

7 Porter and Vigarello, "Corps, santé et maladies," 358.

8 Françoise Loux and Philippe Richard, *Sagesses du corps. La santé et la maladie dans les proverbes français* (Paris: Maisonneuve & Larose, 1978), 304–10.

9 Jacques Léonard, *Archives du corps. La santé au XIXe siècle* (Rennes: Ouest-France, 1986), 116.

10 Loux and Richard, *Sagesses du corps*, 304; Pitrè, *Medicina popolare siciliana*, 167–8.

11 Françoise Loux and Jean Cuisenier, *Le Corps dans la société traditionnelle* (Paris: Berger-Levrault, 1979), 91; Françoise Loux, *Le jeune enfant et son corps dans la médecine traditionnelle* (Paris: Flammarion, 1978), 204–5.

12 Léonard, *Archives du corps*, 117.

13 Ibid., 115.

14 Jean-Pierre Goubert, *The Conquest of Water: The Advent of Health in the Industrial Age* (Cambridge: Polity Press, 1989), 218.

15 Manuel Frey, *Der reinliche Bürger. Entstehung und Verbreitung bürgerlicher Tugenden in Deutschland, 1760–1860* (Göttingen: Vandenhoeck & Ruprecht, 1997), 62.

16 Ibid., 320–3.

17 Paolo Sorcinelli, *Storia sociale dell'acqua. Riti e culture* (Milan: Mondatori, 1998), 5–28.

18 Emmanuel Le Roy Ladurie, "Introduction," in Goubert, *The Conquest of Water*, 14.

19 Emiliano Giancristofaro, *Tradizioni popolari d'Abruzzo* ... (Rome: Newton Compton, 1995), 308.

20 Frey, *Der reinliche Bürger*, 56.

21 Paul Sébillot, *Le folklore de France*, vol. 3: *La mer* (Paris: Editions Imago, 1982); *Le folklore de France*, vol 4: *Les eaux douces* (Paris: Editions Imago, 1982).

22 Goubert, *The Conquest of Water*, 244–5.

23 William Brockie, *Legends & superstitions of the County of Durham* [1886] (Wakefield: EP, 1974), 231–2; Joseph McKenzie McPherson, *Primitive Beliefs in the North-East of Scotland* (London and New York: Longmans, Green, 1929), 37–60; Ruth L. Tongue and Katharine Mary Briggs, *Somerset Folklore* (London: Folk-Lore Society, 1965), 218–20; Tony Deane and Tony Shaw, *The Folklore of Cornwall* (Totowa: Rowman and Littlefield, 1975), 157–9.

24 Goubert, *The Conquest of Water*, 217.

25 Alain Corbin, *The Foul and the Fragrant: Odor and the French Social Imagination* (Cambridge, MA: Harvard University Press, 1986), 37.

26 Anne-Laure Lallouette, "Bains et soins du corps dans les textes médicaux (XIIe-XIVe siècles)," in *Laver, monder, blanchir. Discours et usages de la toilette dans l'occident médiéval*, ed. Sophie Albert (Paris: Presses de l'Université Paris-Sorbonne, 2006), 33–49.

27 Frey, *Der reinliche Bürger*, 111–32.

28 Ernst Gerhard Eder, *Bade- und Schwimmkultur in Wien. Sozialhistorische und kulturanthropologische Untersuchungen* (Vienna: Böhlau, 1995), 118.

29 Frey, *Der reinliche Bürger*, 129.

30 Virginia Smith, *Clean: A History of Personal Hygiene and Purity* (Oxford: Oxford University Press, 2007), 248–9.

31 Philip D. Curtin, *Death by Migration: Europe's Encounter with the Tropical World in the Nineteenth Century* (Cambridge: Cambridge University Press, 1989).

32 Peter M. Dunn, "Dr William Buchan (1729–1805) and His Domestic Medicine," *Archives of Disease in Childhood: Fetal and Neonatal Edition* 83 (2000): F71–F73; Richard L. Bushman and Claudia Bushman, "The Early History of Cleanliness in America," *Journal of American History* 74 (1988): 1223.

33 Quoted in Smith, *Clean*, 255.

34 Quoted in ibid., 254.

35 Ibid., 247–8; Olivier Faure, "Le regard des médecins," in *Histoire du corps*, vol. 2: *De la Révolution à la Grande guerre*, ed. Alain Corbin, Jean-Jacques Courtine, and Georges Vigarello (Paris: Seuil, 2005), 47–8.

36 Corbin, *The Foul and the Fragrant*, passim.

37 Smith, *Clean*, 256–63.

38 Vigarello, *Concepts of Cleanliness*, 170–2.

39 Corbin, *The Foul and the Fragrant*, 71–2.

40 L.W.B. Brockliss, "The Development of the Spa in Seventeenth-Century France," in *The Medical History of Waters and Spas*, ed. Roy Porter (London: Wellcome Institute for the History of Medicine, 1990), 23–47.

41 C.F. Mullett, "Public baths and health in England, 16th–18th century," *Bulletin of the History of Medicine: Supplements*, no. 5 (1946).

42 Douglas Peter Mackaman, *Leisure Settings: Bourgeois Culture, Medicine, and the Spa in Modern France* (Chicago: University of Chicago Press, 1998); Frey, *Der reinliche Bürger*, 219–33.

43 Vigarello, *Concepts of Cleanliness*, 168–9.

44 Alain Corbin, *Le Territoire du vide. L'Occident et le désir du rivage (1750–1840)* (Paris: Aubier, 1988).

45 John Hassan, *The Seaside, Health, and the Environment in England and Wales since 1800* (Aldershot: Ashgate, 2003), 15–30.

46 Smith, *Clean*, 244–6; Vigarello, *Concepts of Cleanliness*, 191; Léonard, *Archives du corps*, 123–5.

47 Bushman and Bushman, "The Early History of Cleanliness in America," 1215.

48 Smith, *Clean*, 244.

49 W. Kaschuba, "Deutsche Sauberkeit – Zivilisierung der Körper und der Köpf," in *Wasser und Seife, Puder und Parfüm. Geschichte der Körperhygiene seit dem Mittelalter*, ed. Georges Vigarello (Frankfurt: Campus, 1988), 292–326; Frey, *Der reinliche Bürger*, passim.

50 Vigarello, *Concepts of Cleanliness*, 156–60.

51 Bushman and Bushman, "The Early History of Cleanliness in America," 1219–22.

52 Kaschuba, "Deutsche Sauberkeit," 302; Eder, *Bade- und Schwimmkultur in Wien*, 122–3.

53 Corbin, *The Foul and the Fragrant*, 142–60; Olivier Le Goff, *L'invention du confort. Naissance d'une forme sociale* (Lyon: Presses Universitaires de Lyon, 1994), 34–7; Frey, *Der reinliche Bürger*, 261–75; Eder, *Bade- und Schwimmkultur in Wien*, 122–9.

54 Edwin Chadwick, *Report on the Sanitary Condition of the Labouring Population of Great Britain*, ed. M.W. Flinn [1842] (Edinburgh: Edinburgh University Press, 1965), 424–5.

55 "First Annual Report of the Whitechapel Association for Promoting Habits Tending to the Cleanliness, Health and Comfort of the Industrious Classes in the Parish of Whitechapel" (Whitechapel [London]: School-Press, 1850).

56 Francesco del Teglia, *Della Bellezza e del bello e onesto Orgolio che decorosamente ha da guernirla e difenderla* (Florence: Bernardo Paperini, 1726).

57 Antoine Le Camus, *Abdeker ou l'art de conserver la beauté* (Paris: Louis-Étienne Ganeau, 1754), 118–24; for the broader context see Mohja Kahf, *Western Representations of the Muslim Woman: From Termagant to Odalisque* (Austin: University of Texas Press, 1999), 111–75.

58 *Leibdiener der Schönheit. Oder neuentdekte Geheimnisse von der Schönheit des Frauenzimmers...* (Bremen: H. Jäger, 1751); *Fuer Damen, und andere Frauenzimmer. Eine Sammlung der wichtigsten, groesstentheils bisher geheim gehaltenen Kunststücke und Mittel, wodurch sie ihre Schoenheit erhoehen und erhalten...* (Salzburg, 1790); *L'Arte di conservare ed accrescere la bellezza delle donne, scritta da un filantropo subalpino* (Turin: M. Morano, 1804); Johann Bartholomäus Trommsdorff, *Kallopistria, oder die Kunst der Toilette für die elegante Welt: Eine Anleitung zur Verfertigung unschädlicher Parfüms und Schönheitsmittel...* (Vienna: Anton v. Haykul, 1805).

59 Auguste Caron, *The lady's toilette, containing a critical examination of the nature of beauty ... an historical sketch of the fashions of France and England* (London: W.H. Wyatt, 1808), 36.

60 Ibid., 141–7, 199.

61 *La Bellezza ed i Mezzi di Conservarla, ossia La Toletta delle Signore* (Milan: Giovanni Pirotta, 1827), 49–58; Mme Celnart, *Manuel des dames, ou L'art de la toilette* (Paris: Roret, 1827), 43–4.

62 A. Debay, *Hygiène de la beauté, résumé de tous les moyens hygiéniques propres à conserver, à développer la beauté du corps et à remédier aux imperfections naturelles ou acquises* (Brussels: Meline, Cars, et cie., 1846), 127–46.

63 Ibid., 135.

64 Ovid, *Metamorphoses*, trans. A.D. Melville (Oxford: Oxford University Press, 1986), 55–8.

65 Titian, *Diana and Actaeon*, 1556–59. National Gallery, London.

66 Michaela Bauks, "Nacktheit und Scham in Genesis 2–3," in *Zur Kulturgeschichte der Scham*, ed. Michaela Bauks and Martin F. Meyer (Hamburg: Felix Meiner, 2011), 17–34.

67 Wolfgang Pircher, "Artemis, Bathseba und Susana im Bade. Verletzte Intimität," in *Das Bad. Eine Geschichte der Badekultur im 19. und 20. Jahrhundert*, ed. Herbert Lachmayer, Sylvia Mattl-Wurm, and Christian Gargerle (Salzburg: Residenz Verlag, 1991); Nadeije Laneyrie-Dagen and Georges Vigarello, *La Toilette: Naissance de l'intime: The Invention of Privacy*, Paris Musée Marmottan Monet (Paris: Éditions Hazan, 2015), 25–7.

68 Hans Peter Duerr, *Der Mythos vom Zivilisationsprozess*, vol. 1: *Nacktheit und Scham* (Frankfurt am Main: Suhrkamp, 1988), 94–5.

69 Eder, *Bade- und Schwimmkultur in Wien*, 211–12.

70 Ibid., 235–43; Jean-Claude Bologne, *Histoire de la pudeur* (Paris: O. Orban, 1986), 43–4; Duerr, *Der Mythos vom Zivilisationsprozess*, vol. 1, 95–101.

71 Léonard, *Archives du corps*, 123.

72 Georg M.C. Brandes, *Voltaire*, vol. 1 (New York: Tudor, 1920), 384.

73 Norbert Elias, *The History of Manners* (Oxford: Blackwell, 1978), 138.

74 Duerr, *Der Mythos vom Zivilisationsprozess*, vol. 1, 109.

75 Vigarello, *Concepts of Cleanliness*, 174; Odile Arnold, *Le corps et l'ame. La vie des religieuses au 19. siècle* (Paris: Seuil, 1984); Monique Eleb and Anne Debarre, *L'invention de l'habitation moderne: Paris, 1880–1914* (Paris: Hazan, 1995), 222.

76 Corbin, *The Foul and the Fragrant*, 177–9; Vigarello, *Concepts of Cleanliness*, 174–5.

77 Giuseppe Tomasi di Lampedusa, *Il Gattopardo*, 87 ed. (Milano: Feltrinelli, 2006), 47.

78 Léonard, *Archives du corps*, 118.

79 A. Béal, *Passe-temps d'un praticien d'Auvergne, causeries sur l'hygiène... et autres sujets joyeux, rédigées conformément aux us et coutumes régionales* (Paris: A. Maloine, 1900), 232.

80 Anna Davin, *Growing Up Poor: Home, School, and Street in London, 1870–1914* (London: Rivers Oram Press, 1996), 51–2; Reinhard Sieder, "'Vata, derf i aufstehn?': Childhood Experiences in Viennese Working-Class Families around 1900," *Continuity and Change* 1, no. 1 (1986): 69–70; Lucinda McCray Beier, *For Their Own Good: The Transformation of English Working-Class Health Culture, 1880–1970* (Columbus: Ohio State University Press, 2008), 231.

81 Eder, *Bade- und Schwimmkultur in Wien*, 234, qtd from Hermann Glaser, *Maschinenwelt und Alltagsleben. Industriekultur in Deutschland vom*

Biedermeier bis zur Weimarer Republik (Frankfurt am Main: Krüger, 1981), 123.

82 Maud Pember Reeves, *Round About a Pound a Week* [1913] (London: Virago, 1979), 55–6.

83 Sorcinelli, *Storia sociale dell'acqua*, 32–38; Paolo Sorcinelli, "L'acqua e il corpo tra igiene e salute," in *Storia dell'acqua. Mondi materiali e universi simbolici*, ed. Vito Teti (Rome: Donzelli, 2003), 293–308.

84 Emmanuel Le Roy Ladurie, *Montaillou: The Promised Land of Error*, trans. Barbara Bray (New York: Vintage, 1979), 141–2.

85 Frey, *Der reinliche Bürger*, 322.

86 Guy Thuillier, *Pour une histoire du quotidien au XIXᵉ siècle en Nivernais* (Paris: Mouton, École des hautes Études en Sciences Sociales, 1977), 50–1.

87 Ibid., 54.

88 Alexandre Layet, *Étude sur la vie matérielle des campagnards en Europe: médecine sociale, hygiène et maladies des paysans* (Paris: G. Masson, 1882), 309.

89 Antonin Baratier, *Hygiène générale. L'École de village au point de vue de l'hygiène publique et privée* (Paris: G. Maurin, 1899), 19–20.

90 Frey, *Der reinliche Bürger*, 323.

91 Léonard, *Archives du corps*, 116, 300.

92 Renato Bellabarba, *Il ciclo della vita nella campagna marchigiana. Contributo allo studio delle tradizioni popolari* (Florence: L.S. Olschki, 1979), 117.

93 Chadwick, *Report on the sanitary condition*, 315–16.

94 Jean-Marie Martin, "Purificazione: il bagno," in *Anima dell'acqua* (Rome: "L'Erma" di Bretschneider, 2008), 284–92.

95 Lallouette, "Bains et soins du corps," 33–49.

96 Jacques Le Goff, *Il corpo nel Medioevo* (Rome: Laterza, 2005), 128–30; Marie Guérin-Beauvois et Jean-Marie Martin, eds., *Bains curatifs et bains hygiéniques en Italie de l'antiquité au Moyen Âge* (Rome: École française de Rome, 2007).

97 Ludovica Sebregondi, "Immagini di bagni e terme," in *Segrete delle acque. Studi e immagini sui bagni, Secoli XIV–XIX*, ed. Paolo Viti (Florence: Leo S. Olschki, 2007), 93–104. Duerr, *Der Mythos vom Zivilisationsprozess*, Bd. 1., 38–73.

98 Frey, *Der reinliche Bürger*, 59–61.

99 Smith, *Clean*, 242–3.

100 Vigarello, *Concepts of Cleanliness*, 103.

101 Bologne, *Histoire de la pudeur*, 37; Pierre-Simon Girard, "Recherches sur les établissements de bains publics à Paris depuis le IVe siècle jusqu'à présent," *Annales d'hygiene publique* 7 (1832): 42.

102 Louis F. Benoiston de Châteauneuf, *Recherches sur les consommations de tout genre de la ville de Paris en 1817 comparées a ce qu'elles étaient en 1789*, Pt. II, 2 ed. (Paris: Chez l'Auteur, Chez Martinet, 1821), 141–2.

103 Vigarello, *Concepts of Cleanliness*, 156–8.

104 Girard, "Recherches sur les établissements"; Ambroise Tardieu, "Bains," in *Dictionnaire d'hygiène publique et de salubrité* (Paris: J.-B. Baillière et fils, 1862), 184–93; Julia Csergo, *Liberté, égalité, propreté: La morale de l'hygiène au XIXe siècle* (Paris: Albin Michel, 1988), 322–3, 334.

105 Michel Lévy, *Traite d'hygiène publique et privée*, vol. 2 (Paris: J.-B. Baillière, 1862), 775.

106 Girard, "Recherches sur les établissements," 51.

107 Frey, *Der reinliche Bürger*, 219–33.

108 Bushman and Bushman, "The Early History," 1215.

109 Ibid., 1228–31; Harold Donaldson Eberlein, "When Society First Took a Bath," in *Sickness and Health in America: Readings in the History of Medicine and Public Health*, ed. Judith Walzer Leavitt and Ronald L. Numbers (Madison: University of Wisconsin Press, 1978), 331–41.

110 Vigarello, *Concepts of Cleanliness*, 190.

111 Leslie Tomory, *The History of the London Water Industry, 1580–1820* (Baltimore: Johns Hopkins University Press, 2017), 223–9.

112 Eder, *Bade- und Schwimmkultur in Wien*, 75–204.

113 Léonard, *Archives du corps*, 122.

114 Edmond Auguste Texier, *Tableau de Paris*, 2 vols. (Paris: Paulin et Le Chevalier, 1852), II: 2–9.

115 Davide Lombardo, "Se baigner ensemble. Les corps au quotidien et les bains publics parisiens avant 1850 selon Daumier," *Histoire urbaine*, no. 31 (2011): 47–68.

116 Georges Vigarello, "Le corps travaillé: Gymnasts et sportifs au XIXe siècle. I. Traditions renouvelées?," in *Histoire du corps*, vol. 2, 327–9.

117 Texier, *Tableau de Paris*, I: 200–2.

118 Ann Elizabeth Fowler La Berge, *Mission and Method: The Early Nineteenth-Century French Public Health Movement* (Cambridge and New York: Cambridge University Press, 1992), 252–3.

119 Frey, *Der reinliche Bürger*, 235–40.

120 Gottfried Pirhofer, Ramon Reichert, and Martina Wurzacher, "Bäder für die Öffentlichkeit – Hallen und Freibäder als urbander Raum," in *Das Bad: eine Geschichte der Badekultur im 19. und 20. Jahrhundert*, ed. Herbert Lachmayer, Sylvia Mattl-Wurm, and Christian Gargerle (Salzburg: Residenz, 1991), 156–9.

CHAPTER TWO

1 Alain Corbin, *The Foul and the Fragrant: Odor and the French Social Imagination* (Cambridge, MA: Harvard University Press, 1986), ch. 9.

2 Ibid., 155–6.

3 *Baths and Wash-houses for the Labouring Classes. Statement of the preliminary measures adopted for the purpose of promoting the establishment of baths and wash-houses for the labouring classes; including a report of the proceedings at a public meeting held in the Mansion House ... Oct. 16, 1844, etc* (London: Blades & East, 1845); Metropolitan Working Classes' Association for Improving the Public Health, "Bathing and personal cleanliness" (London: J. Churchill, 1847). See also Alfred Ebsworth, *Facts and inferences drawn from an inspection of the public baths and wash-houses in this metropolis* (London: n.p., 1853).

4 Tom Crook, "Schools for Moral Training of the People: Public Baths, Liberalism, and the Promotion of Cleanliness in Victorian Britain," *European Review of History* 13, no. 1 (2006), 21–47.

5 Edwin Chadwick, *Report on the sanitary condition of the labouring population of Great Britain*, ed. M.W. Flinn [1842] (Edinburgh: Edinburgh University Press, 1965), 316–18.

6 Edward H. Gibson, "Baths and Washhouses in the English Public Health Agitation, 1839–1848," *Journal of the History of Medicine and Allied Sciences* 9, no. 4 (1954), 394. Great Britain, "First Report of the Commissioners for Inquiring into the State of Large Towns and Populous Districts," Command Papers; Reports of Commissioners, Cmd. 572 (London: William Clowes & Sons, 1844), 197. For an overview of the Victorian public bath movement, see Lee Jackson, *Dirty Old London: The Victorian Fight against Filth* (New Haven: Yale University Press, 2014), 134–54.

7 Sally Sheard, "Profit Is a Dirty Word: The Development of Public Baths and Wash-Houses in Britain, 1847–1915," *Social History of Medicine* 13, no. 1 (2000), 70.

8 Gibson, "Baths and Washhouses"; Anthony S. Wohl, *Endangered Lives: Public Health in Victorian Britain* (London: Dent, 1983), 72–6.

9 Ebsworth, *Facts and Inferences*, Appendix A.

10 Agnes Campbell, *Report on public baths and wash-houses in the United Kingdom*, Carnegie United Kingdom Trust Report (Edinburgh: T. & A. Constable, 1918), 7–11.

11 Committee for Promoting the Establishment of Baths and Wash-Houses for the Labouring Classes, *Public baths and wash-houses: suggestions for building and fitting up parochial or borough establishments: with detailed calculations of the working expenses and earnings of such establishments* (London, 1850), 5.

12 Britain, "First Report."

13 France, *Bains et Lavoirs Publics. Commission instituée par ordre de M. le Président de la République. Ministère de l'Agriculture et en Commerce* (Paris: Gide et J. Baudry, 1850), ii.

14 Adolphe Chauveau, "Bains et lavoirs du Temple," *Journal du droit administratif* 3 (1855), 271–4; Jaimee Grüring, "Dirty Laundry: Public Hygiene and Public Space in Nineteenth-Century Paris" (PhD thesis, Arizona State University, 2011), 111–18.

15 Julia Csergo, *Liberté, égalité, propreté. La morale de l'hygiène au XIXe siècle* (Paris: Albin Michel, 1988), 152–61.

16 Achille Penot, *Les Cités ouvrières de Mulhouse et du département du Haut-Rhin. Nouvelle édition, augmentée de la description des bains et lavoirs établis à Mulhouse* (Mulhouse: L.L. Bader, 1867).

17 Csergo, *Liberté, égalité, propreté*, 162–82.

18 Richard J. Evans, *Death in Hamburg: Society and Politics in the Cholera Years, 1830–1910* (Oxford and New York: Clarendon Press, 1987), 118.

19 Barbara Hartmann, *Das Müller'sche Volksbad in München* (Munich: Tuduv, 1987).

20 Ibid., 7–14.

21 Dirk Meyhöfer, "Public Swimming Baths: A Building Type of the Second German Kaiserzeit," in *The Water Temple: Gründerzeit and Jugendstil Public Baths*, ed. Kristin Feireiss (London: Academy Editions, 1994), 11–23.

22 Friedrich Renk, "Öffentliche Bäder," *Handbuch der Hygiene und der Gewerbekrankheiten*, ed. Max von Pettenkofer and Hugo Wilhelm von Ziemssen (Leipzig: F.C.W. Vogel, 1882), 394.

23 Brian K. Ladd, "Public Baths and Civic Improvement in Nineteenth-Century German Cities," *Journal of Urban History* 14, no. 3 (1988), 382–3.

24 Gottfried Pirhofer, Ramon Reichert, and Martina Wurzacher, "Bäder für die Öffentlichkeit – Hallen und Freibäder als urbander Raum," in *Das Bad. Eine Geschichte der Badekultur im 19. und 20. Jahrhundert*, ed. Herbert Lachmayer, Sylvia Mattl-Wurm, and Christian Gargerle (Salzburg: Residenz, 1991), 168.

25 Ira Spieker, "'Jedem Deutschen wöchentlich ein Bad': Die Popularisierung von Volksbädern um die Jahrhundertwende und ihre Einrichtung im ländlichen Raum," in *Reinliche Leiber, schmutzige Geschäfte. Körperhygiene und Reinlichkeitsvorstellungen in zwei Jahrhunderten*, ed. Regina Löneke and Ira Spieker (Göttingen: Wallstein, 1996), 117.

26 Francesco Freschi, *Dizionario di Igiene pubblica e di Polizia Sanitaria* (Turin: G. Favale, 1857), I: 510–17.

27 Giovanni Fanelli, *Firenze architettura e città* (Florence: Mandragora, 2002), 430.

28 Giuseppe Ravaglia, "Intorno alla Utilità e alla Convenienza che anche a Bologna sorga tra breve Un Bagno Pubblico" (Bologna: Azzoguidi, 1882).

29 Ravaglia, "Guiseppe Garibaldi e un bagno pubblico a Bologna" [1885], in Guiseppe Mattioli and Luigi Guadagini, eds., *Bagno pubblico Garibaldi* (Bologna: Azzoguidi, 1890).

30 *I bagni popolari di Torino* (Turin: Tipografia Cooperativa, 1888); Alessia Giachetti, "Bagni e lavatoi pubblici in Torino," diss., Faculty of Architecture (Turin: Politecnico di Torino, 2003).

31 Paul Ginsborg, *A History of Contemporary Italy: Society and Politics, 1943–1988* (London: Penguin, 1990), 195–6.

32 Chiara Prosperini, *Le città sotterranee di Cleopatro Cobianchi. Architettura e igiene tra le due guerre* (Pisa: Edizioni ETS, 2003).

33 Richard L. Bushman and Claudia Bushman, "The Early History of Cleanliness in America," *Journal of American History* 74 (1988), 1215.

34 "Bains chauds et froids," *Gazette de Québec*, 4 May 1818.

35 Marilyn T. Williams, *Washing "the Great Unwashed": Public Baths in Urban America, 1840–1920* (Columbus: Ohio State University Press, 1991), 16; Raymond Vézina, "Bains publics de Montréal, 1835–2002" (Montreal: SPAG, 2002).

36 *Report on public baths and public comfort stations* (New York: Mayor's Committee on Public Baths and Public Comfort Stations, 1897), 17.

37 Williams, *Washing "the Great Unwashed,"* 38.

38 Peter Ward, *A History of Domestic Space: Privacy and the Canadian Home* (Vancouver: UBC Press, 1999), 57–60; William James Thomson, *Velocipede Rink and Baths*, http://www.torontopubliclibrary.ca/detail.jsp?Entt=RD-MDC-PICTURES-R-5356&R=DC-PICTURES-R-5356 (1896).

39 Jos van den Bongaardt, *Elke week een goed bad! Geschiedenis en architectuur van de badhuizen van Amsterdam. Een eeuw volksbadhuizen* (Amsterdam: Stadsuitgeverij Amsterdam, 1990), 24–52.

40 Williams, *Washing "the Great Unwashed,"* 57, 80, 92–3, 108, 121.

41 *Report on public baths and public comfort stations*, 18.

42 Ebsworth, *Facts and inferences*, Appendix A. The data are only for par-
    ishes for which the numbers of bathers were reported.

43 Campbell, *Report on public baths and wash-houses*, 7–11; Virginia Smith,
    Clean: A History of Personal Hygiene and Purity (Oxford: Oxford
    University Press, 2007), 312.

44 Williams, *Washing "the Great Unwashed,"* 38.

45 Ibid., 65.

46 Hartmann, *Das Müller'sche Volksbad in München*, 10.

47 Maud Pember Reeves, *Round About a Pound a Week* [1913] (London:
    Virago, 1979), 55.

48 "Cleanliness for the Collier," *The Lancet (London)* 177, no. 4572 (1911),
    1022–3.

49 Ernst Gerhard Eder, *Bade- und Schwimmkultur in Wien. Sozialhistorische
    und kulturanthropologische Untersuchungen* (Vienna: Böhlau, 1995), 167.

50 Philip D. Curtin, *Death by migration: Europe's Encounter with the
    Tropical World in the Nineteenth Century* (Cambridge: Cambridge
    University Press, 1989).

51 William A. Hammond, *A treatise on hygiene, with special reference to the
    military service* (Philadelphia: J.B. Lippencott, 1863), 233–41; John
    Ordronaux, *Hints on health in armies, for the use of volunteer officers*,
    2nd ed. (New York: D. Van Nostrand, 1863), 33–4.

52 W.H. Van Buren, *Rules for Preserving the Health of the Soldier*, 2d ed.
    (Washington, 1861); United States Sanitary Commission, *Camp Inspection
    Return* (Washington, 1861); United States Sanitary Commission, *Revised
    General Instructions for Camp Inspections* (Washington,1862).

53 Hammond, *A treatise on hygiene*, 238–9.

54 Ladd, "Public Baths and Civic Improvement," 383.

55 Charles Detienne, *Hygiène de l'armée, ou, Préceptes d'hygiène militaire. A
    l'usage des officiers et des sous-officiers de l'armée* (Liège: H. Dessain,
    1849), 92–103.

56 Hammond, *A treatise on hygiene*, 239–40.

57 Great Britain, "General Report of The Commission appointed for improv-
    ing the sanitary condition of Barracks and Hospitals," Cmd. 2839
    (London: HMSO, 1863), 47.

58 Csergo, *Liberté, égalité, propreté*, 135–48; Georges-Henri Tellier, *La Santé
    du soldat, manuel d'hygiène pratique à l'usage des hommes de troupe*
    (Paris: H. Charles-Lavauzelle, 1902), 14–23; Steven Zdatny, "The French
    Hygiene Offensive of the 1950s: A Critical Moment in the History of
    Manners," *Journal of Modern History* 84, no. 4 (2012), 903–6.

59 G.H.J. Evatt, "The Sanitary Care of the Soldier by His Officer," *Journal of the Royal Army Medical Corps* 18 (1912), 208.

60 Michel Foucault, *Discipline and Punish: The Birth of the Prison* (New York: Vintage Books, 1995), 293–4.

61 Michael Ignatieff, *A Just Measure of Pain: The Penitentiary in the Industrial Revolution, 1750–1850* (New York: Pantheon Books, 1978), 101.

62 "Report of the Committee for the Relief of the Poor and Destitute of the city of Toronto and rules and regulations of the House of Refuge & Industry established under their care, January 1837" (Toronto: J.H. Lawrence, 1837).

63 M.A. Crowther, *The Workhouse System, 1834–1929: The History of an English Social Institution* (London: Batsford Academic and Educational, 1981), 195–6.

64 Chadwick, *Report on the sanitary condition*, 315–16.

65 Georges Vigarello, *Concepts of Cleanliness: Changing Attitudes in France Since the Middle Ages* (Cambridge: Cambridge University Press, 1988), 157; Françoise de Bonneville, *The Book of the Bath* (London: Thames and Hudson, 1998), 82–116.

66 Jean-Pierre Goubert, *The Conquest of Water: The Advent of Health in the Industrial Age* (Cambridge: Polity Press, 1989), 241; Williams, *Washing "the Great Unwashed,"* 12.

67 Smith, *Clean*, 288; Bushman and Bushman, "The Early History," 1227.

68 Bonneville, *The Book of the Bath*, 109–12; Monique Eleb and Anne Debarre, *L'invention de l'habitation moderne. Paris, 1880–1914* (Paris: Hazan, 1995), 221–9; Vigarello, *Concepts of Cleanliness*, 186–7; Nadeije Laneyrie-Dagen and Georges Vigarello, *La Toilette. Naissance de l'intime. The invention of privacy*, Paris Musée Marmottan Monet (Paris: Éditions Hazan, 2015).

69 Xavier Rey, *Degas et le nu* (Paris: Gallimard; Musée d'Orsay, 2012); Laneyrie-Dagen and Vigarello, "La Toilette," 153–62.

70 F.W. Hunt, "The Sanitary Arrangement of Houses in London during the Last One Hundred and Twenty Years," in *The Health Exhibition Literature*, vol. 2: *Health in the Dwelling* (London: William Clowes and Sons, 1884), 171–3.

71 John Burnett, *A Social History of Housing, 1815–1985*, 2nd ed. (London: New York: Methuen, 1986), 206.

72 Stefan Muthesius, *The English Terraced House* (New Haven: Yale University Press, 1982), 61.

73 Robert Owen Allsop, *Public Baths and Wash-houses* (London: E. & F.N. Spon, 1894), 1–2.

74 Hermann Muthesius, *The English House* [1904] (New York: Rizzoli, 1979), 93.

75 Asher Benjamin, *The American Builder's Companion* [1827] 6th ed. (New York: Dover, 1969); A.J. Downing, *The Architecture of Country Houses* (New York: D. Appleton, 1859).

76 Alison K. Hoagland, *The Bathroom: A Social History of Cleanliness and the Body* (Santa Barbara: Greenwood, 2018), 10–29.

77 Ward, *A History of Domestic Space*, 51–60.

78 Georges Vigarello, *Le propre et le sale. L'hygiène du corps depuis le Moyen Âge* (Paris: Seuil, 1985), 186–7.

79 Csergo, *Liberté, égalité, propreté*, 261.

80 Guy Thuillier, *Pour une histoire du quotidien au XIXᵉ siècle en Nivernais* (Paris: Mouton, École des hautes Études en Sciences Sociales, 1977), 51.

81 M.J. Daunton, *House and Home in the Victorian City: Working-Class Housing 1850–1914* (London: Edward Arnold, 1983), 246.

82 Karl Bücher, *Die Wohnungs-Enquête in der Stadt Basel vom 1.–19. Februar 1889, im Auftrage des Regierungsrathes bearbeitet von Karl Bücher* (Basel: H. Georg, 1891), 103.

83 Hans J. Teuteberg and Clemens Wischermann, *Wohnalltag in Deutschland, 1850–1914: Bilder, Daten Dokumente* (Münster: Coppenrath, 1985), 138.

84 Clemens Wischermann, *Wohnen in Hamburg vor dem Ersten Weltkrieg* (Münster: Coppenrath, 1983), 462.

85 Charles O. Hardy and Robert René Kuczynski, *The Housing Program of the City of Vienna* (Washington, DC: Brookings Institution, 1934), 15.

86 Carol Schade, *Woningbouw voor arbeiders in het 19de-eeuwse Amsterdam* (Amsterdam: Van Gennep, 1981), 158–61, 198–9; Nancy Stieber, *Housing Design and Society in Amsterdam: Reconfiguring Urban Order and Identity, 1900–1920* (Chicago: University of Chicago Press, 1998), 75.

87 Geneviève Heller, *"Propre en ordre." Habitation et vie domestique 1850– 1930, l'exemple vaudois* (Lausanne: Éditions d'en Bas, 1979), 208.

88 Williams, *Washing "the Great Unwashed,"* 28; Massachusetts, "A tenement house census of Boston. Section II. Sanitary Condition of Tenements," ed. Bureau of Statistics of Labor (Boston: Wright and Potter, 1893), 117.

89 Michael Honhart, "Company Housing As Urban Planning in Germany, 1870–1940," *Central European History* 23, no. 1 (1990), 3–21.

90 Walter Lionel George, *Labour and Housing at Port Sunlight* (London: Alston Rivers, 1909), 76, 88.

91 Budgett Meakin, *Model factories and villages: Ideal Conditions of Labour and Housing* (Philadelphia: G.W. Jacobs, 1905), 439–40.

92 Ibid., 382–409.

93 Ibid., 371–2; Cedric Bolz, "From 'Garden City Precursors' to 'Cemeteries for the Living': Contemporary Discourse on Krupp Housing and Besucherpolitik in Wilhelmine Germany," *Urban History* 37, no. 1 (2010), 90–116.

94 Renate Köhne-Lindenlaub, *The Villa Hügel: An Entrepreneur's Residence in the Course of Time* (Munich and Berlin: Alfried Krupp von Bohlen und Halbach-Stiftung; Deutscher Kunstverlag, 2003), 38–9.

95 Christian Legrand, Krzysztof Kazimierz Pawłowski, and Bruno Voisin, *Le logement populaire et social en Lyonnais, 1848–2000* (Lyon: Aux arts, 2002), 90, 101–2, 443.

96 Gian Franco Elia, *Il villaggio e la fabbrica. Insediamenti industriali in Gran Bretagna e in Italia. Aspetti della struttura sociale* (Bologna: Editrice Compositori, 1999), 78–82.

97 Csergo, *Liberté, égalité, propreté*, 213–14.

98 Daniel Roche, *A History of Everyday Things: The Birth of Consumption in France, 1600–1800* (Cambridge: Cambridge University Press, 2000), 157. One cubic metre is the equivalent of five or six full bathtubs today.

99 Goubert, *The Conquest of Water*, 51.

100 R.H. Barrow, *I Romani*, trans. Bice Salmaggi (Milan: Oscar Mondadori, 1962), 132.

101 Roche, *A History of Everyday Things*, 148.

102 Elsbeth Kalff, *Le logement insalubre et l'hygiénisation de la vie quotidienne Paris, 1830–1990* (Paris: L'Harmattan, 2008), 81–5; Fabienne Chevallier, *Le Paris moderne. Histoire des politiques d'hygiène, 1855–1898* (Rennes: Presses universitaires de Rennes, 2010), 132–4.

103 Csergo, *Liberté, égalité, propreté*, 216, 227–32.

104 Antonio Cavalieri Ducati, "Dei servizi pubblici acquedotto e fognatura nel comune di Bologna. Relazione dell'ing. cav. A. Cavalieri-Ducati, letta nell'assemblea pubblica del 7 maggio 1902 e discussione / Societa tecnica emiliana" (Bologna: Monti, 1902), 7–8; Massimo Marcolin, "La riattivazione dell'acquedotto romano ad opera di Antonio Zannoni. Il dibattito cittadino ed il ruolo dell'Amministrazione comunale (1860–1890)," in *Acquedotto 2000. Bologna, l'acqua del duemila ha duemila anni* (Casalecchio di Reno: Grafis, 1985), 137–56.

105 Massimo Marcolin, "Crescita urbana e diffusione del servizio idrico. Lenta penetazione sul territorio ed evoluzione verso la gestione pubblica

(1881–1945)," *Acquedotto 2000: Bologna, l'acqua del duemila ha due-mila anni* (Casalecchio di Reno: Grafis, 1985), 167–8, 176.

106 Direzione generale della statistica, "Risultati dell'inchiesta sulle condizioni igeniche e sanitarie dei Communi del Regno" (Rome: Tipografia S. Michele, 1886), vol. 1, 49, 74; Simone Neri Serneri, "The Construction of the Modern City and the Management of Water Resources in Italy, 1880–1920," *Journal of Urban History* 33, no. 5 (2007), 813–27; Giorgio Bigatti, "Strategie di approvvigionamento e gestione dei servizi idrici nell'Italia liberale," *Ricerche storiche* 30, no. 3 (2000).

107 "Strategie di approvvigionamento e gestione dei servizi idrici nell'Italia liberale," 675–6; Simone Neri Serneri, "Resource Management and Environmental Transformations: Water Incorporation at the Time of Industrialization: Milan, 1880–1940," in *Resources of the City: Contributions to an Environmental History of Modern Europe*, ed. Dieter Schott, Bill Luckin, and Geneviève Massard-Guilbaud (Aldershot, England: Ashgate, 2005), 149–67.

108 Leslie Tomory, *The History of the London Water Industry, 1580–1820* (Baltimore: Johns Hopkins University Press, 2017), 181–92.

109 Goubert, *The Conquest of Water*, 42; F.L. Small, *The Influent and the Effluent: The History of Urban Water Supply and Sanitation* (Winnipeg: Underwood McLellan, 1974), 138–9.

110 John von Simson, "Water Supply and Sewerage in Berlin, London, and Paris," in *Urbanisierung im 19. und 20. Jahrhundert : Historische und geographische Aspekte*, ed. Hans J. Teuteberg (Cologne: Böhlau, 1983).

111 Giorgio Bigatti, *L'acqua e il gas in Italia. La storia dei servizi a rete, delle aziende pubbliche e della Federgasacqua* (Milan: F. Angeli, 1997), 35–83; Reinhard Spree, *Health and Social Class in Imperial Germany: A Social History of Mortality, Morbidity, and Inequality* (Oxford: Berg, 1988), 133–43; Barbara Orland, *Wäsche waschen. Technik- und Sozialgeschichte der häuslichen Wäschepflege* (Reinbek bei Hamburg: Rowohlt, 1991), 114–29; Johann Friedrich Geist and Klaus Kürvers, *Das Berliner Mietshaus, 1862–1945. Eine dokumentarische Geschichte von "Meyer's-Hof" in der Ackerstraße 132–133, der Entstehung der Berliner Mietshausquartiere und der Reichshauptstadt zwischen Gründung und Untergang* (Munich: Prestel, 1984), 248–9.

112 Direzione generale della statistica, "Risultati dell'inchiesta sulle condizioni igeniche e sanitarie dei Communi del Regno," 1: 49; Serneri, "The Construction of the Modern City"; Bigatti, "Strategie di approvvigiona-mento e gestione dei servizi idrici nell'Italia liberale," 813–27.

113 Bushman and Bushman, "The Early History"; Maureen Ogle, "Domestic Reform and American Household Plumbing, 1840–1870," *Winterthur Portfolio* 28, no. 1 (1993).

114 Martin V. Melosi, *The Sanitary City: Urban Infrastructure in America from Colonial Times to the Present* (Baltimore: Johns Hopkins University Press, 2000), 117; Letty Anderson, "Water-Supply," in *Building Canada: A History of Public Works*, ed. Norman R. Ball (Toronto: University of Toronto Press, 1988), 200; Leo G. Denis, *Water Works and Sewerage Systems of Canada* (Ottawa: Commission of Conservation, 1916).

115 Alois Grünberg, "Die Assanierung von Wien vom medizinal statistischen Standpunkte," in *Die Assanierung von Wien*, ed. Theodor Weyl (Leipzig: W. Engelmann, 1902), 170.

116 Peter Münch, *Stadthygiene im 19. und 20. Jahrhundert. Die Wasserversorgung, Abwasser- und Abfallbeseitigung unter besonderer Berücksichtigung Münchens* (Göttingen: Vandenhoeck & Ruprecht, 1993), 196.

117 Teuteberg and Wischermann, *Wohnalltag in Deutschland,* 138–9.

118 Evans, *Death in Hamburg,* 128–9.

119 Paul Bairoch and Gary Goertz, "Factors of Urbanisation in the Nineteenth Century Developed Countries: A Descriptive and Econometric Analysis," *Urban Studies* 23, no. 4 (1986), 285–305.

120 Roger-Henri Guerrand, *Les lieux: Histoire des commodités* (Paris: La Découverte, 1997), 13.

121 James H. Winter, *London's Teeming Streets, 1830–1914* (London and New York: Routledge, 1993), 118–19.

122 Bettina Bradbury, "Pigs, Cows, and Boarders: Non-Wage Forms of Survival among Montreal Families, 1861–91," *Labour/Le Travail* 14 (1984), 9–46.

123 Guerrand, *Les lieux,* 122.

124 Gérard Jacquemet, "Urbanisme parisien: La bataille du tout-à-l'égout à la fin du XIXe siècle." *Revue d'histoire moderne et contemporaine* 26, no. 4 (1979), 505–48; Chevallier, *Le Paris moderne,* 229–80. See also Donald Reid, *Paris Sewers and Sewermen: Realities and Representations* (Cambridge, MA: Harvard University Press, 1991), chaps. 1–6.

125 Stephen Halliday, *The Great Stink of London: Sir Joseph Bazalgette and the Cleansing of the Victorian Capital* (Thrupp: Sutton, 1999); Goubert, *The conquest of water,* 58–67; Münch, *Stadthygiene im 19. und 20. Jahrhundert*; Vögele, *Urban Mortality Change in England and Germany, 1870–1913* (Liverpool: Liverpool University Press, 1998), 262–5; Paul

Kortz, "Entwässerung," in *Die Assanierung von Wien*, ed. Theodor Weyl
(Leipzig: W. Engelmann, 1902); Sylvia Mattl, "Die Assanierung Wiens," in
Das Bad: Körperkultur und Hygiene im 19. und 20. Jahrhundert, ed.
Sylvia Mattl-Wurm and Ursula Storch (Vienna: Eigenverlag der Museen
der Stadt Wien, 1991), 53–63; Sylvia Mattl-Wurm, "Die Assanierung der
Großstadt. Von Wiener und anderen Wässern," in *Das Bad. Eine
Geschichte der Badekultur im 19. und 20. Jahrhundert*, ed. Herbert
Lachmayer, Sylvia Mattl-Wurm, and Christian Gargerle (Salzburg:
Residenz, 1991), 136–50; Melosi, *The Sanitary City*, 149–74; Douglas
Baldwin, "Sewerage," in *Building Canada: A History of Public Works*, ed.
Norman R. Ball (Toronto: University of Toronto Press, 1988), 221–44;
Jamie Benidickson, *The Culture of Flushing: A Social and Legal History of
Sewage* (Vancouver: UBC Press, 2007), 98–127.

126 Evans, *Death in Hamburg*, 132–3.

127 Grünberg, "Die Assanierung von Wien," 167.

128 Serneri, "The Construction of the Modern City"; Bigatti, "Strategie di
approvvigionamento."

129 Melosi, *The Sanitary City*, 151–2.

130 Denis, *Water Works and Sewerage Systems of Canada*.

131 Mark Girouard, *The Victorian Country House* (New Haven: Yale
University Press, 1979), 22; Mark Girouard, *Life in the French Country
House* (London: Cassell, 2000), 219–39.

132 F.W. Hunt, "The Sanitary Arrangement of Houses in London during the
Last One Hundred and Twenty Years," *The Health Exhibition Literature*,
vol. 2: *Health in the Dwelling* (London: William Clowes and Sons, 1884),
171–3.

133 Maureen Ogle, *All the Modern Conveniences: American Household
Plumbing, 1840–1890* (Baltimore: Johns Hopkins University Press, 1996),
8–35.

134 May N. Stone, "The Plumbing Paradox: American Attitudes toward Late
Nineteenth-Century Domestic Sanitary Arrangements," *Winterthur
Portfolio* 14, no. 3 (1979), 297.

135 Small, *The Influent and the Effluent*, 138–9.

136 Csergo, *Liberté, égalité, propreté*, 222.

137 Burnett, *A social history of Housing*, 214–15; Eleb and Debarre,
L'invention de l'habitation moderne, 408–11; Ogle, *All the Modern
Conveniences*, 69–71.

138 Muthesius, *The English House*, 235–7.

139 Stone, "The Plumbing Paradox," 307–9.

140 Hoagland, *The Bathroom*, 31–41.

141 Eleb and Debarre, *L'invention de l'habitation moderne*, 224–5, 408–11.

142 Vigarello, *Concepts of Cleanliness*, 105–6; see also Luciano Spadanuda, *Storia del bidet. Un grande contenitore ideologico* (Rome: Castelvecchi, 1998).

143 For examples see: Paolo Sorcinelli, *Storia sociale dell'acqua. Riti e culture* (Milan: Mondatori, 1998), Figure 25.

144 Vigarello, *Concepts of Cleanliness*, 162.

145 Fanny Beaupré and Roger-Henri Guerrand, *Le confident des dames. Le bidet du XVIIIe au XXe siècle. Histoire d'une intimité* (Paris: La Découverte, 1997), 87.

146 Eva B. Ottillinger, "Vom Waschtisch zum Badezimmer," in *Das Bad. Körperkultur und Hygiene im 19. und 20. Jahrhundert*, ed. Sylvia Mattl-Wurm and Ursula Storch (Vienna: Eigenverlag der Museen der Stadt Wien, 1991), 71–85.

147 Beaupré and Guerrand, *Le confident des dames*, 49.

148 Jean-Pierre Goubert, "Le bidet, ou le mot impudique," in *Du luxe au confort*, ed. Goubert (Paris: Belin, 1988), 158–64.

149 Sorcinelli, *Storia sociale dell'acqua*, Figures 15, 16, 17.

150 Ibid., 72; Paolo Sorcinelli, *Avventure del corpo. Culture e pratiche dell'intimità quotidiana* (Milan: Mondadori, 2006), 39–42.

151 Smith, *Clean*, 203; Lawrence Stone, *The Family, Sex, and Marriage in England, 1500–1800* (New York: Harper and Row, 1977), 486; Stone, "The Plumbing Paradox," 308; Sorcinelli, *Storia sociale dell'acqua*, 78.

152 Iris Origo, *Images and Shadows: Part of a Life* (London: John Murray, 1970), 66.

153 Beaupré and Guerrand, *Le confident des dames*, illustrations between 108 and 109; Ottillinger, "Vom Waschtisch zum Badezimmer."

154 Csergo, *Liberté, égalité, propreté*, 270; Beaupré and Guerrand, *Le confident des dames*, 82, 129.

155 Thuillier, *Pour une histoire du quotidien*, 52.

156 A. Béal, *Passe-temps d'un praticien d'Auvergne, causeries sur l'hygiène... et autres sujets joyeux, rédigées conformément aux us et coutumes régionales* (Paris: A. Maloine, 1900), 232–3.

157 Peter Feldbauer, *Stadtwachstum und Wohnungsnot: Determinanten unzureichender Wohnungsversorgung in Wien 1848 bis 1914* (Vienna: Verlag fur Geschichte und Politik Wien, 1977), 164.

158 Enrica Asquer, *La rivoluzione candida. Storia sociale della lavatrice in Italia (1945–1970)* (Rome: Carocci, 2007), 41.

159 Geist and Kürvers, *Das Berliner Mietshaus*, 467; Teuteberg and Wischermann, *Wohnalltag in Deutschland*, 134.

160 Great Britain, "Census of England and Wales, 1911, Vol. VIII. Tenements in the Administrative Counties and Urban and Rural Districts" (London: HMSO, 1913), iv, 624.

161 T.C. Smout, *A Century of the Scottish Peoples, 1830–1950* (London: Collins, 1986), 34.

162 Massachusetts, "A tenement house census of Boston. Section I. Tenements, Rooms, and Rents," ed. Bureau of Statistics of Labor (Boston: Wright and Potter, 1892), 570–1; Ward, *A History of Domestic Space*, 18–24.

163 Geist and Kürvers, *Das Berliner Mietshaus*, 531.

164 Theodor Weyl, *Die Assanierung von Paris*, ed. Theodor Weyl (Leipzig: W. Engelmann, 1900), 34.

165 Csergo, *Liberté, égalité, propreté*, 168–75.

166 Reinhard Sieder, "'Vata, derf i aufstehn?': Childhood Experiences in Viennese working-class families around 1900," *Continuity and Change* 1, no. 1 (1986), 69–70. See also Jerry White, *Rothschild buildings: Life in an East End Tenement Block, 1887–1920* (London: Routledge and Kegan Paul, 1980), 47–9; Reeves, *Round about a Pound a Week*, 55–6; Anna Davin, *Growing Up Poor: Home, School, and Street in London, 1870–1914* (London: Rivers Oram Press, 1996), 51–2.

167 Reeves, *Round about a Pound a Week*, 56.

168 Pauline Laure Marie Pange, *Comment j'ai vu 1900* (Paris: B. Grasset, 1962), 196.

169 Ibid.

170 Girouard, *Life in the French Country House*, 219–39.

171 Ladd, "Public Baths and Civic Improvement," 383.

172 Eleb and Debarre, *L'invention de l'habitation moderne*, 238.

173 D. Glassberg, "The Design of Reform: The Public Bath Movement in America," *American Studies* 20, no. 2 (1979), 7.

174 Smith, *Clean*, 312.

175 Williams, *Washing "the Great Unwashed,"* 30; Campbell, *Report on Public Baths and Wash-Houses*, 16–18.

CHAPTER THREE

1 Daniel Roche, *The Culture of Clothing: Dress and Fashion in the "Ancien Régime"* (Cambridge and New York: Cambridge University Press, 1994), 371–5.

2 Georges Vigarello, *Concepts of Cleanliness: Changing Attitudes in France since the Middle Ages* (Cambridge: Cambridge University Press, 1988), 39–77. See also C. Willett Cunnington and Phyllis Cunnington, *The History of Underclothes* (London: Faber and Faber, 1981).

3 Vigarello, *Concepts of Cleanliness*, 60.

4 Kathleen M. Brown, *Foul Bodies: Cleanliness in Early America* (New Haven: Yale University Press, 2009), 109–14.

5 Roche, *The Culture of Clothing*, 164–7, 180.

6 Paolo Sorcinelli, *Storia sociale dell'acqua. Riti e culture* (Milan: Mondatori, 1998), 52–4; Paolo Sorcinelli, *Avventure del corpo. Culture e pratiche dell'intimità quotidiana* (Milan: Mondadori, 2006), 43–4; see also Luciano Spadanuda, *Storia delle mutande* (Rome: Coniglio, 2005), 5–48.

7 Philippe Perrot, *Le travail des apparences, ou les transformations du corps féminin. XVIIIe-XIXe siècle* (Paris: Seuil, 1984), 74.

8 Raffaella Sarti, *Vita di casa. Abitare, mangiare, vestire nell'europa moderna* (Rome: Laterza, 2003), 252–3.

9 Gustave Bienaymé, "Le coût de la vie à Paris à diverses époques. Le blanchissage," *Journal de la société statistique de Paris* 44 (1903), 54.

10 Roche, *The Culture of Clothing*, 386.

11 Edmond Auguste Texier, *Tableau de Paris*, 2 vols. (Paris: Paulin et Le Chevalier, 1852), vol. 1, 332.

12 Philippe Perrot, *Fashioning the Bourgeoisie: A History of Clothing in the Nineteenth Century* (Princeton: Princeton University Press, 1994), 146–9.

13 Émile Zola, *L'Assommoir* [1876] (London: Penguin, 1970), 135–67.

14 Rosita Levi Pisetzky, *Il costume e la moda nella società italiana* (Turin: G. Einaudi, 1978), 290, 300, 311.

15 Sabine Schachtner, "Der Wäscheberg. Textilien in ländlichen Haushalten vor der Industrialisierung," in *Die Grosse Wäsche*, ed. Elisabeth Helming (Cologne: Rheinland, 1988), 31–7.

16 Ibid.; Perrot, *Fashioning the bourgeoisie*, 161–2.

17 Francesco Roncati, *Compendio di igiene. Per uso dei medici* (Naples: Vincenzo Pasquale, 1870), 345–6; Sorcinelli, *Storia sociale dell'acqua*, 53–4.

18 Alain Corbin, "Le grand siècle du linge," *Ethnologie française* 16, new series, no. 3 (1986), 299; Guy Thuillier, *Pour une histoire du quotidien au XIXe siècle en Nivernais* (Paris: Mouton, École des hautes Études en Sciences Sociales, 1977), 51.

19 Walter Artelt, "Kleidungshigiene im 19. Jahrhundert," in *Städte-, Wohnungs- und Kleidungshygiene des 19. Jahrhunderts in Deutschland. Vorträge eines Symposiums vom 17. - 18. Juni 1967 in Frankfurt am Main*, ed. Walter Artelt et al. (Stuttgart: Enke, 1969); Patricia A. Cunningham, *Reforming women's fashion, 1850–1920: Politics, Health, and Art* (Kent: Kent State University Press, 2003).

20 Publio Torelli, *Compendio d'igiene popolare per uso delle società operarai e delle scuole feriale* (Macerata: Bianchini, 1864); Angelo Prioli, *Nozioni d'igiene popolare ad uso delle scuole diurne e seriali e delle famiglie italiane* (Turin, 1880); Louis Coltman Parkes, *The Elements of Health: An Introduction to the Study of Hygiene* (London: J. & A. Churchill, 1895); Giulia Ferraris Tamburini, *Come devo governare la mia casa? Libro per la famiglia, nel quale si tratta dell'abitazione, arredamento della casa, amministrazione, governo della servitù, ecc.* (Milan: Ulrico Hoepli, 1898); D.H. Bergey, *The Principles of Hygiene: A Practical Manual for Students, Physicians, and Health Officers* (London and Philadelphia: W.B. Saunders, 1901).

21 Evelyn Bernette Ackerman, *Health Care in the Parisian Countryside, 1800–1914* (New Brunswick: Rutgers University Press, 1990), 19; Thuillier, *Pour une histoire du quotidien*, 51; Schachtner, "Der Wäscheberg."

22 Great Britain, General Board of Health, *Report of the General Board of Health on the Supply of Water to the Metropolis* (London: HMSO, 1850), 71–2.

23 Brown, *Foul Bodies*, 151, 238.

24 Pierre Jakez Hélias, *The Horse of Pride: Life in a Breton Village* (New Haven: Yale University Press, 1978), 2.

25 Karin Hausen, "Große Wäsche. Technischer Fortschritt und sozialer Wandel in Deutschland vom 18. bis ins 20. Jahrhundert," *Geschichte und Gesellschaft* 13, no. 3 (1987), 289; Schachtner, "Der Wäscheberg."

26 Roche, *The Culture of Clothing*, 367–70.

27 Giorgio Riello, *Cotton: The Fabric That Made the Modern World* (Cambridge: Cambridge University Press, 2013), 214.

28 Quynh Delaunay, *La machine à laver en France. Un objet technique qui parle des femmes* (Paris: L'Harmattan, 2003), 13–14.

29 Jules Michelet, *Le peuple*, 3rd ed. (Paris: Hachette, 1846), 80.

30 Ibid., 9.

31 Schachtner, "Der Wäscheberg"; Barbara Orland, *Wäsche waschen: Technik- und Sozialgeschichte der häuslichen Wäschepflege* (Reinbek bei Hamburg: Rowohlt, 1991), 71.

32 Jacques Léonard, *Archives du corps. La santé au XIXe siècle* (Rennes: Ouest-France, 1986), 135–9; Hélène Fatoux, *Histoire d'eau en Seine-et-Marne. 1 Sources, rivières, canaux, étangs, abreuvoirs, l'eau potable, puits briads, réservoirs, fontaines, lessive au village, lavandières, lavoirs* (Le-Mée-sur-Seine: Amatteis, 1987), 193–8; Yvonne Verdier, *Façons de dire, façons de faire. La laveuse, la couturière, la cuisinière* (Paris: Gallimard, 1979), 108–21.

33 Suzanne Tardieu-Dumont, "Le trousseau et la 'grande lessive,'" *Ethnologie française* 16, new series, no. 3 (1986), 281–2.

34 Frédéric Le Play, *Les ouvriers européens. Études sur les travaux, la vie domestique, et la condition morale des populations ouvrières de l'Europe. Précédées d'un exposé de la méthode d'observation* (Paris: l'Imprimerie impériale, 1855), 39; Michel Verret, "Les cycles du linge," *Ethnologie française* 16, new series, no. 3 (1986), 223.

35 Hélias, *The Horse of Pride*, 2–4, 166–7.

36 Verdier, *Façons de dire*, 130–5.

37 Ibid., 135.

38 Helene Grünn, *Wäsche waschen. Volkskunde aus dem Lebensraum der Donau* (Vienna: Niederösterreichisches Heimatwerk, 1978), 24–44; Orland, *Wäsche waschen*, 21–48.

39 Renato Bellabarba, *Il ciclo della vita nella campagna marchigiana. Contributo allo studio delle tradizioni popolari* (Florence: L.S. Olschki, 1979), 78; Enrica Asquer, *La rivoluzione candida. Storia sociale della lavatrice in Italia (1945–1970)* (Rome: Carocci, 2007), 42–4.

40 Virginia Smith, *Clean: A History of Personal Hygiene and Purity* (Oxford: Oxford University Press, 2007), 232; Pamela Sambrook, *The Country House Servant* (Stroud: Sutton, 1999), 126; Caroline Davidson, *A Woman's Work Is Never Done: A History of Housework in the British Isles, 1650–1950* (London: Chatto & Windus, 1982), 136–63.

41 Leonore Davidoff and Catherine Hall, *Family Fortunes: Men and Women of the English Middle Class 1780–1850* (London: Hutchinson, 1987), 386.

42 Davidson, *A Woman's Work Is Never Done*, 138–49; Patricia E. Malcolmson, *English Laundresses: A Social History, 1850–1930* (Urbana: University of Illinois Press, 1986), 3–5.

43 Jean-Pierre Goubert, *The Conquest of Water: The Advent of Health in the Industrial Age* (Cambridge: Polity Press, 1989), 71, 76.

44 Toni Nicolini and Andrea Micheli, *I lavatoi dei navigli di Milano. Milano, Pavia e dintorni* (Milan: Skira, 2000).

45 Paul Sébillot, "Lavandières et blanchisseuses," in *Légendes et curiosités des métiers* (Paris: Flammarion, 1895), 6; Françoise Loux and Philippe

Richard, *Sagesses du corps. La santé et la maladie dans les proverbes français* (Paris: Maisonneuve & Larose, 1978), 122–4; Verdier, *Façons de dire*, 136–41; Fatoux, *Histoire d'eau en Seine-et-Marne*, 198.

46 Sarah Hewett, *Nummits and crummits; Devonshire customs, characteristics, and folk-lore* [1900] (Norwood: Norwood Editions, 1973), 54.

47 Françoise Wasserman, *Blanchisseuse, laveuse, repasseuse. La femme, le linge et l'eau* (Fresnes: Écomusée, 1986), 20.

48 Grünn, *Wäsche waschen*, 155–7.

49 Sébillot, "Lavandières et blanchisseuses"; M. Placucci, "Usi e preguidizi de' contadini della Romagna," in *Romagna tradizionale. Usi e costumi, credenze e pregiudizi*, ed. Paolo Toschi (Bologna: Licinio Cappelli, 1952), 136; L. De Nardis, "A la garboja. 500 note sulle tradizioni popolari romagnole," in *Romagna tradizionale*, 270.

50 Loux and Richard, *Sagesses du corps*, 124.

51 Verdier, *Façons de dire*, 135, 143.

52 Marguerite Perrot, *Le Mode de vie des familles bourgeoises 1873–1953* (Paris: Presses de la Fondation nationale des sciences politiques, 1982), 272–3.

53 Roche, *The Culture of Clothing*, 282.

54 Horn, *The Rise and Fall of the Victorian Servant* (Stroud: Sutton, 2004), 23.

55 Sambrook, *The Country House Servant*, 148–246; Isabella Mary Beeton, *Book of household management ... also, sanitary, medical, & legal memoranda; with a history of the origin, properties, and use of all things connected with home life and comfort* (London: S.O. Beeton, 1861), 1008–13.

56 Horn, *The Rise and Fall*, 77.

57 Great Britain, *Report of the General Board of Health on the Supply of Water to the Metropolis* (London: H.M.S.O., 1850), 80.

58 Ibid., 8.

59 Josef Kurz, *Kulturgeschichte der häuslichen Wäschepflege. Frauenarbeit und Haushaltstechnik im Spiegel der Jahrhunderte* (Heidelberg: Braus im Wachter, 2006), 26.

60 Great Britain, *Report of the General Board of Health*, 159–60.

61 Ibid., *Appendix III: Reports and Evidence – Medical, Chemical, Geological, and Miscellaneous*, 15.

62 Anna Davin, *Growing Up Poor: Home, School, and Street in London, 1870–1914* (London: Rivers Oram Press, 1996), 186.

63 Rosmarie Beier, "Leben in der Mietskaserne. Zum Alltag Berliner Unterschichtsfamilien in den Jahren 1900 bis 1920," in *Hinterhof, Keller,*

und Mansarde. Einblicke in Berliner Wohnungselend 1901–1920, ed. Gesine Asmus (Reinbek bei Hamburg: Rowohlt, 1982), 257.

64 For descriptions, see Davidson, *A woman's work is never done*, 145–9; Susan Strasser, *Never Done: A History of American Housework* (New York: Pantheon Books, 1982), 104–8; M.J. Daunton, *House and Home in the Victorian City: Working-Class Housing 1850–1914* (London: Edward Arnold, 1983), 242–4; Jerry White, *Rothschild Buildings: Life in an East End Tenement Block, 1887–1920* (London: Routledge and Kegan Paul, 1980), 46–47; Hilde David, "'Die Waschfrau war abends kaputt,'" in *"Das Paradies kommt wieder..." Zur Kulturgeschichte und Ökologie von Herd, Kühlschrank und Waschmaschine*, ed. Museum der Arbeit (Hamburg: VSA, 1993), 108–13; Hausen, "Große Wäsche," 290–2.

65 Johann Friedrich Geist and Klaus Kürvers, *Das Berliner Mietshaus, 1862–1945. Eine dokumentarische Geschichte von "Meyer's-Hof" in der Ackerstraße 132–133, der Entstehung der Berliner Mietshausquartiere und der Reichshauptstadt zwischen Gründung und Untergang* (Munich: Prestel, 1984), 531; Asquer, *La rivoluzione candida*, 45; Monique Eleb and Anne Debarre, *L'invention de l'habitation moderne. Paris, 1880–1914* (Paris: Hazan, 1995), 411–14.

66 Massachusetts, "A tenement house census of Boston. Section II. Sanitary Condition of Tenements," ed. Bureau of Statistics of Labor (Boston: Wright and Potter, 1893), 132–3.

67 Maud Pember Reeves, *Round about a Pound a Week* [1913] (London: Virago, 1979), 33.

68 Geist and Kürvers, *Das Berliner Mietshaus*, 543.

69 Agnes Campbell, *Report on Public Baths and Wash-Houses in the United Kingdom*, Carnegie United Kingdom Trust Report (Edinburgh: T. & A. Constable, 1918), 45–53.

70 This estimate is based on the following: greater London population – 7 million, estimated mean household size – 4.5, estimated number of households – 1.6 million, number of public laundry visits – 964,000 (Campbell, *Report on Public Baths and Wash-Houses*, 48), number of visits per household per year – 0.6, number of weekly household visits – 964,000/52 = 18,500, estimated proportion of households making weekly visits – 1.2 percent.

71 Campbell, *Report on Public Baths and Wash-Houses*, 51.

72 Barbara Hartmann, *Das Müller'sche Volksbad in München* (München: Tuduv, 1987), 7; Brian K. Ladd, "Public Baths and Civic Improvement in Nineteenth-Century German Cities," *Journal of Urban History* 14, no. 3

(1988), 390; Octave Du Mesnil, *Rapport sur la création de bains et lavoirs populaires* (Melun: Imprimerie administrative, 1893), 75.

73 Alessia Giachetti, "Bagni e lavatoi pubblici in Torino," diss., Faculty of Architecture (Turin: Politecnico di Torino, 2003).

74 Vittorio Puntoni, "Le condizioni igieniche di alcuni lavatoi di Bologna" (Bologna: Gamberini e Parmeggiani, 1916), 19.

75 J. Moisy, *Les eaux de Paris. Les journaux et leurs communiqués. Les tarifs 1846, 1852, 1853, 1860, 1862, convention de 1867. Bains et lavoirs* (Paris: Savy, 1868), 189.

76 Ambroise Tardieu, "Lavoirs," in *Dictionnaire d'hygiène publique et de salubrité* (Paris: J.-B. Baillière et fils, 1862), II, 546.

77 Moisy, *Les Eaux de Paris*, 176–7.

78 J. Moisy, *Les Lavoirs de Paris* (Paris: E. Sausset, 1884), 20.

79 Chambre syndicale des maîtres de lavoirs – Paris (1) Seine, "Recensement des lavoirs de Paris. Année 1896 / demandé par l'administration municipale à la Chambre syndicale des maîtres de lavoirs" (Paris: P. Debreuil, 1896).

80 Du Mesnil, *Rapport*, 75–6.

81 Fatoux, *Histoire d'eau en Seine-et-Marne, 3 Les Bateaux-lavoirs* (Le-Mée-sur-Seine: Amattis, 1989).

82 France, Agriculture et Commerce – Ministère, *Bains et lavoirs publics. Commission instituée par ordre de M. le Président de la République* (Paris: Gide et Baudry, 1850), 91.

83 For example, Grünn, *Wäsche waschen*, 55.

84 For example, see Katherine W. Rinnie, "The Landscape of Laundry in Late Cinquecento Rome," *Studies in the decorative arts* 9, no. 1 (2001); Douglas Biow, *The Culture of Cleanliness in Renaissance Italy* (Ithaca: Cornell University Press, 2006), 95–143.

85 Malcolmson, *English Laundresses*, 19.

86 Tardieu, "Lavoirs"; Moisy, *Les lavoirs de Paris*, 24–5.

87 Malcolmson, *English Laundresses*, 23–34; Strasser, *Never Done*, 106–9; Brown, *Foul Bodies*, 218–19, 265–8; France, *Bains et Lavoirs Publics*, 48–55; Moisy, *Les lavoirs de Paris*, 24–9.

88 Ibid., 22; Alessandro Schiavi, *L'industria del bucato in Milano. Inchiesta compiuta in occasione di uno sciopero* (Milan: Società umanitaria, 1906), 5–7.

89 Malcolmson, *English Laundresses*, 7; Hausen, "Große Wäsche," 284.

90 Moisy, *Les lavoirs de Paris*, 22.

91 Zola, *L'Assommoir*.

92 Moisy, *Les lavoirs de Paris*.; Malcolmson, *English Laundresses*, 23–34; Hausen, "Große Wäsche"; Orland, *Wäsche waschen*, 150–60; Wasserman, *Blanchisseuse, laveuse, repasseuse*.

93 Orland, *Wäsche waschen*, 158.

94 Malcolmson, *English Laundresses*, 11; Schiavi, *L'industria del bucato*, 10.

95 Birgit Bolognese-Leuchtenmüller, "Die Wiener Wäschermadln. Von der Kultfigur des Biedermeier zur Lohnarbeiterin," in *Wien wirklich. Ein Stadtführer durch den Alltag und seine Geschichte*, ed. Renate Banik-Schweitzer and Peter Lachmit (Vienna: Verlag für Gesellschaftskritik, 1983), 155–61.

96 Louis Figuier, *Les merveilles de l'industrie, ou description des principales industries modernes. Industries chimiques* (Paris: Furne Jouvet et Cie, 1873), vol. 3, 504–22; Moisy, *Les lavoirs de Paris*, 27–65; Marie-Cécile Riffault, "De Chaptal à la Mère Denis. Histoire de l'entretien du linge domestique," *Culture technique* 3 (1980); Delaunay, *La machine à laver en France*, 21–4; Malcolmson, *English Laundresses*, 126–56; Arwen Mohun, *Steam Laundries: Gender, Technology, and Work in the United States and Great Britain, 1880–1940* (Baltimore: Johns Hopkins University Press, 1999); Orland, *Wäsche waschen*, 160–7; Schiavi, *L'industria del bucato*, 24–8; J. Piet, *Blanchisseries, désinfection, lavoirs publics. Installations, procédés et appareils spéciaux* (Paris: s.n., 1892); Thomas Bewick, *1800 Woodcuts by Thomas Bewick and His School* (New York: Dover, 1962), Plate 133; Bettina Rinke, "Weiße Wäsche aus Bielefeld: Die Geschichte der industriellen Wäscheproduktion am Beispiel der Wäschefabrik Winkel," in *Reinliche Leiber, schmutzige Geschäfte. Körperhygiene und Reinlichkeitsvorstellungen in zwei Jahrhunderten*, ed. Regina Löneke and Ira Spieker (Göttingen: Wallstein, 1996), 160–73.

97 Wasserman, *Blanchisseuse*, 59–84; Malcolmson, *English Laundresses*, 8–9; Orland, *Wäsche waschen*, 152.

98 Moisy, *Les lavoirs de Paris*, 28–9.

99 Malcolmson, *English Laundresses*, 103–22; Mohun, *Steam Laundries*, ch. 5; Schiavi, *L'industria del bucato*.

100 Henry McDonald, "McAleese Report Finds Police Also Bore Responsibility in 'Enslavement' of More Than 30,000 Women in Institutions," *Guardian*, 5 February 2013.

101 Michael G. Mulhall, *Mulhall's Dictionary of Statistics*, 2nd ed. (London: George Routledge, 1886), 289, 497.

102 N.F.R. Crafts, "Regional Price Variations in England in 1843: An Aspect of the Standard-of-Living Debate," *Explorations in Economic History* 19,

no. 1 (1982), 58; Gregory Clark, "The condition of the Working Class in England, 1209–2004," *Journal of Political Economy* 113, no. 6 (2005), 1330–2.

103 Louis René Villermé, *Tableau de l'état physique et moral des ouvriers employés dans les manufactures de coton, de laine et de soie [1840]* (Paris: Études et documentation internationales, 1989), 178–9.

104 Le Play, *Les ouvriers européens. Études sur les travaux, la vie domestique, et la condition morale des populations ouvières de l'Europe/ Précédées d'un exposé de la méthode d'observation, passim.*

105 Ibid., *passim.*

106 Ibid., 272–5.

107 Ibid., 266–71.

108 France, *Bains et Lavoirs Publics*, iv, 46–64.

109 Great Britain, *Report of the General Board of Health*, 71–5.

110 Perrot, *Le travail des apparences*, 107–16.

111 Malcolmson, *English Laundresses*, 7.

112 Great Britain, *First report from His Majesty's commissioners for inquiring into the condition of the poorer classes in Ireland*, House of Commons Papers, Reports of Commissioners (London: HMSO, 1835), 194.

113 Le Play, *Les ouvriers européens*, 40.

114 Louis-Sébastien Mercier, *Tableau de Paris*, vol. 5 (Amsterdam: n.p., 1782), 118.

CHAPTER FOUR

1 Charles X. Cornu, *Les savons et les détergents* (Paris: Presses universitaires de France, 1970), 48–54; J.A. Hunt, "A Short History of Soap," *Pharmaceutical Journal* 263, no. 7076 (1999), 986.

2 F.W. Gibbs, "The History of the Manufacture of Soap," *Annals of Science* 4, no. 2 (1939), 169–71; Douglas Biow, *The Culture of Cleanliness in Renaissance Italy* (Ithaca: Cornell University Press, 2006), 12–14.

3 Gibbs, "The History of the Manufacture of Soap," 172–6; John U. Nef, "A Comparison of Industrial Growth in France and England from 1540 to 1640: III," *Journal of Political Economy* 44, no. 5 (1936), 643–66.

4 Gibbs, "The History of the Manufacture of Soap," 176; P.A.R. Puplett, *Synthetic Detergents: A Study of the Development and Marketing of a New Product* (London: Sidgwick and Jackson, 1957), 12–16.

5 M. Duhamel du Monceau, *L'art du savonnier* (1774); Jean-Pierre Joseph d' Arcet, Claude-Hugues Lelièvre, and Bertrand Pelletier, *Rapport sur la*

fabrication des savons, sur leurs différentes espèces, suivant la nature des huiles et des alkalis qu'on emploie pour les fabriquer; et sur les moyens d'en préparer partout, avec les diverses matières huileuses et alkalines, que la nature présente, suivant les localités (Paris, 1794); Sigismund Friedrich Hermbstaedt, *Die Wissenschaft des Seifesiedens oder chemische Grundsätze der Kunst alle Arten Seife zu fabriciren. Für Seifensieder und Hauswirthinnen welche diese Kunst verständig ausüben wollen* (Berlin: Nicolai, 1808).

6 Louis Figuier, *Les merveilles de l'industrie, ou description des principales industries modernes: Industries chimiques* (Paris: Furne Jouvet et Cie, 1873), I: 411–12.

7 Gibbs, "The History of the Manufacture of Soap," 181–90.

8 Michael Stephen Smith, *The Emergence of Modern Business Enterprise in France, 1800–1930* (Cambridge, MA: Harvard University Press, 2006), 280.

9 Louis F. Benoiston de Châteauneuf, *Recherches sur les consommations de tout genre de la ville de Paris en 1817 comparées a ce qu'elles étaient en 1789*, 2 ed. (Paris: Chez l'Auteur, Chez Martinet, 1821) Pt. I, 112.

10 Pierre-Paul Zalio, "Le 'Savon de Marseille': Contribution à une sociologie économique des produits," in *La qualité des produits en France (XVIIIᵉ-XXᵉ siècles)*, ed. Alessandro Stanziani (Paris: Belin, 2003), 95–111.

11 Figuier, *Les merveilles de l'industrie*, 412.

12 Emmanuelle Dutertre, *Savons et savonneries. Le modèle nantais* (Nantes: Éditions Memo, 2005); Figuier, *Les merveilles de l'industrie*, 403–13; Smith, *The Emergence of Modern Business Enterprise*, 281.

13 Stephen Dowell, *A History of Taxation and Taxes in England: From the Earliest Times to the Present Day*, vol. IV: *Taxes on Articles of Consumption* (London: Longmans, Green, 1884), 218–34.

14 Great Britain, Progress of the consumption of soap from 1830 to 1835, both inclusive, extracted from the seventeenth report of the Commissioners of Excise Inquiry (S.l.: s.n., 1836).; Michael G. Mulhall, *Mulhall's Dictionary of Statistics*, 2nd ed. (London: George Routledge, 1886), 419; W.J. Corlett, *The Economic Development of Detergents* (London: Duckworth, 1958), 24; Charles Wilson, *The History of Unilever: A Study in Economic Growth and Social Change* (London: Cassell, 1954), I: 9.

15 Ibid., I: 9–20; see also Albert Edward Musson, *Enterprise in Soap and Chemicals: Joseph Crosfield & Sons, Limited, 1815–1965* (Manchester: Manchester University Press, 1965).

16 Samuel Colgate, "American Soap Factories," in *1795–1895: One Hundred Years of American Commerce*, ed. Chauncey Mitchell Depew (New York: D.O. Haynes, 1895), 422.

17 Richard L. Bushman and Claudia Bushman, "The Early History of Cleanliness in America," *Journal of American History* 74 (1988), 1233–5; Secretary of the Treasury United States, *Documents relative to the manufactures in the United States* (New York: B. Franklin, 1833; repr., 1969)., *passim.*

18 William Jackson, *Document 3, No. 11*, ed. US Secretary of the Treasury, vol. 1, *Documents Relative to the Manufactures in the United States* (New York: B. Franklin, 1833; repr., 1969). vol. 1, 88.

19 Figuier, *Les merveilles de l'industrie*, 413.

20 N.F.R. Crafts, "Real Wages, Inequality, and Economic Growth in Britain, 1750–1850: A Review of Recent Research," in *Real Wages in nineteenth and Twentieth Century Europe: Historical and Comparative Perspectives*, ed. Peter Scholliers (New York: Berg, 1989), 90–5; Gregory Clark, "The Condition of the Working Class in England, 1209–2004," *Journal of Political Economy* 113, no. 6 (2005), 1327.

21 Frédéric Le Play, *Les ouvriers européens. Études sur les travaux, la vie domestique, et la condition morale des populations ouvrières de l'Europe. Précédées d'un exposé de la méthode d'observation* (Paris: l'Imprimerie impériale, 1855), 49–57.

22 Clark, "The condition of the working class in England," 1330–32; Jeanne Singer-Kérel, *Le coût de la vie à Paris de 1840 à 1954. Recherches sur l'économie française* (Paris: A. Colin, 1961), 490–1; Vera Mühlpeck, Roman Sandgruber, and Hannelore Woitek, "Index Verbraucherpreise 1800 bis 1914," in *Geschichte und Ergebnisse der Zentralen amtlichen Statistik in Österrreich 1829–1979* (Vienna: Österreichischen Statistischen Zentralamt, 1979), 166–67; Benedetto Barbieri, *I consumi nel primo secolo dell'Unita d'Italia, 1861–1960* (Milan: Giuffré, 1961), 101.

23 N.F.R. Crafts and Terence C. Mills, "Trends in Real Wages in Britain, 1750–1913," *Explorations in Economic History* 31, no. 2 (1994), 176–94; Charles H. Feinstein, "Pessimism Perpetuated: Real Wages and the Standard of Living in Britain during and after the Industrial Revolution," *Journal of Economic History* 58, no. 3 (1998), 625–58; Richard Eugene Sylla and Gianni Toniolo, *Patterns of European Industrialization the Nineteenth Century* (London: Routledge, 1991), 118–20; Stefano Finoaltea, "Production and Consumption in Post-Unification Italy: New Evidence, New Conjectures," *Rivista di Storia Economica* 18, no. 3 (2002), 268–76; Wilfried Feldenkirchen and Susanne Hilger, *Menschen und Marken: 125 Jahre Henkel, 1876–2001* (Düsseldorf: Henkel KGAA, 2001), 19.

24 Mulhall, *Mulhall's Dictionary of Statistics*, 419; Michael G. Mulhall, *The Dictionary of Statistics* (London: George Routledge and Sons, 1892), 542; Maria Ragno, *L'industria dei saponi ed affini in Italia e all'estero* (Rome: Federazionale nazionale fascista degli industriali dei prodotti chimici, 1936), 65–6; Walther G. Hoffmann, ed. *Das Wachstum der Deutschen Wirtschaft seit der Mitte des 19. Jahrhunderts* (Berlin: Springer, 1965), 676–7.

25 Christina Brede, *Das Instrument der Sauberkeit. Die Entwicklung der Massenproduktion von Feinseifen in Deutschland 1850 bis 2000* (Münster: Waxman, 2005), 72.

26 Musson, *Enterprise in Soap and Chemicals*, 22; H.R. Edwards, *Competition and Monopoly in the British Soap Industry* (Oxford: Clarendon Press, 1962), 135.

27 Corlett, *The Economic Development of Detergents*, 61–2; for a more extensive contemporary description see Figuier, *Les merveilles de l'industrie*, 411–66.

28 Smith, *The Emergence of Modern Business Enterprise in France, 1800–1930*, 281.

29 United States Department of the Interior, "Report of the Manufactures of the United States at the Tenth Census (June 1, 1880)," ed. Census Office (Washington: Government Printing Office), 13.

30 J.R. Nottingham & Co., comp., *Digest of trade-marks registered in the United States Patent office for soap* (Washington, DC: Age Printing Co., 1896).

31 Davis Dyer, Frederick Dalzell, and Rowena Olegario, *Rising Tide: Lessons from 165 Years of Brand Building at Procter & Gamble* (Cambridge, MA: Harvard Business School Press, 2004), 23–31.

32 Alfred D. Chandler and Takashi Hikino, *Scale and Scope: The Dynamics of Industrial Capitalism* (Cambridge, MA: Belknap Press, 1994), 64, 152.

33 Nottingham, *Digest of trade-marks registered in the United States Patent office for soap*.

34 Geoffrey Jones, *Beauty Imagined: A History of the Global Beauty Industry* (Oxford and New York: Oxford University Press, 2010), 75–6.

35 Musson, *Enterprise in Soap and Chemicals*, 64.

36 Mulhall, *The Dictionary of Statistics*, 542.

37 For a recent, unconventional biography of Lever see Brian Lewis, *So Clean: Lord Leverhulme, Soap and Civilisation* (Manchester: Manchester University Press, 2008).

38 Great Britain, "Report on the Soap Industry," Cmd. 1126 (London: HMSO, 1921), 6; Wilson, *The History of Unilever*, I: 21–44, 59–88, 115–24;

Corlett, *The Economic Development of Detergents*, 48–58; Edwards, *Competition and Monopoly*, 143–51; Chandler and Hikino, *Scale and Scope*, 264.

39 Edwards, *Competition and Monopoly*, 146–51; Dyer, Dalzell, and Olegario, *Rising Tide*, 24–32, 35–8.

40 Figuier, *Les merveilles de l'industrie*, 413.

41 Wilson, *The History of Unilever*, II: 213–17.

42 Hoffmann, *Das Wachstum der Deutsechen Wirtschaft*, 361–2, 683–4.

43 Brede, *Das Instrument der Sauberkeit*, 73.

44 Wolfgang Feiter, *80 Jahre Persil: Produkt- und Werbegeschichte* (Düsseldorf: Henkel, 1987), 13–23; Chandler and Hikino, *Scale and Scope*, 431–2; Feldenkirchen and Hilger, *Menschen und Marken*, 22–41.

45 *Archivio di statistica* (Rome: Elziveriana, 1879), 489–90.

46 Ragno, *L'industria dei saponi*, 34–5, 42.

47 Barbieri, *I consumi nel primo secolo*, 101.

48 Giovanni Leone, *Il Saponaro* (Naples: Rogiosi, 2006).

49 Ramon Ramon i Muñoz, "Los Rocamora, la industria jabonera barcelonesa y el mercado colonial antillano (1845–1913)," *Revista de historia industrial* 5 (1994), 151–62.

50 Figuier, *Les merveilles de l'industrie*, 411–13; Dutertre, *Savons et savonneries*.

51 Vittorio Scansetti, *L'industria dei saponi*, 3rd ed. (Milan: Hoepli, 1920), 516–20.

52 Tihomir J. Markovitch, *L'industrie française de 1789 à 1964. Analyse des faits*, vol. II (Paris: Institut de science économique appliquée, 1966), Table de base XV – Corps gras.

53 Smith, *The emergence*, 282.

54 Zalio, "Le 'Savon de Marseille,'" 117–20.

55 Williams Haynes, *American Chemical Industry* (New York: Van Nostrand, 1945), VI: 81–3, 341–5; Wilson, *The History of Unilever*, I: 57, 120–1; Musson, *Enterprise in Soap and Chemicals*, 84, 193, 198–9; Dyer, Dalzell, and Olegario, *Rising Tide*, 47, 50.

56 Richard Evely, "The Battle of the Detergents," *Cartel*, January 1954, 12.

57 Victor S. Clark, *History of Manufactures in the United States*, vol. 1: *1607–1860* (Washington, DC: Carnegie Institution of Washington, 1916), 97, 99, 114.

58 Wilson, *The History of Unilever*, II: 223–4.

59 Musson, *Enterprise in Soap and Chemicals*, 100.

60 Wilson, *The History of Unilever*, I: 89–111; Chandler and Hikino, *Scale and Scope*, 264–5.

61 Feiter, *80 Jahre Persil*, 30–1; Musson, *Enterprise in Soap and Chemicals*, 199–201.

62 Feldenkirchen and Hilger, "Chronik," *Menschen und Marken*, 14–33.

63 Ekkehard Bornhofen, *90 Jahre Persil. Rechtsprobleme einer grossen Marke* (Düsseldorf: Henkel KGAA, 1997).

64 Brede, *Das Instrument der Sauberkeit*, 80.

65 Wilson, *The History of Unilever*, I: 107–10, 188–91.

66 Musson, *Enterprise in Soap and Chemicals*, 199–201, 304–5, 330.

67 Wilson, *The History of Unilever*, I: 283, 288–9, 309; II, 348–9.

68 C.J.S. Warrington and R.V.V. Nichols, *A History of Chemistry in Canada* (Toronto: Pitman and Sons, 1949), 323–6; Wilson, *The History of Unilever*, I: 105, 193–6.

69 Ibid., I: 104–5, 202–6, 285–7; Mira Wilkins, *The History of Foreign Investment in the United States, 1914–1945* (Cambridge, MA: Harvard University Press, 2004), 145–6, 228, 325, 401.

70 Wilson, *The History of Unilever*, II: 343–4; Mira Wilkins, *The Maturing of Multinational Enterprise: American Business Abroad from 1914 to 1970* (Cambridge, MA: Harvard University Press, 1974), 16–17, 83; Chandler and Hikino, *Scale and Scope*, 189, 385, 388.

71 Ibid., 385.

72 Wilson, *The History of Unilever*, I: 159–87, 227.

73 Ibid., II, 213–30.

74 Dyer, Dalzell, and Olegario, *Rising Tide*, 51–2.

75 Evely, "The Battle of the Detergents," 13.

76 Ragno, *L'industria dei saponi*, 65–6.

77 D.K. Fieldhouse, *Unilever Overseas: The Anatomy of a Multinational, 1895–1965* (London: Croom Helm; Stanford: Hoover Institution Press, 1978).

78 Britain, "Report on the Soap Industry," 16–19.

79 Barbara Orland, *Wäsche waschen: Technik- und Sozialgeschichte der häuslichen Wäschepflege* (Reinbek bei Hamburg: Rowohlt, 1991), 183–4; Brede, *Das Instrument der Sauberkeit*, 76–7.

80 Ibid., 83–4; Feldenkirchen and Hilger, *Menschen und Marken*, 88–90.

81 Ragno, *L'industria dei saponi*, 30; Italy, Ministero delle corporazioni, *Disciplina della produzione e del commercio de saponi* (Rome: Istituto poligrafico dello stato, 1939); Confederazione generale dell'industria italiana, *Relazione al comitato corporativo olii, grassi e saponi su la disciplina della produzione saponiera* (Rome: La Confederazione, 1940); US Office of Price Administration, "Wartime Control of Supply and Distribution in Italy" (1943), 14.

82 League of Nations, *Wartime Rationing and Consumption* (Geneva, 1942); Hanna Diamond, *Women and the Second World War in France, 1939–48: Choices and Constraints* (Harlow: Pearson Education, 1999), 63–4; Ina Zweiniger-Bargielowska, *Austerity in Britain: Rationing, Controls, and Consumption, 1939–1955* (Oxford: Oxford University Press, 2000), 144–5.

83 Chandler and Hikino, *Scale and Scope.*

84 R. Church and C. Clark, "Product Development of Branded, Packaged Household Goods in Britain, 1870–1914: Colman's, Reckitt's, and Lever Brothers," *Enterprise and Society* 2, no. 3 (2001), 503–42; Diana Twede, "The Birth of Modern Packaging," *Journal of Historical Research in Marketing* 4, no. 2 (2012), 245–72; Juliann Sivulka, *Stronger Than Dirt: A Cultural History of Advertising Personal Hygiene in America, 1875–1940* (Amherst: Humanity Books, 2001), 59–106; Lewis, *So Clean,* 58–74; Pamela Walker Laird, *Advertising Progress: American Business and the Rise of Consumer Marketing* (Baltimore: Johns Hopkins University Press, 1998), 13–37. For an exploration of the broader cultural meanings of this transformation, see Thomas Richards, *The Commodity Culture of Victorian England: Advertising and Spectacle, 1851–1914* (Stanford: Stanford University Press, 1990).

85 Chandler and Hikino, *Scale and Scope,* 148.

86 Ibid.

87 Sivulka, *Stronger Than Dirt,* 52–4.

88 Wilson, *The History of Unilever,* vol. 1, 17; Sivulka, *Stronger Than Dirt,* 93–8; Mike Dempsey, *Bubbles: Early Advertising Art from A. & F. Pears Ltd* (London: Fontana, 1978).

89 Vincent Vinikas, *Soft Soap, Hard Sell: American Hygiene in an Age of Advertisement* (Ames: Iowa State University Press, 1992), 3–19; Sivulka, *Stronger Than Dirt,* 71–98; Dyer, Dalzell, and Olegario, *Rising Tide,* 26–31, 35–8.

90 Wilson, *The History of Unilever,* vol. 1, 38–41.

91 Lever Brothers Ltd., *Sunlight Household Hints and General Information: Sunlight Soap: The Soap We Use and How We Use It* (Warrington, 1889); *Sunlight Household Hints: A Useful Book of Reference and Handy Guide in Domestic Matters;* Procter & Gamble, *Something about Soap* (Cincinnati: Procter & Gamble, 1881); Mary Beals Vail, *Approved Methods for Home Laundering* (Cincinnati: Procter & Gamble, 1906); Dyer, Dalzell, and Olegario, *Rising Tide,* 36–7.

92 Musson, *Enterprise in Soap and Chemicals,* 103.

93 Jutta Reinke, "Die 'Weisse Dame.' Persil. Eine Waschmittelwerbung macht Geschichte," in *Oikos. Von der Feuerstelle zur Mikrowelle. Haushalt und*

Wohnen im Wandel, ed. Michael Andritzky (Giessen: Anabas, 1992), 439–41; Brede, *Das Instrument der Sauberkeit,* 247–78; Feiter, *80 Jahre Persil,* 27–8.

94 Musson, *Enterprise in Soap and Chemicals,* 100; Dyer, Dalzell, and Olegario, *Rising Tide,* 26–8.

95 T.R. Nevett, *Advertising in Britain: A History* (London: Heinemann on behalf of the History of Advertising Trust, 1982), 72–4; Lewis, *So Clean,* 68.

96 Dyer, Dalzell, and Olegario, *Rising Tide,* 35–6.

97 Wilson, *The History of Unilever,* 1:43; Edwards, *Competition and Monopoly,* 149.

98 Reinke, "Die 'Weisse Dame,'" 439.

99 Dyer, Dalzell, and Olegario, *Rising Tide,* 40; Lewis, *So Clean,* 56–7.

100 Roy Church, "Advertising Consumer Goods in Nineteenth–Century Britain: Reinterpretations," *Economic History Review* 53, no. 4 (2000), 621–45; Brede, *Das Instrument der Sauberkeit,* 247–78; Ute Daniel, "Der unaufhaltsame Aufstieg des sauberen Individuums: Seifen- und Waschmittelwerbung im historischen Kontext," in *Stadtgesellschaft und Kindheit im Prozeß der Zivilisation. Konfigurationen städtischer Lebensweise zu Beginn des 20. Jahrhunderts,* ed. Imbke Behnken (Opladen: Leske + Budrich, 1990), 49.

101 Lewis, *So Clean,* 74–5.

102 Feldenkirchen and Hilger, *Menschen und Marken,* 34.

103 Sivulka, *Stronger Than Dirt,* 87–8, 125–7; Dyer, Dalzell, and Olegario, *Rising Tide,* 36–8.

104 "Bubbles," *Illustrated London News,* 5 December 1887.

105 Lewis, *So Clean,* 65.

106 Dempsey, *Bubbles;* Lewis, *So Clean,* 65.

107 Brede, *Das Instrument der Sauberkeit,* 259, 277.

108 Ibid.; Daniel, "Der unaufhaltsame Aufstieg," 54; Dutertre, *Savons et savonneries,* 71–2; Lori Anne Loeb, *Consuming Angels: Advertising and Victorian Women* (New York: Oxford University Press, 1994), 62; Sivulka, *Stronger Than Dirt,* 93–8.

109 Loeb, *Consuming Angels,* 97.

110 Sivulka, *Stronger Than Dirt,* 125; Loeb, *Consuming Angels,* 16–18.

111 Ibid., 11.

112 Sivulka, *Stronger Than Dirt,* 138–56.

113 Ibid., 143–55; Laird, *Advertising Progress,* 291, 297–8.

114 Sivulka, *Stronger Than Dirt,* 151.

115 Lewis, *So Clean,* 78.

116 Sivulka, *Stronger Than Dirt,* 101.

117 Loeb, *Consuming Angels,* 149–54; Anne McClintock, *Imperial Leather: Race, Gender, and Sexuality in the Colonial Contest* (New York: Routledge, 1995), 207–31; Lewis, *So Clean,* 78–9.

118 Sivulka, *Stronger Than Dirt,* 98–106.

119 Lewis, *So Clean,* 80–1.

120 Loeb, *Consuming Angels,* 107–10.

CHAPTER FIVE

1 "By order of Monsignore Illmo Ermo, President of the Streets, it is expressly prohibited to any person to throw rubbish of any sort or manure in this place under penalty of ten scudi and otherwise under the authority of Signore Illma in conformity with the edict of 11 May 1740."

2 George Rosen, *History of Public Health* (New York: MD Publications, 1958), 131–91; Geoffrey Bilson, *A Darkened House: Cholera in Nineteenth-Century Canada* (Toronto: University of Toronto Press, 1980); Anthony S. Wohl, *Endangered Lives: Public Health in Victorian Britain* (London: Dent, 1983), 142–65; John Duffy, *The Sanitarians: A History of American Public Health* (Urbana: University of Illinois Press, 1990), 35–51; Gérard Jorland, *Une société à soigner. Hygiène et salubrité publiques en France au XIXe siècle* (Paris: Gallimard, 2010), 19–83.

3 Rosen, *History of Public Health,* 192–293; Wohl, *Endangered Lives,* passim; William Coleman, *Death Is a Social Disease: Public Health and Political Economy in Early Industrial France* (Madison: University of Wisconsin Press, 1982), 95–306; Duffy, *The Sanitarians,* 66–192; Eduard Simon Houwaart, *De hygiënisten. Artsen, staat & volksgezondheid in Nederland 1840–1890* (Groningen: Historische Uitgeverij, 1991); Lion Murard and Patrick Zylberman, *L'hygiène dans la République. La santé publique en France, ou l'utopie contrariée (1870–1918)* (Paris: Fayard, 1996); Jorland, *Une société à soigner,* 87–201; Eugenia Tognotti, "Scoperte mediche e risposta istituzionale alla sfida delle malattie infettive tra '800 e '900," in *Salute, malattia e sopravvivenza in Italia fra '800 e '900,* ed. Marco Breschi and Lucia Pozzi (Udine: Editrice Universitaria Udinese, 2007), 15–35; Axel C. Hüntelmann, *Hygiene im Namen des Staates. Das Reichsgesundheitsamt 1876–1933* (Göttingen: Wallstein, 2008).

4 Rosen, *History of Public Health,* 225.

5 Simon Szreter, "The Importance of Social Intervention in Britain's Mortality Decline c. 1850–1914: A Re-interpretation of the Role of Public Health," *Social History of Medicine* 1, no. 1 (1988), 1–38.

6 Quoted in Pierre Guillaume, *Le rôle social du médecin depuis deux siècles: 1800–1945* (Paris: Association pour l'étude de l'histoire de la sécurité sociale, 1996), 95.

7 For example, see W.D. Foster, *A History of Medical Bacteriology and Immunology* (London: W. Heinemann Medical Books, 1970); Patrice Debré, *Louis Pasteur* (Baltimore: Johns Hopkins University Press, 1998); Pierre Darmon, *L' homme et les microbes XVIIe–XXe siècle* (Paris: Fayard, 1999).

8 Oliver W. Holmes, "The Contagiousness of Puerperal Fever," *New England Quarterly Journal of Medicine and Surgery* 1, no. 4 (1843), 503–30; Ignác Fülöp Semmelweis, *The Etiology, Concept, and Prophylaxis of Childbed Fever* [1861] (Madison: University of Wisconsin Press, 1983); John Snow, *On the Mode of Communication of Cholera* (London: John Churchill, 1855).

9 Joseph Lister, "On the Antiseptic Principle in the Practice of Surgery," *British Medical Journal* 2, no. 351 (1867), 246–8.

10 Semmelweis, *The Etiology*.

11 Michael Worboys, *Spreading Germs: Disease Theories and Medical Practice in Britain, 1865–1900* (Cambridge: Cambridge University Press, 2000), 1–42.

12 Ibid., 3–4.

13 Ibid., 109–10, 234.

14 Bruno Latour, *The Pasteurization of France* (Cambridge, MA: Harvard University Press, 1988), 3–150; Nancy J. Tomes, "American Attitudes toward the Germ Theory of Disease: Phyllis Allen Richmond Revisited," *Journal of the History of Medicine and Allied Sciences* 52, no. 1 (1997), 17–50; Alain Contrepois, "The Clinician, Germs, and Infectious Diseases: The Example of Charles Bouchard in Paris," *Medical History* 46, no. 2 (2002), 197–220; Anne I. Hardy and Mikael Hård, "Common Cause: Public Health and Bacteriology in Germany, 1870–1895," *East Central Europe* 40, no. 3 (2013), 319–40.

15 Arthur Newsholme, *Hygiene: A Manual of Personal and Public Health* (London: George Gill, 1892).

16 Ephrem Aubert and A. Lapresté, *Cours élémentaire d'hygiène, rédigé conformément aux programmes officiels des écoles normales primaires* (Paris: E. André fils, 1893), 146–8.

17 Lister, "On the Antiseptic Principle."

18 Worboys, *Spreading Germs*, 73–107, 150–92, 186–90.

19 Tomes, "American Attitudes," 46.

20 Nancy Tomes, *The Gospel of Germs: Men, Women, and the Microbe in American Life* (Cambridge, MA: Harvard University Press, 1998), 103–6.

21 Dorothy Porter, "Introduction," in *The History of Public Health and the Modern State*, ed. Porter (Amsterdam: Rodopi, 1994), 1–5.

22 Ibid., 9.

23 For a general overview of these differences see the various essays in ibid.

24 Tognotti, "Scoperte mediche," 26–7.

25 Wohl, *Endangered Lives*, 179–204.

26 Celia Davies, "The Health Visitor as Mother's Friend: A Woman's Place in Public Health, 1900–14," *Social History of Medicine* 1, no. 1 (1988), 39–59.

27 Quoted in ibid., 43.

28 Wohl, *Endangered Lives*, 36–8, 67–71; Anne Hardy, *The Epidemic Streets: Infectious Disease and the Rise of Preventive Medicine, 1856–1900* (Oxford: Clarendon Press, 1993), 275–6.

29 Barbara Gutmann Rosenkrantz, *Public Health and the State: Changing Views in Massachusetts, 1842–1936* (Cambridge, MA: Harvard University Press, 1972), 130–1; Tomes, *The Gospel of Germs*, 150–4, 185–8; Elizabeth Fee, "Public Health and the State: The United States," in *The History of Public Health*, ed. Porter, 234–75.

30 Alan M. Kraut, *Silent Travelers: Germs, Genes, and the "Immigrant Menace"* (New York: Basic Books, 1994).

31 C.-E.A. Winslow, *The Evolution and Significance of the Modern Public Health Campaign* [1923] (New Haven: Yale University Press, 1984), 56–9; Kraut, *Silent Travelers*, 212.

32 Jay Cassel, "Public Health in Canada," in *The History of Public Health*, ed. Dorothy Porter, 288–9.

33 Mary Lynn Stewart, *For Health and Beauty: Physical Culture for Frenchwomen, 1880s–1930s* (Baltimore: Johns Hopkins University Press, 2001), 61.

34 Matthew Ramsey, "Public Health in France," in *The History of Public Health*, ed. Porter, 71.

35 Walter Douglas Hogg, *L'hygiène scolaire dans les établissements d'enseignement secondaire de la Grande-Bretagne. Rapport adressé à M. le ministre de l'Instruction publique, des beaux-arts et des cultes* (Paris: A. Colin, 1892).

36 Ibid., 28.

37 Abram de Swaan, *In Care of the State: Health Care, Education, and Welfare in Europe and the USA in the Modern Era* (Cambridge: Polity Press, 1988), 85–117.

38 Jean-Pierre Goubert, The Conquest of Water: The Advent of Health in the Industrial Age (Cambridge: Polity Press 1989), 146; Stewart, For Health

and Beauty, 56–74; Julia Csergo, "Propreté et enfance au XIXe siècle," in *Éducation à la santé, XIXe–XXe siècle*, ed. Didier Nourrisson (Rennes: Éd. de l'École nationale de la santé publique, 2002), 43–56; Steven Zdatny, "The French Hygiene Offensive of the 1950s: A Critical Moment in the History of Manners," The Journal of Modern History 84, no. 4 (2012), 901–3.

39 France, Ministère de l'instruction publique, *Hygiène des écoles primaires et des écoles maternelles* (Paris: Imprimerie nationale, 1884).

40 Ibid., 18–20.

41 Gaetano Bonetta, *Corpo e nazione. L'educazione ginnastica, igienica e sessuale nell'Italia liberale* (Milan: F. Angeli, 1990), 281–5.

42 Angelo Celli, *La scuola e l'igiene sociale. Note del Prof. Angelo Celli* (Naples, 1893).

43 Arthur Newsholme, *School Hygiene: or The Laws of Health in Relation to School Life* (Boston: D.C. Heath, 1889), 102.

44 Carl Ernst Bock, *Bau, Leben und Pflege des menschlichen Körpers in Wort und Bild* (Leipzig: Keil, 1869); Hans-Jürgen Apel and Jürgen Bennack, eds., *Hygiene in preussischen Schulvorschriften: Eine Zusammenstellung unter besonderer Berücksichtigung der Rheinlande 1800–1945* (Cologne & Vienna: Böhlau, 1986), 17.

45 Alfred Baur, *Gesundheitsregeln für Schulkinder* (Munich: Seitz & Schauer, 1905), 14–15.

46 L.A. Parravicini, *Manuale de pedagogia* (Livorno: Giacomo Antonelli, 1850), 10–11, quoted in Bonetta, *Corpo e nazione*, 286.

47 Jörg Vögele, *Urban Mortality Change in England and Germany, 1870–1913* (Liverpool: Liverpool University Press, 1998), 203.

48 Armand Lévy, "L' enseignement de l'hygiène individuelle dans les écoles" (Faculté de Médecine de Paris, 1902), 27–32.

49 Ibid., 31–2; David S. Barnes, *The Great Stink of Paris and the Nineteenth-Century Struggle against Filth and Germs* (Baltimore: Johns Hopkins University Press, 2006), 175–6.

50 Goubert, *The Conquest of Water*, 154.

51 Anna Davin, *Growing Up Poor: Home, School, and Street in London, 1870–1914* (London: Rivers Oram Press, 1996), 134–5.

52 Great Britain, "Annual Report for 1910 of the Chief Medical Officer of the Board of Education," ed. Board of Education, House of Commons, Parliamentary Papers (1911), 236–8.

53 Italia, Ministero della pubblica istruzione, "Regolamento generale per l'istruzione elementare. Decreto 6 febbraio 1908, N. 150" (Turin: G.B. Paravia, 1909), Art. 197.-

54 France, Ministère de l'instruction publique, *Hygiène des écoles primaires*, 15–16; Goubert, *The Conquest of Water*, 150.

55 Ibid., 149–50.

56 Apel and Bennack, *Hygiene in preussischen Schulvorschriften*, 13–14; Thilo Rauch, *Die Ferienkoloniebewegung. Zur Geschichte der privaten Fürsorge im Kaiserreich* (Wiesbaden: Deutscher Universitäts-Verlag, 1992), 155–61; Hideharu Umehara, "Gesunde Schule und gesunde Kinder: Schulhygiene in Düsseldorf 1880–1933," PhD diss. (Düsseldorf: Heinrich-Heine-Universität Düsseldorf, 2011), 35–45; Duffy, *The Sanitarians*, 183, 210.

57 Bernard Harris, *The Health of the Schoolchild: A History of the School Medical Service in England and Wales* (Buckingham: Open University Press, 1995), 6–47; Worboys, *Spreading Germs*, 234.

58 Wohl, *Endangered Lives*, 331–5; J.M. Winter, *The Great War and the British People* (London: Macmillan, 1986), 8–18.

59 Great Britain, "Report of the Royal Commission on Physical Training (Scotland)," House of Commons, Parliamentary Papers (1903), Cmd. 1507 & 1508; "Report of the Inter-departmental Committee on Physical Deterioration," Parliamentary Papers (1904), Cmd. 2715; "Report of the Inter-departmental Committee on Medical Inspection and Feeding of Children Attending Public Elementary Schools," Parliamentary Papers (1906), Cmd. 2773 & 2784; "Report on Children under Five Years of Age in Public and Elementary Schools, by Women Inspectors of the Board of Education," ed. Board of Education (London: HMSO, 1906), Cmd. 2726.

60 Harris, *The Health of the Schoolchild*, 48–69.

61 Great Britain, Department of Education and Science, *The School Health Service, 1908–1974: Report of the Chief Medical Officer of the DES and Presenting an Historical Review by Dr. Peter Henderson* (London: HMSO, 1975), 4–5.

62 Pamela Horn, *The Victorian and Edwardian Schoolchild* (Gloucester: Sutton, 1989), 81.

63 Britain, "Report of the Royal Commission on Physical Training (Scotland)," vol. I, Table III, 81, 104.

64 "Report of the Inter-departmental Committee on Medical Inspection," 24–5; J.S. Hurt, *Elementary Schooling and the Working Classes, 1860–1918* (London: Routledge and Kegan Paul, 1979), 131–5.

65 Kraut, *Silent Travelers*, 234–54.

66 Lillian D. Wald, "Medical inspection of public schools," *The Annals of the American Academy of Political and Social Science* 25 (1905), 91, 94; Kraut, *Silent Travelers*, 236.

67 Ibid., 249.

68 Hardy, *The Epidemic Streets*, 268.

69 Lucinda McCray Beier, *For Their Own Good: The Transformation of English Working-Class Health Culture, 1880–1970* (Columbus: Ohio State University Press, 2008), 300–1.

70 Wald, "Medical inspection of public schools," 295.

71 Giuseppe Tropeano, *Per l'educazione igienica popolare* (Naples: Detken e Rocholl, 1910), 18, quoted in Bonetta, *Corpo e nazione*, 291.

72 Britain, "Report of the Inter-departmental Committee on Medical Inspection," 25.

73 Ramsey, "Public Health in France," 90.

74 Britain, "Report of the Inter-departmental Committee on Physical Deterioration," II: 344.

75 Antonin Baratier, *Hygiène générale. L'école de village au point de vue de l'hygiène publique et privée* (Paris: G. Maurin, 1899), 19–25.

76 Murard and Zylberman, *L'hygiène dans la République*, 352.

77 Goubert, *The Conquest of Water*, 158–64.

78 A. Peracchia, quoted in Bonetta, *Corpo e nazione*, 290.

79 Rosenkrantz, *Public Health and the State*, 168.

80 Oscar Lassar, "Über den Stand der Volksbäder," *Gesundheits-Ingenieur* 25, no. 6 (1902), 94–6; Herbert D.P.H. Jones, *School Hygiene: A Handbook for Teachers of All Grades, School Managers, etc.* (London: J.M. Dent, 1907), 86–8; Britain, "Annual Report for 1910 of the Chief Medical Officer of the Board of Education," 33–6; Alessandro Lustig, *Igiene della scuola ad uso degli insegnanti delle scuole primarie e secondarie e delle scuole normali e di pedagogia*, 2nd ed. (Milan: Vallardi, 1911), 179–83; Henri Méry and Joseph Génévrier, *Hygiène scolaire* (Paris: J.B. Baillière, 1914), 61–8; Jos van den Bongaardt, *Elke week een goed bad! Geschiedenis en architectuur van de badhuizen van Amsterdam. Een eeuw volksbadhuizen* (Amsterdam: Stadsuitgeverij Amsterdam, 1990), 15–23; Horn, *The Victorian and Edwardian Schoolchild*, 79.

81 Goubert, *The Conquest of Water*, 167–8; Bonetta, *Corpo e nazione*, 313.

82 John R. Gillis, *Youth and History: Tradition and Change in European Age Relations, 1770–present* (New York: Academic Press, 1974), 95–183.

83 Robert Stephenson Smyth Baden-Powell, *Scouting for Boys: A Handbook for Instruction in Good Citizenship* (London: C. Arthur Pearson, 1908).

84 The American manual, *Boy Scouts of America*, was written principally by the naturalist and writer Ernest Thompson Seton, with additions from Baden-Powell. Born in England and raised in Canada, Seton looked to nature and Native society as guides to young life. He seems to have had

only passing interest in health and hygiene. Seton and Baden-Powell, *Boy Scouts of America: A Handbook of Woodcraft, Scouting, and Life-Craft* (New York: Doubleday, Page, 1910).

85 Baden-Powell, *Scouting for Boys*, ed. Elleke Boehmer (Oxford: Oxford University Press, 2004), xi, n1.

86 Ibid., 163–88.

87 Ibid., 174, 182.

88 *Brownies or Blue Birds: A Handbook for Young Girl Guides* (London: C.A. Pearson, 1920); *Girl Guiding: A Handbook for Guidelets, Guides, Rangers, and Guiders* (London: C.A. Pearson, 1926); *Aids to Scoutmastership: A Handbook for Scoutmasters on the Theory of Scout Training* (London: Jenkins, 1930).

89 *Scouting for Boys*, 26th ed. (London: C.A. Pearson, 1951).

90 For example, see *Das Pfadfinderbuch. Nach General Baden-Powells Scouting for Boys*, trans. Adolf Lion (Munich: Gmelin, 1909); *Eclaireurs. Un programme d'éducation civique*, trans. Pierre Bovet, 3rd ed. (Neuchâtel: Delachaux et Niestlé, 1920); *L'esplorazione per giovani. Manuale per la formazione di buoni Cittadini*, trans. M. Di Carpegna (Rome: Tip. Ed. Laziale, A. Marchesi, 1920).

91 Martin Kitchen, *The German Officer Corps 1890–1914* (Oxford: Clarendon, 1968), 139–42; Gillis, *Youth and history*, 149–55.

92 Kenny Cupers, "Governing through Nature: Camps and Youth Movements in Interwar Germany and the United States," *Cultural Geographies* 15, no. 2 (2008), 184.

93 Rauch, *Die Ferienkoloniebewegung*, 173.

94 Cristiano Focarile, *La funzione sociale della cooperazione fascista per il potenziamento della stirpe* (Rome: Esperienza cooperativa, 1930), 31; Rauch, *Die Ferienkoloniebewegung*, 167–74.

95 Laura Lee Downs, *Childhood in the Promised Land: Working-Class Movements and the Colonies de Vacances in France, 1880–1960* (Durham: Duke University Press, 2002), 45.

96 Comando Generale P.N.F. Gioventù Italiana del Littorio, *Regolamento delle colonie estive* (Rome: Unione editoriale d'Italia, 1939), 39; Giuseppe Sangiorgi, "Igiene individuale," in *Trattato d'igiene*, ed. Ernesto Bertarelli (Milan: Treves, 1938), 67–75; Elena Mucelli, *Colonie di vacanza italiane degli anni '30. Architetture per l'educazione del corpo e dello spirito* (Florence: Alinea, 2009), 29.

97 David I. Macleod, *Building Character in the American Boy: The Boy Scouts, YMCA, and Their Forerunners, 1870–1920* (Madison: University of Wisconsin Press, 1983), 234–7.

98 Abigail Ayres Van Slyck, *A Manufactured Wilderness: Summer Camps and the Shaping of American Youth, 1890–1960* (Minneapolis: University of Minnesota Press, 2006), 158–67.

99 Hardy, *The Epidemic Streets*, 278; Tomes, *The Gospel of Germs*, 141–6.

100 Goubert, *The Conquest of Water*, 167; Nancy Tomes, "The Private Side of Public Health: Sanitary Science, Domestic Hygiene, and the Germ Theory, 1870–1900," *Bulletin of the History of Medicine* 64, no. 4 (1990), 520–2; idem, *The Gospel of Germs*, 52–67.

101 Frank R. Keefer, *A Text-Book of Military Hygiene and Sanitation* (Philadelphia: W.B. Saunders, 1914), 32–4.

102 William Daly Paley, "9th Infantry Boys' Morning Wash" (Edison Manufacturing Co., 1898), http://hdl.loc.gov/loc.mbrsmi/sawmp. 1329.

103 Alfons Labisch, "Doctors, Workers, and the Scientific Cosmology of the Industrial World: The Social Construction of 'Health' and the 'Homo Hygienicus,'" *Journal of Contemporary History* 20, no. 4 (1985), 604–7; Ute Frevert, "Professional Medicine and the Working Classes in Imperial Germany," *Journal of Contemporary History* 20, no. 4 (1985) 649–51; Reinhard Spree, *Health and Social Class in Imperial Germany: A Social History of Mortality, Morbidity, and Inequality* (Oxford: Berg, 1988), 178–83; Harry Hendrick, "Child Labour, Medical Capital, and the School Medical Service, c. 1890–1918," in *In the Name of the Child: Health and Welfare, 1880–1940*, ed. Roger Cooter (London and New York: Routledge, 1992), 45–71.

CHAPTER SIX

1 Peter Ward, *A History of Domestic Space: Privacy and the Canadian Home* (Vancouver: UBC Press, 1999), 58; US Census Bureau, "Historical Census of Housing Tables, Plumbing Facilities," https://www.census.gov/hhes/www/housing/census/historic/plumbing.html.

2 "American Housing Survey for the United States: 2001" (Washington, DC: US GPO, 2002), 46.

3 Alexander Kira, *The Bathroom* (New York: Viking, 1976), 8.

4 Great Britain, "Census" (1951), England and Wales, Housing Report, Table 11, Private Households by Availability of Certain Household Arrangements.

5 Office of Population and Census Surveys Great Britain, *1991 Census: Housing and Availability of Cars*, Table 3, Housing Characteristics (1991).

6 Charles O. Hardy and Robert René Kuczynski, *The Housing Program of the City of Vienna* (Washington, DC: The Brookings Institution, 1934), 54–72, 99–101; Eve Blau, *The Architecture of Red Vienna, 1919–1934* (Cambridge, MA: MIT Press, 1999).

7 Ronald V. Wiedenhoeft, *Berlin's Housing Revolution: German Reform in the 1920s* (Ann Arbor: UMI Research Press, 1985); Karin Kirsch and Gerhard Kirsch, *The Weissenhofsiedlung: Experimental Housing Built for the Deutscher Werkbund, Stuttgart, 1927* (New York: Rizzoli, 1989).

8 Silbermann and Brüning, *Der Deutschen Badezimmer. Eine soziologische Studie*, 26; Christina Trupat, "'Bade zu Hause!' Zur Geschichte des Badezimmers in Deutschland seit der Mitte des 19. Jahrhunderts," *Technikgeschichte* 63 (1996), 219–36.

9 Barbara Orland, *Wäsche waschen. Technik- und Sozialgeschichte der häuslichen Wäschepflege* (Reinbek bei Hamburg: Rowohlt, 1991), 232; Silbermann and Brüning, *Der Deutschen Badezimmer*, 26.

10 European Communities Commission, *Family Budgets: Comparative Tables: Germany, France, Italy, United Kingdom* (Luxembourg: Office des publications officielles des Communautés européennes, 1984), 36; idem, *Family Budgets: Comparative Tables: Netherlands, Belgium, Ireland, Denmark, Greece, Spain* (Luxembourg: Office des publications officielles des Communautés européennes, 1986), 94.

11 Silbermann and Brüning, *Der Deutschen Badezimmer*, 37, 40–1.

12 Ina Merkel, *Utopie und Bedürfnis. Die Geschichte der Konsumkultur in der DDR* (Cologne: Böhlau, 1999), 317.

13 Bogdan Mieczkowski, *Personal and Social Consumption in Eastern Europe: Poland, Czechoslovakia, Hungary, and East Germany* (New York: Praeger, 1975), 30.

14 Jacques Méraud, *Les besoins des Français* (Paris: Economica, 1990), 46; Jacques Rouaud, *60 ans d'arts ménagers*, vol. 2: *1948–1983. La consommation* (Paris: Syros Alternatives, 1993), 74; Steven Zdatny, "The French Hygiene Offensive of the 1950s: A Critical Moment in the History of Manners," *The Journal of Modern History* 84, no. 4 (2012), 913–17; Nicole C. Rudolph, *At Home in Postwar France: Modern Mass Housing and the Right to Comfort* (New York: Berghahn, 2015), 18.

15 Institut national de la statistique et des études économiques, "Enquête sur les budgets familiaux 1963–1964. Resultats relatifs à l'ensemble des ménages" (Paris: Imprimerie nationale, 1964), Tableau 3.IV; Rudolph, *At Home in Postwar France*, 118–28.

16 Antonella De Michelis, "The Garden Suburb of the Garbatella, 1920–1929: Defining Community and Identity through Planning in Post-War Rome," *Planning Perspectives* 24, no. 4 (2009), 516.

17 Marco Giardini, *Per Bologna. Novant'anni di attività dell'Istituto autonomo case popolari: 1906–1996* (Bologna: IACP, 1996), 102–4, 148–9, 244.

18 Luciano Bergonzini, *Un'indagine sulle condizioni igieniche delle abitazioni in Italia* (Bologna: L. Cappelli, 1957), 29.

19 Méraud, *Les besoins des Français*, 46; Istituto nazionale di statistica, *Struttura socioeconomica e condizione abitava della popolazione residente. Fascicolo nazionale II. Italia. 14e censimento generale della popolazione e delle abitazioni* (Rome: ISTAT, 2006), 153.

20 Fanny Beaupré and Roger-Henri Guerrand, *Le confident des dames. Le bidet du XVIIIe au XXe siècle. Histoire d'une intimité* (Paris: La Découverte, 1997), 10–11; Valeria Robecco and Angela Puchetti, "In Usa è scoppiata la febbre del bidet. Con 300 anni di ritardo," *Business Insider Italia*, 21 April 2017.

21 Alison K. Hoagland, *The Bathroom: A Social History of Cleanliness and the Body* (Santa Barbara: Greenwood, 2018), 65–82.

22 Méraud, *Les besoins des Français*, 46; Zdatny, "The French Hygiene Offensive," 914–15.

23 Donald S. Pitkin, *The House That Giacomo Built: History of an Italian Family, 1898–1978* (Cambridge: Cambridge University Press, 1985), 125–6.

24 Ibid., 134.

25 US Department of Labor, Bureau of Labor Statistics, "Cost of Living in the United States, 1917–1919" [computer file]. Also additional files (Ann Arbor, MI: Inter-university Consortium for Political and Social Research 1986), variables 378 and 379.

26 Political and Economic Planning, *The Market for Household Appliances. A Study of the Market for Household Appliances Produced by the Light Engineering Industries before the War. The Design of the Appliances Then Available, and the Market as It May Exist in the Next Ten Years* (London: Political and Economic Planning, distributed by Oxford University Press, 1945), 158–9.

27 "Bollettino della Doxa," 31 January 1957, 16–17.

28 Istituto nazionale di statistica, *Indagine speciale su alcuni aspetti delle condizioni igieniche e sanitarie della popolazione* (Rome: ISTAT, 1960), 36.

29 Institut national de la statistique et des études économiques, "Enquête sur les budgets familiaux 1963–1964. Resultats relatifs à l'ensemble des menages" (Paris: Imprimerie nationale, 1964), Tableau 3.IV.

30 Lawrence Wright, *Clean and Decent: The Fascinating History of the Bathroom and the Water Closet, and of Sundry Habits, Fashions, and Accessories of the Toilet, Principally in Great Britain, France, and America* (London: Routledge and Kegan Paul, 1960), 187–98; Stefan Muthesius, *The English Terraced House* (New Haven: Yale University Press, 1982), 60–1; John Burnett, *A Social History of Housing, 1815–1985*, 2nd ed. (London and New York: Methuen, 1986), 215.

31 Geneviève Heller, *"'Propre en ordre.' Habitation et vie domestique 1850–1930, l'exemple vaudois* (Lausanne: Éditions d'en Bas, 1979), 206; Trupat, ""Bade zu Haus!," 229–30.

32 United States Department of Labor. Bureau of Labor Statistics, "Cost of Living in the United States, 1917–1919" [computer file] (Ann Arbor, MI: Inter-University Consortium for Political and Social Research, 1986), ICPSR08299-v5, variable 388.

33 Larry Weingarten and Suzanne Weingarten, "The History of Domestic Water Heating," PM *Engineer* 4, no. 8 (1998); Hoagland, *The Bathroom*, 36–7.

34 Hermann Muthesius, *The English House* [1904] (New York: Rizzoli, 1979), 235.

35 Sue Bowden and Avner Offer, "Technological Revolution That Never Was: Gender, Class, and the Diffusion of Household Appliances in Interwar England," in *The Sex of Things: Gender and Consumption in Historical Perspective*, ed. Victoria De Grazia and Ellen Furlough (Berkeley: University of California Press, 1996), 248.

36 Political and Economic Planning, *The Market for Household Appliances*, 159.

37 Burnett, *A Social History of Housing*, 215.

38 "Bollettino della Doxa," 31 January 1957, 17.

39 Burnett, *A Social History of Housing*, 232; Kira, *The Bathroom*, 8.

40 John Bongaarts, "Household Size and Composition in the Developing World in the 1990s," *Population studies* 55, no. 3 (2001), 264–5.

41 For the Canadian example, see Ward, *A History of Domestic Space*, 8–46.

42 Ibid., 47–88; Hoagland, *The Bathroom*, 83–99.

43 Louis P. Cain, *Sanitation Strategy for a Lakefront Metropolis: The Case of Chicago* (DeKalb: Northern Illinois University Press, 1978), x, Table 1.

44 Peter Münch, *Stadthygiene im 19. und 20. Jahrhundert. Die Wasserversorgung, Abwasser- und Abfallbeseitigung unter besonderer Berücksichtigung Münchens* (Göttingen: Vandenhoeck & Ruprecht, 1993), 379.

45 Carlo Bima, *L'acqua a Torino* (Moncalieri: Grafiche Jemma, 1970), 180.

46 Jean-Pierre Goubert, *The Conquest of Water: The Advent of Health in the Industrial Age* (Cambridge, UK: Polity Press, 1989), 196.

47 Michael G. Mulhall, *The Dictionary of Statistics*, 4th ed. (London: George Routledge and Sons, 1899), 818.

48 Martin V. Melosi, *The Sanitary City; Urban Infrastructure in America from Colonial Times to the Present* (Baltimore: Johns Hopkins University Press, 2000), 215.

49 Ibid., 299, 375.

50 European Environmental Agency, "Indicator Fact Sheet Signals 2001 – Chapter Households, YIR01HH07 Household water consumption" (2001), 2–3.

51 Goubert, *The Conquest of Water*, 169–259.

52 Melosi, *The Sanitary City*, 375–6; American Public Works Association, "Community Water Supply," in *History of Public Works in the United States, 1776–1976*, ed. Ellis L. Armstrong, Michael C. Robinson, and Suellen M. Hoy (Chicago: The Association, 1976), 217–46.

53 Goubert, *The Conquest of Water*, 180.

54 Ibid., 187.

55 Mass Observation, "An Enquiry into People's Homes: A Report Prepared by Mass-Observation for the Avertising Service Guild" (London: J. Murray, 1943), 217–18.

56 "People and homes" (1943), in *Mass Observation Online*, 217.

57 "Washing habits" (1949), in *Mass Observations Online*, 1.

58 Françoise Giroud, "La Française est-elle propre?," *Elle*, 22 October 1951; Zdatny, "The French Hygiene Offensive," 923–4.

59 Jean Maudit, "Les françaises sont-elles devenues propres?," *Elle*, 20 January 1986. See also Nathalie Mikaïloff, *Les Manières de propreté. Du Moyen Âge à nos jours* (Paris: Maloine, 1990), 172–7.

60 Patrick Miler, Patrick Mahé, and Richard Cannavo, *Les Français tels qu'ils sont. La fameuse enquête "France-Soir"–IFOP [Institut français d'opinion publique], le dossier complet* (Paris: Fayard, 1975), 123, 125.

61 Marilyn Langford, *Personal Hygiene Attitudes and Practices in 1000 Middleclass Households* (Ithaca: Cornell University Agricultural Experiment Station, New York State College of Agriculture, 1965), 106.

62 Reinhold Bergler, *Sauberkeit. Norm, Verhalten, Persönlichkeit. Beträge zur empirischen Sozialforschung* (Bern: Hans Huber, 1974), 184.

63 Ibid., 182.

64 Ibid., 190.

65 Bergler, "Körperhygiene und Sauberkeit im internationalen Vergleich," *Zentralblatt für Bakteriologie, Mikrobiologie und Hygiene. Serie B, Umwelthygiene, Krankenhaushygiene, Arbeitshygiene, präventive Medizin* 187, nos. 4–6 (1989), 484–5.

66 Gérard Nirascou, "Moins d'une Français sur deux se lave complètement chaque jour," *Le Figaro*, 20 November 1998.

CHAPTER SEVEN

1 Union pour l'étude du marché de l'électricité, "Évolution des applications domestiques de l'électricité en France et dans quelques pays d'Europe" (Paris, 1955), 18.

2 European Communities Commission, *Family Budgets: Comparative Tables: Germany, France, Italy, United Kingdom* (Luxembourg, 1984), 36–9; idem, *Family Budgets: Comparative Tables: Netherlands, Belgium, Ireland, Denmark, Greece, Spain* (Luxembourg, 1986), 94.

3 Jacob Christian Schäffer, *Die bequeme und höchstvortheilhafte Waschmaschine* (Regensburg: Heinrich Gottfried Zunfel, 1766); "Neu erfundene Englische Patent-Waschmaschine," *Journal des Luxus und der Moden* 6 (March 1791), 169–73; Sigfried Giedion, *Mechanization Takes Command: A Contribution to Anonymous History* (New York: Oxford University Press, 1948), 560–8.

4 Carl Christian Schäfer, *Gründliche und durch Erfahrung erprobte Anweisung, sich seine Seife selbst zu bereiten so wohl aus Fett und Oel, als auch aus fettigen Abfällen und andern Gegenständen, sowie Vorschriften zu den vorzüglichsten Waschmethoden und Seifen surrogaten, nebst Beschreibung der neuesten und vorzüglichsten Wasch-, Mang- und Plättmaschinen ...*, 2 ed. (Coburg: J.G. Riemann'schen, 1840), 75–92; Barbara Orland, *Wäsche waschen: Technik- und Sozialgeschichte der häuslichen Wäschepflege* (Reinbek bei Hamburg: Rowohlt, 1991), 89; Maureen Ogle, "Domestic Reform and American Household Plumbing, 1840–1870," *Winterthur Portfolio* 28, no. 1 (1993), 141.

5 Orland, *Wäsche waschen*, 93–103.

6 Todd S. Goodholme, ed., *A Domestic Cyclopedia of Practical Information* (New York: Henry Holt, 1878), 596, quoted in May N. Stone, "The Plumbing Paradox: American Attitudes toward Late Nineteenth-Century Domestic Sanitary Arrangements," *Winterthur Portfolio* 14, no. 3 (1979), 304.

7 *100 Jahr Miele im Spiegel der Zeit* (Gütersloh: Miele & Cie, 1999), 16.

8 Françoise Wasserman, *Blanchisseuse, laveuse, repasseuse. La femme, le linge et l'eau* (Fresnes: Écomusée, 1986), 85.

9 *100 Jahr Miele im Spiegel der Zeit*, 23; Rosmarie Beier, "Leben in der Mietskaserne. Zum Alltag Berliner Unterschichtsfamilien in den Jahren 1900 bis 1920," in *Hinterhof, Keller und Mansarde. Einblicke in Berliner Wohnungselend 1901–1920*, ed. Gesine Asmus (Reinbek bei Hamburg: Rowohlt, 1982), 247.

10 David E. Nye, *Electrifying America: Social Meanings of a New Technology, 1880–1940* (Cambridge, MA: MIT Press, 1990), 262.

11 Jacques Rouaud, *60 ans d'arts ménagers*, vol. 1 : *1923–1939. Le confort* (Paris: Syros Alternatives, 1989), 83–9; Maurice Lévy-Leboyer and Henri Morsel, *Histoire générale de l'électricité en France*, vol. 2: *L'interconnexion et le marché, 1919–1946* (Paris: Fayard, 1994), 1273.

12 Orland, *Wäsche waschen*, 209–22.

13 Ibid., 206.

14 Jennifer Ann Loehlin, *From Rugs to Riches: Housework, Consumption and Modernity in Germany* (Oxford: Berg, 1999), 61.

15 Sue Bowden and Avner Offer, "Household Appliances and the Use of Time: The United States and Britain since the 1920s," *Economic History Review* 47, no. 4 (1994), 744; Political and Economic Planning, *The Market for Household Appliances: A Study of the Market for Household Appliances Produced by the Light Engineering Industries before the War; the Design of the Appliances Then Available, and the Market as It May Exist in the Next Ten Years* (London: Political and Economic Planning, distributed by Oxford University Press, 1945), xxviii.

16 Susan Strasser, *Never Done: A History of American Housework* (New York: Pantheon Books, 1982), 118.

17 F.G. Adams and D.S. Brady, "The Diffusion of New Durable Goods and Their Impact on Consumer Expenditures," *Proceedings of the Business and Economic Statistics Section, American Statistical Association*, 1963, 86.

18 Paul Bairoch, "The Main Trends in National Economic Disparities since the Industrial Revolution," in *Disparities in Economic Development since the Industrial Revolution* (Springer, 1981), 10; Vera Zamagni, "An International Comparison of Real Industrial Wages, 1890–1913: Methodological Issues and Results," in *Labour's Reward: Real Wages and Economic Change in Nineteenth- and Twentieth-Century Europe*, ed. Peter Scholliers and Vera Zamagni (Aldershot: Edward Elgar, 1995), 112; Peter Scholliers, "Some Conclusions and Suggestions for Further Research," in *Labour's Reward*, 232; Kevin H. O'Rourke and Jeffrey G. Williamson, *Globalization and History: The Evolution of a Nineteenth-Century Atlantic Economy* (Cambridge, MA: MIT Press, 1999), 17, 19; Stefano Finoaltea, "Production and Consumption in Post-Unification Italy:

New Evidence, New Conjectures," *Rivista di Storia Economica* 18, no. 3 (2002), 268–76; Charles Feinstein, "Changes in Nominal Wages, the Cost of Living and Real Wages in the United Kingdom over Two Centuries, 1780–1990," in *Labour's Reward*, 29–32; Jeffrey G. Williamson, "Globalization, Convergence, and History," *Journal of Economic History* 56, no. 2 (1996), 277–306; Bowden and Offer, "Household Appliances and the Use of Time," 732.

19 L. Needleman, "The Demand for Domestic Appliances," *National Institute Economic Review* (1960), 24–44.

20 *100 Jahr Miele im Spiegel der Zeit*, 23.

21 William J. Hausman, Peter Hertner, and Mira Wilkins, *Global Electrification: Multinational Enterprise and International Finance in the History of Light and Power, 1878–2007* (New York: Cambridge University Press, 2008), 27–8.

22 Union pour l'étude du marché de l'électricité, "Évolution des applications domestiques de l'électricité en France et dans quelques pays d'Europe" (Paris: Union pour l'étude du marché de l'électricité, 1955), 9; Union pour l'étude du marché de l'électricité, "Évolution des applications domestiques de l'électricité en France et dans quelques pays d'Europe" (Paris: Union pour l'étude du marché de l'électricité, 1961), 5; Thomas Anthony Buchanan Corley, *Domestic Electrical Appliances* (London: Jonathan Cape, 1966), 19; Lévy-Leboyer and Morsel, Histoire générale, 2: 1194–5; Bowden and Offer, "Household appliances," 745; Sven Tetzlaff, "'Laß mich hinein ...!' Die Eroberung der Haushalte durch die Elektrizitätswirtschaft," in *"Das Paradies kommt wieder ..." Zur Kulturgeschichte und Ökologie von Herd, Kühlschrank und Waschmaschine*, ed. Museum der Arbeit (Hamburg: vsa, 1993), 10–25.

23 Orland, *Wäsche waschen*, 197–209.

24 Sue Bowden and Avner Offer, "Technological Revolution That Never Was: Gender, Class, and the Diffusion of Household Appliances in Interwar England," in *The Sex of Things: Gender and Consumption in Historical Perspective*, ed. Victoria De Grazia and Ellen Furlough (Berkeley: University of California Press, 1996), 252–3.

25 *United States of America, Plaintiff, v. Lever Brothers Company and Monsanto Chemical Company, Defendants* (1963), 15.

26 "Statistical Abstract of the United States," (Washington: US GPO, 1966), 754; Joy Parr, *Domestic Goods: The Material, the Moral, and the Economic in the Postwar Years* (Toronto: University of Toronto Press, 1999), 218–42.

27 Canada, Statistics Canada, *Household Facilities and Equipment, 1977–1981* (Ottawa: Statistics Canada, n.d.), 29.

28 Jacques Rouaud, *60 ans d'arts ménagers*, vol. 2: *1948–1983. La consommation* (Paris: Syros Alternatives, 1993), 121–3. Andre Charlot was a French comic actor and impresario.

29 Orland, *Wäsche waschen*, 241–2. For general accounts of the development of the washing machine, see, for Germany, Hans Harder and Albricht Löhr, "Der Wandel der Waschverfahren im Haushalt seit 1945," *Tenside Detergents* 18, no. 5 (1981), 246–52; Ingo Braun, *Stoff, Wechsel, Technik. Zur Soziologie und Ökologie der Waschmaschinen* (Berlin: Sigma, 1988), 25–38; Gudrun Silberzahn-Jandt, *Wasch-Maschine. Zum Wandel von Frauenarbeit im Haushalt* (Marburg: Jonas, 1991), 16–34; and Ursula Schneider, "Waschmachinen. Von der 'Befreiung der Frau' und den unsichtbaren Folgen," in *"Das Paradies kommt wieder..." Zur Kulturgeschichte und Ökologie von Herd, Kühlschrank und Waschmaschine*, ed. Museum der Arbeit (Hamburg: VSA, 1993), 114–27; for France, Quynh Delaunay, *La machine à laver en France. Un objet technique qui parle des femmes* (Paris: L'Harmattan, 2003), 41–88; Delaunay, *Société industrielle et travail domestique. L'électroménager en France, XIXe–XXe siècle* (Paris: L'Harmattan, 2003), 348–83; for Italy, Valeriano Balloni, *Origini, sviluppo e maturità dell'industria degli elettrodomestici* (Bologna: Il Mulino, 1978), 42–6, 98–104; and Enrica Asquer, *La rivoluzione candida. Storia sociale della lavatrice in Italia (1945–1970)* (Rome: Carocci, 2007), 11–38.

30 Communautés européennes. Commission, *Répercussions du marché commun dans le secteur des biens de consommation électrotechniques; principaux résultats d'une étude empirique* (Brussels: Commission des communautés européennes, 1970), 33.

31 Delaunay, *La machine à laver en France*, 112.

32 Ibid., 64; François Dupuy and Jean-Claude Thoenig, *La loi du marché. L'électroménager en France, aux Etats-Unis et au Japon* (Paris: L'Harmattan, 1986), 14.

33 Donald S. Pitkin, *The House That Giacomo Built: History of an Italian Family, 1898–1978* (Cambridge: Cambridge University Press, 1985), 146, 153.

34 Ellen Ross, *Love and Toil: Motherhood in Outcast London, 1870–1918* (New York: Oxford University Press, 1993), 137–8.

35 Joann Vanek, "Time Spent in Housework," *Scientific American* 231, no. 5 (1974), 116–20.

36 Ruth Schwartz Cowan, *More Work for Mother: The Ironies of Household Technology from the Open Hearth to the Microwave* (New York: Basic Books, 1983), 98–9; Silberzahn-Jandt, *Wasch-Maschine*, 40; Bowden and Offer, "The Technological Revolution That Never Was."

37 Yannick Lemel, *Les Budgets-temps des citadins* (Paris: I.N.S.E.E., 1974), 13; Marie Térèse Huet, Yannik Lemel, and Caroline Roy, "Les emplois du temps des citadins: résultats de l'enquête emplois du temps 1974–1975," in *Archives et documents*, ed. Institut national de la statistique et des études économiques (1982), Tables 8, 32, 154, 178; Sándor Szalai, *The Use of Time: Daily Activities of Urban and Suburban Populations in Twelve Countries*, vol. 5 (The Hague: Mouton, 1972), 576–7; John P. Robinson, *How Americans Use Time: A Social-Psychological Analysis of Everyday Behavior* (New York: Praeger, 1977), 63; Martha S. Hill, "Patterns of Time Use," in *Time, Goods, and Well-Being*, ed. F. Thomas Juster, Frank P. Stafford, and University of Michigan Survey Research Center (Ann Arbor: Institute for Social Research, University of Michigan, 1985), 171–3.

38 "Wash-House Blues," *Observer*, 13 January 1974, 3.

39 For example, see Victoria Kelley, *Soap and Water: Cleanliness, Dirt, and the Working Classes in Victorian and Edwardian Britain* (London and New York: I.B. Tauris, 2010).

40 Yvonne Verdier, *Façons de dire, façons de faire. La laveuse, la couturière, la cuisinière* (Paris: Gallimard, 1979), 116.

41 Jean Pearson, *Memories of Monday: A Lighthearted Account of Washday as Seen through the Eyes of Many Who Laboured before the Days of Washing Machines* (York: Sessions, 1986), 2–3.

42 Claudia Brush Kidwell and Margaret C.S. Christman, *Suiting Everyone: The Democratization of Clothing in America* (Washington: Smithsonian Institution Press, 1974), 65–203; Rachel Worth, *Fashion for the People: A History of Clothing at Marks & Spencer* (Oxford: Berg, 2007); Gilles Lipovetsky, *The Empire of Fashion: Dressing Modern Democracy* (Princeton: Princeton University Press, 1994), 55–64; Philippe Perrot, *Fashioning the Bourgeoisie: A History of Clothing in the Nineteenth Century* (Princeton: Princeton University Press, 1994), 58–79.

43 Orland, *Wäsche waschen*, 261–4.

44 Braun, *Stoff, Wechsel, Technik*, 97–100; Lipovetsky, *The Empire of Fashion*, 88–128.

45 Braun, *Stoff, Wechsel, Technik*, 99–100.

46 Luciano Spadanuda, *Storia delle mutande* (Rome: Coniglio, 2005), 74–7.

47 Françoise Giroud, "La Française est-elle propre?," *Elle*, 22 October 1951, 14–16; Steven Zdatny, "The French Hygiene Offensive of the 1950s: A Critical Moment in the History of Manners," *The Journal of Modern History* 84, no. 4 (2012), 923–4.

48 Braun, *Stoff, Wechsel, Technik*, 98.

49 Jean Maudit, "Les françaises sont-elles devenues propres?," *Elle*, 20 January 1986, 40–3; Reinhold Bergler, "Körperhygiene und Sauberkeit im internationalen Vergleich," *Zentralblatt für Bakteriologie, Mikrobiologie und Hygiene. Serie B, Umwelthygiene, Krankenhaushygiene, Arbeitshygiene, präventive Medizin* 187, no. 4–6 (1989), 477–8, 489.

50 Christina Brede, *Das Instrument der Sauberkeit. Die Entwicklung der Massenproduktion von Feinseifen in Deutschland 1850 bis 2000* (Münster: Waxman, 2005), 76–7, 83–4.

51 Edgar George Thomssen and John W. McCutcheon, *Soaps and detergents* (New York: MacNair-Dorland, 1949), 397–9; Charles Wilson, *The History of Unilever: A Study in Economic Growth and Social Change* (London: Cassell, 1954), 2: 351–2; P.A.R. Puplett, *Synthetic Detergents: A Study of the Development and Marketing of a New Product* (London: Sidgwick and Jackson, 1957), 18–22; Willard M. Bright, "Synthetic Detergents: Development and Use in Domestic Washing-Products," *Journal of the American Oil Chemists' Society* 34, no. 4 (1957), 170–2; W.J. Corlett, *The Economic Development of Detergents* (London: Duckworth, 1958), 104–21; H.R. Edwards, *Competition and Monopoly in the British Soap Industry* (Oxford: Clarendon Press, 1962), 205–15; Albert Edward Musson, *Enterprise in Soap and Chemicals: Joseph Crosfield & Sons, Limited, 1815–1965* (Manchester: Manchester University Press, 1965), 333, 354–6; Edgar Woollatt, *The Manufacture of Soaps, Other Detergents, and Glycerine* (Chichester: E. Horwood, 1985), 21; A. Davidsohn and B.M. Milwidsky, *Synthetic Detergents*, 7th ed. (Harlow: Longman Scientific & Technical, 1987), 1–9; Orland, *Wäsche waschen*, 185–91; Gisela Utesch, "Waschmittel. Saubermacher und Gewässerverschmutzer zugleich," in *"Das Paradies kommt wieder...,"* 144; Davis Dyer, Frederick Dalzell, and Rowena Olegario, *Rising Tide: Lessons from 165 Years of Brand Building at Procter & Gamble* (Cambridge, MA: Harvard Business School Press, 2004), 68–70.

52 Wolfgang Feiter, *80 Jahre Persil. Produkt- und Werbegeschichte* (Düsseldorf: Henkel, 1987), 60–3; Wilfried Feldenkirchen and Susanne Hilger, *Menschen und Marken. 125 Jahre Henkel, 1876–2001* (Düsseldorf: Henkel KGaA, 2001), 125.

53 Puplett, *Synthetic detergents*, 32; Charles Wilson, *Unilever 1945–1965: Challenge and Response in the Post-War Industrial Revolution* (London: Cassell, 1968), 194; Orland, *Wäsche waschen*, 260–1.

54 United States District Court S.D. New York, *United States of America, Plaintiff* v. Lever Brothers Company and Monsanto Chemical Company, Defendants, 1963, 13; Great Britain, Monopolies Commission, "Household Detergents: A Report on the Supply of Household Detergents" (London: HMSO, 1966), 30; Centro studi sviluppo industria chimica, *I detergenti sintetici nell'industria italiana* (Florence: Vallecchi, 1971), 52–3; Jean Pierre Berlan, *Unilever, une multinationale discrète* (Paris: Les Éditions du Cerf, 1978), 28; Luigi Lipparini and Massimo M. Sabbatini, *I prodotti detergenti. Tecnologia, mercato ed ecologia* (Bologna: CLUEB, 1982), 80–8.

55 Edwards, *Competition and Monopoly*, 200–5.

56 Ibid., 203–4.

57 Davidsohn and Milwidsky, *Synthetic detergents*, 5–8; Terrance Kehoe, "Merchants of Pollution? The Soap and Detergent Industry and the Fight to Restore Great Lakes Water Quality, 1965–1972," *Environmental History Review* 16, no. 3 (1992), 21–46.

58 Great Britain, "Prices of Household and Toilet Soaps, Soap Powders and Soap Flakes, and Soapless Detergents," ed. National Board for Prices and Incomes (London: HMSO, 1965), 10.

59 Richard Evely, "The Battle of the Detergents," *Cartel*, January 1954; Spencer Klaw, "The Soap Wars: A Strategic Analysis," *Fortune*, June 1963, 123–5; Woollatt, *The Manufacture of Soaps*, 111–13; Dyer, Dalzell, and Olegario, *Rising Tide*, 84.

60 R.W. Evely, "Evolution of Concentration in the Soap and Detergents Industry for the United Kingdom" (Brussels: Commission of the European Communities, 1978), 47.

61 Centro studi sviluppo industria chimica, *I detergenti sintetici*, 50–51; Lipparini and Sabbatini, *I prodotti detergenti*, 68–78.

62 Klaw, "The Soap Wars," 123.

63 Great Britain, "Prices of Household and Toilet Soaps," 13; Evely, "Evolution of Concentration," 50.

64 Edwards, *Competition and monopoly*, 249.

65 Great Britain, "Prices of Household and Toilet Soaps," 13.

66 Evely, "Evolution of Concentration," 55.

67 Geoffrey Heyworth, *Distribution* (Lever Brothers & Unilever Ltd., 1951), 8–9.

68 Hilde Schmidt, "Die Weisse Dame im Wandel der Jahrzehnte," in *Werbung mit Plakaten von gestern bis heute*, ed. Frieder Mellinghoff et al. (Düsseldorf: Henkel KGAA, Stabsstelle Öffentlichkeitsarbeit, Werksarchiv, 1978); Marc Martin, *Trois siècles de publicité en France* (Paris: O. Jacob, 1992), 21; Dirk Reinhardt, *Von der Reklame zum Marketing. Geschichte der Wirtschaftswerbung in Deutschland* (Berlin: Akademie, 1993), 231–369.

69 Dyer, Dalzell, and Olegario, *Rising Tide*, 62–3; "Procter & Gamble," *Fortune* 19, no. 4 (1939), 154–6.

70 Feiter, *80 Jahre Persil*, 49.

71 Thomas R. Tibbetts, "Expanding Ownership of Household Equipment," *Monthly Labor Review* 87, no. 10 (1964), 1133–4; Peter Ward, *A History of Domestic Space: Privacy and the Canadian Home* (Vancouver: UBC Press, 1999), 70–1.

72 Audits of Great Britain, "AGB Home Audit: Report on Consumer Durables Establishment as at 30 June 1970" (1970); Fernand Pascaud, "La consommation des ménages de 1959 à 1972" (Paris: Institut national de la statistique et des études économiques, 1974), 25; Carmela D'Apice, *L'arcipelago dei consumi. Consumi e redditi delle famiglie in Italia dal dopoguerra ad oggi* (Bari: Di Donato, 1981), 53; European Commission, *Family budgets ... Germany, France, Italy, United Kingdom*, 36–9; Christopher Duggan, *A Concise History of Italy* (Cambridge: Cambridge University Press, 1994), 274–5; Arne Andersen, *Der Traum vom guten Leben. Alltags- und Konsumgeschichte vom Wirtschaftswunder bis heute* (Frankfurt am Main: Campus, 1997), 119.

73 Francesco Alberoni et al., *Pubblicità e televisione. Saggi* (Rome: ERI, 1968), 119.

74 Klaw, "The Soap Wars," 124.

75 Brian Henry, "The History," in *British Television Advertising: The First 30 Years*, ed. Henry (London: Century Benham, 1986), 46, 76–9.

76 Martin, *Trois siècles de publicité en France*, 333–5, 357–8.

77 Terrence H. Witkowski and Joachim Kellner, "Convergent, Contrasting, and Country-Specific Attitudes toward Television Advertising in Germany and the United States," *Journal of Business Research* 42, no. 2 (1998), 168.

78 Antonio Valeri, *Pubblicità italiana. Storia, protagonisti e tendenze di cento anni di comunicazione* (Milan: Edizioni del Sole—24 ore, 1986), 207–21; Varni Codeluppi, "Il sogno del consumo. Arretratezze e ritardi del sistema pubblicitario italiano," in *Dreams. I sogni degli italiani in 50 anni di pubblicità televisiva*, ed. Gianni Canova (Milan: Mondadori, 2004), 75.

79 Klaw, "The Soap Wars," 124.

80 Vicenzo Marchianò, "25 anni di investimenti pubblicitari," in *Cent'anni di pubblicità nello sviluppo economico e nel costume italiano* (Turin: Sipra, 1975), 518.

81 Lisa Lebduska, "Ivory Soap and American Popular Consciousness: Salvation through Consumption," *Journal of Popular Culture* 48, no. 2 (2015), 385–7.

82 Schmidt, "Die Weisse Dame"; Jutta Reinke, "Die 'Weisse Dame.' Persil. Eine Waschmittelwerbung macht Geschichte," in *Oikos: von der Feuerstelle zur Mikrowelle. Haushalt und Wohnen im Wandel*, ed. Michael Andritzky (Stuttgart: Anabas, 1992), 440–4.

83 For example, see Adam Arvidsson, *Marketing Modernity: Italian Advertising from Fascism to Postmodernity* (London: Routledge, 2003), 67–70.

84 *Carosello… e poi a letto. La storia della televisione italiana, 1957–1977* (Rome: RAI, 1957–77), disc 1, track 1, Il teatrino di Olà.

85 David Bernstein, "The Television Commercial: An Essay," in *British Television Advertising: The First 30 Years*, ed. Brian Henry (London: Century Benham, 1986), 281.

86 Laura Minestroni, *Dash. Più bianco non si può. Storia cultura e comunicazione di una marca che è cresciuta insieme a noi* (Milan: F. Angeli, 2010), 45–158.

87 For examples, see the digitized advertisements curated by the John W. Hartman Center for Sales, Advertising, and Marketing History, Duke University Library: http://library.duke.edu/digitalcollections/advertising.

88 Winston Fletcher, *Powers of Persuasion: The Inside Story of British Advertising: 1951–2000* (Oxford: Oxford University Press, 2008), 55.

89 Henry, "The History," 77–8; Peter Woodhouse, "Copy Controls from Within," in *British Television Advertising*, 376–7.

90 Aldo Grasso, *Storia della televisione italiana*, new ed. (Milan: Garzanti, 2004), 764.

91 Gian Luigi Falabrino, *Effimera & bella. Storia della pubblicità italiana. Venezia 1691–Roma 2001*, 2nd ed. (Milan: Silvana, 2001), 217–18.

92 Piero Dorfles, *Carosello* (Bologna: Il mulino, 1998), 37–54; Codeluppi, "Il sogno del consumo," 71–9; Chiara Giaccardi, "Immagini di identità. Pubblicità televisiva e realtà sociale," in *Dreams. I sogni degli italiani*, 81–95; Grasso, *Storia della televisione italiana*, 698–9, 774; Daniele Pittèri, "Le relazioni pericolose. Economia politiche ed economia simboliche nella pubblicità televisiva," in *Dreams*, 65–9.

93 Roland Barthes, "Soap-Powders and Detergents," in *Mythologies* (New York: Hill and Wang, 1972), 36–8.

94 Paul W. Farris and Mark S. Albion, "The Impact of Advertising on the Price of Consumer Products," *The Journal of Marketing* 44, no. 3 (1980), 17–35.

95 "World Soap, Detergent Growth Rate Slows," *Journal of the American Oil Chemists' Society* 61 (1984), 1405.

CHAPTER EIGHT

1 Francesco Alberoni, *Consumi e società* (Bologna: Il mulino, 1964), 40–1.

2 Jon S. Cohen and Giovanni Federico, *The Growth of the Italian Economy, 1820–1960* (New York: Cambridge University Press, 2001), 30–45, 87–106.

3 Kathy Lee Peiss, *Hope in a Jar: The Making of America's Beauty Culture* (New York: Metropolitan Books, 1998).

4 Geoffrey Jones, "Blonde and Blue-Eyed? Globalizing Beauty, c. 1945–c. 1980," *The Economic History Review* 61, no. 1 (2008), 127–31.

5 Umberto Eco, *Storia della bellezza* (Milan: Bompiani, 2004), 425.

6 Georges Vigarello, *Histoire de la beauté. Le corps et l'art d'embellir de la Renaissance à nos jours* (Paris: Seuil, 2004), 189–252; Giuseppe Minoia, "Il ruolo della pubblicità nell'educazione dei comportamenti," in *La scatola nera della pubblicità*, ed. Aldo Grasso (Turin: Silvana, 2000), 77.

7 Emmanuelle Dutertre, *Savons et savonneries. Le modèle nantais* (Nantes: Éditions Memo, 2005), 70–1, 74; Morag Martin, *Selling Beauty: Cosmetics, Commerce, and French Society, 1750–1830* (Baltimore: Johns Hopkins University Press, 2009), 18.

8 Erasmus Wilson, "Toilet Soaps," *Journal of Cutaneous Medicine and Diseases of the Skin* 1 (1868), 446–8; Heinrich Auspitz, *Die Seife und ihre Wirkung auf die gesunde und kranke Haut* (Vienna: Tendler, 1867).

9 Great Britain, "Reports on the Paris Universal Exhibition, 1867," vol. 1, Cmd. 3968 (London: HMSO, 1867–68), 577.

10 W.J. Corlett, *The Economic Development of Detergents* (London: Duckworth, 1958), 86–93; Albert Edward Musson, *Enterprise in Soap and Chemicals: Joseph Crosfield & Sons, Limited, 1815–1965* (Manchester: Manchester University Press, 1965), 86; Christina Brede, *Das Instrument der Sauberkeit. Die Entwicklung der Massenproduktion von Feinseifen in Deutschland 1850 bis 2000* (Münster: Waxman, 2005), 64–70; Geoffrey Jones, *Beauty Imagined: A History of the Global Beauty Industry* (Oxford; New York: Oxford University Press, 2010), 77–8.

11 Williams Haynes, *American Chemical Industry* (New York: Van Nostrand, 1945), 82.

12 Brede, *Das Instrument der Sauberkeit*, 253–4; Jones, *Beauty Imagined*, 77–8.

13 Brede, *Das Instrument der Sauberkeit*, 263.

14 H.R. Edwards, *Competition and Monopoly in the British Soap Industry* (Oxford: Clarendon Press, 1962), 238.

15 Charles Wilson, *The History of Unilever: A Study in Economic Growth and Social Change* (London: Cassell, 1954), II: Appendix 11; Corlett, *The Economic Development of Detergents*, 25, 40.

16 Musson, *Enterprise in Soap and Chemicals*, 192–3.

17 Andrew Marshall Knox, *Coming Clean: A Postscript after Retirement from Unilever* (London: Heinemann, 1976), 155–6. At that price the queen's soap cost the equivalent of two days' wages for a London carpenter. See also Edward H. Hunt, "Industrialization and Regional Inequality: Wages in Britain, 1760–1914," *Journal of Economic History* 46, no. 4 (1986), 964.

18 Haynes, *American Chemical Industry*, 82.

19 Wilson, *The History of Unilever*, vol. 1, 286–7, 301; Haynes, *American Chemical Industry*, 345.

20 Wilfried Feldenkirchen and Susanne Hilger, *Menschen und Marken. 125 Jahre Henkel, 1876–2001* (Düsseldorf: Henkel KGaA, 2001), 44.

21 Mike Dempsey, *Bubbles: Early Advertising Art from A. & F. Pears Ltd* (London: Fontana, 1978).

22 Dirk Reinhardt, *Von der Reklame zum Marketing. Geschichte der Wirtschaftswerbung in Deutschland* (Berlin: Akademie, 1993), 397–412; Lori Anne Loeb, *Consuming Angels: Advertising and Victorian Women* (New York: Oxford University Press, 1994), 60–71; Brede, *Das Instrument der Sauberkeit*, 263–78.

23 Pamela Walker Laird, *Advertising Progress: American Business and the Rise of Consumer Marketing* (Baltimore: Johns Hopkins University Press, 1998), 297–8; Denise H. Sutton, *Globalizing Ideal Beauty: How Female Copywriters of the J. Walter Thompson Advertising Agency Redefined Beauty for the Twentieth Century* (New York: Palgrave Macmillan, 2009), 99–121; Regina Lee Blaszczyk, *American Consumer Society, 1865–2005: From Hearth to HDTV* (Wheeling: Harlan Davidson, 2009), 120–3; Jones, *Beauty Imagined*, 82–3.

24 Sutton, *Globalizing Ideal Beauty*, 113.

25 Ibid., 107.

26 Ibid., 99.

27 David R. Foster, *The Story of Colgate-Palmolive: One Hundred and Sixty-Nine Years of Progress* (New York: Newcomen Society in North America, 1975), 10–16.

28 Jones, *Beauty Imagined*, 81.

29 Olivier Darmon, "Lux story," *Bon à tirer*, no. 84 (1986), 52–9; Joanna E.
Di Domenico, "Advertising in Italian Women's Magazines 1915–1980:
Gender and Evolving Ideologies of the Middle-Class Italian Woman"
(PhD diss., University of Strathclyde, 2004), 332–77; Christina Burr,
"'The Beauty Soap of Film Stars': Lux Toilet Soap, Star Endorsements,
and Building a Global Beauty Brand," in *Globalizing Beauty:
Consumerism and Body Aesthetics in the Twentieth Century*, ed.
Hartmut Berghoff and Thomas Kühne (New York: Palgrave Macmillan,
2013), 171–89.

30 Burr, "'The Beauty Soap of Film Stars,'" 175.

31 Ibid., 172.

32 Di Domenico, "Advertising in Italian Women's Magazines," 356–69;
Brede, *Das Instrument der Sauberkeit*, 310–14.

33 Auguste Caron, *The lady's toilette, containing a critical examination of the
nature of beauty ... an historical sketch of the fashions of France and
England* (London: W.H. Wyatt, 1808), 199; Mme Celnart, *Manuel des
dames, ou L'art de la toilette* (Paris: Roret, 1827), 12–13; *La Bellezza ed i
Mezzi di Conservarla, ossia La Toletta delle Signore* (Milan: Giovanni
Pirotta, 1827), Chapter 1; A. Debay, *Hygiène de la beauté, résumé de tous
les moyens hygiéniques propres à conserver, à développer la beauté du
corps et à remédier aux imperfections naturelles ou acquises* (Brussels:
Meline, Cars, et cie., 1846), 40; Odile Arnold, *Le corps et l'ame. La vie
des religieuses au 19. siècle* (Paris: Seuil, 1984), 77; Ulla Gosmann, "'So
viel Unheil quillet aus dem schmutzigen Unterrocke!': Ratschläge zur
Körper- und Schönheitspflege im 'hygienischen' 19. Jahrhundert," in
*Reinliche Leiber, schmutzige Geschäfte. Körperhygiene und
Reinlichkeitsvorstellungen in zwei Jahrhunderten*, ed. Regina Löneke and
Ira Spieker (Göttingen: Wallstein, 1996), 101–2.

34 A.T. Schofield, *Manual of Personal and Domestic Hygiene*, vol. 2 (London:
Allman & Son, 1891), 29; William Allen Pusey, *The Care of the Skin and
Hair* (New York and London: D. Appleton, 1912), 144–5; W. Allan
Jamieson, *The Care of the Skin in Health* (London: Henry Frowde Hodder
and Stoughton, 1912), Chapter 3; Colombano Bertaccini, *Nozioni elemen-
tari d'igiene, ad uso delle scuole e delle famiglie* (Bologna: Licino Cappelli,
1922), 67–9.

35 Antonin Baratier, *Hygiène générale. L'école de village au point de vue de
l'hygiène publique et privée* (Paris: G. Maurin, 1899), 20–1.

36 J.S. Hurt, *Elementary Schooling and the Working Classes, 1860–1918*
(London: Routledge and Kegan Paul, 1979), 133–5.

37 Guy Thuillier, *Pour une histoire du quotidien au XIXe siècle en Nivernais* (Paris: Mouton, École des hautes Études en Sciences Sociales, 1977), 166.

38 Anna Davin, *Growing Up Poor: Home, School, and Street in London, 1870–1914* (London: Rivers Oram Press, 1996), 140.

39 For a brief description of shampoos, their composition and function, see R.P.R. Dawber, *Shampoos – Scientific Basis and Clinical Aspects* (London: Royal Society of Medicine Press, 1996), 11–17.

40 Feldenkirchen and Hilger, *Menschen und Marken*, 12.

41 "Shampoo," in *Encyclopedia of Hair: A Cultural History*, ed. Victoria Sherrow (Westport: Greenwood Press, 2006), 349.

42 National Museum of American History, "Halo Shampoo," http:// americanhistory.si.edu/collections/search?custom_search_id= collections-search&edan_local=1&edan_q=halo+shampoo&op=Search.

43 Wilson, *The History of Unilever*, vol. 2, 351–2.

44 Cynthia C. Urbano, "50 Years of Hair-Care Development," *Cosmetics and Toiletries* 110, no. 12 (1995), 85; Angela G. Liljequist, "'Soft, Glossy Tresses': Shampoo Advertisements, White Women's Hair, and the Late- and Post–World War II Domestic Ideal" (PhD diss., University of Kansas, 2015), 70–1.

45 Maison G. De Navarre, "25 Years of Cosmetic Progress," *American Perfumer and Essential Oil Review* (1953), 268–9.

46 R. Richard Riso, "Trends in Shampoos," *Cosmetics and Toiletries* 95, no. 5 (1980), 77.

47 De Navarre, "25 Years of Cosmetic Progress," 269; Riso, "Trends in Shampoos," 77.

48 Thomas Went, *Vereinheitlichung der Werbung im Rahmen der internationalen Marktbearbeitung. Eine empirische Analyse am Beispiel des Shampoo-Marktes* (Frankfurt am Main: P. Lang, 2000), 228; Jones, "Blonde and Blue-Eyed?," 139.

49 "The Second 'John Bull' Census: Report on Household Toilet, Home Equipment, Clothing, and Footwear Markets" (London: Odhams, 1937), 54–5.

50 Françoise Giroud, "La Française est-elle propre?," *Elle*, 22 October 1951, 14–16.

51 *Bollettino della Doxa* 14, no. 19 (1960), 186.

52 Reinhold Bergler, *Sauberkeit. Norm, Verhalten, Persönlichkeit. Beträge zur empirischen Sozialforschung* (Bern: Hans Huber, 1974), 196.

53 Jean Maudit, "Les françaises sont-elles devenues propres?," *Elle*, 20 January 1986, 43.

54 Peter Gorle, *The West German Consumer: A Statistical Profile* (London: Metra Consulting Group, 1975), 244, 257; Nathalie Mikaïloff, *Les Manières de propreté. Du Moyen Âge à nos jours* (Paris: Maloine, 1990), 178; Jones, "Blonde and Blue-Eyed?," 134.

55 John Pepper, *What Really Matters: Service, Leadership, People, and Values* (New Haven: Yale University Press, 2007), 59–61.

56 Riso, "Trends in Shampoos," 77–8.

57 Pepper, *What Really Matters*, 59–61.

58 Riso, "Trends in Shampoos."

59 "Highlights on Breck Annual Survey," *American Perfumer and Cosmetics* (1962), 56.

60 Caron, *The lady's toilette*, 234.

61 D.A. Cameron, *Plain advice on the care of the teeth; with a popular history of the dentist's art, and a chapter to mothers on the management of children during the first dentition* (Glasgow: Richard Griffin, 1838), 3–4.

62 Caron, *The lady's toilette*, 237; Celnart, *Manuel des dames*, 21–35; Cameron, *Plain advice*, 26–33; Debay, *Hygiène de la beauté*, 49–50; *How to Behave: A Pocket Manual of Etiquette, and Guide to Correct Personal Habits, Etc.* (Glasgow: John S. Marr, 1865), 20–1; Gualtiero Lorigiola, *Studi fisiognonomici sulla bocca e precetti per l'igiene della bocca e dei denti* (Padua: s.n., 1865); Anna M. Galbraith, *Hygiene and Physical Culture for Women* (New York: Dodd & Mead, 1895), 165–6; René Vaucaire, *La femme sa beauté, sa santé, son hygiène* (Paris: Rueff, 1896), 57–73; Mary S. Haviland, *Modern Physiology, Hygiene, and Health. Primer* (Philadelphia: Lippincott, 1921), 124.

63 Simon Hillson, "The Current State of Dental Decay," in *Technique and Application in Dental Anthropology*, ed. Joel D. Irish and Greg C. Nelson (Cambridge: Cambridge University Press, 2008), 123.

64 Ibid., 118–28.

65 Peter Miskell, "Cavity Protection or Cosmetic Perfection? Innovation and Marketing of Toothpaste Brands in the United States and Western Europe, 1955–1985," *Business History Review* 78, no. 1 (2004), 34–5.

66 Alyssa Picard, *Making the American Mouth: Dentists and Public Health in the Twentieth Century* (New Brunswick: Rutgers University Press, 2009), 5.

67 Great Britain, "Report of the Inter-departmental Committee on Medical Inspection and Feeding of Children Attending Public Elementary Schools," vol. 2, Appendix VI, Parliamentary Papers (1906), Cmd 2784, 277–83, esp. 280.

68 Picard, *Making the American Mouth*, 2.

69 B. Sommer, "L'Hygiène dentaire scolaire dans quelques pays," *Ondontologie* 42, no. 15 (1909), 102–13.

70 M. Jessen, "L'Hygiène dentaire à l'école," *Ondontologie* 40, no. 22 (1908), 448–55.

71 Hans-Jürgen Apel and Jürgen Bennack, eds., *Hygiene in preussischen Schulvorschriften. Eine Zusammenstellung unter besonderer Berücksichtigung der Rheinlande 1800–1945* (Cologne & Vienna: Böhlau, 1986), 251–7.

72 Picard, *Making the American Mouth*, 14–41.

73 Miskell, "Cavity Protection or Cosmetic Perfection?," 37.

74 Foster, *The story of Colgate-Palmolive*, 10; Jones, *Beauty Imagined*, 79–80.

75 Thomas Gubig and Sebastian Köpcke, *Chlorodont. Biographie eines deutschen Markenproduktes* (Dresden: Werksarchiv Dental-Kosmetik, 1996).

76 "The Second 'John Bull' Census," 26–7.

77 Neil H. Borden, *The Economic Effects of Advertising* (Chicago: R.D. Irwin, 1942), 302; Miskell, "Cavity Protection or Cosmetic Perfection?," 36.

78 Borden, *The Economic Effects of Advertising*, 298–300.

79 Ibid., 300; Miskell, "Cavity Protection or Cosmetic Perfection?," 37.

80 Borden, *The Economic Effects of Advertising*, 302; Miskell, "Cavity Protection or Cosmetic Perfection?," 32–3.

81 Ibid., 33.

82 Charles Frederick Higham, *Advertising: Its Use and Abuse* (London: Williams & Norgate, 1925), 16–17.

83 Borden, *The Economic Effects of Advertising*, 294–6; Vincent Vinikas, *Soft Soap, Hard Sell: American Hygiene in an Age of Advertisement* (Ames: Iowa State University Press, 1992), 93–4; Miskell, "Cavity Protection or Cosmetic Perfection?," 39; "The Second 'John Bull' Census," 26–7, 66–7.

84 Borden, *The Economic Effects of Advertising*, 297–8.

85 Gorle, *The West German Consumer*, 247, 252; Reinhold Bergler, "Körperhygiene und Sauberkeit im internationalen Vergleich," *Zentralblatt für Bakteriologie, Mikrobiologie und Hygiene. Serie B, Umwelthygiene, Krankenhaushygiene, Arbeitshygiene, präventive Medizin* 187, nos. 4–6 (1989), 483; Miskell, "Cavity Protection or Cosmetic Perfection?," 42–3.

86 Thuillier, *Pour une histoire du quotidien*, 166; Charles X. Cornu, *Les Savons et les détergents* (Paris: Presses universitaires de France, 1970), 111; Mikaïloff, *Les Manières de propreté: Du Moyen âge à nos jours*, 180; Bergler, "Körperhygiene und Sauberkeit im internationalen Vergleich," 483.

87 Istituto nazionale di statistica, *Indagine speciale su alcuni aspetti delle condizioni igieniche e sanitarie della popolazione*, notes and reports 1960/10 (Rome: ISTAT, 1960), 31; Mikaïloff, *Les Manières de propreté*, 180.

88 Miskell, "Cavity Protection or Cosmetic Perfection?," 39–40; Jones, "Blonde and Blue-Eyed?," 137. P&G strengthened its German presence substantially in 1987 by buying Blendax.

89 Miskell, "Cavity Protection or Cosmetic Perfection?," 44–50; Davis Dyer, Frederick Dalzell, and Rowena Olegario, *Rising Tide: Lessons from 165 Years of Brand Building at Procter & Gamble* (Cambridge, MA: Harvard Business School Press, 2004), 141–58.

90 Miskell, "Cavity Protection or Cosmetic Perfection?," 58.

91 Dwight E. Robinson, "Fashions in Shaving and Trimming of the Beard: The Men of the Illustrated London News, 1842–1972," *American Journal of Sociology* 81, no. 5 (1976), 1133–41.

92 Françoise Loux, *Le Corps dans la société traditionnelle* (Paris: Berger–Levrault, 1979), 91–2.

93 Georges-Henri Tellier, *La santé du soldat, manuel d'hygiène pratique à l'usage des hommes de troupe* (Paris: H. Charles-Lavauzelle, 1902), 17; Nancy Tomes, *The Gospel of Germs: Men, Women, and the Microbe in American Life* (Cambridge, MA: Harvard University Press, 1998), 104, 126–7, 159; Christopher Oldstone-Moore, "Mustaches and Masculine Codes in Early-Twentieth-Century America," *Journal of Social History* 45, no. 1 (2011), 50–1.

94 Ibid., 51–2.

95 Frank Gnegel, "Bart und Rasur. Beards and Shaving," *Eine Kulturgeschichte der Schönheitspflege. A Cultural History of Beauty Care* (Heidelberg: Edition Braus, 2003), Wella Museum ed., 137; Oldstone-Moore, "Mustaches and Masculine Codes," 53.

96 Frank Gnegel, *Bart ab: zur Geschichte der Selbstrasur* (Cologne: DuMont, 1995), 35–48; Gnegel, "Bart und Rasur," 134–6; Franco Lorenzi, *Rasoi e lame. Barbe e baffi* (Milan: Silvana, 2003), 33–81.

97 Russell B. Adams, *King C. Gillette, the Man and His Wonderful Shaving Device* (Boston: Little, Brown, 1978).

98 George B. Baldwin, "The Invention of the Modern Safety Razor: A Case Study of Industrial Innovation," *Explorations in Entrepreneurial History* 4, no. 2 (1951), 96–7.

99 Gnegel, *Bart ab*, 44–62.

100 Gordon McKibben, *Cutting Edge: Gillette's Journey to Global Leadership* (Cambridge, MA: Harvard Business School Press, 1998), between 52 and 53.

101 R.W. Evely and Ian Malcolm David Little, *Concentration in British Industry: An Empirical Study of the Structure of Industrial Production, 1935–51* (Cambridge: Cambridge University Press, 1960), 198–203; McKibben, *Cutting Edge*, 23–36.

102 Jones, "Blonde and Blue-Eyed?," 138.

103 Adams, *King C. Gillette*, 55–6.

104 Baldwin, "The Invention of the Modern Safety Razor," 93; McKibben, *Cutting Edge*, 18.

105 Mass Observation, "Personal appearance" (1939), 27–47.

106 Ibid., 47.

107 Ibid., 33–4; Edward Norworth, "Dry Shavers: Imports Live at Peace with Domestic Brands," *Barron's National Business and Financial Weekly*, 23 August 1954, 13; Alfred R. Zipster, "Electric Shavers as Big Business: $100,000,000 Sales Seen in 1954," *New York Times*, 28 February 1954; Gnegel, *Bart ab*, 67–113; Gnegel, "Bart und Rasur," 38–140; Lorenzi, *Rasoi e lame*, 171–85.

108 "The Second 'John Bull' Census," 56–9.

109 Jones, "Blonde and Blue-Eyed?," 136.

110 Alain Corbin, *The Foul and the Fragrant: Odor and the French Social Imagination* (Cambridge, MA: Harvard University Press, 1986).

111 H.E. Jass, "The History of Antiperspirant Product Development," *Cosmet Toilet 95*, no. 7 (1980), 25–31; K. Laden, "Introduction and History of Antiperspirants and Deodorants," in *Antiperspirants and Deodorants*, ed. Karl Laden and Carl B. Felger (New York: Marcek Dekker, 1988), 1–13; Karl Laden, "Antiperspirants and Deodorants: History of Major HBA Market," in *Cosmetic Science and Technology Series*, ed. Laden (New York: Marcel Dekker, 1999), 1–15.

112 Laird, *Advertising Progress*, 301–3.

113 Laden, "Antiperspirants and Deodorants," 3.

114 *Bollettino della Doxa* 15, nos. 1–2 (1961), 6, 14; Jones, "Blonde and Blue-Eyed?," 135; Bollettino della Doxa 20, nos. 10–11 (1966), 89–90; Gorle, *The West German Consumer*, 248; Paul Irlinger, Catherine Louveau, and Michèle Métoudi, *Les pratiques sportives des français. Usages sportifs du temps libéré* (Paris: Institut national du sport et de l'éducation physique, Laboratoire de sociologie, 1987), 577–8; Bergler, "Körperhygiene und Sauberkeit," 487.

115 Valentino Ostermann, *La vita in Friuli. Usi, costumi, credenze popolari*, ed. Giuseppe Vidossi, 2nd ed. (Udine, 1940), 358; Adalberto Pazzini, *La medicina popolare in Italia. Storia, tradizioni, leggende* (Trieste: F. Zigiotti, 1948), 318–19; L. De Nardis, "A la garboja. 500 note sulle tradizioni

popolari romagnole," in *Romagna tradizionale. Usi e costumi, credenze e pregiudizi*, ed. Paolo Toschi (Bologna: Licinio Cappelli, 1952), 207.

116 Corbin, *The Foul and the Fragrant*, 44; Birgit Ohlsen, "Weibliche Praxis und ärztlicher Diskurs. Zur Geschichte der Menstruationshygiene," in *Reinliche Leiber, schmutzige Geschäfte: Körperhygiene und Reinlichkeitsvorstellungen in zwei Jahrhunderten*, ed. Regina Löneke and Ira Spieker (Göttingen: Wallstein, 1996), 239–40.

117 Vern Bullough and Martha Voght, "Women, Menstruation, and Nineteenth-Century Medicine," *Bulletin of the History of Medicine* 47, no. 1 (1973), 66–82, esp. 69–73; P. Crawford, "Attitudes to Menstruation in Seventeenth-Century England," *Past and Present* 91, no. 1 (1981), 47–73; Sharra Louise Vostral, *Under Wraps: A History of Menstrual Hygiene Technology* (Lanham: Lexington Books, 2008), 21–58; Julie-Marie Strange, "'I Believe It to Be a Case Depending on Menstruation': Madness and Menstrual Taboo in British Medical Practice, c. 1840–1930," in *Menstruation: A Cultural History*, ed. Andrew Shail and Gillian Howie (Houndmills: Palgrave Macmillan, 2005), 102–16.

118 Ohlsen, "Weibliche Praxis," 238.

119 A. Béal, *Passe-temps d'un praticien d'Auvergne, causeries sur l'hygiène... et autres sujets joyeux, rédigées conformément aux us et coutumes régionales* (Paris: A. Maloine, 1900), 231–6.

120 Sabine Hering and Gudrun Maierhof, *Die unpässliche Frau. Sozialgeschichte der Menstruation und Hygiene* (Pfaffenweiler: Centaurus, 1991), 37, 60–1; Joan Jacobs Brumberg, "'Something Happens to Girls': Menarche and the Emergence of the Modern American Hygenic Imperative," *Journal of the History of Sexuality* 4, no. 1 (1993), 114–15.

121 Ohlsen, "Weibliche Praxis," 244; Vostral, *Under Wraps*, 64.

122 Thomas Heinrich and Bob Batchelor, *Kotex, Kleenex, Huggies: Kimberly-Clark and the Consumer Revolution in American Business* (Columbus: Ohio State University Press, 2004), 62–3.

123 Ohlsen, "Weibliche Praxis," 252–4; Sharra L. Vostral, "Masking Menstruation: The Emergence of Menstrual Hygiene Products in the United States," in *Menstruation: A Cultural History*, 247–8.

124 Ohlsen, "Weibliche Praxis," 252; Lucinda McCray Beier, *For Their Own Good: The Transformation of English Working-Class Health Culture, 1880–1970* (Columbus: Ohio State University Press, 2008), 216–18.

125 Heinrich and Batchelor, *Kotex, Kleenex, Huggies*, 95–100, 173.

126 Vostral, "Masking Menstruation," 245.

127 Hering and Maierhof, *Die unpässliche Frau*, 74; Ohlsen, "Weibliche Praxis," 254.

128 Hering and Maierhof, *Die unpässliche Frau*, 98–148; Ohlsen, "Weibliche Praxis," 254–5; Shelly M. Park, "From Sanitation to Liberation? The Modern and Postmodern Marketing of Menstrual Products," *Journal of Popular Culture* 30, no. 2 (1996), 149–68; Vostral, "Masking Menstruation"; Vostral, *Under Wraps*, 65–8.
129 Ohlsen, "Weibliche Praxis," 254.
130 Heinrich and Batchelor, *Kotex, Kleenex, Huggies*, 175.
131 Marc Martin, *Trois siècles de publicité en France* (Paris: O. Jacob, 1992), 305.
132 Jones, *Beauty Imagined*, 89.

CONCLUSION

1 Jean-Pierre Goubert, *The Conquest of Water: The Advent of Health in the Industrial Age* (Cambridge: Polity Press, 1989).
2 Philippe Perrot, *Le travail des apparences, ou les transformations du corps féminin: XVIIIe-XIXe siècle* (Paris: Seuil, 1984), 137.
3 Thomas Piketty, *Capital in the Twenty-First Century* (Cambridge, MA: Harvard University Press, 2017), 123–5.
4 Sándor Szalai, *The Use of Time: Daily Activities of Urban and Suburban Populations in Twelve Countries* (The Hague: Mouton, 1972), 576–7.
5 John P. Robinson, Vladimir G. Andreyenkov, and Vasilly D. Patrushev, *The Rhythm of Everyday Life: How Soviet and American Citizens Use Time* (Boulder: Westview Press, 1989), 100; C. Roy, "Les soins personnels," *Données sociales* (1984), 400–1; Istituto nazionale di statistica, *L'uso del tempo in Italia* (Rome, 1993), 42, 52, 62, 72.
6 Robert Musil, *The Man without Qualities* (London: Picador, 1997), 265.
7 Roland Barthes, "Soap-powders and Detergents," in *Mythologies* (New York: Hill and Wang, 1972), 36–8.
8 Mary Ruebush, *Why Dirt Is Good: 5 Ways to Make Germs Your Friends* (New York: Kaplan, 2009).
9 Elaine Larson, "Hygiene of the Skin: When Is Clean Too Clean?," *Emerging Infectious Diseases* 7, no. 2 (2001): 225–30.
10 Sandy Skotnicki and Christopher Shulgan, *Beyond Soap: The Real Truth about What You Are Doing to Your Skin and How to Fix It for a Beautiful, Healthy Glow* (Toronto: Penguin Canada, 2018).
11 Kira Cochrane, "Could You Give Up Washing?," *The Guardian*, 2 November 2010.

INDEX

Abdeker ou l'art de conserver la beauté, 27–8
advertising, effects of, 48, 103, 156, 175, 230–4. *See also* detergents: advertising; soap marketing and advertising
Agree Shampoo, 214
Alberoni, Francesco, 202
Amsterdam: bathrooms, 67; public baths, 58
antiperspirants. *See* deodorants
Artemis and Actaeon, 29–30
Auspitz, Heinrich, 204

Baden-Powell, Robert, 151–2
Barthes, Roland, 198–9, 236
bathing: ambivalence and resistance, 29–35, 38; and behaviour change, 60–3; compulsory, 60–4; equipment, 64; frequency, 36–8, 82–3, 169–73; institutional, 60–3; medical understanding, 18–23; medieval, 38–9; military, 20, 60–2; river, 43–4; therapeutic, 12
bathrooms: diffusion of, 158–63; in eighteenth and nineteenth century, 64–9; fixtures, 77; hygiene practices in absence of, 80–3
baths, public: in Amsterdam, 58; attendance, 58–9; in England, 51–3; in Germany, 42, 53, 55; in Italy, 56–7; medieval, 39–40; in North America, 42, 57–8; in Paris, 40–1; eighteenth-century revival, 40–3; in Vienna, 41–2
beauty: feminine, 26–9; changing standards, 204; and cosmetics industry, 203–4; and hair care, 212, 215–16; and toilet soap, 126–8, 207–10
beauty soap. *See* toilet soap
Berlin: *bains à domicile*, 42; bath and washhouse, 54; bathrooms (1880), 67; sewers, 74; water supply, 95; working-class housing, 80
bidet, 77–9, 162
Bologna: bathrooms, 162; *lavatoio*, plate 6; public bath, 56, 57; water supply, 70
Boston: housing, 80; public baths, 58; school medical inspections, 147; tenement bathrooms, 67

"Bubbles," 127, plate 7. *See also* Millais, John Everett

Buchan, William, 20

Camay Soap, 206, 208

Caron, Auguste, 28

Carosello, 195, 197–8

cesspits, 74

Chadwick, Edwin, 26, 38. See also *Report on the Sanitary Condition of the Labouring Population of Great Britain*

Châtelet, Marquise du, 32

Chicago: bathrooms, 67; public baths, 58–9; school medical inspections, 147; water consumption, 167

Chlorodont, 218–19

cholera, 21, 25, 49, 50, 133, 134

cleanliness, 11–12; fear of, 16–17; medical opinion on, 19–20

clothing: frequency of changing, 87–8; linen as a cleaning agent, 84–9; symbolic value of clean clothes, 24, 84, 86, 184–5; twentieth-century innovations in, 184–8

Colgate & Co., 114

Colgate Dental Cream, 218

Colgate Palmolive, 189, 190; toilet soaps, 205–6; shampoos, 213

Corbin, Alain, 50, 226

cotton textiles and clothing, 88–9

Crest Toothpaste, 221

Crosfield's soaps, 119, 125

Daumier, Honoré, 44

David and Bathsheba, 30–1

Degas, Edgar, 64

dental care, 216–22; dental health, 216–18; oral hygiene education, 218

deodorants, 225–6

detergents: advantages, 190–1; advertising, 192–201, plate 12; competition for markets, 188–92; consumption, 200–1; development of, 188–9, 191–2; Persil, 191, 196–7, plate 12. *See also* Barthes, Roland

Diana and Actaeon. *See* Artemis and Actaeon

disease: childhood skin diseases, 147; early theories of, 133–4; fear of among the poor, 25–6; germ theory, 135–8; miasmatic theory, 21, 25, 74, 132

Dove Soap, 210

Eco, Umberto, 204, 210

Fa Toilet Soap, 206

filth, protective and curative qualities of, 16

folklore and health, 14–16

Giroud, Françoise, 170–1, 213

Goethe, Johann Wolfgang von, 31–2

hair care: advice literature on, 210–11; school hygiene teaching, 212; shampoo, 212–16; traditional practices, 211–12; washing frequency, 213–14

Hamburg: bathrooms, 67; bath and washhouse, 54; waste water, 72

handwashing, children, plates 3, 9

health, traditional knowledge. *See* folklore and health
Heilsame Dreck-Apotheke, 16
Henkel, Fritz, 116, 189–90
Hitlerjugend, 152
Holmes, Oliver Wendell, 135
household electrification, 179–80
housing conditions, working class, 80–1
Hugo, Victor, 32
hygiene, personal: and advice literature, 26–9; beliefs and customs, 13–18; concept of, 22; medical understandings of, 18–23; and public policy, 138–41; and social class, 23–6; traditional practices, 35–8

Ivory Soap, 114, 126, 196

Jungdeutschlandbund, 152

King, John, Suffolk river bath, 40
Koch, Robert, 135

Ladies Sanitary Association, 139–40
laundries, commercial, 98–9; Magdalene, 103
laundry: *bateaux-lavoirs*, 98–9; costs, 104–6; popular beliefs, 92–3; traditional village customs, 89–94; urban practices, 94–9; upper classes, 93–4
laundry facilities. *See* washhouses
laundry trades, 99–104; female employment in, 100–2; and mechanization, 102–3
lavatoio, plates 6, 10. *See also* washhouses

lavoir, plate 5. *See also* washhouses
Le Camus, Antoine, 27
Lever, William Hesketh, 115
Lever Brothers, 115–16; advertising budget, 125; and Vinolia soaps, 205–6
lice, 11, 35–6, 211–12, plate 1
Lifebuoy soap, 129
Lindley, William, 54
linen, and cleanliness, 12, 85
Lister, Joseph, 135, 137
London: bathing frequency, 81, 170; bathrooms, 65; childhood skin diseases, 147; children and lice, 211; laundry costs, 104–5; household plumbing, 76; housing conditions, 26, 80; laundry industry, 103; public bath movement, 52, 58; river bathing, 43; sanitation, 73; soap making, 108, 110; soiled clothing in, 90; washhouses, 97, 184; water supply, 70–1, 90
Louis XIV, 11–12
Lux Toilet Soap, 209

Marie Antoinette, 33
menstrual hygiene, 226–9
Millais, John Everett, 127
modesty, and bathing, 29–35
Montreal, public baths, 57
Munich: housing conditions, 80; water consumption, 167; water supply, 72
Muthesius, Hermann, 65–6, 77, 165

New York: bath houses, 42, 58; bathrooms, 67; public baths, 59; school medical inspections, 147,

148; sea bathing, 23; water system, 76
nudity and bathing, 29–35

odour, offensive and threatening, 21, 49–50

Pacentro, 174, plate 10
Palmolive Soap, 128, 205
Pantene Shampoo, 215
Paris: *bains à domicile*, 42; *bateaux-lavoirs*, 99–100; bath houses, 40–1; bath and wash-house, 53; bathing costs, 41; bathing frequency, 82; bathing in bourgeois homes, 64, 66; laundry facilities, 96; *lavoirs*, 99–100; price of soap in, 112; river bath-ing, 43; Salon des arts ménagers, 177; sewers, 74; soap consump-tion, 109; soap production, 110; underwear fashions, 86–7; water supply, 69–70, 81
Pasteur, Louis, 135
Paullini, Christian Franz, 16
Pears Soap, 124–5, 127–8, 205, 207, plate 7
Pepys, Elizabeth, 12
Pepys, Samuel, 11–12
Persil: advertising, 125–6, 193, 196–7; Roland Barthes on advertise-ments, 198–9; international expansion, 119–20; as a laundry detergent, 191; as a laundry soap, 116–17; Persil whiteness, 197; die Weiße Dame, 196–7, plate 12
plumbing fixtures, 75–80. *See also* bidet
Potevin, Jean-Jacques, 40

Procter & Gamble: advertising, 124–5, 191–4; international expansion, 120, 121; market share, 120; origins, 114; product innovation, 191; and shampoos, 212–13, 215; and synthetic detergents, 189–90; and toilet soaps, 205–6, 213; and tooth-paste, 221. *See also* Ivory Soap
proverbs, health, 14–16
public health and the state, 138–41

razor blades, 222–5
Renk, Friedrich, 55
Report on the Sanitary Condition of the Labouring Population of Great Britain, 49, 51, 53, 63, 134. *See also* Chadwick, Edwin
Revson, Charles, 203

Salon des arts ménagers, 177, 181
sanitary movement, nineteenth century, 132–5
sanitation, public, 50, 72–4
Schicht, Georg, 116
Schicht, Johann, 116
schools: influence on pupils' hygiene, 149–50; oral hygiene education in, 218; and personal hygiene, 141–50; pupils' health and hygiene, 146–7; surveillance and resistance, 148–9
Scout movement, 150–2
Semmelweis, Ignàz, 135–6
sewers, urbanization and, 72–5
shampoo: advertising, 214–15; development of, 212–13; and feminine beauty, 216; mar-kets, 213–14. *See also* hair care